Yut Di - One Earth

by
E.H.K. Ho

Wholesale discounts for book orders are available through Ingram or Spring Arbor Distributors.

ISBN

978-1-77302-056-3 (paperback)

978-1-77302-057-0 (ebook)

978-1-77302-058-7 (hardcover)

Published in Canada.

First Edition

Table of Contents

Dedication

This book is dedicated to the Chinese laborers who helped to build the Canadian Pacific Railway and the 81,000 Chinese immigrants who paid the Head Tax in Canada.

Acknowledgements

MANY FRIENDS HAVE CONTRIBUTED TO THE WRITING AND completion of this book. They helped me find and access information, made critical suggestions, helped to edit mistakes and gave me constant encouragement to complete the task at hand. I owe a great debt of gratitude to numerous friends for their support.

First and foremost, I have to thank my wife, Sylvia, for her love, understanding and devotion, without her support this book would never have been written. If I have been unjustly harsh on the Brits, being married to one for 37 years has fueled the angst. Secondly, I would like to thank all my clients who helped to support my family and I during my many years as a real estate professional. I have always felt deeply honoured by those who trusted me to serve them.

I started writing this book over 10 years ago. I may not have continued without the encouragement of my friends – Donovan & Lynn Saul, Gale & Alyce Christenson, Gloria Giggilo and especially Lyndell & Lekh Goorachurn, who typed and deciphered my early hand-written notes. Aware of my personal shortcomings, I thought if I told friends and acquaintances that I was writing a book that I would be too embarrassed not to complete the task. I shared my manuscript at different phases of development with numerous friends to gain support and to measure their response.

The people who I am most indebted to are those who assisted me with research and editing – Dr. Jennifer Clayton, Annette Wetherly, Bill Murphy-Dyson, Charles Araujo, and Desmond Fisher as well as the Tellwell Talent Inc. staff – Tim Lindsay, Jordan Mitchell, Raeanne Pearce, Mitchel Moylan, Erin Ball, Sandy Ibrahim, Francesca Jackman & Liviu Peicu. The computer age blossomed during the early development of my manuscript. I would like to thank my son, Sean Ho, my daughter, Kirsten Ho-Chan, and my dear friends David Purser, Brian Yee, Charles & Daniel Araujo for their technical support and their patience with my ineptitude. Many contributors worked with me at DFH Real Estate Ltd. in Victoria. I would like to thank & acknowledge Nanci Sebo (Golddesk Digital Design) for her technical support, Ron Cunningham and Myles Christenson for their generosity and Brian Graves for his editorial advice.

I would also like to acknowledge friends who encouraged me and helped to inspire thoughts and ideas during the gestation of the manuscript – Brian Sharp, David Purser, Charles Araujo, Johanne Amonson, Ken Chow, Kathleen Lee, Dan & Sandy Ho, Alex Cordero, Henry Leong, John & Rosa Lapointe, Sey Beilihis Baileys, John MacMillan, Bart & Johanne Guisnet, Deborah Wright, Goldie Carlow, Dave Cutler, Daniel Hsu, Barry & Annie Fisher, Henry Van Der Vlugt, Kevin Sing, Valerie Sing Turner, Frank Chan, T.W. Patterson, Prof. Robert C H Sweeny, Fred & Jenny Peters, Peter & Graeme Sykes, Jack Etkin.

I would also like to acknowledge my grand-daughters, Makena, Brooklyn & Elsa and thank them for renewing my hope for the future.

Introduction

GLANCING BACK AT THE EARLIEST DAYS OF MY CHILDHOOD, I remember growing up in Victoria and attending North Ward Elementary School which no longer exists today. The school area was inhabited by a multi-cultural mix of Euro-Canadians, East Indians, First Nations and the Chinese. The borders of the school area also encompassed Chinatown. When I became of school age like most of the other Chinese at the school I was a new immigrant, having arrived in 1951 at the age of three. My mother was born and raised in Canada and was sent back to China to complete her schooling. During the Second World War she was denied the right to re-enter Canada. She had married a Chinese national and somehow lost the right of re-entry. After the Exclusion Act was repealed in 1947 and persistent lobbying by my grand-parents supported by their church, my mother was permitted to re-enter Canada with my father, my sister and me in 1951.

My mother's family was already established in Victoria outside of Chinatown so I lost the ability to speak proper Chinese much too quickly. By the time I reached elementary school I was considered by the other Chinese to be a "banana" – yellow on the outside and white on the inside. Many of the Chinese students were a year or two older because they were new arrivals and held back temporarily due to their inability to speak English. Though I was never shunned completely by the dominant Chinese faction, I was never made to feel fully accepted because I spoke "Chinglish" a mixed bag

of Chinese and English. During those early years, I did everything I could to fit in with the majority composed mostly of Euro-Canadians. For a while I rejected almost everything that was Chinese and what I remember most was that I hated being Chinese. I hated that the Chinese kids all seemed poor, ignorant, and underprivileged. I hated that they were the targets of verbal and physical abuse for no apparent reason except for being different. I hated how they acted in an ever-pleasing, acquiescent manner. After all, they were inferior, weren't they? I knew that I wasn't – so how could I be one of them? I just wanted to be like my white friends who did whatever they wanted without any forethought of public opinion and who had such easy access to doors closed to the Chinese. It wasn't until junior high school when I found others like myself that I realized the error in my thinking. Embarrassed now by my early ignorance, I would like to share some of my acquired enlightenment with others who may journey down a similar path. It never occurred to me to explore the questions of why the Chinese were treated this way or how they were affected until much later in my life.

My father passed away in 1991. I was devastated by the loss of the one person who truly believed in me. He always felt strongly that I had a gift, but during his lifetime he could never determine what it was. Little did I know that his passing would help to awaken latent potential. I never realized how much that he had meant to me until he was there no more. Now who would answer all those questions I should have asked? Who was this man? Why was his simple gentle philosophy ingrained in me? What factors influenced the choices he made? He worked doing menial jobs to feed his family as a janitor at a nurses' residence and then as a central supply technician at a local hospital. During his early youth in China he was trained to be an artist. His private tutor was a great master named Wong Bo Bick, who supposedly became the private tutor of Soong May-ling or Madam Chiang Kai Shek. Wong Bo Bick was purported to be one of the most prominent Chinese landscape painters of his era. My father never spoke or permitted his old friends or family members to speak about any of his training or artwork while he was alive. My aunts later said that my father worked on several paintings with Wong Bo Bick that later became prominent. The paintings were destroyed during China's Cultural Revolution since possession of them by family members would have had dire consequences. Why did my father never speak of this? Was the pain of his unfulfilled destiny too hurtful

for him to bear? I never heard him complain about the twists of fate that he always accepted with quiet dignity. I never realized or understood the extent of his talent until he was gone. The back cover of my book displays a painting dedicated to my father by his former tutor Wong Bo Bick. By doing this, his friends, acquaintances and family members will know that "I am my father's son and his life flows through mine."

After the death of my father, my only solace came from reading about the past and about others who may have travelled a path similar to that of my father. But what did I really know about my father's early life? He left so many blanks. He was never really that vocal about the past and he always believed "pain and sorrow need not be shared with others." Anyways, I was a very poor listener in those days, even at the best of times. But all the reading that I undertook to appease my sorrow after his passing culminated in the writing of this book. I have tried to honour my father by commemorating the wisdom, perseverance, and achievement of others like him who survived and triumphed in the face of racial intolerance, political disempowerment and socio-economic injustice.

In this book I have attempted to present a view of the past from a Chinese perspective. Why did the early Chinese cross the Pacific? Why was the Chinese Immigration Act of 1885 passed, imposing the Head Tax? How did it affect those who paid it? How did our Fathers of Confederation justify it? Though the central characters are creations of my imagination I have, to the best of my abilities, remained consistent with historical events as they occurred during this era. Some Chinese person may have lived through similar experiences but it is doubtful whether any lived through them all.

Writing this book has been an odyssey of self-discovery. I feel as if I have awakened from a life-long nap with new insight. Now who else is still asleep? How can I inspire them? Discovering what my forefathers may have experienced in the past makes me feel even more grateful for my presence, here and now, but they paid the price. For anyone offended by my exposé of the past, I can only respond: How would you liked to have been Chinese during those times?

"New ideas can only flourish inside an open mind. To view history from a Chinese perspective, this book proceeds in the traditional style of Chinese literature. A journey of 200 years begins at the back of the book."

P.S. The electronic version of this book is printed in a conventional format.

Prologue

History is written by the victors not the victims.

AT THE BEGINNING OF THE NINETEENTH CENTURY, CHINA WAS the richest country on earth. Between 1740 and 1800, the population of China increased from 143 million to nearly 300 million. By the 1850s the Qing or Manchu Dynasty had ruled over China for 200 years. The Manchus had invaded from the north, driving the armies of the Ming Dynasty south until they finally reached Guangdong province. Many Ming loyalists fled overseas in hopes of one day returning to topple the Qing dynasty. After defeating the Ming forces, the Manchus attempted to quash the hopes of Ming loyalists from forming a resistance movement overseas by passing an edict preventing their countrymen from going abroad. The penalty for those violating the law was decapitation. For 200 years the Ming loyalists dreamed of the time when the Mandate of Heaven would pass from their Manchu oppressors. When the British defeated the Qing in the Opium Wars the Ming loyalists saw it as a sign that the time had come.

The Opium War started over the confiscation and destruction of British opium by Chinese government authorities in 1837. The principal underlying issues concerned the removal of trade barriers and the administration of Chinese justice. A trade imbalance created by the ever-growing demand

for Chinese imports drained the coffers of the British monarchy. Dealing with the threat of colonial rebellions further diminished the coffers of the royal exchequer. The use of opium in China was changing from a medicinal use to a recreational use for the rich. The British decided to capitalize on the growing appetite for opium in China to correct their imbalance in trade. Hundreds of thousands of acres of the richest land of the Ganges and the plains of India were converted from mostly cotton-growing to the cultivation of poppies administered by the British East India Company. Opium was manufactured in Bengali by the East India Company under a royal charter originally granted by Queen Elizabeth in 1600. Massive cargoes of opium were stored and delivered to islands off the coast of China. Transport of shipments of opium to the coastal regions of China was protected by the British fleet. They were then picked up by Chinese traders who smuggled them for inland distribution. Prior to the American Revolution (1775-1783), fewer than 200 chests had flowed into China annually. Shipments rose to 2000 chests in 1800, 3,211 chests in 1816, 16,000 chests in 1831, and 40,000 chests in 1838. After the Opium War, shipments rose to 70,000 chests.

When the Emperor's own son died of an overdose the Emperor decided to put an end to the trade. The Emperor appointed Lin Tse-Hsü as Imperial Commissioner and sent him to Canton with instructions to negotiate an end to the importation of opium into China. Upon his arrival in 1839 Lin attempted to initiate an exchange of Chinese tea for British-held opium. The English merchants refused to co-operate. After a month and a half of negotiation Charles Elliot, the British Superintendent of Trade in China convinced the British traders to relinquish 20,000 chests of opium each bearing approximately 55 kilograms of opium with the promise of reimbursement from the British government. Once the cargo was received by government authorities, a labour force of 500 mixed 2.6 million pounds of opium with lime and salt over 23 days and jettisoned it into the open sea off the shores of Hong Kong. Prior to the outbreak of the Opium War, Lin Tse-Hsu wrote and published an open letter in Canton, addressed to Queen Victoria to explain and to justify his actions. It has never been chronicled whether the letter was ever received by Queen Victoria, but the letter may have changed the history of the world as we know it today. The following is a summary of the letter:

A Communication to Your Majesty, Queen Victoria:

The Way of Heaven is fairness to all; it does not suffer us to harm others to benefit ourselves. Men are alike in this regard all over the world, they cherish life and hate what endangers life. For the betterment of all nations our great Emperor wishes to appease and resolve the growing tensions between China and the other nations of the world. If there is profit China will share it with the peoples of the world; if there is harm it will be removed for the sake of humanity. Our belief is that what is just and fair for one nation is just and fair for all nations of the world.

The benefits from trade has been mutually enjoyed by both our countries for two hundred years but there appear among us purveyors of opium who wish only to profit and disregard the harm to the people of the Celestial Kingdom. His Majesty the Emperor has sent me to resolve this matter. Those people in China who sell opium or smoke opium will receive the death penalty. If foreign traders who have been caught selling opium repent for their crime and confirm their compliance to our laws, we will accept this as an expression of remorse and repentance and they will be exonerated.

The wealth of our culture is being exploited to profit these individuals. The profit made by these traders is a result of our culture and ingenuity. Opium is being produced by the British East India Company in India. We are aware that very little of their produce reaches the shores of your homeland and that the use of opium is constrained and very limited in your country. Since you must realize how harmful this drug is to others then how can you knowingly allow those under your rule to participate in this enterprise? Of all that China exports to foreign countries there is not a single thing which is not beneficial to all people. How can you allow your countrymen to continue growing, manufacturing and selling products injurious to our people? All goods imported into China are non-essential, if we close our borders to foreign trade, how will the rest of the world endure without tea, silk, satin, chinaware, ginger, cinnamon, etc.?

After this correspondence has been received you must clearly understand our concern and the need for the severity of our new laws. We ask for your co-operation to advise your subjects to discontinue & terminate this activity. Please communicate your response to our request as soon as possible so our countries may continue to live in peace and harmony.

Lin Tse-Hsu

Imperial Commissioner of the Celestial Court

Financially unable to reimburse British merchants over the loss of their goods, the British government sent warships instead of money. Superior military expertise and technology overwhelmed the military forces of the Qing government with ease. The Opium War which started in 1839 was the first Anglo–Chinese war. It ended in 1842 after the Manchu government negotiated a peace settlement, the Treaty of Nanking, which entitled the British to an indemnity, unconditional access to 5 treaty ports in Canton, Amoy, Foochow, Ningbo and Shanghai and the cession of Hong Kong. Under the indemnity, the Qing government would pay 6 million taels (Chinese currency - 1.3 oz of silver) in ransom for Canton and an indemnity totaling 33 million taels in reparation for the cost of the war. A document supplemental to the Treaty of Nanking bestowed extraterritorial rights to British citizens and most favoured nation status with lower tariffs and higher import quotas to Britain. With extraterritorial right, foreign nationals were above Chinese law and native Chinese were relegated to second-class citizens in their own country. By granting most favoured nation status to the British, China could not fix her own tariffs to protect her own industries. Mass-produced goods from the industrialized West flooded Chinese markets disrupting the centuries-old handicraft economy. Though opium was not mentioned in the treaty, it was free to flow into China because under extraterritorial rights, foreign national were exempt from Chinese laws. Following the British lead, France and USA concluded similar treaties with China in 1844 as more western powers seized the opportunity to exploit and humiliate the "sick man of Asia". Like the carcass of a roast pig, western powers sectioned port cities into their own separate domains of influence. The motto of the French Revolution "Liberty, Equality & Brotherhood" and the "inalienable rights to life, liberty and the pursuit of happiness" from the Declaration of Independence rang hollow beyond the borders of France and America.

The Second Opium War provided the British with an excuse to confront the Chinese on issues of obstruction and non-compliance relating to the Treaty of Nanking. A vessel carrying opium was apprehended by the Chinese coastguard. The British claimed the ship was theirs though it bore no national flag. Even though a formal apology was delivered to the British consul in Canton, British warships attacked Canton and continued bombarding the region even though the Chinese offered no resistance. It was an era of gunboat diplomacy and protest was useless. The British were

later joined by the French, Russians and the Americans in their war effort which concluded with additional rights being granted to the foreign powers with the legalization of the opium trade, access to 10 more ports, cession of Kowloon to Britain, diplomatic representation, freedom for Christian churches to evangelize in China. In addition the British were given the right to participate in the coolie trade. Laborers were indentured based on unpaid debts, family needs, and false promises and transported throughout the Pacific region. England and France received 8 million taels of silver in war reparation. Between 1860 and 1881, the use of opium in China exploded to epic proportions. It was estimated that one third of the male population of China were regular users of opium by 1881. The opium trade had a catastrophic effect on the framework of China's economy, culture, and traditions. Chinese society imploded in unbridled misery under an avalanche of opium. Farmland lay dormant from neglect. Crops remained in the field with no one to harvest. Sons and daughters stole from their parents and wives from their husbands to satisfy their hunger for opium. Farmers sold their land to pay their debts and that of their children and grand-children. Landless farmers turned to banditry. Parents sold and indentured their children into servitude as servants, prostitutes and coolie laborers. Instead of raising daughters in poverty who were considered physically subordinate to males for working the fields, parents would drown them at birth because feeding too many endangered survival of the rest and they wanted to avoid subjecting their daughters to a life of hopeless misery as slaves or prostitutes. Cities and villages were filled with walking skeletons. The dead and dying cluttered the streets, the fields, the countryside, the riverbanks, unattended and abandoned.

The British House of Commons conducted an inquiry on the opium trade. It agreed with the East India Company's justification that if they did not produce opium, someone else would. It was the same plea used by slave traders and others involved with immoral endeavors: "I did not create the vice, I only service it". When the early missionaries arrived in China they were asked: "Why should we replace our traditional gods with Christianity? How could the government of your country that professed to be Christian legalize the importation of opium into China? How could those who import opium for the sake of personal gain knowing that it is harmful to others believe in a religion better than our own?"

The Qing government shifted the burden of indemnities of the Opium War onto the peasants forcing them to pay higher taxes. Civil unrest became rampant. Many secret societies such as the Triads, the Ke-Loa Brotherhood, the Red Turbans, and the White Lotus were formed to oppose the Qing government. The White Lotus uprising lasted 9 years and was brutally suppressed by government forces. The 1850 Taiping Rebellion was a civil war in southern China led by Hong Xiu Quan Li a Christian-inspired fanatic who professed to be the brother of Jesus Christ. He amassed millions of hopeless and starving followers disenchanted with the Qing dynasty, their corrupt officials, and their humiliating defeats at the hands of foreign powers. The government backed by British and French forces, finally crushed the rebellion in 1864. It is estimated that over 20 million died in one of the deadliest conflicts in history. The estimated population of China decreased from approximately 400million in1820 to approximately 370 million in1881.

With millions homeless and starving, the southern maritime provinces were the most adversely affected. The people of the south searched for a way out of their plight of misery and suffering. Peasants who had farmed the same land for centuries could no longer support their families. The people of the southern provinces were the first to receive the news about the discovery of gold in America, a new country with abundant resources that valued freedom, justice and human equality. To escape the misery and hopelessness, many chose to defy authority and face decapitation. The men of southern China flocked to the shores of California in search of work and wealth, to ensure the survival of their families.

Glossary of Terms:

Please note that Chinese terms are written in my Sam Yup dialect of Cantonese.

Aiya : exclamation equivalent to "my goodness"

Amah : live-in nanny dedicated to a child's upbringing

Bao : a steamed rice bun with assorted fillings

Barracoon : a cage used to hold prisoners

Boo How Doy : highbinder – a hired assassin

Cohong : trading company authorized by the Emperor of China

Daifow : literally "big port" refers to San Francisco

Dim Sum : literally "touch the heart", a lunch of gourmet pastries

Erhu : musical stringed instrument played with a bow

Fan Yuen Gok : corner park

Guangdong : a coastal province in Southern China

Gum San : literal translation "gold mountain" refers to North America

Han : Chinese with common Yangtze (Yellow) River basin ancestry

Highbinder : hired assassins who wear a belt to hold their weapons

Huabiao : ornamental pillar to signify clan affiliations

Huiguan : district brotherhood society based on clan, district and/or dialect

Jok Kay : literally "capture the flag" , Chinese chess game

Jook : Chinese porridge

Kowtow : a kneeling bow signifying respect

Lofan : people of European descent

Loungei : literally "woman with open legs", prostitute

Lycee : gifts of money generally given to the young

Moksi : priest (literally – "revered one")

Mui Jeh : little sister, also used as slang for prostitute

Pailou : monumental gate commemorating the past

Pia Hua : literally "forcing out", evicting undesirables by force

Qing Dynasty : Manchurian rulers of China from 1644 to 1911

Sam Yup : a district of Guangdong – literally "the 3 counties"

Sanfow : literally "third port" refers to Marysville

Sifu : teacher – learned one

Skookum : native term for strong, powerful, brave

Sto:lo : native inhabitants of Fraser River – "the river people"

Sze Yup : a district of Guangdong – literally "the 4 counties"

Tien Gow : Chinese dominoes game

Tong Yun : Chinese people

Tong Yun Gai : literally "Chinese street" refers to Chinatown

Tong : another term for Huiguan

Yeefow : literally "second port" refers to Sacramento

Maps & Photos

Chapter 1

New Horizons

MAY 1880

THE PAST 18 YEARS HAD BEEN HAPPY AND PROSPEROUS YEARS for Dai Woo Cheung and his family. In the fall of 1862 he had returned triumphantly to his village in the Pearl River Delta of Guangdong Province in southern China. As a man of wealth he wasted no time in starting new business ventures exporting Chinese products to Gum San, Gold Mountain, the term for North America because the mountains were said to be filled with gold. His wealth and influence grew as the situation in China worsened. The Pearl River Delta region was overburdened with homeless peasant families in desperate need of food, shelter and protection from armed factions. Food production could not keep pace with the growing demand, as rebel and government forces fed themselves at the expense of farmers and merchants. Disease, famine and natural disasters such as floods, typhoons, earthquakes, droughts and pestilence added more fuel to civil unrest. The Qing dynasty was devastated by the lack of funds since the coffers of imperial China had been depleted by the Taiping Rebellion and the reparations paid to foreign government for the Opium Wars. Government corruption was rampant under the shadow of western domination. Burdened by taxes

1

levied years in advance, farmers could no longer feed their families. Opium was openly available on the streets of every major city in China as merchants of misery enlarged their spheres of profit. The fabric of traditional Confucian values was unraveling under a barrage of new western concepts and ideals. Centuries of Chinese infrastructure was crumbling as government magistrates struggled to restore control. The dreams of the current horrors in China that had haunted Dai Woo Cheung and his father many years before had now come to fruition. These premonitions had helped to drive him harder to relocate his clan to the new world before the foreseen catastrophes deepened in severity. Cheung did not know when these events would come to pass, but he knew that his clan had to be prepared for a time of great turbulence.

In preparation, Cheung demanded that all family members under the age of 30 learn the language of the New World. He insisted the young become God Worshippers and he made the children attend the nearest American missionary school to learn math, science and English. Many rebelled, but his relentless pursuit for their conversion won over in time. His continual praise and rewards for those who excelled succeeded in motivating family members to learn new concepts despite the taunting and ridicule of the villagers and their children. As his business ventures grew more prosperous and employed more and more of the villagers, even his harshest critics were silenced by his success. Cheung never argued or justified his actions but to those who would say that he was being contemptuous of his culture and ancestral traditions he would simply say "If we waste the present by dwelling too much on the past, the future will hold little promise for our children." Though few understood the warning hidden in his words, nobody doubted the sincerity of his convictions. For it seemed everyone else was only concerned with the restoration of those harmonious days of the past. Had not China always enlightened and swayed her conquerors with the superiority of her wisdom and culture? Why should these barbarians from the West be any different from the Manchus or the Mongols? Cheung never questioned the wisdom of his civilization. However, his most vivid dreams rarely lied and when his father shared similar dreams the path for the clan's future seemed clear. He would fulfill his promise to his father.

The ship swayed monotonously back and forth. Cheung remembered his first journey to Gold Mountain as a twelve-year-old boy with his father

during the California Gold Rush of 1849. He was happy that his son was spared the hardship of his first crossing. The pain of those times still danced in his mind even though he forced himself to focus on the present.

Their destination was the port of Victoria on Vancouver Island in the province of British Columbia. Cheung had visited there once before during the early days of the Fraser River Gold Rush. For most travelers from Asia to Canada , it was the first port of entry before the long journey to the gold fields. Fort Victoria had been a sleepy little trading post for the Hudson's Bay Company prior to the discovery of gold. Then in 1858, Governor James Douglas of Vancouver Island and New Caledonia published a newspaper announcement in San Francisco stating that anyone coming to the Fraser River in search of gold had to apply for a mining license in Fort Victoria. The town's population quickly exploded as the weak, the strong, the ignorant, the wise, the lawful, the lawless, the virtuous, and the virtueless converged on Fort Victoria from every crevice of humanity.

Fort Victoria was ruled by British law that offered better protection for the Chinese. California in contrast was ruled only by the passion, desires and greed of ruthless men with guns. California offered no protection to anyone who was too timid to use a bullet to satisfy their desires and resolve their misunderstandings. Although the American influence seemed to be growing when Cheung departed in 1862, working and living in a British colony was by far a healthier and safer proposition for all Chinese in con-trast to life in California. The people of the town had welcomed the Chinese and had encouraged them to set up residences and businesses. They were respected for their knowledge, their craftsmanship, their honesty, their sobriety and their industriousness. The town had grown greatly in size during his visits from 1858 to 1862 and Cheung looked forward to seeing it once more. He had heard from others that the attitude of the townspeople had changed towards the Chinese but he knew from past experience that you could not believe those returning from Gold Mountain in bitter dis-appointment because most would colour their misfortune with a coarse brush. How could these good people turn against the Chinese? When he and others first arrived in 1858, a period of adjustment was to be expected because there were some differences in culture and philosophy but there was nothing insurmountable that knowledge, understanding and good lead-ership could not overcome. Were all men not brothers in the same universe?

The leaders of this country under British rule would surely be men of principle and wisdom and would understand the basic fundamentals of human co-existence.

Wing had never been away from home for any longer than a few days. It had been 10 days since he had left the great port of Canton. The trip on the lorcha from Canton to Hong Kong took 2 days. They boarded the steam ship "Strathearn" when they reached the port of Hong Kong. The main cargo were coolies (indentured laborers, derived from Kuli an Indian word meaning "bitter strength") heading to Gold Mountain.

Wing sought to understand the purpose of the journey to Gum San and why he was chosen for the journey. Father had said that the laborers occupied the lower level of the ship and that we would not see them until we arrived at our destination. He also said that we may see many poor people during our journey but we could do very little to help them because every man has his own fate and we must not disturb or alter the fate of others unless you expect to assume some responsibility for those you have affected. Feeding a poor man today may be a noble act of kindness but if this man cannot feed himself who will feed his wife and children and their children's children tomorrow? And what if the person you save becomes evil? Who will undo his evil deeds or his children's evil deeds? The accumulated responsibility was too much to bear. It is much wiser to only help the few you know and trust. Why was father talking like this? Back in the village, father was always prepared to help almost anyone in need. Did the villagers not always come to him first in times of famine, flood, sickness and drought? Something was amiss; this journey was such a mystery. There were so many questions, but his father only answered in riddles. His father never volunteered answers when he could encourage his children to ponder and reason for themselves. And there was always a reward when he was pleased with the use of logic and common sense. But why was I chosen for this journey? Of the three sons why was I selected for the journey? Is this a reward or a punishment? I am the youngest son just 12 years old. Why not eldest brother Yuen who is 17 years old, or Hong, who is 15 years old? I so wish that he had taken one of them. I am so scared that I will disappoint him. My brothers are much bigger, much stronger, much smarter and much, much braver. I cry every time I think of home. This ship keeps moving up and down and I keep dreaming I will be tossed over the side and

left to drown. What really grieves me the most is that I miss my little sister May Yun. I wonder if she has found those toys I made for her. I hid them before I left in all her secret spots in the inner courtyard. I am sure she will cry whenever she thinks of me. Good, fill the ocean with your tears, May Yun. I wish it were you on this floating dragon and not me. After father's sudden announcement that her favourite playmate had been selected to journey with him to Gold Mountain he remembered the last days of tears and anguish that his little sister suffered through prior to his departure. No beloved sister, it is better me than you. Why should I curse you with my pain when you would lovingly endure it? Anyway you could never digest this food. It is truly barbaric – blood-soaked slices of beef, baked egg and flour pudding, tasteless boiled vegetables and potatoes ground in milk and butter. Father said that my stomach will get used to it. If only its passage did not offend my mouth and tongue first. Maybe the food is better on the lower level with the laborers. I overheard one of the stewards say that they eat rice every day. Why is it forbidden for me to go below?

It had been another restless night with little sleep for Cheung and his son. The ocean appeared to be calmer this morning as Cheung peered out the porthole. Wing looked forward to going to the dining lounge to eat break-fast. Pork sausages, bacon, scrambled eggs, baked beans and toast with butter and jams was the meal Wing found to be the most palatable. It was still a little early to get up. Wing lingered in a lazy drowse trying hard to recapture glimpses of his home in China while his father studied foreign newspapers and books that he had received from his friends the American missionaries who taught at the school his children had attended. They had come to visit father regularly and they were always invited for dinners, parties and the many different Chinese festivals. Father spoke very highly of these friends because he felt those who would leave the comfort of their home, family, rel-atives and friends to be surrounded by poverty, ignorance and despair must be men and women of great virtue. For what did they receive in return? The satisfaction of knowing they had benefited others they did not know and who may or may not be thankful for being helped? It is no use Wing thought, my sleep won't return. I can leave this ship only in my sleep. Now even that has forsaken me.

"Good morning, illustrious father." (italicized print - signifies dialogue spoken in Chinese, but paraphrased into English)

"Good morning, beloved third son, did your bed sheets have another successful night?"

Slightly embarrassed, Wing defended his past mishap, "Father, before this journey I have never slept on a ship. I did not know I would have such silly dreams. You do not help my situation by reminding me of this small problem. It's been many days now without a reoccurrence. Please let us not mention it again even in jest."

Observing the earnestness of his son, Cheung realized that his son was paying too dearly for his amusement, "It will be as you wish, my son."

Suddenly there were three solid raps on the cabin door. Already dressed and washed Cheung opened the door and found Mr. Osgood, the chief steward of the dining lounge. He was a giant of a man by Chinese standards. He was maybe 40 years old, stood over six feet tall, slender build, short dark curly hair, meticulously groomed with a well-trimmed short mustache and beard, high cheek bones, and grayish-blue eyes. In a courteous but formal tone Mr. Osgood said, "Mr. Dai, sorry to disturb you so early in the morning, but Captain Anderson requested that we change the seating arrangements temporarily. He asked for your permission to do so."

"Mr. Osgood, do you know why?"

"Sorry Mr. Dai, the Captain never explains his reasoning. He just commands and I obey, but I am sure he means well."

"Well, as long as it is only temporary you have my approval, Mr. Osgood."

"Jolly good, can the Captain expect you for breakfast at 8 o'clock? He wanted to personally introduce you to the other guests at your new table."

Cheung pondered momentarily. "The Captain wants me to meet someone." The Captain seemed to be a good man. Although his conversations with him were always brief and formal, Cheung assumed this from the respect that he gave and received in return from his subordinates. Cheung answered "My son and I will be there at eight o'clock."

"Very well Mr. Dai, thank you very much and sorry once again for calling on you so early."

Overhearing the conversation, Wing quickly washed and started to dress. The new clothes were so uncomfortable. How could one ever feel comfortable in them? Silk was so much more comfortable and cooler for summer use. You do nothing but sweat profusely in garments made of cotton and wool and they were so much heavier than silk. I will never get used to these

clothes. Why does father insist we wear them? The American missionaries never wore Chinese garments when they came to visit our home. Why should we adopt their clothing when we are visiting their country? Well, father, what riddles will you answer me with today? With his face contorted as he struggled with his collar and tie Wing queried, "*Father why do we wear these foreign clothes when we can wear our own? Surely, they can tell we are Chinese. Why must we try to look like them when it is quite obvious that we are not? I did not see the American missionaries wearing Chinese garments when they lived amongst us.*"

"*My son, I can see that you have thought long and hard before asking me these questions. Let me ask you this. If we are emulating them, what does that tell you?*"

"*Their society is superior to ours?*"

"*Perhaps, perhaps not, until the Opium Wars, our society had survived for many generations in relative peace. One of the most important goals in life is the quest for knowledge. We must always strive to learn from those that we respect and admire. Knowledge always improves an individual's opportunities and the chance of survival during a crisis. During my travels and my association with foreigners, I have learnt many things. I have learnt how to read and write the English language, which has helped me to understand their history. When the population of a nation in the West grew too large to support itself within its own boundaries it took over the land of its neighbors, just as our early ancestors did. As a consequence, the nations of the West had to develop military expertise to survive because they were perpetually at war. Our country went through a similar pattern of warring states before the Mongols united China under a single power. This has not occurred in the West. With limited military threats our rulers allowed natural disasters, disease and famines to curb our populations. Meanwhile western technology had advanced, applying and improving many things that their early traders brought back from China, like making paper, printing, gun powder, and the compass. At this time, Western technology may have advanced past us, but history will judge which path would have been best for the future of humanity. Their military might and skill is superior, but their philosophy and their right of conquest is contrary to our belief in peaceful co-existence. The biggest and strongest are not always the wisest. Without wisdom, power is temporary. The West must be truly admired for their remarkable technological advances but victims do not remain weak forever. Their philosophy of perpetual greed is fraught with envy, hatred and violence, which can only lead to ever-growing conflict. The Han (largest ethnic group*

in China with ancestry originating from the Yangtze River basin) have always believed that trading with others for what was needed and allowing nature to run its course was a more enlightened strategy for peace. The Manchus have grown arrogant and underestimated the advances in western technology. China will never be the same and must learn from mistakes of the past. The world has changed and China must change with it or become a victim subject to the whim of others."

"Sorry to interrupt father but why must we wear these clothes?"

"Son, you are not listening. Think again of what I spoke and you will find the answer. Now tell me of your dreams. What did you see?"

"Sorry father I cannot remember anything right now. The less I dream of being on the ocean the better." Yes, thought Wing, I did have a silly dream of swimming helplessly in the ocean but why should I tell you when you never answer my questions. Why did I ever ask? It is too early for a headache. If the ocean becomes angry again, I may give up another offering to the goddess of the sea.

Noting a tone of rebelliousness in his son's words, Cheung implored "My son, you cannot close the door to your dreams. They are the windows to the future. To deny what you may have seen in your dreams may put us in danger."

Another answer, thought Wing, not about the clothes but an earlier question. Was I chosen to come on this journey for my dreams? Too bad my beloved father; the less you know of my dreams the sooner I will be home playing with May Yun. As much as I respect and honour you, I prefer to be home and I regret ever telling you of my dreams of savages, wild dogs, hateful foreigners and Chinese laborers building a path through immense forested mountains for an iron dragon.

Cheung took out his pocket watch and opened the ornate gold cover. "We'd better leave for the dining lounge, my obedient son."

"Yes I am ready, father."

On the way to the dining room, Cheung led the way as Wing followed. They walked along the portside outer deck to catch some fresh air and the blurred image of the morning sun as it peered through the slowly rising morning mist.

"You know my son this ship is made of iron. Did you know that iron could float on water?"

"Yes father it has to do with the theory of displacement. Anything will float as long as it weighs less than the same volume of water. The American school taught us this."

"Son, you are very clever, but remember that there is a big difference between intelligence and wisdom."

"And what is that, honourable father?"

"My beloved son, they taught you everything except what is really the most essential to your education. That is learning how to think instead of what to think. Do you understand the difference?"

"What is the difference?" He is not going to answer, thought Wing, maybe another riddle at best.

Cheung noticed the indifference in his son's eyes, *"My clever son, life is filled with choices. Wisdom is knowing how to make the best decision, based on knowledge and past experience lacking in youth. Learning from one's own mistakes and the mistakes of others is crucial in the quest for wisdom."*

Surprised at receiving an answer instead of a riddle, Wing pondered the answer.

"My son, the customs and traditions of the west are different from ours so you must learn when to follow the Book of Rites and when to emulate western customs. (The centuries-old Book of Rites was the book that regulated public, social and domestic conduct for the Chinese. To respect your elders, walk behind them slowly; anyone twenty years older must be treated as your father; anyone ten years older must be treated as a brother; anyone five years older walk side by side. Follow your teacher, never pass or speak with others without the teacher speaking first. When approaching a teacher, speak not until the teacher has spoken.) *Among our countrymen, you must follow traditional rules. Among non-Chinese, the traditional rules of conduct will only arouse curiosity, laughter and potential abuse. Newly-arrived Chinese immigrants will follow tradition, but our westernized compatriots will follow local customs. You must decide how to act with each faction."*

Wing moved gingerly forward to walk beside his father. "Thank you, father, I will try not to disappoint you." Cheung smiled in response.

The dining room was filled with passengers eating breakfast as the entrance door opened. Onlookers fell silent momentarily to gawk at the new arrivals. It was the first time, the pair appeared dressed in western attire. Both wore dark blue single breasted morning waistcoats with matching

open-V vests and Victorian trousers, white collared shirts, black ties and black leather shoes. The handsome pair stood much taller than the average Chinese. The father had a dark complexion; a lean athletic built and stood 5 foot 7inches in height. The son was slender and stood 5 foot 3 inches in height. Both wore pigtails but unlike most Chinese men, they walked confidently in long strides, instead of the short shuffle adopted by the Chinese to appear subservient to their Manchu masters. Under Qing rule, all Chinese males were forced to wear pigtails or queues as a symbol of Han submission to Manchu domination. Not wearing one identified radicals and was considered an act of treason, which was punishable by the immediate loss of one's head.

Upon their arrival in the dining room Captain Anderson left his officers' table to greet the pair. The Captain was a handsome, dark-complexioned man of average height, approximately fifty years of age, stocky framed with short white hair, a small white moustache and bushy eyebrows with deep wrinkles around his eyes and on his forehead. His probing blue eyes perpetually darted from crew member to crew member, who would nod in recognition of his authority whenever eye contact was exchanged. He had a very formal but courteous manner, a charming smile but a booming voice of command.

"Good morning Mr. Dai and young Master Wing. I hope that you are enjoying the voyage. There are some passengers that I would like you to meet. I arranged a separate table so that you have a chance to converse and get acquainted."

I hope this plan works, thought the Captain, who had been approached by the chief steward concerning complaints from the other passengers that they wished not to be dining with people of inferior origins especially the Chinese. The Captain had thought that he had curtailed this problem early in the voyage when a Mrs. Winifred Simpson first brought the matter to him. He had bluntly refused her request to have the Chinese shunted to the lower deck. Then she had rallied support from some of the other passengers, one of them supposedly knew the owner of the Line, so he was forced to make a token concession to appease the hag and her hen cronies before matters escalated. In the meantime she had found more that offended her as she added Jews to her list of untouchables (Indian term for lower cast).

I will definitely have to redirect her energies elsewhere or this voyage will become mayhem if she continues to stir the pot.

The Captain led Cheung and his son through the spacious dining lounge which housed built-in booths for six people along the outer periphery and tables to seat four people everywhere else. In the far back corner Wing could see a large middle-aged gentleman with a full beard and mustache. He wore a skullcap and was dressed in a white shirt with a black jacket and trousers. Sitting next to him was a pretty dark-haired girl of about ten years of age with radiant white skin and pretty green eyes that seemed to dance. She was dressed in a blue and white gingham dress. Wing had noticed her from the first day he boarded the ship. She smiled each time their eyes met but he always turned away when his interest became too tactless. Why did she always stare at him? Don't these lofan (Europeans) teach their children proper conduct? As the Captain led them closer and closer to the table of dreaded interest Wing thought, no, not that table, but it was too late.

"Mr. Dai and young master Wing please let me introduce you to Rabbi Nathan Beilihis and his daughter Rachel. The Rabbi and Rachel are also on their way to Victoria and have spent the last ten years living in China. My table is signaling me that breakfast is ready and they cannot start without me. So please, excuse me."

Rachel smiled at Wing and greeted him spritely in Chinese, *"Good morning, Mr. Dai and Wing. How are you? Would you like to call me by my Chinese name?"*

Shocked by her fluency in Chinese and her impudence, speaking before their elders, Wing pondered, she assumes that I am too ignorant to be able to speak English. Wing whispered in his father's ear *"Pardon me, father, am I permitted to speak English very quietly?"* Cheung nodded his approval but signaled with his hand to lower his voice, as Wing whispered, "My full name is Dai Wing Sing. I will use your English name, Lachel."

Rachel Louisa erupted into hysterical laughter and knocked over an empty glass.

"I knew you couldn't say my name. So I tried to save you the embarrassment. You can't pronounce your R's because there are no R's in the Chinese language."

"Rachel Louisa, we're in public and you're embarrassing Wing," warned the Rabbi.

"Father, I'm sorry... but I can't help it," as Rachel frantically struggled to regain her ten-year-old composure.

"Lachel, Lachel – what is wrong with that? Silly name anyway. What is your Chinese name?" whispered Wing whose anger has dissipated into amusement at his own inability. His teachers had tried to teach him to pronounce his R-words. He thought that he had finally mastered it while others could not, but now he realized that his teachers had just given up. I will work harder because if this girl is laughing at me, how much more laughter will I cause during the rest of the journey.

"My Chinese name is May Yun."

"That is my sister's name. It means pretty and graceful. She is ten years old." whispered Wing.

"So am I," Rachel whispered in response.

"Please do sit down, Mr. Dai, Wing. I am sorry, Wing, if my daughter's outburst caused you any embarrassment. My daughter and I are fluent in Cantonese and English. We can converse in either English or Chinese which ever you feel most comfortable with. Rachel has lived all her life in China and has only recently learned to pronounce her R's properly. By the way Wing, you have no idea how much training it took for Rachel to learn to say her own name properly."

Wing burst into laughter, "You could not say your own name?"

"We never used my English names before we found out that we were leaving for the New World. We spoke only Chinese until I started learning English two years ago. Let us all agree to just call me by my middle name, Louisa, or May Yun. It will be much easier." said Louisa, somewhat disarmed by Wing's infectious laughter. He reminded her of Leung, the eldest son of her Amah (a live-in nanny dedicated to nurturing a child from birth until marriage) who grew up with her and was her closest companion since birth. The only thing different was that he was much better looking, more poised, more confident, but he had the same high pitched laugh Leung used to emit just before he yielded to her childish whims. Wing was very tall for a Chinese boy and wore a long braided queue of straight black hair that hung midway down his back. His brown eyes were soft and kind, and he appeared bewilderingly confident.

Louisa had been very homesick since the start of the voyage. She had cried almost every day after leaving her home in Canton. When she first

spotted Wing, she had tried to get her father to inquire about him and arrange for an introduction but he had refused. He had wanted her to learn to play with the other children on board. But they shunned her because she was not like them. She was not used to being dominated by older children and she would not submit to the whims of older peers even if they were bigger. She had resigned herself to isolation from the other children until she overheard Mrs. Simpson talking with her friends concerning having to sit in the dining hall with those filthy Chinese and despicable Jews. Then she had approached Mr. Osgood with a proposed solution for all involved. But what did Mrs. Simpson mean "filthy Chinese"? I have lived in China. The Chinese are not filthy, except for beggars. "Despicable Jews?" I must ask father what "despicable" means.

"Mr. Dai may I ask you the purpose of your voyage?" inquired the Rabbi.

"I am a merchant, Rabbi, and I have a store in Victoria that requires my personal attention. We export Chinese goods from China to Gold Mountain. May I ask you the reason for your journey?"

"Yes, I am to be the new Rabbi for the Congregation Emanu- El in the city of Victoria. My brother is a businessman in New York and he informed me of the posting about nine months ago and I applied to the Jewish Congress in New York and was informed that my application was accepted a few months ago."

"So the rest of the family will follow?"

"No Mr. Dai. My wife Miriam, who rests in God's sanctuary died during childbirth. The rest of our household consisted of our Amah and her two children and our cook and his wife who served as our maid. We tried to bring them with us but they chose to remain in the Middle Kingdom (China - the Chinese considered China as the center of human endeavours) and serve the new Rabbi. My daughter and I miss them dearly. They were our family but China was their home and even their love for us could not take them away from the Middle Kingdom."

As the steward approached the Rabbi greeted him "Good morning, Samuel. This is Mr. Dai and his son Wing."

Samuel Harper, a slightly balding, solidly-built, middle-aged man of about 40 years old, stood about five feet eight inches tall and had a cheerful outward disposition. But his eyes never stayed focused on anyone or

anything for too long because he was constantly checking to see who was watching him.

"Good morning Rabbi. Miss Rachel. Pleased to meet you Mr. Dai, Master Dai. I have already ordered for you, Rabbi and Miss Rachel. What would you like to order Mr. Dai and Master Dai?"

"We will have the same."

"The Rabbi and Miss Rachel do not eat pork so we replace bacon and sausages with a slice of beef liver and kidney pie with scrambled egg and baked beans. Do you still want to have the same Mr. Dai and Master Dai?"

Cheung looked in his son's pleading eyes and understood his dilemma."I will have the same but my son will have ---."

The Rabbi interjected, turning towards Cheung. "Mr. Dai, others eating pork does not disturb our appetite in the least. We have lived among the Chinese too long, not to understand that pork is your meat of preference and that the ship only serves it one meal a day. Please have bacon and sausages. When they dined with us our servants ate it at our table all the time. No harm was done."

The Rabbi's understanding of his dilemma and his tactful solution allowed Cheung to save face. The Rabbi had won the admiration of Cheung and also Wing's stomach. Looking at Samuel's nametag, Cheung ordered, "Mr. Harper, we will be pleased to have the regular breakfast with tea. Thank you Rabbi for your understanding."

The Rabbi and Louisa smiled in response. After the completion of breakfast the fathers walked and talked together as Wing and Louisa followed. The morning mist had completely lifted and the weather had finally taken a turn for the better. Both fathers were relieved to find their children happily occupied outside their cabins and each father had found another to exchange their thoughts and ideas on philosophy, politics, culture and history.

Settlements of Jewish people existed in China as early as the Tang Dynasty. Jewish colonies were readily accepted because they shared a common sense of morality and values. Their ideology concerning the value of family, community, education and business were very similar to Chinese ideals. The major chasm between the two cultures was religion. The Jews believed in only one true God. And they tolerated no other beliefs. They believed that they were the chosen people and this belief bound them as a

group against outside forces, but alienated them from mainstream society. In contrast, Chinese religious beliefs centered on ancestral worship. They believed that the spirit of ancestors influenced fate and each individual was accountable to those who passed before them in the next realm, for their conduct during their lifetime. Competition for power and wealth between religious sects never played a significant role in China's past. Taoism and Confucianism were philosophical ideologies without deities. Philosophers, rather than prophets, advocated self-enlightenment and living in harmony within the framework of society. Gods existed in superstitious folklore and were thought to control fate and the forces of nature. Throughout the history of China, religious wars never occurred until Christianity arrived and demanded exclusivity. As early as the 7th century, colonies of Jews had migrated and lived amongst the Chinese. They were treated with respect and dignity by their hosts. With each successive generation, their bloodlines became more diluted until those with Jewish blood could no longer be distinguished amongst the Chinese.

During the voyage, the relationship between the patriarchs grew stronger in mutual admiration and respect. Each had a passion for chess. The Rabbi played the European game and Cheung only played the Chinese form. But since the Chinese game was more complex, it was decided that the Rabbi would teach Cheung the European game. The Rabbi was amazed at how quickly his friend adapted to his game. Soon they became inseparable opponents sitting on the sundeck or in the reading lounge from sunrise to sunset.

Wing and Louisa became constant companions. Louisa was up, washed and ready earlier than before. She would occupy herself reading or looking out the porthole until her father gave permission to leave for the dining lounge. Louisa adopted the routine of rousing the Dai's before breakfast so that Wing could accompany her to the dining lounge.

At first they were accompanied by their parents. As time passed, Wing and Louisa were left to their own devices. They seldom played with other children. There were only six to eight others who frequented the play area and the leaders were a pair of thirteen year-old bullies, one was George, a tall, solidly-built lad and the other was a bigger chubby lad named Michael, the son of Mrs. Simpson. He branded Wing and Louisa with his mother's venom, labeling them as lower-class heathen savages not fit to play with. Seeing that his size and age were an obvious advantage, he and his followers

harassed the two constantly at every possible opportunity. The two had never been exposed to this type of treatment and were ill-prepared to resolve this problem until the solution came, as a result of necessity.

One day the conspirators trapped Wing and Louisa in an isolated portion of the sundeck. The two oldest boys had contrived a plan. Surrounded by a band of children ranging in age from eight to thirteen years, Michael addressed Wing and Louisa."Now the two of you will do as we bid or we'll throw you over. Speak up, Chink or I'll smash you in the face."

Wing did not respond as he sized up the group consisting of five boys, two girls. A pair of 13 year olds Michael and George were the oldest and biggest, then an 11-year-old named Simon and a pair of timid 8-year-olds. Michael's sister Winnie was a gawky-looking 11-year-old. The other girl was a mouthy little nine-year-old named Millicent.

"You touch him Michael Simpson, and I'll tell the Captain and he'll have you flogged," shouted Louisa defiantly as she grasped Wing's left arm to leave.

"You'll be swimming with the sharks before the Captain even hears a word from that big mouth," retorted Michael.

Little Millicent spoke, "Michael, make them do it. I want to see her catch leprosy. My mother said they're all diseased so anyone who kisses a Chink will get leprosy."

"That's right," said Simon, turning to Louisa. "We want you to kiss the Chink."

Louisa thought what a lot of hogwash. She had played with all these children early on in the voyage until there were whispers of her inferior lineage and the older children started to order her around like a servant. Up until that time all three of the older boys were charmed by her striking beauty and self-assured countenance. The girls were envious as her control over the boys had continued to grow. All may have been eventually resolved by her charm had she not cavorted with an even lower outcast in their eyes. Now they were joined in their efforts to make the pair grovel.

But Wing did not look afraid. Louisa knew he would not speak because he had told her that his father had forbidden him from speaking English to strangers for some reason that she could not understand. Wing just stood in front of Louisa, measuring their adversaries. Michael was biggest but was fat and slow. George looked the strongest and most athletic. Simon appeared afraid and harmless, hiding behind the older boys. The girls were too selfish

and pampered to risk getting hurt or dirty and the rest were insignificant. His father's words echoed in his mind, "Avoid confrontation under all circumstances even at the cost of personal injury".

"Go on kiss the Chink," repeated Michael.

The children started to chant "Kiss the Chink. Kiss the Chink."

Louisa suddenly struggled in front of Wing, turned, peered into his eyes, took his face in both hands, smiled at him and then softly kissed him on the lips.

"My God did you see that?" shouted George.

"Now you're a leper," said Simon.

They all started to dance and chant, "You're a leper. You're a leper. You're a leper," as they followed Louisa's every movement around the sundeck.

Then someone shouted "Throw the leper over."

The group tried to grab Louisa, but Wing stepped in front of her. Suddenly, the older boys grabbed Wing and started raining blows from fists and knees as Louisa was held back by the two girls.

Louisa screamed, "No! No!" as the girls allowed Louisa a full view of the beating.

After a barrage of blows by the older boys, Wing struggled to his feet with his face bruised and bleeding. He appeared defenseless but had deflected the most damaging blows and skillfully cushioned what he could not avoid. The group turned its attention onto Louisa. Wing struggled to stand in front once again and he tried to lead her away, as she sobbed at the brutality. Then Michael seized Louisa by her left shoulder from behind with his left hand. Wing who was in front looped his right thumb around Michael's left thumb and gave it a severe outward twist. Michael wielded at the pain.

Wing waited patiently to see what George was going to do. George looked at Michael in bewilderment; he approached the defenseless prey, expecting to give him a thrashing. As he leaned over to grab the victim, Wing blocked his outstretched arms, sidestepped, and delivered a well-placed blow to George's nose, which spurted a stream of blood.

The group gathered to survey the damage to George's nose. Michael and Simon on each side of George faded back, shocked at the sudden change of circumstances. Before the group could recover Wing seized the advantage of surprise. He quickly moved forward and kicked Michael in the groin then delivered a fist into Simon's solar plexus.

Michael doubled over in agony, clasping his privates. Simon slumped back with one knee on the ground, gasping for air. George covered his bleeding nose, as Wing approached him to nullify any further aggression, he cowered and then raised his hand, to signal that he had had enough. The rest looked on in awe. The girls quickly released Louisa then the others cleared a path, as the victors calmly walked through the gathering, in triumph. Louisa's once tear-filled eyes brightened in jubilation and disbelief.

Louisa mulled over the sequence of events that altered their fate. As Wing led her back to her cabin, Louisa questioned Wing, "How did you learn to fight like that, Wing? Why did you let them beat you up if you can fight so well?" asked Louisa.

"Are you hurt? I guess not if you can ask all these questions. Why do you ask so many questions? Why did you kiss me? Never mind. I don't want to know."

"You are not answering my questions. That was stupid, taking a beating like that. You were trying to avoid fighting by letting them beat you up. When they threatened me, you thought that I was in danger, so you decided to fight."

"Lachel Louisa, you think too much. When are you going to teach me how to say your real name properly?"

"I like the way you say it already. Let's get back to how you learned to fight so well. That was amazing. That Michael is twice your size."

"Louisa you must say nothing about this to my father. He will never understand my use of the forbidden art. He said it can only be used to save my own life. Any other use is frivolous and unjustified. Physical violence must always be the last resort. Saving you from harm is not a permitted use."

"Oh! So you admit you did it for me. I must be truly special." Louisa beamed proudly.

"Sorry, I must wash up and change my clothes before my father sees me like this." Wing hurried off.

From that day on, the other children no longer tormented Wing and Louisa. However, the course of their friendship had drastically changed. Each looked at the other differently than before. In his eyes, she was no longer just a playmate, replacing his sister in the courtyard of his mind. She had faced public humiliation kissing him in front of others, to save him from physical injury. Both understood that public displays of affection were forbidden in

Chinese society. How could such a young girl have so much courage standing up to so many others ? She was truly admirable. His mother, his sister and his aunt had never kissed him on the lips, only on the forehead or cheek. While the incident shocked him, he was not offended and the experience still lingered in his mind. After all, the kiss was not unpleasant.

Even though Louisa was shocked by the brutality of the beating, she was enchanted by Wing's humility and maturity as well as his self-discipline and his alarming physical prowess. She understood that she thought and acted above expectations for her age. She recognized the same quality in Wing. His hidden physical talent was cloaked by a quiet demeanor. It captured her imagination and curiosity. How and why does a twelve year old boy from China learn to speak English? Or learn the legendary art of ancient heroes? What else are you hiding, Dai Wing Sing? Smiling to herself, Louisa reflected on the events of the day. He didn't kiss back. Maybe I did it all wrong? It must take a lot of practice to do it right. Amah Lee Que said some practice a lifetime but never master the art. Was she referring to me? She had smiled and winked at her husband when she had spoken these words. Well I hope not because I really enjoyed the shocked look in his eyes when I kissed him. Amah always said the eyes are the windows to the soul and if you do not like what you see then find another window.

Sequestered above, Samuel the steward, watched the whole sequence of events from an elevated perch outside the officers' quarters. He was casually smoking a pipe of tobacco while waiting for the officers to finish their afternoon tea when the mêlée erupted below him. He watched the whole episode in amusement. He thought that little Chinaman had impressive pluck and self-discipline! I thought that he was only twelve. You can never tell the age of these chinks. He must be much older than he looks. But Miss Louisa, a man could sell his soul to possess you - that milky white skin, the long silky, black hair, those long, curly eyelashes and those sparkling green eyes!

At dinnertime, Wing and Louisa were queried about the events of the day after seeing Wing's obvious facial injuries. Since neither would break the bond of silence, both parents agreed that Wing and Louisa would not be permitted to play together until the shroud of secrecy was lifted. They would see each other only during mealtimes, but would not be allowed to speak. Both were to stay in their respective cabins unless they were accompanied by their father. While both parents agreed that the punishment was

just, neither understood that imposed isolation would create greater endearment, as Wing and Louisa communicated with their eyes. Each longed to see the other during mealtimes. And they constantly smiled at each other during breakfast, luncheon, afternoon tea and dinner, until they received a parental look of disapproval. There always seemed to be a hidden joke between the two and anything occurring by accident or out of the ordinary would cause hysterical laughter from both simultaneously. Unbeknownst to the fathers, notes were being secretly passed between the two. As time passed, both parents knew that enforced separation was becoming futile. Cheung noticed that Wing and Louisa behaved differently towards the other children. Previous to Wing's injuries, Wing and Louisa would always evade eye contact with the other children, in passing. Now, they would stare back defiantly, until the others cowered and looked away. Yes, there had been a conflict with the others thought Cheung, and my disrespectful son and his companion triumphed. In the days that followed, Wing received several parental lectures reminding him of the dangers of using unwisely the secret forbidden art and the importance of respect for his elders.

Chapter 2

Trouble Below

MIDWAY ON THE VOYAGE, THE PEACE AND TRANQUILITY OF the early morning was broken by three forceful raps on the door of the Dai cabin. Cheung answered the door."Oh, good morning Captain Anderson is there anything wrong?"

"Mr. Dai, I must talk with you on a matter of the utmost importance. May I please come in?"Cheung stepped aside to let the Captain in. He continued, "Mr. Dai. May I ask you? Are you a doctor of Chinese medicine? I have you listed as a merchant but one of the Chinese passengers below said you are a doctor."

"No, I am not a doctor Captain."

"Well, Mr. Dai, are you familiar with Chinese herbs and remedies?"

"Captain I do have some knowledge of Chinese medicine and I have helped others during times of necessity when there is no one else available. But who aboard would have knowledge of this?"

"One of the passengers in steerage, Mr. Dai, has an accident. He does not trust our ship's physician to treat his wound. Would you please come down to the lower deck to see if you can help us out?"

On his first crossing, Cheung had experienced what it meant to be in steerage. Though he was curious of who knew him down below, he was also

wary of the health problems of infectious diseases, posed to himself and ultimately to his son. Surely, the sanitation and the living conditions for the passengers in steerage must be greatly improved from his youthful experience, 30 years ago. His first voyage to California during the gold rush, still plagued his dreams. So, before making any commitment to help the Captain, he inquired further. "What seems to be the problem Captain? I will not jeopardize the safety of my son."

"Mr. Dai I would not ask that of anyone. One of the boys below was involved in an accident and is bleeding from a bad gash in his leg, He is from your village and he noticed you boarding the ship in Canton. He will not permit the ship's physician to treat him and Mr. Dai, please rest assured that we have no known infectious diseases on board and I will be personally accompanying you."

Wing listened intently. The Captain was unaware that he could understand and speak English since Wing never spoke it openly in public. Having dressed and washed quickly while the two adults conversed, he prepared to satisfy his curiosity about the lower deck.

"Shall we go now Captain? I will bring some of my remedies."Cheung quickly fetched a small brown paper packet labeled in Chinese from his black leather travelling bag."What did you say this man's name was Captain?"

"Way Chuk Yee. Apparently you helped him as a little boy back in China when he was sick with a fever."

Wing whispered in his father's ear. *"Father it's my friend from our village, Loun An (nickname - "dragon eye", also name of a fruit). He taught me how to swim two summers ago. He told me that he was leaving for Gold Mountain to build a path for an iron dragon. What luck to be on the same ship! Please father, may I come? I am truly sorry for my acts of disobedience. I am still very young and have much to learn. Please father, he and I are very good friends."*

"Captain, do you foresee any danger below?"

"No, Mr. Dai. It's safe there but unfortunately it is very hot and foul-smelling but not dangerous."

"May my son come with us, Captain? That injured boy may be his friend."

"Yes, let's go. By the way, does Master Wing understand English?"

"Captain, life is full of surprises. The difference between a victim of circumstance and a master of fate is careful preparation."

Surprised by the form of Cheung's reply the Captain thought to himself, you did not answer my question but again I do not think you meant to. Of course he understands English. The Captain remembered Wing being close by when he was approached by Mrs. Simpson and her hens. Wing must have overheard the reason for changing the seating in the dining room.

Wing tried to memorize the way down through the bowels of the ship so he could return on his own at another time to search for better cuisine. As they descended below through a labyrinth of gangways, doors and ramps, Wing searched for guides to help him remember the path. He thought maybe I can borrow something from Loun An to mark the way back. If I borrow an ink brush then I will have to carry an ink bottle. All I really need is a small piece of cloth dipped in ink but that would mark my clothes and hands. Better not. I have been enough trouble. Maybe if I can impress father, he will let me play with Louisa again, although it is fun writing notes and passing them under the table.

The drone of the engine grew louder as the group descended through narrow passage-ways into the heart of the vessel. When they arrived at the entrance to steerage on the lower deck they encountered a guard at the door. He snuffed out his pipe at the approach of the Captain and stood and saluted.

"The doctor is still in there, Captain. But the injured boy is still resisting. And the other passengers have rallied behind him."

The door was locked from the outside. The sentry unlocked and opened the door. The foul odour of vomit and human excrement jolted the visitors as they quickly covered their noses to avoid gagging. The visitors and their clothes were already soaked in perspiration from their climb down and the heat from the nearby engine room. The passengers were all young Chinese males. When they saw their compatriots they quickly rallied around the visitors shouting their complaints about food and living conditions onboard, all at the same time in a mixture of different dialects.

The facility appeared to be a gigantic iron cavern with vertical metal poles spaced at regular intervals. Between the poles were suspended hammocks three high. The passengers were all young men ranging from 14 years to 40 years of age. It was very warm due to the closeness to the engine room; the topless passengers were dressed only in loincloths or baggy cotton pants rolled up to the knees. The whole room vibrated with the churning and

hissing of the nearby engine. The room was fairly dark, except for the light coming from a few elevated portholes and the odd oil lamp. In various areas there were blankets suspended over ropes. These must be the toilet areas thought Cheung. There were at least four to five hundred men crowded in the metal cavern. Comparing these lodgings with his first ocean crossing in a wooden-hulled ship Cheung thought yes, these metal ships have more space but they just pack more into them. Not much had changed for passengers in steerage. Cheung watched the effect of these sights on his son who bravely tried to hold back his tears of compassion at seeing others endure such hardship and suffering but the sight was almost too much for a child of twelve with limited experience in human misery. Cheung knew it was something that Wing must see and experience to prepare him for the future. You have been truly fortunate my son but look and learn from these harsh realities as fate smiles kindly on very few.

All of a sudden from the distant corner came a yell, "*Up your mother's butt you white demon. Don't touch me. Leave me alone.*"

Wing recognized the voice as the visitors pushed through the crowd to the injured victim. No longer holding his nose Wing rushed over to see his friend."*My friend, are you badly hurt? I am happy to see you.*"

"*Wing, I am happy to see you too,*" replied Loun An.

"*Loun An please watch your language. My father is here.*"

As Cheung approached he gently waved his son aside. "*My son I have heard this language often. Now let me see your injury.*" He looked down at Loun An who was sitting in a corner with a cleaver close by.

The left pant leg of his cotton trouser was stained and dripping with blood and the ship's physician was sitting on a stool looking exasperated and sweating profusely.

Covering his nose with a perfumed handkerchief, the Captain spoke, "Doctor Mason this is Mr. Dai and his son Master Wing. They are familiar with the injured passenger. Mr. Dai has some knowledge of Chinese medicine which may be useful."

"Glad to meet you Mr. Dai, young master" responded Dr. Mason through a perfumed handkerchief. "I don't think the femoral artery has been severed but the wound needs cleaning and a fresh dressing. As soon as I pulled out the scalpel to cut away his pant leg, he started to balk."

"He was going to kill me," shouted the injured victim. *"A friend from our village told me his cousin in Gold Mountain wrote and told him when you get injured and can no longer work for them they just kill you."*

"He's not going to kill you. He was only going to cut your pant leg to treat your injury. Now let me see it," said Cheung in a calming voice and setting Loun An's cleaver aside.

The doctor already had a towel, a basin of clean water and dressings sitting on a small metal tray. As the doctor stood up, the injured man was helped onto the empty stool, his leg elevated on a large inverted bucket so that it was lying straight. The doctor started to wash it off but felt nauseous. He quickly searched for his perfumed handkerchief to avoid vomiting. Cheung quickly moved closer and gestured that he would take over treating the injured man. The doctor consented watching closely the technique of his Chinese counterpart. Instead of cutting the garment Cheung motioned Wing to come forward to help Loun An remove his pants. I should have understood this injured man only owned one pair of pants thought Doctor Mason in retrospect. Cheung scrubbed his hands fastidiously then started to clean the wound. Doctor Mason was amazed with Cheung's understanding of medical technique.

"Thank you, Mr. Dai, can I have a closer look at the wound?"

He probed and inspected the wound "No damage to the femoral. I will wash and dress it if I can just rest for a minute."

"Doctor Mason, I can do it for you. I've adjusted to the smell. Why don't the rest of you go out and catch some fresh air. Is this your solution for cleansing the wound over here?" said Cheung pointing to a bottle marked "alcohol". Doctor Mason responded with a nod.

"Thank you very much Mr. Dai," replied the Captain as he escorted Doctor Mason towards the locked door. He rapped three times, a small window opened from the other side, the door was unlocked and the two departed.

"Wing, why do you not leave? And you no longer hold your nose at the smell," said Cheung suddenly very proud of his son.

"Father, I thought that if you could bear the stench so must I. The more that you resist the smell the more difficult it will be to bear. I think that you once told me about this in a story from your journey to Gold Mountain." Wing reminded his father.

"*You are a good listener, my son. I feel very proud that you can learn from a story I told you, so long ago.*"

Loun An fidgeted impatiently as father and son conversed.

"*This is going to sting.*" Loun An grimaced in pain as Cheung cleansed the wound with alcohol. Doctor Mason returned to survey his counterpart at work. Cheung opened the brown paper packet and took out the shavings from a deer horn and spread it over the deep diagonal gash on the left side of Loun An's left calf. Then he applied a clean dressing and wrapped the wound snugly.

Wing spotted a bloody cloth that was used by his father to compress the wound before bandaging and thought just what I need.

Cheung warned Loun An "*Your injury is deep, you must wash your pants and keep these dressings as clean as possible. I will be back to see you soon to change your dressings. By the way how did this happen?*"

"*Mr. Dai it was just a silly accident. You see that fool over there*" he pointed at a young boy of approximately 16 years of age." *He was chasing some rats that had found some food he had been hiding and he tripped over something and the cleaver fell out of his hand and somehow the blade hit my leg. It was an accident and I bear him no malice since he promises to do my share of the chores and agrees to serve me my meals until I am recovered from my injury. His mother must certainly have been a donkey and he must have come out of her wrong end.*" Loun An spoke purposely loud enough that his perpetrator could overhear the conversation.

Loun An addressed Wing "*Wing you did not tell me that you were going to Gold Mountain. Why didn't you tell me?*"

Wing had been quietly analyzing and trying to make sense out of the deplorable living conditions in steerage. He was shocked back to reality by his friend's questions.

"*Loun An I did not know that I was coming until after you had already left for Canton. But I am happy to see you, maybe I can come back to visit you.*"

The window opened the entry door and the Captain shouted "Mr. Dai are you finished yet?"

As Cheung and his son proceeded towards the door, they are followed by their countrymen who bombard them with questions and requests. When Cheung approached the door, he turned towards the gathering and spoke out "*If anyone needs my help, I will return tomorrow.*"

Cheung rapped three times on the door; the sentry unlocked the door, as father and son exited.On the other side the Captain said "Mr. Dai thank you very much. I don't know what might have happened if you weren't available. Is there any way I can show my gratitude?"

"Captain, may I tour your kitchen after lunch today?"asked Cheung. The Captain acknowledged consent.

"Then that is thanks enough" replied Cheung.

Doctor Mason said "That boy's gash was pretty deep; he should have had stitches. His wound will surely infect under those conditions. He doesn't have much of a chance, surrounded in that filth."

"Can I have permission to go back to steerage whenever I wish, Captain? To check and change the dressings."

"I will arrange an escort whenever you find the time, Mr. Dai," replied Captain Anderson.

On the way back Wing marked the walls and doors with the blood-soaked face cloth. He had lost his appetite temporarily with the shock of what he saw and smelt, but the thought of rice rekindled his interest since it was almost lunchtime and breakfast had been missed.

When they returned to their cabin Cheung said "*The Captain knows you understand and probably assumes you can also speak English. He watched your response to what he told me. His knowing is of no consequence but you must learn to look ignorant whenever strangers speak English and not react to what is spoken. Your eyes must be distant and you must wear a blank look. Remember anyone that knows that you understand or speak English knows that you have attended a school that only the rich can afford. You will be worth a very big ransom. Please try to be more careful. Now, I wish to express how happy I am with your conduct on the lower deck. So I will talk to Nathan about allowing you and Louisa to play together again, and maybe the two of you can stop passing notes under the table.*"

Surprised by his father's discovery, Wing replied sheepishly, "*Yes, father.*"

After quickly washing and changing for lunch, Cheung and Wing proceeded to the dining room. On their way they visited the Beilihis' cabin just as Louisa and Nathan stepped out their cabin door. The Rabbi was pleasantly surprised. He said "We missed you this morning. The chief steward said that you and Wing were off doing a favour for the Captain. I hope everything worked out."

"Nathan I will tell you of our experience later, but may I talk to you in private for a moment?" The two men conferred for a short while, then returned to address their children. "Well, Nathan and I are in full agreement that any further extension of our ban will be lifted immediately and the two of you can resume playing together as long as there is no more trouble with any of the other passengers."

Louisa squealed. "Oh thank you, father and thank you Mr. Dai." Then she turned to Wing and asked. "How did you manage to do that?"

Wing just smiled and whispered privately to Louisa, "They know about our notes at mealtimes. You weren't careful enough. I hope they didn't read any of them. You should not have made fun about how they eat. It was disrespectful"

Louisa replied, "It was fun, wasn't it? If they saw anything, then it was probably your fault. By the way, I'm ahead in our wagering game. You owe me six favours and I am going to make a list right after lunch of what you have to do for me, to even the score now that the game is over."

Wing felt duped by someone two years his junior." What are you talking about? Favours? We were just having fun. Were we not?" But she knew that he would submit as he started to emit that high-pitched laugh of submission.

Everything seemed to be back to normal as lunch was finally completed. The Captain approached the table and addressed the table. "I hope that you all enjoyed your lunch. Mr. Dai, I have arranged that tour of the galley for you. We can go now if you are not otherwise engaged."

Cheung excused himself from the table and accompanied the Captain. Once in the galley Cheung saw what he had hoped to find – food waste. The Captain escorted Cheung around the galley and gave him a description of the machinery and its capacity. Mr. Cheung walked about casually and surveyed it himself. The Captain thought to himself, he is looking for something but he is too polite to be direct. I may really need him if any more problems arise during the voyage on the lower deck. The ship is dangerously over-burdened with too much human cargo. If anything provokes the Chinese below, we could encounter more problems than we may have anticipated. The Chinese in steerage respect and trust this man. I must do all I can to win his co-operation.

Cheung stopped at a large container of food refuse, beside the dishwashing counter. He looked at the Captain who was leading him and inquired,

"What happens to this bucket of food remnants? Is it all dumped into the sea?"

"Yes Mr. Dai it is in our regulations. They'll go rotten otherwise and the rat problem would escalate unless it is dumped."

So you have rats even on the upper decks of this iron ship thought Cheung." It just seems so wasteful when you feed the Chinese what? Maybe, rice and tea?"

Cheung had hoped that conditions for those in steerage had improved, but he could see very little progress from thirty years ago. The Captain was embarrassed by his duplicity with the shipping line's inhumanity. The Captain thought this man understands how dangerously over-subscribed we are on board.

"Captain, do you think that your galley workers could sort out the meat and vegetables into separate buckets and at the end of the day, maybe I could carry them down to the Chinese passengers in steerage?"

The Captain smiled in admiration and thought what a brilliant idea. What better way would there be to pacify the Chinese down below. "It's against the shipping line's health regulations, Mr. Dai. But I agree with you, it is an awful waste which could be put to good use on the lower deck. I think that we can make an exception under the current circumstances, as long as we keep it quiet and no one finds out. I will make the arrangements. I will send someone with you to carry the buckets. After the dining lounge is closed for the evening, I will send someone to your cabin, who will lead you down to the lower deck. The buckets will be waiting for you with the sentry on duty. We can commence the project this evening, Mr. Dai, if you wish."

Pleasantly surprised at the Captain's prompt compliance, Cheung quickly added "Captain, can I also request some large candles, a large bucket of water and mop to be provided to the steerage passengers on a daily basis? The candles will burn off some of the noxious fumes and the passengers can mop the deck when it is soiled. I will bear the costs for all that I have requested. Can the toilet buckets be emptied daily?"

Captain Anderson replied "All will be done as you have requested Mr. Dai at the shipping line's expense."

Starting that evening Mr. Osgood the chief steward knocked on the Dai's' cabin door. It was around eight p.m. The steward led Cheung down below. Two large sealed buckets were brought down by galley staff and left with

the sentry in advance. Mr. Osgood waited at the door with the sentry as Cheung entered the steerage chamber with the two sealed buckets. After a few visits, Mr. Dai became familiar with the way down to steerage and convinced the steward to relax on the upper deck while he proceeded down below on his own. During his visits he treated many with medical problems, lectured on personal health, and answered questions about Gold Mountain, the local customs and the laws of its inhabitants.

Wing questioned his father on his evening outings but Cheung decided that the less his son knew the better for all concerned. Although he wanted his son to view the conditions below, he feared that Wing would be too easily swayed by his sympathy for the steerage passengers. One evening, Wing decided to follow his father. As he followed, he knew immediately that his father's path was the same as the one he had secretly marked with Loun An's blood. His markings were still on the doors, railings and walls. He kept a good distance back from his father to avoid detection. When his father came to the steerage entrance he saw him enter with two buckets. What was in those buckets? Then he remembered his father's tour to the ship's galley. Could that be food in those buckets father? He thought to himself, beware father you may become responsible for all those lives. Who will undo their evil? I had better get back to the upper deck before Louisa comes looking for me. I was supposed to meet her on the starboard outer deck to watch the sunset. I hope she is not still waiting for me.

Meanwhile, on the starboard outer deck, Louisa watched the moon and stars as she laid face up on a box platform which housed safety equipment. Where are you Wing? I have been to your cabin twice already and nobody was there. What a beautiful night! I know you'll come soon. Suddenly a pair of hands grasped her from behind. Before she could scream, a hand covered her mouth and she was suspended with her legs dangling helplessly in mid-air. A voice whispered "You had better co-operate or I will throw you over right now. Do you understand?" She consented with a nod as a hand groped the secret crevices of her body.

Wing came around the corner. Louisa, upon seeing Wing, started to resist again. She bit down hard on the hand covering her mouth and shouted, "Wing! Help!"

Wing realized right away that he was over-matched by the adult. He saw Samuel, grimacing from the bite with one hand and holding Louisa around

the waist with the other. The scene flashed in his mind. I have seen this before. Oh no, that silly dream! He assessed the situation wondering what to do. He could see panic and fear in the eyes of the assailant who was desperate and sweating profusely, gesturing with his hand to keep quiet or over she would go.

Suddenly Samuel's eyes narrowed. He decided on a course of action. He would throw her over and blame the little Chink who couldn't speak English. Louisa screamed "Wing help me! Get help! Quick!" as Samuel approached the side railing.

In one swift moment Louisa was tossed over. She shouted "Wing, Wing. Save me!" There was a distant splash. Wing ran towards the bow of the ship, seized a life preserver nearby and tossed it as far as he could in Louisa's direction.

He shouted "Swim to the life-preserver, Louisa!"

He then spotted an alarm bell nearby and ran towards it, dodging Samuel who was in close pursuit. Samuel whispered, "So, you can speak English. You devious little bastard."

Wing reached the bell and rang it vigorously, until Samuel seized him. Several passengers and crew started heading in the direction of the commotion. From the bridge the Captain responded to the alarm and spotted the last seconds of Wing's scuffle with the steward. Samuel dislodged Wing from the bell. As Wing continued to flay, Samuel carried him to the side rail and threw him into the sea. The Captain ordered, "Halt the engines. Lower a lifeboat and be quick about it. Bring me that steward right now." He pointed at Samuel from the outer deck of the bridge.

Louisa clung to the life preserver. The night was calm and the sky was clear otherwise she would not have seen the life preserver. The water was very cold.

In the distance she heard a faint voice, "Louisa Louisa. Where are you?"

She screamed, "Wing, I'm over here. Can you hear me?"

"Keep shouting. I will follow your voice. Try to follow mine."

After several minutes of yelling, the two finally found each other. Wing swam towards the sound of Louisa's voice. Louisa was shivering badly, her teeth were starting to clatter. Exhausted from the cold, Wing finally reached the life preserver that Louisa clung to.

"Hey what happened back there Louisa? Why did you make Samuel so angry?"

"Wing I don't really understand what he wanted, but he tried to touch me all over in my most private areas. I hate him. I hope he dies."

"Louisa, are you okay? Sorry I was late. Maybe if I had been on time this would not have happened."

"What has happened is our fate. I think we were meant to die together."

"I think you have been reading too many Chinese romance novels. No one is going to die. Oh look the ship has stopped and is reversing. They are sending out a search party. Do you have anything light-coloured that we can wave so they will be able see us, when they get close?"

"No I'm wearing dark clothing except for my bloomers."

"Oh, they will do."

"Hey you have a white shirt on."

"Look Louisa. I am exhausted from swimming around trying to find you while you have been floating on this life preserver. My arms feel very heavy. I don't have the strength to take off my jacket My arms and back have started to cramp."

Louisa struggled for a few minutes as Wing clutched the life preserver with his left hand and the back of Louisa's dress with the other hand. "Okay here are my bloomers."

"Now let's try to kick our legs and steer ourselves towards the ship. My father said under cold conditions you must remember to keep moving and never let yourself fall asleep. So keep talking."

The pair thrashed through the water towards the ship. Louisa's outer extremities were starting to grow numb as the power in her legs gradually dissipated. Her eyes struggled to stay open, her breathing became shallow, her voice grew faint and nearly indiscernible. She could no longer kick her legs.

Wing tried to coax her to remain conscious. "Keep moving your arms and legs. Don't stop." Desperate to keep her awake, he thought momentarily."By the way, what were those 6 favours that I still owe you?"

Louisa's eyes opened slightly and in a quivering voice she said, "I wanted you to kiss me."

"Okay I am ready. Are you?" Wing said in an animated voice to keep her conscious.

Louisa was embarrassed and giggled coyly. She perked up slightly but her eyes struggled to stay open. "Yes, I've been ready since that first time, when you didn't kiss me back. Now … now do it right or I'll… go nighty.. night."

Wing flipped the life-preserver over Louisa's head and overlapped her arms. Her arms started to slip off the life-preserver. He feared that she might sink into the abyss. He decided to fasten her to the life-preserver by using her bloomers to secure her to the flotation device with a double knot. From outside of the life–preserver Wing faced Louisa. He leaned forward then kissed her eyes, her nose, her cheeks, and then her lips. Her lips were cold. His tongue explored the inner recesses of her mouth which was only slightly warm. Fearing for her life he took a deep breath and blew hard into her cold mouth to share his warmth. He saw a faint smile appear on her face and her eyes opened a bit wider. Good ,he thought, this could keep her from falling asleep because if she fell asleep she would die. I have to keep her awake.

"Keep moving. Now how was that Louisa?"

In a weakened voice "Pret-ty good. I think you can do bet-ter. Do you mind not try-ing to blow air down my my throat this time. I still have … have five more to go. Re-mem-ber no blo-wing or it doesn't count."

"Okay here comes number two."

Wing kissed her again but this time with warmth and softness. He sucked as hard as he could, as if he were removing the cold from her lungs and into his.

"Wing, that was bet-bet-ter, much bet-ter."

"I think I can do better still. Want to try four more, Louisa?"

"Sure, why… why not?"

Then her eyes started to roll back. Wing thought no, no, do not go to sleep. He shook her frantically with no response. Suddenly Wing heard the distant screaming of men in a life-boat.

"Master Wing. Master Wing."

He yelled "Here, here."

He tried to paddle closer to the rescue vessel but his legs had grown too numb. His hands were also numb. All he could muster was shouting "Here."

Wing shook her and whispered "Louisa wake up, Louisa. Louisa wake up."

Even though his strength to retain his hold of the life-preserver was dwindling, Wing tried to nudge Louisa with his face.

Louisa's eyes opened slightly for a few seconds and she said in a dying whisper, "Wing, always …. always remem..ber me." Her eyes rolled back and her head slumped forward.

Wing whispered in her ear "No, no Louisa come back. Louisa come back."

His father had told him that when the spirit leaves its physical being, it must be coaxed back before it departs completely. Within minutes, the search party in the lifeboat reached the pair. The rescuers were shocked to discover Louisa since they were only expecting a single victim. When the rescuers finally pulled the victims out of the water Wing quickly lost consciousness and was covered with blankets. The life-boat reached the ship and docked at the bottom of a gang-way. Louisa's body was carried up the gang-plank on a stretcher. Wing was carried up next. A crowd of people surrounded the two. Once he arrived on the main deck Wing recovered consciousness. Cold and shivering he saw Louisa's cold body next to him. His eyes filled with tears. Cheung sat quietly beside his son and tried to sympathize with him. Crouched beside Louisa, Nathan shook his head at the sight of his daughter's lifeless body. He quietly sobbed as other passengers surrounded him offering their sympathy.

Wing turned to his father and pleaded "*Father, is there anything you can do? Please, father we must bring her back. Please father, do something! Do not let her die! This is not her fate! My dreams reveal otherwise. Please believe me!*"

Cheung immediately approached Captain Anderson and spoke with him privately. The Captain whispered instructions to Mr. Osgood who complied and departed in haste. The Captain returned and took Cheung aside "Everything will be ready for you as soon as you arrive at the bath-house facility."

A young seaman picked up the limp body and quickly carried her to the ladies' bathhouse. Cheung followed closely behind. Mr. Osgood was standing at the entrance to the bathhouse. Cheung thanked the seaman and relieved him of the drowned victim. Steam poured out, as the door was opened. A large tub filled with hot water had been prepared. Cheung immersed the clothed body into the tub elevating her head. Supported by Nathan, Wing arrived at the bathhouse shortly after. Cheung turned to Wing. "You must call her back."

As Wing called out repeatedly "Louisa, Louisa. Come back...", Cheung opened her mouth placed his mouth over hers and filled her lungs with

warm air. When Cheung tired, Nathan continued. The process was continued for half an hour with no response. Appearing to surrender to the inevitable, Cheung looked at Wing with remorse. Wing shook his head and refused to yield to the outcome. "Father, she survives in my dream. I know she will live." He continued to struggle forward painfully on deadweight legs towards the top end of the tub where Cheung was still holding Louisa's head. Wing shouted out louder than before "Louisa, come back, you have to come back."

Nathan and Cheung were startled by Wing's tenacity. Suddenly a finger twitched. Wing pointed at Louisa's left hand. The others saw more fingers start to move, then the arms, then a gasp for air, followed by coughing. Louisa's eye-lids opened. Her eyes rolled forward. Cheung and Nathan were awestruck, Wing smiled as he gently caressed the revived spirit. Nathan raised his arms and cried out, "Oh, merciful God, thank you for returning my daughter."

Louisa forced a smile at Wing. Barely conscious, she whispered to Wing, "I came back for you!" Then she dropped off into a restful slumber, breathing soundly.

Tired but relieved, father carried his son to the men's bathhouse. Cheung had requested a tub of hot water to be prepared for his son. Wing fell asleep in the bath. He was lifted out, dried and carried to his bed by his father. Cheung looked at his son and thought to himself, my son, you have saved a life. Her life is now your responsibility. Your fate and mine may have been greatly altered by what has transpired tonight.

Chapter 3

A New Commitment

WING HAD BEEN SO EXHAUSTED BY THE ORDEAL, HE SLEPT FOR two days. When he woke up his first thought was to visit Louisa. Had it been just a terrible dream or did it really happen? His legs and arms ached so much, it confirmed what had occurred. He noticed that the clothes and shoes he had worn last were missing from the closet, which further reinforced the reality. He washed and dressed as quickly as he could, to check on Louisa. With aching joints, he struggled down the hallway as people whispered behind him. Some clapped. Some shouted "well-done boy". He tried to ignore them, as many stopped him to pat him on the back. He didn't understand what they are doing, but he had to see Louisa, right away. When he arrived, he tapped gently at the cabin door. Nathan answered the door and picked him up in his massive arms and hugged him warmly.

"Wing, I am indebted to you for the rest of my life. If there is ever anything I can do for you, please let me know, you need not ask more than once."

Louisa called out "Wing, are you alright? I am famished but they won't let me have anything but chicken soup and some bread to eat. I think that I'm ready to go out and play but they won't let me leave the cabin for one more day. How do you feel? You look a bit tired."

"Louisa, did it all really happen? It all seemed like a crazy dream. Everything went by so fast. Are you alright? Will you recover completely?"

"Wing, I am fine. I feel fully recovered now."

Nathan's eyes filled with tears of joy. He decided that he would allow the two a chance to discuss their experience in private. He retreated to the dining room to join Cheung for lunch. As the door closed behind Nathan, Wing took Louisa's face in his hands and gently kissed her forehead. She smiled at him with an impish look. "I am not counting that one. You still owe me five."

"Four" said Wing.

"Second one didn't count. I think I was dead. So you're back up to five." Louisa giggled with girlish glee, rosy cheeks and a sparkle in her eyes.

"Louisa, did you really die? How did it feel?"

"Actually it felt wonderful. You know I don't think I will ever fear death again. I thought that I was going to finally see my mother. All I have are photos. I have dreamed of meeting her my whole life. I have always felt her presence. I wanted so much to tell her how much I love her and how much I missed her. I wanted to feel her arms around me and the warmth of her embrace. I did not want to come back, until I heard you calling for me. "

Wing tried to deflect the gravity of Louisa's words. "What did you see?"

"It was not so much what I saw, Wing, it was how I felt. It was such a wonderful feeling that if it had not been for your calling me back, I would not have returned."

"Well, I'm truly sorry to have brought you back. Why did you listen to me? You don't generally listen to me," said Wing whimsically.

"Because I don't want you to forget me… Ever! And that's why I'm here. I grew up with Chinese philosophy and I know that you're responsible for me for the rest of your life. Dai Wing Sing, I want to tell you right now that you and I are bound forever, and I will never let you forget it. My life belongs to you." She smiled softly as she spoke but both understood her intent.

"Louisa, you think that I didn't know the responsibility, tied with saving your life. I fully intended to assume this responsibility, before I tossed you the life-preserver. I risked all for you, against all my father's teachings. Louisa, let us not speak of this responsibility as a burden with which I am laden. I accept it freely without regret."

Louisa beamed with joy over Wing's eloquent reply, and stumbled out of bed falling into Wing's arms. Aroused by his words, she kissed him as he lifted her back onto her bed and covered her with the blanket. "I think you had better rest until tomorrow. I will visit you later. I have not seen my father yet."

"Please thank him for me. I was barely conscious during his earlier visits."

As he entered the dining room, Wing found his father having lunch and talking with Nathan. They smiled and waved as he gingerly walked through the dining room. Other passengers stopped eating, to greet him with "well done", "good job lad", "very admirable my boy". Some shook his hand; others patted him on the back as he made his way through the dining lounge, even Mrs. Simpson. Others seated in the dining room called out "Here, here," and clapped in a show of support.

When he reached the table, Cheung smiled and said *"My son, I am glad to see you have recovered from your ordeal. Don't let the other passengers sway your sense of judgment. None of these people were your friends before the rescue, so why would their opinions matter now? How do you feel? You were very fortunate to survive. I feared for your safety."*

"Father, I feel fine except for a little soreness. I am sorry to have scared you but I knew that we would both survive. Can we speak about it later? " Cheung gestured his approval.

A new steward took Wing's order and soon he was eating with great relish. Cheung asked, *"And how is Louisa? Nathan tells me you were visiting with her. How is her colour this morning?"*

"She looked and sounded fine, father. She asked me to thank you for helping with her treatment after the rescue."

"I saw her yesterday and this morning. Nathan has thanked me enough. Let us just be thankful you both survived with no ill-effects."

"I'm sure that she will be fine" said Nathan.

Doctor Mason approached the table to talk to the Dai's and Nathan. "Good day everyone. Mr. Dai, what your son did was truly brilliant and courageous in that frigid water. Can you express to him my deepest admiration? But I am dying of curiosity as to your treatment for Louisa and her recovery. Maybe I can learn something from eastern medicine and save more lives in the future. Whose idea was that bathtub of hot water? I have never heard of or seen such a treatment. I wish that I had come up to the ladies' bathhouse

to observe. I had abandoned all hope for her after I examined her body on deck. She was officially dead according to western medicine; there was no pulse, no breathing, and I could hear no heartbeat. Now she is recovering with no damage to her brain after being dead for at least half an hour. What a miracle! Was the treatment your idea Mr. Dai?"

Cheung answered "Yes, Doctor Mason. It was my idea. I worked strictly on intuition. Both Nathan and I thought that she had passed away, but my son was determined to restore her."

"That makes it even more amazing Mr. Dai. In addition, Mr. Way's leg is completely healed in just a few days. I have never seen anything like it. What did you put on that wound for it to heal so soon? I've never seen such a large gash close so quickly."

"Chinese herbs mixed with the shavings of deer antlers, Doctor Mason. You can acquire it from most Chinese herbalists. Sorry, my supply has been used up by those on the lower deck or I would give you some. There should be some in Victoria. I will try to send some to you."

"Yes, please, can you send it to me through our shipping line office, Mr. Dai? I would love to have it analyzed. When I watched you treat Mr. Way, I couldn't help but notice your techniques resembles that of Western medicine."

"Doctor Mason, like you I try to learn from other medical practitioners. I've adopted techniques from the West. The local missionary school had an attendant doctor who would sometimes assist our local people when Eastern medicine failed. Sometimes I served as an assistant as well as a translator. This doctor and I became very good friends and we exchanged many ideas on medical treatments. Eastern and western medicine serve the same purpose and each can learn from the other. Neither eastern or western medical science should ever pre-judge what is new or different, based on its source. Medical treatments and remedies should be judged on their effectiveness."

"Thank you Mr. Dai, I am in full agreement. Anyway, I had better continue my tour of the sick passengers. Rabbi, can you tell Louisa I will be a little late this afternoon? Sorry to have interrupted your meal but I could not hold back my curiosity any longer. Thank you for your indulgence. I look forward to talking with you again, Mr. Dai."

Inspired by the exchange, Doctor Mason bowed respectfully then departed.

"Good man that Doctor Mason" declared Nathan.

"Yes, maybe we can exchange some ideas and knowledge before the end of the voyage. There are only a couple of weeks remaining" said Cheung.

The next day the Captain dropped in to see both Louisa and Wing, individually. He questioned both at length and was satisfied with their version of the events. Samuel the steward was put under mandatory custody for the duration of the voyage. Since the Qin Dynasty (221BC), the Han had never believed his obvious lies. The steward was a new crew member. None of the other stewards liked or trusted him. He was a festering sore that had to be lanced sooner or later. What a miracle it was that those children had survived. The death of one or both would have stirred up a lot of trouble. Mrs. Simpson would have of course rallied support behind the steward. If only Wing had survived, he would have been heavily burdened to prove his innocence.

Though happy to have his daughter back, Nathan was very concerned about his daughter's growing infatuation with Wing. After the close encounter with death her inquiries had taken a different tone. These were questions of a personal nature, only a mother could comfortably answer. He felt so inadequate to answer such questions, but knew her precocious mind would find solutions, if not by advice then by trial and error. After the death of his wife, he had carefully selected a very capable and wise woman to serve as an amah for Louisa because he was determined that his daughter needed a good role model to become a woman of strength and wisdom. However, there would be an overabundance of confidence and willfulness accompanying these qualities. Once she made a decision, her will was unbending. Now this young boy had won her heart. The societal consequences of such a relationship could lead to eventual catastrophe. Cheung must have also selected a very perceptive amah for his children. If Louisa's infatuation grew stronger she may become blind to more compatible opportunities. He had no antagonism with her present heart's passion since she was still a child. Wing may appear to be a child but he has been prepared for a life meant to deal with challenges which his daughter need not face. However, without Wing's efforts, she would be dead. When the alarm had sounded, Nathan immediately started searching for his daughter and when he could not find

her, he was sickened by the thought that they could be together. When he saw her limp body hoisted up from the lifeboat he had given her up for dead. How they saved her was beyond belief. Perhaps this is the will of God. Maybe it would be best to leave it in His hands.

Walking back to the cabin after lunch Wing was quiet, pensive and troubled. He has something to say to me thought Cheung; I will be patient and wait. When the Dai's returned to their cabin, Wing was very nervous and obviously was thinking hard on how to approach his father. *"Father I have something that I must confess. I had dreams that I never told you about. When you asked me each morning about my dreams I lied because I was angry at having to leave our home in China. I now know that I erred and that it almost cost my life as well as that of Louisa. Father I did dream about the rescue before it happened. Not in detail with recognizable faces but the event was fairly similar."*

Cheung put his hand on his son's shoulder and sighed. *"My son I knew that you had dreams because of the restlessness with which you slept. You also speak when you dream but I never knew that there could be such danger for you on board this ship, or I would have been more insistent on you revealing your dreams to me. I have been negligent as your father for not relating to you sooner about how I also have been affected by my dreams and also those of my father's, and now maybe yours. I realized that you were unhappy with leaving home. I waited too long for your anger and defiance to subside to emphasize the significance of your dreams. We must learn from our mistakes. So now, my son, tell me what you saw in your dreams, what happened during the incident and how you prepared for the occurrence of that which you dreamt."*

"Father," Wing began, *"my dreams are always in scattered fragments. Some are very vivid but most are not. In the morning there are very few that I can remember in any great detail, but the dream of being thrown into the ocean was too vivid to dismiss. I could not see the face of who threw me or why I was being thrown. I also saw Louisa being thrown into the sea but only glimpses of her recovery. I could not see how you were going to save her. I just knew you would. That is why I was so determined to continue."*

Cheung interrupted *"But, son, how did you prepare for your dream?"*

Dejectedly, Wing hung his head.*"Father I did nothing."* His eyes became misty and the tears streamed from his eyes. Cheung gently hugged his smitten son remembering a similar incident with his own father. After a few minutes Wing regained partial composure and spoke. *"Father I am so sorry*

but I realize now the importance of these dreams. I will hide my dreams from you no more."

Cheung smiled with compassion. "My son, are you sure that you did nothing? Now think hard."

"Well father," started Wing his eyes distant as he tried to visualize the past events. Then abruptly he exclaimed smiling "Oh yes father I did do something. After the dream I walked around the passenger deck to try to find the location of where my dream had occurred. I noted the placement of the alarm bell and the life preservers." Wing smiled at himself with satisfaction.

Cheung patted Wing on the back, and then rested his arm around his son's shoulders. "You now see the power of your dreams and the need to learn to use them wisely."

"Father, when I spoke to Louisa today she told me that death was nothing to fear. She said that it felt wonderful. Is that so father?"

"It may be so, my son. Louisa's experience is very rare and I only know what has been recounted to me by superstitious villagers near our home. I have no concept of the realm beyond life."

"Is that not the domain of God? Is there a heaven or a hell as stated in the Holy Bible?"

"My son, I sent you to the missionary school to learn English, math and science. If I forbade the missionaries from teaching you their religion I would not have been permitted to enroll you into the school. So it was a necessary exchange for your education. Now, is there a God, a heaven, a hell? I have seen no evidence of the existence of any of these things. I think that God was created out of the human manifestation with the fear of death. Everyone must choose for themselves what they must personally believe. It is my belief that no truthful man of sound mind has ever seen or spoken to God and, as far as I know, God has never written any books. I find the Christian concept of God very difficult to accept. An all-knowing being that sees and hears everything we do or say does not seem logical. Now imagine an ant-hill. To those ants I am like God because I have the power to influence their existence. I may be able to help them, hinder them or destroy them. How can I know what each ant is doing, saying or thinking at any one moment in time? Now imagine a million ant-hills. Now imagine these ants are people. Can you see my problem with God? If he exists why should he care about one individual ant?"

"But Father, someone must have created the Universe?"

"My son, the fundamental paradox of Christianity is based on a God that has always existed and will always exist. Common sense dictates that everything has a beginning and an end. Nothing has always existed and everything must have an end. Nothing lasts forever, not even heaven. Without a parent how does a being like God learn right from wrong or good from evil? How does he learn the value of love and compassion without a mother or father? If you continue to follow others, when will you learn how to lead? My son each individual must find their own truth by learning from others, through intuition or through the use of common sense and logic. Life is all about making decisions, the more you know the better prepared you are to make the wisest choice."

Shocked into silence, Wing was confused and uncertain whether to be angry at his father's duplicity with the missionary school or grateful for his analysis of Christianity.

The remaining days of the voyage were peaceful and serene as the ship drew closer and closer to its destination. Cheung's relationship with both Captain Anderson and Doctor Mason grew closer as Cheung was often invited to join them in the officers' mess for tea. The Captain and Doctor were very interested in Chinese viewpoints on a variety of subjects. The group spent many hours discussing and debating the merits of religion, history, science, medicine, culture, philosophy and the future of humanity.

One day during tea, Captain Anderson remarked, "Mr. Dai, both the doctor and I are vehemently opposed to the profiteers feeding off the avails of the opium trade in China. We are embarrassed at how our country has allowed this evil trade to continue. How do you think this will affect future relations between our countries?"

"Captain, I am afraid the Chinese have a long memory but we are not an aggressive race. The major difference between eastern and western philosophy is that the west thinks in terms of now while we think in terms of after. Western society is a system based on the accumulation of ever-increasing wealth and power. More is never enough. This creates endless conflict which could lead to eventual disaster. Western politicians are too blinded by ambition to care about what may lie ahead. The Chinese will follow the path that is best for future generations. Peace and goodwill ensures a healthy future for everyone. Violence only ensures future conflict. China sees itself as the Middle Kingdom, the center of the universe. Our rulers hold the Mandate of Heaven as long as they govern wisely for the benefit of all. China must

lead by example to serve as a role model for the world to follow, even in defeat. Our ancestors have always strived to live in peace, even at the cost of being ruled by others. China is a land of peasant farmers. When threatened by outside forces, the country may on occasion participate in wars but only in defense of itself and its neighbors. Any land lost must be repatriated in time, but trade and diplomacy have always been used to deal with matters outside of our borders. The Chinese have never invaded or colonized land belonging to others. The Mongols and Manchus have during their dynastic reigns but they were not indigenous. Independent colonies of Chinese may exist outside of China but they were formed without government design. We have always traded fairly with others for anything we needed from outside. Throughout history China has never deviated from the doctrine of peaceful co-existence and non-aggression."

Stunned by Cheung's historical knowledge and understanding, Doctor Mason responded "Yes, Mr. Dai, I have been reading about Chinese traders in the journal accounts of Marco Polo, the man who discovered China."

Cheung reflected for a moment, thinking how to avert discord, but decided to enlighten his hosts. "Doctor Mason, I am sorry but the west never discovered the east, the east was trading with the west long before Marco Polo and his two uncles arrived at the court of Kublai Khan. The route that Marco Polo and his companions travelled was called the Silk Road which had been utilized by nomadic Arab traders for centuries prior to the Polo quest to China. According to our historical documents, Emperor Wu Ti sent his ambassador Chang Chien on a trade mission to the west two hundred years before the birth of Christ. The Emperor was curious about animals he had heard about that a man could ride at great speed. Chang's mission was to investigate and procure horses and expertise for Emperor Wu Ti. When Chang returned he conveyed to the Emperor the immense opportunity for trade between east and west. As many as ten caravans of several hundred men travelled to the west each following year. Composed of traders, diplomats, poets, soldiers and Buddhist missionaries, the caravans were sent to educate and trade with the west. Many never returned. Some returned after eight to nine years. This is thought to be the origin of the Silk Road. The art of making silk was kept secret by the Chinese for many centuries. The ancient Romans and Greeks possessed silk garments. How do

you think they acquired them when they had not the knowledge to produce silk? Your historical records and ours conflict."

The Captain smiled, "Mr. Dai, I think our friend Doctor Mason is a little overwhelmed by your knowledge of Chinese history. Do you have any knowledge concerning the exploration on the Pacific Northwest? Are you familiar with the voyages of Captain John Meares?"

"No, Captain Anderson, why do you ask?"

"In 1788, Meares left Canton with two vessels in January and landed at Nootka Sound on Vancouver Island in May. On board his ship the *Felice Adventurer* and the accompanying ship, the Iphigenia Nubian, were approximately 55 Chinese artisans and laborers who were contracted to help build a trading post and a dockyard. They also built a sloop, the *North West America*, the first sailing ship built in the Pacific Northwest. In 1789, Meares arranged to have 70 more Chinese workers transported to Nootka Sound. Shortly after their arrival, the settlement was seized by the Spanish. It is unclear what exactly happened to the Chinese afterwards."

"Captain, I visited Fort Victoria during the Fraser River Gold Rush. I often wondered about the similarity in facial features between some of the natives and our people. I think some of these stranded Chinese laborers must have found wives and produced children in the native community."

"Meares was British but operated under a Portuguese flag to circumvent the monopoly of the East India Company which prohibited any British subjects from operating in the Pacific Northwest without being licensed by the British. Even though his claims were grossly exaggerated, it helped to establish territorial rights for the British. This historical incident is known as the Nootka Crisis and it almost caused a war between Britain and Spain."

"Captain, it would be interesting to know how these Chinese artisans might have influenced the native communities with their knowledge and expertise. I would venture to guess that artwork and construction would have been radically affected."

"Mr. Dai, I suppose it may have been."

Chapter 4

Arrival In Victoria

THE ANTICIPATION OF THE *Strathearn's* CREW AND PASSENGERS grew with each passing day as all waited the sounding of the ship's horn at the first sight of Victoria Harbour. Then on July 10th the klaxon shattered the afternoon interlude. Excitement spread throughout the ship. After the initial revelry of seeing land, the passengers all returned to their cabins to pack their belongings in preparation for disembarkment. The fathers had tentatively agreed to visit each other as soon as they had settled in their planned accommodation. Soon all the passengers were dressed in their finest garments with bags in hand on the main deck. From the distance all could hear the cheering of the crowd lining the docking facilities. As they approached closer, the cheering grew louder and louder. Once close enough to see the faces of those on shore, Wing and Cheung could see a noisy mob of angry faces. Both were shocked at the reception, as were Nathan and Louisa. Soon the voices of the crowd could be heard above the drone of the ship's engines. All could now make out the chant of the angry crowd, "Go home, Chinks! Go home, Chinks!"

Cheung thought to himself. Why did I not listen? How could I have brought my son here?

The Captain thought giving Samuel to the authorities here would serve no purpose if this demonstration of public sentiment was any indication of what was occurring here. Judging from the hatred and anger he saw in the sea of faces, he feared for the immediate safety of his Chinese passengers. He decided that he would keep them on board until the demonstrators departed.

The excitement once in the young eyes of Wing and Louisa turned to horror and dread, as they exchanged glances. Louisa dropped her bag and clutched Wing's hand. Cheung watched in horror, as he and Wing were singled out by the crowd as the targets for insults, eggs and rocks. The crowd was somewhat quelled when some of the other passengers were mistakenly hit by eggs. The Dai's were smeared by some well-aimed eggs. Cheung was jarred backwards, bleeding and stunned. A thrown rock had hit him in the forehead. Wing was horrified but held back his tears in defiance. He had never experienced such intense hatred. The passengers surrounding the Dai's quickly dispersed in all directions. Louisa recognized the crowd's hesitation to risk hitting anyone other than their Chinese targets. She quickly seized the initiative and moved directly in front of the Dai's with her arms spread open. Stunned by the ten year old's courage, the barrage of eggs and rocks ceased.

An altercation at the back of the mob seemed to change the focus of the crowd. As the people at the front of the mob turned to investigate, Mr. Osgood quickly appeared, "Mr. Dai, the Captain has asked me to escort you to Dr. Mason's office. Will you please follow me? I will have someone look after your bags. You can leave them here."

The steward tried to lead Wing and Cheung away but Louisa grasped Wing's hand. Nathan leaned over to her, "Louisa, they are safe now. You will see them on shore. We must go. There are people waiting for us." She reluctantly relinquished Wing's hand. Rushing to evade the angry mob, Nathan quickly led Louisa down the gangway.

Tears started to appear in Wing's eyes. He was in shock, but he would not give the angry crowd the satisfaction of seeing him lose his composure. As he turned he noticed that his father was injured and bleeding. Suddenly, he was blinded by a flash of light and his body crumbled onto the deck.

"Master Wing, are you alright?" an English-speaking voice called out. Then the pungent odour of smelling salts caught Wing's nostrils as he

winced in response. "How are you feeling, lad? You were hit by a rock on the back of the head."

Both father and son looked haggard and their clothes were covered with bloodstains and the remnants of eggs. Wing looked around for his father. Cheung smiled at him and nodded his approval to speak English.

"Doctor, I am fine."

The doctor was surprised to hear such perfect English emanating from Wing. He shook his head thinking he should have known.

It was early evening. Father and son were in Doctor Mason's quarters. The Captain entered the door. "Mr. Dai," said the Captain. "I had one of my officers go ashore to do some reconnaissance in town for you and Master Wing. Apparently, there is a lot of racial discord in the City, presently. If I were you, I would not stay there any longer than necessary. Safety will be a major concern. There may be little or no legal protection for you in this town." The Captain placed a hand on Cheung's shoulder in an act of friendship, "Please, Mr. Dai, leave as soon as possible. I tell you this as a friend. Have a look at the local newspaper describing our arrival yesterday."

Cheung read the long *Daily Colonist* article, July 11, 1880 :

"Yesterday afternoon the British bark *Strathearn* Captain Anderson, whose arrival from Hong Kong with 473 Chinamen on board ... When the first detachment of the immigrants left the wharf for their quarters a number of young men availed themselves of what they deemed to be a rare opportunity to "have some fun" and commenced to throw stones at the celestials and otherwise annoy them. But they caught a tartar in the person of a heathen Chinee who has lived in this city for some time past and instead of their going "for that heathen Chinee", the heathen went for them, demonstrating the mutability of things mundane."

With a dressing on his forehead Cheung looked at his son and was deep in thought. What of my dreams? I should turn back now if it means endangering my family but it surely cannot be worse here than what is taking place now in China. No I must at least remain long enough to investigate the present danger and future possibilities for our family.

Cheung noticed Wing inquisitively looking at the Captain, "My son, you can speak English. We are among friends."

"Father, how long have I been asleep?"

"You have been unconscious for almost three hours. Captain, you suspected Wing could speak English, didn't you?"

The Captain smiled in response. "Yes, I suspected it but certainly not as well as he does. Your comment about a victim of circumstance and a master of fate was the first clue. The crew also told me that they heard him utter a few words during the rescue." Cheung returned the Captain's smile.

Turning to Doctor Mason, Cheung asked "Will he be alright Doctor? Do you think there will be any lasting effects?"

"No Mr. Dai. I think he should recover fully. I am so sorry about this whole incident. I can not understand what happened. Victoria was supposed to be the British Jewel of the Pacific. I am embarrassed at the behavior of these people."

"Doctor Mason, you can bear no responsibility for these people. Just as I bear none for those in steerage."

Captain Anderson interjected, "Apparently, the search for gold on the riverbanks of the Fraser River has waned and the town is full of disenchanted miners and adventurers who are out of work and have a lot of idle time to infect others with their misery. They feel the Chinese are here to take jobs that would otherwise be theirs. So they are handing out as much abuse and pain as possible to discourage them from coming here. I can not understand this because in the local paper, the railway company is offering jobs to anyone willing to work. Apparently, there are not enough laborers in the whole province to complete the western portion of the railway. The crew members that I sent ashore saw notices posted throughout the port."

A crew member knocked and entered the doctor's office. Saluting the Captain he said, "Sir, no sign of anyone waiting for Mr. Dai. And the Customs House said that they are not taking any more Chinese immigrants to process until tomorrow at one o'clock because they will be up until midnight with those they have now in their holding facilities on shore."

The Captain said, "Sorry, Mr. Dai, I hope you and Master Wing won't mind staying another night on board. I know the chief immigration officer in charge at the Customs House. Perhaps I can summon him to come aboard for lunch and he can process you while he is here." Cheung consented.

The less visibility tomorrow for the Dai's the better, thought the Captain. The Captain added, "Mr. Dai I have had one of the cabins made ready for you and Master Wing. Your bags will be waiting inside. If you leave your

clothing in a bundle outside your cabin door I will send someone to fetch and clean them overnight. They will be ready for you in the morning."

During the distraction that erupted on the street behind the main crowd, the crew seized the opportunity to quickly herd most of the Chinese passengers from the lower deck into the Customs House where they all waited to be processed then transferred to the mainland. No one could discern from aboard ship what distracted the mob. Whatever caused the disturbance on shore saved the crew from an over-abundance of grief, thought the Captain.

Cheung pondered; I wonder what happened to my shop manager Quan Li? I gave him strict instructions to wait for us upon arrival. The afternoon events and the newspaper article flashed through his mind. Did my instructions put you in danger, old friend?

The evening meal with the Captain and Doctor Mason was a solemn affair. Most of the crew except a skeleton staff was on shore leave. Very little was spoken. All were very concerned over the day's events. Once the meal was over Wing and Cheung retired to their cabin. Neither could sleep as both reflected on the day's events. Wing thought, what is the reason for such intense hate directed towards us? Is it something our people have done? Is it something my father has kept from me? But I cannot ask him because he may lose face. So much hate. His sullenness abated temporarily with the image of Louisa standing in front of the angry mob – a beacon of light in a sea of darkness. So young, so brave, so beautiful, how could I ever forget you?

Cheung thought methodically, if Quan Li was not waiting for us, either he left early seeing the danger or he was the man injured by the crowd, as described in the newspaper article. He suspected the latter. Please forgive my ignorance, Quan Li. All that I heard from those who returned with stories of hatred and violence were true. I should have listened. I only believed what I saw in my dreams.

As the Dai's approached the Captain's table the next morning the Captain thought they looked better but not rested. "Mr. Dai, Master Wing. Let me introduce you to my good friend Mr. Nigel Thompson, the chief immigration officer for the Port of Victoria."

The three exchanged handshakes then sat down for lunch. Thompson saw two Chinese dressed in Western clothing. Though bloodied by yesterday's attack they appeared confident and composed. Both were taller than

most Chinese and they walked with longer and more deliberate strides. The father had a bandage beside his left eye and the son had a large dressing on the back of his head.

With a subdued smile, Thompson said, "Mr. Dai, the Captain has told me so much about the two of you. I wish to express my regret over your ordeal of yesterday. I hope that you will allow me to be of assistance if the need ever arises. Right now it is not safe for any Chinese person in Victoria. They lost the right to vote in 1875. Some local politicians disturbed by a predecessor's success by solicitation of the Chinese vote rallied the locals to disenfranchise the Chinese and because of this, their rights have steadily diminished. The most popular political platform is hate-mongering against the Chinese who are being blamed for every social, economic and moral wrong in the city. Mr. Dai I wish you and Master Wing to know that I harbour no such feelings but I am afraid to say my opinion carries little weight with the locals. But please do not judge them harshly. They are just simple folk stirred up by the local newspapers and unscrupulous politicians who want to further their personal political aspirations. I expect this current anti-Chinese trend will hopefully soon pass since the amount of available labour is in very short supply. In 1871, the Dominion government promised to build a ribbon of steel to connect us from coast to coast, otherwise we may not have joined Confederation. The government has taken its time executing their promise and the locals grow impatient over its lack of progress. A high portion of the non-native residents in the province are American gold miners, and if this railway is not completed soon, our regional allegiance could easily shift southward. Without Chinese labour to help build the railway, this land will surely become a part of the United States. The Americans purchased Alaska in 1867 from the Russians. We may become just the next addition to the American doctrine of Manifest Destiny, proposed by John O'Sullivan. Do you think that they had any intention to leave Alaska separate and isolated from the rest of America? And if our province joins the United State where will the fragmentation of Canada end? What happens with the construction of the Canadian railway may determine whether or not Canada survives as a nation, Canadians should be welcoming the Chinese laborers as their saviours but politicians will do whatever has mass support to win themselves votes. I would think that attitudes will change once the railway is completed and the country recognizes what the Chinese will have contributed."

Cheung looked at Mr. Thompson with respect and admiration. "Yes, I see why you and the wise Captain are close friends. Thank you for your assessment and your insight. It has provided me a much clearer understanding of the situation than I could have found on my own." Mr. Thompson was surprised by Cheung's fluency.

I don't understand, thought Wing... what is 'vote' and those other words? Oh yes, now I remember. He thought back to his lessons on American history. Now it was coming back to him. The people decide who will represent them in government. That foolish angry mob has a right to select representatives for government? What a pitiful system that gives fools this right. Yes, every man has a right to vote. He remembered questioning his American teachers who devoutly stood behind this fundamental principle. So it must be the same here. He still remembered his difficulty in understanding how all were given this right. He had concluded finally that all who lived there must be very wise like his teachers to be given this right. He realized now that he was wrong.

The chief steward entered the room. "Captain, may I have a word with you?" The Captain rose. He and the chief steward walked away out of hearing distance and talked for a short time. The Captain returned to the table and addressed Cheung, "Mr. Dai, the man on shore awaiting your arrival was attacked by the mob yesterday. He is hurt but will survive. The police took him away and have him housed at the local jail because the hospital won't treat Chinese The police had to find an interpreter last night to find this out. He was still in shock this morning. No one knows what arrangements he has made for you. I will send one of my crew members to try to find you lodgings at a hotel but I should warn you that most of the hotels in town do not allow for Chinese guests, even merchants." Turning to Mr. Thompson, "Can you help, Nigel?"

"Yes I think I can, Thomas. I have a friend with a small rooming house on the outskirts of town. I am sure that she will accommodate you and your son, Mr. Dai, until your lodgings have been sorted out. Her son works for me at the Customs House. Once we finish lunch I'll send her son to check to see if she has a vacancy. By the time he gets back we will have your immigration papers finished and if they have accommodation for you I'll tell him to have a horse and carriage waiting for you outside."

"Thank you, Mr. Thompson. We are forever in your debt." Cheung peered deeply into Nigel Thompson's smiling blue eyes. What an impressive young man thought Cheung.

Thompson was six feet tall with short curly blonde hair, a clean-shaven face and a slender, but muscular build. He walked with the graceful swagger of a tiger. How does a man this young achieve such an important position? He was obviously very intelligent but how could a position with so much responsibility be given to someone with such limited experience? "Mr. Thompson, may I ask you how you became the chief immigration officer at such a young age?"

Thompson looked into Cheung's eyes. From all that was related to him by his friend Captain Anderson, he had already decided that this merchant doctor and his son were two very extraordinary people and that he would like to get to know them better. "Mr. Dai, I have worked for the Customs House since I was 14 years old. I am 20 years of age now. I was forced to find employment to support my mother and sister. My father had worked as a senior clerk for the Hudson's Bay Company. When he saw his friends and co-workers returning rich from the gold fields, the lure for gold finally overwhelmed him. He begged and pleaded with my mother who would never give him her consent to venture to the mainland in search of gold, so he finally abandoned us in the hope of one day returning rich. That was six years ago and no one has heard from him since. Regardless, I worked my way up from a sweeper to a clerk and now I am the chief immigration officer. It's all been made easy for me because it seems that the temptation of gold eventually overcomes even our staunchest employees. I have seen it cause too much misery in my life to be likewise affected. Two years ago when Mr. Robertson, the last chief immigration officer left for the gold fields with two of our long-term employees he recommended me for the job because the federal government wanted someone who wouldn't quit for the gold fields and since I was the only means of support for my mother and younger sister they decided to give me the job."

Cheung thought this young man was no stranger to hardships and dedication. How can you not admire someone who has conquered such adversity? If yesterday's events are a reflection of how we can expect to be treated here we will need knowledgeable, well-informed friends in positions of influence. We must nurture this man's friendship, trust and loyalty at

all cost. Cheung queried, "What of your mother and sister? Are they well Mr. Thompson?"

"Oh they are quite well Mr. Dai. Thank you for asking. My younger sister Pauline is now 16 years of age and has a serious suitor. We all live in a small house that I purchased on the outskirts of town not too far from where I hope you may be residing."

He turned to the Captain, "Perhaps I should send a note to Jonathan now."

The Captain turned to the chief steward and signaled a request for a writing set. The chief steward brought a small silver case on a leather tray to the table. Thompson opened it and quickly scribbled out a message and gave it to the chief steward. "Thomas, can I have this taken to the Customs House and given to Jonathan Beckham?" The Captain looked at the chief steward who passed the note to a subordinate.

After lunch the immigration paperwork was completed. A note arrived for Thompson who read it then looked at Cheung and Wing and smiled. "Your accommodations are confirmed, Mr. Dai, Master Wing. A carriage and driver will be here shortly. We have already given the driver instructions. Should I have a clerk from the money exchange brought aboard or have you already acquired some money Mr. Dai?"

"That won't be necessary, Mr. Thompson. I have been here before and still have some local money. You have been very kind, Mr. Thompson. If there is any way we can return your kindness please don't hesitate to ask."

A steward arrived and whispered in the Captain's ear. The Captain turned and spoke, "Mr. Dai, your carriage has arrived. I'll have someone fetch your luggage."

"Thank you very much Captain" responded Cheung. "You and your crew have been very kind to us. I hope that we have not been too much trouble for you."

"On the contrary, Mr. Dai, you have been a godsend for us. You and I both know that this ship was carrying too much human cargo. Mishaps and misunderstandings can escalate and create serious consequences under these circumstances. The trust and respect that you earned from the passengers in steerage helped us stay in control. We are the first ship to arrive in Victoria from China with laborers for the new railway. You taught me a lesson not only in managing waste but also one in humanity. I will pass it along to the shipping line as well as my peers."

Doctor Mason interrupted, "Mr. Dai, may I also express how thankful I am to have met you and seen your application of eastern medicine. Your treatment of the boy with the deep gash was extraordinary. And that treatment of Miss Louisa's hypothermia was nothing short of raising the dead. There is so much we can learn from each other. If you send me your new address once you are established, I would certainly like to keep up some correspondence." Cheung gestured his agreement to Doctor Mason's request.

Captain Anderson rose. The rest of the table did likewise. "May I walk you to the carriage, Mr. Dai?" Cheung concurred. The Captain, Mr. Thompson and Mr. Dai head out the dining room, and the rest of the party followed. The Captain's face had a troubled look. "Mr. Dai, I didn't know what to do with that damn steward except dropping him off at another port. If I give him to the authorities here, they will just laugh and most likely release him. It does not seem likely that they will deal properly with anyone here for assaulting a Chinese. I already sent someone to the local constabulary to check with the chief of police. So instead of releasing the scoundrel here I will release him in our next port of call, Portland, Oregon, so it will be unlikely that he should bother you or the Beilihis' again."

Mr. Cheung said, "Thank you Captain for your thoughtfulness. I think that is probably the best possible solution available under the circumstances."

The party disembarked and when they reached the carriage, goodbyes were exchanged and the Dai's boarded the carriage and with a crack of the whip, they departed. The Captain watched the fading carriage and turned to Thompson. "Nigel, please keep an eye on them for me and keep me informed of what happens to them. I hope that they return to China soon. This port offers them no safety and I can see a big wave of senseless violence ahead for the Chinese here should Victoria follow the same trend as I have seen in the ports of San Francisco, Seattle and Portland. The streets are filled with too many idle desperate dreamers searching for easy wealth."

Birdseye View of Victoria B.C. 1878

Birdseye View of Victoria B.C. 1889

Chapter 5

Beckham's Boarding House

IT WAS A WARM SUNNY DAY. THE TWO HORSES SPED THROUGH the dirt roads of Victoria. Everything seemed so strange but exciting as Cheung watched his son's reaction to the new sights.

"Father everything is so green. The air smells of mountain pine and salt water. The streets are much wider than those in China. The buildings are spread so far apart. Where are all the people? There are so few on the streets."

Cheung answered. *"This country is young and this town is not as heavily populated as our cities in China, but it has grown greatly since my last visit. There are many new buildings. But let us remember that this is not China. This is a new country with bountiful resources waiting for people to harness and develop it. You and I can observe how wisely this is being done. But remember to keep your mind open and do not be too quick to judge the behavior of those that you do not know and do not fully understand. We must be like the shape of water and conform to the vessel in which it is contained."*

"Father, why are the lofan (Europeans) so much bigger than our people?"

"My son I am not sure. I think that the answer lies in their food and their environment but this is strictly a guess. Now look at yourself and your brothers. You are all larger than most of the other boys of your age in the village. Why do you think this is so?"

"*We have more to eat and better foods than the others.*"

"*Now as a young child I had goldfish. I kept some in a small jar and some in a very big basin. The ones in the small jar were always smaller while the ones in the basin grew much larger even though I fed them equal amounts of food. It was always a mystery to me as a child but perhaps the limits of human growth are also likewise affected. My son, not all of the lofan are larger. The Italian and Portuguese sailors that came to trade in Canton were not as large as the English. Some of the English that I have met were also small in stature. Now if we finally settle in this land I think after awhile our children will be bigger and stronger than those in China. In my dreams of the future I see Chinese doctors, lawyers, politicians, and newspaper editors. Some are very large people. Did you see any of this in your dreams, my son?*"

"*Oh yes father I did but the colours were never this vivid and there were no smells. Is it always so quiet father? In China, everyone must shout to be heard above the noise of others. This quietness here is so different from our villages and cities in China. It gives me a sense of loneliness.*"

Cheung quickly tried to redirect Wing's train of thought, "*See that new building over there. That must be where Nathan works. That symbol above the front door means it is Jewish. Let us try to remember the way.*"

Wing understood Cheung's diversion. His shedding tears in front of the driver would have been an embarrassment for both of them. "*Father, do you think Louisa and her father will be housed there?*"

"*It does not look large enough but we are seeing it only from the front.*"

The carriage moved swiftly through the streets. Wing hung onto the passenger seat with both hands tightly. He had never ridden in anything pulled by a horse and though he felt exhilarated by the speed as his reflexes overcompensated for each movement of the carriage.

Cheung smiled at his son. "*Much faster than a rickshaw, is that not so, my son? Don't worry, you won't fall over. Just relax and let your body yield to the motion of the carriage.*" Wing relaxed. "*Now release the seat and enjoy the ride.*" Within a few minutes, the carriage slowed down, as the driver checked the residential addresses with a piece of paper in his hand. Finding the proper address, he pulled his carriage in front of a large, two-storey, Victorian-style residence. At the bottom of a wide staircase leading to a large porch stood a group of three people who awaited the new guests. The driver unloaded the

baggage and left them at the front entrance. Cheung paid the driver, who cordially tipped his hat and drove away.

A middle-aged lady with a friendly smile approached and introduced herself. "Mr. Dai, my name is Mary Beckham."She shook his hand."I am sorry but I was not given your son's name."

"My son's name is Wing but I am sorry that his English is extremely limited. So I will have to translate if anyone wants to speak with him."

Mary shook Wing's hand and continues with the introductions. She directed Cheung to a well-dressed tall man of 30 years with a full beard. "This is Mr. Gray." Gray hesitated then after a scornful look from the lady, he condescended to shake hands with Cheung and Wing. She next approached a short slightly-bald middle aged man with a well-trimmed moustache. "And this is Mr. Rossini."

Rossini bowed and warmly smiled, "A pleasure Mr. Dai, young master. I can...cannot tell you how excited I am to meet some...someone from China. I have so ma...many questions to ask you a...about your people and your country. I look for...forward to talking with you."Mr. Rossini spoke in a broken Italian accent with exaggerated hand gestures."I am sorry, my...my English, it's not so good." Mr. Rossini's brown eyes smiled behind a pair of bushy black eyebrows.

"Ming," shouted Mary. A head popped out from behind the front door. The face was Chinese. A diminutive man less than five feet tall quickly scurried in front of Mary Beckham. He was dressed in dark blue Chinese silk garments. He walked in a shuffle in the traditional manner. He wore the long ponytail instigated by the Manchus who conquered the Chinese in the 17th century. Ming was hunched over, his head was slightly bowed and his eyes were lowered. Under Manchu rule any display of an aggressive nature was swiftly and severely punished. Direct eye contact, standing too tall, speaking without permission, walking with too long a stride were all considered to be acts of aggression that could send an individual swiftly onward, to visit his ancestors, without his head.

"Boss, what you want I do?"

Mary spoke in a kind and gentle voice. "Ming, can you take these bags upstairs to the rooms we have prepared for our guests?" Ming complied, as he started to haul the baggage up the steps. "This is our slow season and I have several vacancies so I can give you separate quarters. Will that suit

you?" Cheung agreed. "Now, can I give you a tour of the house Mr. Dai, Master Wing, while your bags are being taken upstairs?" Cheung responded with a nod.

Mary Beckham displayed her residence with pride and gave a history of all her collected family heirlooms. She was particularly proud of her collection of Chinese antique porcelains which was displayed along the mantle of the fireplace in the parlor. She said that she acquired them from a friend in Chinatown who was expert on Chinese antiquities. Cheung and Wing were puzzled by the crudeness of the legendary figurines. The residence was two-stories high with a basement primarily used to house the coal bin, the central heating furnace, and a servant's living quarters. The main floor contained a large entry area with a central hallway that led straight through to the back door. The first room to the right of the entry was a large living room with an ornate oak-mantled brick fireplace. A wooden door with leaded glass panels separated the living room and dining room. Dominating the dining room was a long oak table with fourteen chairs. A compact galley kitchen was located on the far side of the dining room. Separated by a leaded glass door and to the left of the front entry was a den with a small brick fireplace. A staircase was located off the main hallway adjacent to the den. The stairs led to the sleeping quarters above while beneath it were stairs leading to the basement. Mrs. Beckham's bedroom was located beside the staircase then a small water closet with a sink followed by a larger water closet containing a bathtub and a sink. After finishing the main floor tour Mrs. Beckham led Cheung and Wing into the backyard. The guests were pleasantly surprised as they stepped onto a brick patio beside a large manicured lawn. It was bordered by an array of multi-coloured flowers and well-pruned fruit trees. The sweet fagrance from the flowers and the sound of honey bees filled the air. A small vegetable and herb garden was located next to the 6 foot cedar fence along the back border. A solitary white-washed outhouse was located in a corner to the left of the back door. Mrs. Beckham led her guests back inside and upstairs where there were five bedrooms and a water closet with a claw-foot cast iron bathtub. Each bedroom was approximately twelve feet by twelve feet and contained bunk beds, a large tall boy, a dresser, a closet and a night table. On the dresser sat a floral porcelain water jug and a matching basin with a cup.

As Mrs. Beckham escorted the pair to their rooms she smiled proudly, "Mr. Dai, Master Wing, I hope that you find these accommodations to your liking. Please let me know if you have any further questions. Dinner will be at five o'clock. So I will leave now so you can settle in. Does young Mr. Wing understand any English Mr. Dai?" Cheung shook his head."Well I am sure we will get along fine. If our English-style cuisine is not to your liking I can have Ming fetch some special provisions and prepare some Chinese dishes for you." Cheung replied with a nod. "He generally eats later in the evening by himself in the kitchen. I let him make whatever he fancies as long as the smell of it does not radiate through the dining room the next morning. Well, I will leave you for now. If you are not at the dining room table by five this evening I will send Ming to knock lightly on your door." Mary smiled, turned and descended down the stairs.

It seemed curious, thought Cheung that no one inquired about our injuries. Mary's son must have already informed them about the incident with the angry mob. Cheung looked at his son, "*Well, my son, I feel very tired. I think that I will take a short rest before dinner. If you are awake, will you wake me at 4:30?*" Cheung pointed to a large grandfather clock standing in the hallway at the far end of the landing."*You see that clock over there? It will chime on the hour and the half hour. If you hear it before I do, please wake me up.*"

Cheung retired to his room. Wing entered his room. A metal travel case was lying on the floor beside the bed. He was restless and excited but was hesitant to explore the residence or the neighbourhood without his father's permission. He decided to unpack his luggage. After sorting and stacking his clothing and accessories, Wing laid on his bed and gazed out the window at the front street and the surrounding neighbourhood. What a paradise of greenery. Everything must grow here. The pine-scented air smelled so much better here than near the harbour. He listened intently to the strange melody of birds foreign to his ears. What kind of birds are they? His eyes searched earnestly but the lush greenery veiled the source of the musical interlude. Wing rested on the bed and shut his eyes to imagine the musical source, then fell asleep.

Wing was jolted back to consciousness by the sound of rapping on his bedroom door. It was now twilight and long past the dinner hour. "*My son please wake up. Your dinner is waiting for you.*"

"Sorry father I must have been very tired. I hope that you did not miss dinner because of me."

"My son no harm was done. Ming woke me at 5 o'clock and told me that he would prepare a dinner for us if we wanted to eat later in the evening with him. I knew you were tired so I didn't wake you. I hope that you are rested and very hungry. Ming has prepared a surprise for you. So let us join him in the dining room. Since there will only be the three of us." Wing quickly jumped off his bed and quickly followed his father down the stairs. He could detect the sweet aroma of freshly-cooked rice. His sense of hunger had been enhanced by the fragrance of familiar cuisine. Once he entered the dining room he was over-whelmed by the sight and smell of a five-course Chinese feast awaiting his arrival. As Wing sat down Ming smiled at his young guest and gave a slight bow of his head then uncovered a large pot of rice. Wing's eyes focused on the rice, as his father filled his son's bowl. Than Cheung offered to fill Ming's bowl but Ming politely gestured that Cheung should serve himself first. Only the close proximity of his father restrained Wing from losing his patience to devour the bowl of rice in front of the cook. Ming smiled as he watched Wing because he understood the effect of being deprived of the traditional staple. Cheung smiled at this son, "Eat my son. Let us not worry about our manners tonight. Ming has prepared a large pot of rice and many special dishes, especially for you."

Wing consumed the first few bowls of rice with only a few spoonfuls of gravy from various dishes. He closed his eyes for short durations of time to allow his senses to fully savour the taste, the smell and texture of the freshly-cooked rice. After three bowls of rice Wing looked up to inspect the other dishes, the dining room and the grinning cook. The dishes were all simple peasant dishes: egg foo young with peas and green onions, white-cut chicken with a green onion, ginger, peanut oil dip, alternating slices of pork belly and taro root , stir fried beef with Chinese broccoli, and a large slab of steamed salmon glazed in a mixture of ginger, green onion, soya sauce and peanut oil. Ming and Cheung talked about China, the weather, the port city and its people. Wing occasionally slowed down and looked up to see two smiling faces then submerged himself again into the feast, ignoring the joy he created for his father and a very gratified host. Everything tasted so good that for a short while when he closed his eyes Wing felt that he was back home again in China. As tears started to form he stopped eating to calm

himself. Recognizing the reason for his momentary sadness Cheung tried to divert Wing's thoughts. "*My son, you must try the salmon. It is very fresh and certainly as good as any that I have ever tasted. The cooking of seafood must be well-timed. It hardens and loses its succulence when it is over-cooked. Ming, you have done an admirable job preparing this dish. Has he not, my son?*"

Drying his tears with a napkin, Wing set aside his sorrow and said, "*Yes, thank you very much Ming. I will always remember this feast. I have never enjoyed a meal in my life so much as this one.*"

"*You are most welcome, Wing. You have given me great pleasure watching you eat my cooking. So please continue. I have made much and there will be too much left over to store in my room in the basement. It will be such a waste to throw out all this excess food. Boss lady is very nice but if she smells something that may upset her guests she will become angry. If she finds any leftovers in her kitchen she will throw them out. So eat as much as you can.*"

Wing continued eating but at a much slower pace. "*Oh yes father this salmon is fit for a king. What a large fish it must have been. This piece was only a small portion of its tail. Our fish in China were never this big. How big do these fish grow, Ming?*"

"*Wing, I have seen these fish almost the same length as our countrymen.*"

"*How do they catch anything that large? They must have to spear them is that not so?*"

"*The natives spear them in the river but I think some people use nets to catch these fish.*"

After seven bowls, Wing's longing for rice has been appeased. "*Ming, if I have another grain of rice I will burst. I never imagined that I could eat so much. I hope that I can still walk after this fine meal.*"

Cheung spoke, "*Ming, thank you again for your kindness. Do you mind if we eat with you every once in a while during our stay here? I will make the arrangements with Mrs. Beckham and let you know in advance. I want Wing to get accustomed to the local food and customs so we can only do it perhaps once a week. Is that okay with you, Ming?*" Ming concurred.

"*Maybe we can all go for a walk and see some of the neighbourhood.*"

Ming looked at Cheung somewhat bewildered. "*Mr. Dai you do not understand what it is like living here. It is not safe for Chinese to walk anywhere but Chinatown at any time. The young men punch and kick us like dogs. The children call us names and throw rocks as their parents watch in silence. I do not*

understand how anyone can allow their children to treat other human beings like this, but they do. The police will do nothing. They sometimes just watch and laugh. If we complain to the police they may take us to jail and we will be forced to pay a fine to be released."

Cheung ruminated over Ming's words, *"Even merchants are treated like this, Ming?"*

Ming answered, *"Mr. Dai, I am not sure the locals care to notice the difference, no matter how well you are dressed, how well you speak their tongue or how you conduct yourself. Some may recognize that you are different, but few will care if it gets in the way of their having fun at your expense."*

Cheung and Wing looked at each other in dismay. The words of Captain Anderson echo in Cheung's mind. "Mr. Dai, go back to China as soon as you can."

Early next morning as Cheung was planning his day he was interrupted by knocking on his bedroom door. "Mr. Dai, it's Mrs. Beckham. You and Master Wing have visitors. I will accompany them to the den. A very distinguished Jewish gentleman and a delightful young girl, as lovely as any flower in my garden."

"I will wake my son. Please tell them that we will be down shortly. It must be Rabbi Beilihis and his daughter, Louisa."

"I think it is. So that is the little girl that I have heard so much about. My son told me the other night about the unfortunate incident when your ship arrived. Our town is over-populated with unemployed and disenchanted Americans from San Francisco who have nothing better to do then create havoc at any opportunity. Please do not judge the locals too harshly. I hope that you slept well and you enjoyed your meal last night. Please do not think ill of me I am not as horrid as Ming may make me out to be. I know it just about kills him to throw out good food but I have to worry about offending the other guests with noxious smells, especially Mr. Gray who is very easily offended."

"Mrs. Beckham, thank you for your concerns but please do not worry. There are good and bad influences everywhere in the world, even in China. I also understand how small matters can affect one's business." Mrs. Beckham departed downstairs.

Cheung tapped on Wing's door , *"My son, are you awake? Did you hear? We have visitors."* Wing jumped out of bed and dressed quickly.

"Nathan and Louisa are here, are they not? I am ready."

As they descended the staircase Cheung inquired, "Any dreams my son?"

"Oh yes father. Very vivid, can we discuss them later?"

Wing impatiently followed his father down the hallway to the den. Sitting on a sofa, Louisa caught a glimpse of Cheung and Wing through the leaded glass door. Her composure was overcome with youthful exuberance. She jumped to her feet, as Mrs. Beckham opened the door.

Louisa approached the doorway timidly, "Uncle Cheung, I am sorry for your injuries. Are they serious?"

Cheung touched the bandage on the side of his forehead, "It is just a minor cut. Neither I nor Wing have any serious injuries." Cheung turned towards Mrs. Beckham. "Please let me introduce you to Rabbi Nathan Beilihis and Louisa, his daughter."

Mrs. Beckham addressed Louisa. "What a pleasure to meet you. The whole town is talking about what a brave little girl you are. My son described the whole incident to me. He said you can also speak Chinese. That is incredible!"

Nathan quipped, "I wish she was as fluent in Hebrew."

Mary Beckham shook Nathan's hand and gave Louisa a warm maternal hug.

Louisa smiled back at Mary. Her eyes met Wing's. She walked around him to peer at the back of his head to check his wound and said in jest, "Why are you always getting hurt? If that head of yours wasn't so big, that rock might have missed."

Everyone laughed but Mrs. Beckham. Feeling that her presence was an imposition, she smiled, "Well I'll leave you now to talk. I look forward to seeing you both again. Please drop by to visit. I'm sure you have a lot to discuss. Incidentally, breakfast will be served at nine o'clock, lunch at noon and dinner at five o'clock but let me know if you wish to bring guests so Ming can properly prepare in advance. It has been a pleasure meeting you Rabbi Beilihis and especially you young lady. I am always in need of female companionship. It is a rare commodity in a town full of men. Please drop in anytime that you wish. I think you and I will become very good friends. My door will always be open to you."

Mary retreated through the leaded glass door. Cheung turned towards Nathan and inquired, "How did the two of you find us so quickly?"

"The day after our arrival I sent someone to inquire about the two of you. Captain Anderson sent us a message to inform us about everything that had transpired after our departure. Then he directed us to contact Mr. Thompson on how to find you. Our new residence is only two blocks away from here. Now Wing, how is your injury? No lasting effects I hope."

"No, Uncle Nathan, I am fine. I can't see it anyway. Father will look after my injury."

"Cheung, Wing, please go and have your breakfast. We have already eaten and apologize to Mrs. Beckham for our calling so early in the morning. We'll get together later. I would have waited till later in the day to visit but this willful daughter of mine would not wait." Wing grinned sheepishly.

"Dai Wing Sing, I will see you after my Hebrew lessons are over. Wing Sing means forever becoming greater, doesn't it? I hope that doesn't refer to the hole at the back of your head" Louisa's hands hide a cheeky smile.

"Louisa, you shouldn't make fun of someone's injury. It is bad luck." said Nathan.

Cheung interceded, "Nathan, we are not superstitious farmers. Your daughter could never offend us."

Nathan looked at the clock in the hallway, "Cheung, Wing, we have to go or Louisa will be late for her lessons." The visitors quickly departed.

As they watched the visitors depart from the front veranda, Cheung turned to Wing. "*Now my son, what of your dreams? Remember to speak only in Chinese in case we are overheard.*"

Wing paused and closed his eyes to revive the images of the night. "*Father the images were so vivid I truly was fearful and deeply troubled by what I saw. I remember being suspended from a rope on the side of an enormous mountain. I had a big hammer in both hands while someone else held a large metal chisel. We dug small holes in the rock wall of a mountain and into the holes I placed small packages which were contained in a pouch attached to the rope from which I was suspended. I am sure it was me but I was much darker and much more muscular. Beneath me were many Chinese workers with picks and shovels laying a path of crushed rocks on which were laid wooden ties traversing the rock path? On top of the wooden ties were two lines of steel rails that stretched as far as the eyes could see. I saw no one that I recognized except the man that worked in the dining room who threw Louisa and me off the floating dragon. He was one of the bosses. I think*"

Loun An was there too but I am not sure. Father that is all I remember. What do you think it all means?"

"I do not know my son but we must take precautions so this will never come into being. We must also take precaution just in case it does. Let us go eat our morning meal and I will think more about it later."

When they arrived in the dining room Cheung and Wing were met by Ming at the hallway entrance. Ming smiled and with a slight nod he directed father and son beside each other across from Rossini and Gray. Mary Beckham was seated at the head of the table. Next to Mary was an adolescent wearing a broad smile. "Mr. Dai and Wing, you have met our other guests already. Let me introduce you to my son, Jonathan." Smiling, Mary beamed with pride. Jonathan was a handsome young man. He had blue eyes, short, dark brown hair, was clean-shaven and five feet eight inches in height. He stood up smiling and warmly shook hands with the new residents.

"Mr. Dai, Master Wing, I stayed a little later this morning hoping to meet you. I am usually gone by the time the rest of the guests come down for breakfast. I have heard many good things about the two of you from Mr. Thompson. I look forward to talking more with you this evening at dinnertime. Please do not think me rude but I really must go. If I run I will just make it on time for work." Jonathan waved as he turned down the hallway and dashed out the front door.

Mrs. Beckham smiled at Cheung and Wing. "He was very anxious to meet the two of you and when you did not come to dinner last night he was very disappointed. He described the whole incident to me with those mindless demonstrators during your arrival in the harbour. He was there when it happened and saw it all. I am sorry, but I am sure you do not want to be reminded. You both must be hungry. Ming will make the eggs any way you please but there is also bacon, pork sausages, baked beans and toast. Most of us eat scrambled eggs at breakfast so there is lots of it already here on the table but if you want your eggs done differently just tell Ming."

"This will be fine Mrs. Beckham."

"The selection of tea with the meals is by consensus but we will try anything at least once. So if you have any special requests please let me know. Right now we have a China Black." Ming poured samples. Cheung and Wing each indicated their approval with a nod. Mr. Rossini made an earnest effort to befriend Wing. Pushing a dish of sausages towards Wing,

he remarked, "You like this? Very good, make you very strong. Master Dai he no speak English?" Cheung shook his head. Rossini continued "Maybe I help him learn?" Cheung smiled at Rossini and turned to Wing, shrugged his shoulders and gestured his approval with open palms.

"Mr Rossini, what do you do?" asked Cheung.

As Rossini gestured with hands and fingers sweeping across an invisible keyboard, "I play and...and teach the piano. In the afternoons, Mrs. Beckham lets me use her..her piano for practice and to give lessons to...to students after school. Sometimes, rich people call me to to play at parties and weddings. Sometimes, I play at...at the hotels."

During the meal, Cheung whispered to Wing, *"My son, I think that you shall be learning to play the piano. Whether you are any good does not matter. He is a very kind man and we will need friends. While you are listening to the conversations, your ignorance will be more convincing if you look at something other than the person speaking then they will think you are disinterested because you don't understand what has been spoken."* Wing complies with a nod.

"Mr. Rossini, would you like to teach my son to play the piano? He enjoys music but has never had the opportunity to learn to play a musical instrument."

"Mr. Dai, I will be honoured to teach your son. When would you like me to to start?"

"I will let him rest one more day. Can he start tomorrow afternoon?"

"That will be..be fine, tomorrow at two o'clock?"

"That will be fine."

Tired of being ignored, Mr. Gray interjected. "So, Dai, what are..."

Mrs. Beckham pointed a disapproving finger as a warning at Gray, to halt his tone of disrespect. Gray paused, somewhat embarrassed, but continued in a less offensive yet still sarcastic tone. "So Mr. Dai, what brings you to Victoria? You are some kind of merchant are you not?"

"I'm sorry, Mr. Gray, what is that you do?"

Agitated by not receiving an answer, Gray snapped back "I asked you first."

"Mr. Gray, it seems that you know more about me than I know about you. I am not trying to be difficult but the situation does not seem equal."

Surprised but unwilling to give in, Gray shrugged his shoulders, finished his breakfast and left the dining room in haste. Amused by how Gray has been upstaged, Mary smiled and lifted her eyebrows at Cheung. The

pervading silence was interrupted only by the sound of the front door slamming shut. With a content smile, Mary broke the silence. "I am sorry, Mr. Dai, at Mr. Gray's behavior. He has only been here a short while but does not like to talk too much about himself. I think he is just another spoiled remittance snob from my homeland whose useless existence became too worrisome for his family to bear any longer. They are sent here subsidized by their families with regular stipends. Because they have usually failed at careers in England, their families send them to the New World to try to teach them the meaning of hard work and self-reliance. They come determined to convince the rest of us about their self-importance. They generally never find work unless their families cut off their stipend. No one will hire them because they are so lazy, willful and arrogant, unless they win the eye of some employer's unwed daughter. The great majority of them leave after two years. Meanwhile they flock together at bars and taverns, drink and gamble away their monthly stipend and then try to borrow as much as they can from the locals based on greatly exaggerated future inheritances. When their time is up they disappear without notice leaving behind hidden debts, broken hearts and misery. I have very little use for them and I will only take them in when they give me payment for room and board in advance. I will never extend them credit under any circumstances no matter what situation arises."

Shocked by Mary's contempt for the English upper class, Cheung turned to Wing. "*I hope that Englishman was not too badly offended by my comments. We do not need any enemies. I will try to make amends when the opportunity arises. My son, there is good in everyone. In some people we have to look harder to find it. Let us try to win over this Englishman. It should be fairly easy because clearly he has very few allies. But we must be patient and wait for the right opportunity. Otherwise he will be distrustful of our motives.*"

"*Father, do you really wish to have him as a friend?*"

"*No my son, but I do not wish to have him as an enemy because I think he is capable of creating mischief. If we become friends he will be less likely to do us harm? Anyone who makes enemies needlessly is a fool. You never know who will be present during a crisis. My son, no one is born good or evil. What we become is a matter of circumstance. What lies ahead is not always predictable and sometimes, even your worst enemy may eventually become your best friend. So never try to judge others when you can seek to understand them. A wise man disarms needless*

animosity." Cheung pauses, "Mrs. Beckham, Mr. Rossini, please excuse us. I am very sorry to have to speak in Chinese to my son at your dining table but I was just explaining to him about what you have said."

"Mr. Dai, we both know that Master Wing cannot communicate otherwise. Your apology is not necessary. Please feel free to converse in your native tongue whenever you like in our presence. Mr. Gray's presence is inconsequential." Mrs. Beckham giggled at her own words of mischief. "By the way, did you know that the Chinese vegetables that you ate last night came from my garden?"

"Mrs. Beckham, we are very fortunate indeed to be staying here. I am surprised you have empty rooms."

"Mr. Dai, this is our slow time. Towards the end of October, the gold miners return to Victoria for the winter. We sometimes have to pack them three and four to a room. They love Ming's cooking and my lodgings. And Mr. Rossini always has a ready audience anytime he wants to practice." Rossini smiled.

"Mrs. Beckham, after the docking incident and my conversations with Captain Anderson and Mr. Thompson, I know that the local people are not very receptive to Chinese immigrants. Will our presence here adversely affect your business?"

"Not at all Mr. Dai. I can pick and choose my boarders. I will take no drunks. If they come back drunk they have to sleep on the porch and they will find their bags beside them when they wake up. We generally have a long waiting list. And everyone knows I will not tolerate drunks."

Chapter 6

Rescuing A Friend

AFTER BREAKFAST WAS FINISHED, CHEUNG AND WING TOOK A carriage into town. Wing sat across from his father in the horse-drawn carriage; he purposely folded his arms in front of his chest. Cheung smiled proudly, as his son remembered to heed his advice.

Wing searched for landmarks to help him remember the route into town. As they rode through the busy streets, people stopped and stared at the novelty of two Chinese dressed in western clothing riding in a horse-drawn carriage.

When the carriage arrived at the Customs House, father and son stepped onto the road. Cheung paid the driver and rewarded him with a generous tip. This should ensure good service in future once he tells his cohorts. The wide-eyed driver finally broke his prolonged silence and warmly thanked Cheung with newly inspired vigor. Then the driver tipped his hat and inquired when and if his services would be needed later. Cheung thanked him but declined. As they crossed the street Cheung and Wing noticed a line-up of people in front of the Custom House. Cheung stopped a young boy to ask him the reason for the line. The boy explained "The mail ship has arrived."

Cheung thought we will not have any mail yet, but if we go to the front of the line to ask to see Mr. Thompson, people may think we are unwilling

to wait our turn. It will be much better to wait in this long line rather than give anyone the wrong impression. A man in the middle of the line pointed at Cheung "Hey ain't they the chinks that arrived on board the Strathearn a couple of days ago?"

"Aye that be them," exclaimed another from further back in the line.

"No little girl to protect you today," yelled another.

"Look at those clothes! They don't belong on chinks. Take them off before we cut off your pigtails." shouted another.

"I saw them arriving by carriage, all prim and proper, acting like royalty," added another near the front.

"Can't you chinks learn anything; you don't get your mail, the same time as your betters. Now off with you before you get a good thrashing."

Cheung surveyed the mounting hostility of the crowd which was only tempered by their fear of losing their place in the line-up. As father and son retreated to safety across the street, they heard a loud but friendly voice, "Mr. Dai, Master Wing." A tall young man with a smiling face waved to them from the front door. Having seen the arrival of the carriage and having watched the rising tensions from his open office window, Nigel Thompson quickly descended down the staircase. From the building entrance, he greeted his friends warmly "Mr. Dai, Wing, so nice to see you again". In stunned silence, Nigel accompanied Cheung and Wing into the Customs House leaving the on-lookers gawking and murmuring in dismay.

After a personal tour of the newly-constructed Customs House, Victoria's newest and proudest landmark, the three entered Nigel's office. "Mr. Dai I am so sorry about the behavior of that crowd. You and Wing must be careful. There is a lot of anti-Chinese sentiment right now with the con-struction of the new railway."

"Mr. Thompson, we appreciate your concern. We just came to thank you for the helping us find lodgings at Mrs. Beckham's rooming house. We are very fortunate to have met you."

Cheung and Wing both gave Nigel a bow of respect with hands in prayer fashion as a gesture of their appreciation for his kindness. Nigel smiled and returned their bow.

"Mr. Dai, when you left for Mrs. Beckham's the other day I asked that driver to give you a tour around town because Jonathan said that your rooms had to be prepared. I hope that was alright?" Cheung gave a nod.

Nigel continued "You had said during lunch that day you left here in 1862. The city has grown immensely since then. Did you see the first paved street in Western Canada? Government Street was paved in the year you departed. The federal government had this extravagant building built in 1874. British Columbia joined Confederation in 1871 so I guess they had to do something to confirm the alliance, and also quell the local anger at no longer being a tax-free port. A lot of residents still don't accept the alliance. They refer to Canada as a separate entity somewhere east of the Rockies. If this long-promised railway which is to connect east and west does not materialize soon the local politicians will rally public support to severe the ties of Confederation. The promise of a national railway was what enticed the masses into Confederation in the first place."

Cheung turned to Wing who has listened carefully but hid his comprehension of the conversation by staring distantly out the front window.

Nigel scrawled an address and a rudimentary map on a piece of paper then handed it to Cheung. "This is the address to my residence and a map of how to get there from your lodgings. Please come to visit me. If you let me know in advance I will have my mother and sister bake some fresh scones to have with tea. I think it will be safer for you to visit me there. But it is not generally this busy here unless the mail ship has arrived. Please excuse that crowd out there. The local newspaper and politicians have incited them into an anti-Chinese frenzy to sell more newspapers and to make political gains at the ballot box. The *British Colonist* reprints every anti-Chinese article it can lay its hands on from American newspapers and especially San Francisco. The frenzy has been a smashing success for both politicians and the newspaper. The owner of the *British Colonist* is Amor de Cosmos, that is Latin for "Lover of the World". He started publishing that scandal sheet in 1864. He has come into prominence by lambasting every established seat of authority in the country. Now he mercilessly defames the Chinese who cannot vote and have little or no legal protection. He caters to the majority of new immigrants who are from south of the border. His American cronies balk at any regulations that put limitations on their godless contrivances."

Memories of his earlier experiences in California flashed quickly through Cheung's mind. No, it could not happen here, not with the British system of justice. If so we must avoid situations that will allow the locals to perpetrate

acts of violence against us. We may not be safe at Mrs. Beckham's. We must search for other options just in case.

"Mr. Thompson, do you think it will be safe for us at our present lodgings? If not where else can you advise us to search for accommodations?"

Nigel paused to think momentarily. "Mr. Dai, I am not sure but I think that you are safe where you are. However, I must warn you that we had a recent incident concerning a Chinese gardener being seriously hurt by children throwing rocks. Mrs. Beckham feared for the safety of her cook after that incident, so she had Jonathan accompany him to Chinatown to do his shopping. Jonathan knows all the local residents and their children. He made sure they understood that there would be an accounting if anything happened to the cook. I will ask him to do likewise for you and Master Wing."

Cheung replied, "This would be a great service but too great a hardship to impose on a friend without some form of remuneration. We can only accept this generous offer if we can give Jonathan something in return."

"Let us not spoil Jonathan," insisted Nigel, "you are staying at his mother's lodging house during her slow season when she has a hard time filling her vacant rooms. Secondly, Jonathan is very well paid and was selected for his job by me. We are very good friends and this will be a very small favour that will inconvenience Jonathan very little. Why don't you arrange a place to meet and schedule your trips to and from town with Jonathan's travels? He comes to work early every morning and generally goes home for lunch. That should pose no problems for anyone. A lot of the time he walks with Ming. The locals all along their route know them now and Ming sometimes travels the streets by himself. If you have any trouble along the way, anyone's mail can be temporarily misdirected, if you understand my logic." Cheung could only smile as Nigel winked.

"Mr. Thompson, I do not know how to express my gratitude. I can only say that if there is any way I can repay your kindness I look forward to the opportunity. Thank you so much."

All three exchanged bows. "Well Mr. Thompson, we have wasted enough of your valuable time. Can you tell us how to get to the jailhouse so that I can rescue my injured employee?"

Nigel pointed to a four-storied building with a domed turret. "That's the courthouse and jail. It's only one block up and two blocks down towards

Chinatown." He looked at his pocket watch."It is lunchtime. I will have Jonathan accompany you. No, I will escort you there, myself."

As the three walked along the dusty streets towards the jail Nigel tipped his hat and briefly stopped to chat with almost everyone he encountered along the way. Brief introductions were made at each encounter. Most of the locals seemed at a loss for words as the three continued on after a tip of the hat or a nod of recognition. Railway notices for laborers were posted on nearly every wall and lamp-post. The three stopped momentarily as Cheung read a notice.

When they reached the jail, Nigel greeted the constable at the front desk. He took a piece of paper out of his pocket and crumpled it."Duck, Will, here comes the ball." The constable looked up, just in time to intercept the crumpled piece of paper tossed at his head. "Hey, good catch. I hope your bat is as sharp on Saturday."

"Nigel, if that is the speed you will be throwing when we play this week, don't count on us buying the drinks after the match." The friends shook hands, "Will, I mean Constable Morrison, these are my friends Mr. Dai and his son Master Wing." Cheung and Wing offer a handshake, but Morrison ignored their request and just looked amusingly at the Chinese. Nigel continued, "They are here to see their injured friend. Mr. Dai is his employer."

"A $2.00 fine has to be paid before you can see him."

"Will, what for? I was there. I saw the whole incident."

"For disturbing the peace."

"Will, that is ridiculous."

Cheung tapped Nigel on the shoulder. With two silver dollars in his hand he placed the coins on the constable's desk. "Mr. Thompson that's fine. Can we see him now?"

While they waited, Cheung turned to Nigel and said warmly, "Mr. Thompson we have taken enough of your time. Please don't increase our indebtedness. We may never be able to return your kindness. We must learn to deal with our own problems."

Nigel begrudgingly yielded to Cheung's request. Shaking his head in disgust, he remarked, "I will trust your judgment Mr. Dai, but please let me know if I can be of any further assistance to you and Master Wing."

Nigel shook hands with Cheung and Wing and then snubbed Morrison who tried to wave good-bye as he departed..

Constable Morrison led Cheung and Wing downstairs to the cell containing Quan Li. When Morrison opened the door Cheung saw his friend covered in a blanket lying on the bed. His face was partially bandaged and a gauzed patch covered his left eye. Quan Li broke out in tears, upon recognition of Cheung. *"My friend I am so happy to know that you were not to badly hurt. I waited for you until I was attacked by the lofan."* His tears started to flow uncontrollably. Cheung sat on the bed and embraced his friend, patting him on the back.

"Quan Li, this is all my fault. I could not see the danger that I was putting you in, because I was blinded by my dreams. Old friend, please forgive me."

"Cheung, how could you know those silly white demons would attack a harmless old man waiting for visitors? I'm so sorry that I was not there to greet you at the dock. The lofan attacked me while I was waiting for you to come off the ship. I saw them throwing eggs at you. When you were hit in the head with a stone I tried to distract them by yelling 'police' thinking that they might disband but it just angered them more. So they turned on me. When I woke up I found myself in jail, and I cannot remember anything else. I am glad you are both safe and not too badly injured. I brought some treats for Wing but they must have been taken away."

Quan Li started to regain his composure. Constable Morrison shook his head and started to leave. When he reached the door he turned and said, "he is free to leave, the sooner the better. Let us know when you are ready to go and we will bring his belongings and have someone escort you out." Morrison departed leaving the cell door ajar.

"Sorry old friend, this is Wing, my third son."

"My father has told me many stories about your early days together when you were mining gold. I feel like I know you already. May I just address you as "uncle" as is the Chinese custom for all family friends."

Quan Li gestured with a nod, *"Yes uncle is fine. Cheung, you have three sons, but why did you bring the youngest?"*

Wing waited patiently for his father's reply.

"Long story, Quan Li. We will have a long talk later. Right now let us leave before they think up more fines for us to pay. Are you badly hurt? Are you able to walk? Have you had anything to eat today?"

"I have only some minor bruises and scrapes. I will be fine. I had some bread and beans early this morning. I think my legs are fine, just old and stiff from sitting and

lying around. I see you were both injured." Quan Li tried to stand with support from his friends. "Yes, I think I can walk without help. Let us go to Chinatown. The food here is not fit for a starving dog."

"Our injuries are minor," said Cheung.

Taking a closer look at Cheung's attire "Aiyah, Cheung, nice clothes but the white demons will not like seeing you dressed in such fancy clothes. There are many in Chinatown who have tried to dress, talk and act as the white demons. Drunks and young ruffians amuse themselves by taunting them and beating them up. These clothes are not safe for you to wear. If we do not act like them, we arouse anger and if we act as they do, we may arouse even more. We cannot please those blinded by hatred."

"You may be right old friend. Our wearing these clothes was for the purpose of escaping notice, not drawing it as we have done. We may have to alter our strategy."

Quan Li struggled to walk. He grimaced and cursed at the initial soreness "Up your mother's butt .... sorry old friend. Old habits are hard to change. Please excuse this unworthy son of a poor farmer."

Wing smiled, "Uncle, my tender ears have heard this much-used phrase often and these young lips may even have uttered them on very rare occasions but of course never in the presence of my illustrious father. So be not afraid of offending me." All burst into laughter.

Quan Li walked gingerly. As he started to move with some fluidity Cheung left the cell. "I will inform the constable at the front desk that we are ready to leave."

When Cheung returned, a young constable was carrying Quan Li's jacket and a cloth bag with a small box inside it. The bloodstained jacket was torn and dirty but the bag and its contents were only slightly damaged. Dressed in dark blue silk trousers and a white short-sleeved cotton undergarment, Quan Li scrutinized his belongings. He shook his head and defiantly muttered that much-used Chinese phrase again as he looked disdainfully at the young constable carrying his possessions. Quan Li quickly put on his tattered dark blue silk jacket. The young constable led the trio out towards the entrance of the jailhouse. Several constables now congregated behind the front desk to observe the rare spectacle of two chinks in western clothing and head bandages with their injured employee. They snickered as they watched the trio and the constable pass by.

"Good riddance. It was really starting to smell like Chinatown in here," quipped an officer, as they all burst into a fit of hysterical laughter. The trio proceeded down the steps to street level. The junior constable, uncertain at the amusement of his cohorts, realized that he was still holding Quan Li's carrying bag. He proceeded out the front door to the landing at the top of the steps and hurled the bag and its contents in the direction of the three pedestrians. The box ruptured upon impact and Chinese biscuits, dried fruits, candies and preserves spilled out along the dirt road in front of the three. More laughter erupted from the open windows of the jailhouse. These were not the same people that I left in 1862, thought Cheung. How can I move my family here if these are the men whom we expect to protect us from crimes and injustice? He looked sadly at his son and fought back his emotions. I cannot trust my dreams. They were so vivid, so real. I saw Chinese doctors, Chinese lawyers, Chinese mayors, Chinese members of parliament, and Chinese representatives of the Queen. How could I be so misled by my dreams? I was so sure. It all happened here. How could I be so wrong?

Wing had never encountered the painful look of despair that now clouded his father's eyes. Afraid his father may lose his composure as the constables and more pedestrians gathered to watch, Wing quickly sprung into action. He picked up the tattered bag and started to gather up any remnants worth salvaging. "Father, these dried lichee nuts, preserved olives and plums are my favourites. Lucky for me, not all of the individual packages have been broken. The almond cookies and jellied candies are still in tin cans. The only loss is a small box of cookies and the fresh fruit which were bruised and over-ripe anyway." Dodging a horse-drawn carriage Wing filled the carrying bag and triumphantly rejoined the two adults at the side of the dirt road with his prize in hand.

Realizing Wing's intent, Cheung recovered. "Thank you my son. You continue to amaze me not only with your insight but with your ability to avoid carriages." Cheung rested his hand on Wing's shoulder. "Well-done, my son."

The three proceeded toward Chinatown. Quan Li led the way through the less traveled alleyways to avoid any further unfortunate encounters. As they approached at the southern outskirts of Chinatown, they encountered a labyrinth of wooden shacks and lean-tos. The stench of human waste and garbage radiated from open ditches. They were greeted by the local Chinese.

Many stopped Quan Li to inquire about his injuries and the new strangers. He briefly summarized his ordeal and introduced his companions. There was no sanitation, only rainfall to cleanse the open trenches of Chinatown. The group leaned against a wall, as a labourer carrying basket-loads of farm produce suspended at both ends of a bamboo pole balanced on his shoulder passed by. The man scurried by with a respectful bow for their courtesy. Workers always had the right of way. The three stopped at the entrance to a narrow alleyway. To the right of the door in the red brick wall was a small trap door which opened; a face peered out at the group. After a minute the iron gate swung open and the group passed through, then the spring-loaded gate snapped shut. Quan Li introduced the newcomers to the gatekeeper , a frail older man with a loosely cropped beard. Bows were exchanged. In a playfully sarcastic tone, Quan Li cursed at the gatekeeper, *"You bucket of cow dung, what took you so long to open the gate? Can you not see my injuries? Can you not see I have important visitors?"*

"Up your mother's butt." The sentry approached and inspected Quan Li's head bandages more closely, he relented."*Quan Li my friend, are your injuries serious?"*

In a grave tone Quan Li said, *"yes very serious, and when I die I plan to come back as an evil spirit to visit you every night."* The four broke out in laughter.

"Okay, just don't wake the fools that share my bed."

Entering the alley, Cheung and Wing saw a long narrow red-brick corridor. The walls and doors of the many established premises were adorned with Chinese signs. *"This is the alley of foolish pleasures (later known as Fan Tan Alley). It is for those who wish to seek lazy wealth without toil, for those who wish to escape the harshness of reality using the milk of paradise (opium) and for those who wish to exercise their manhood in the arms of soiled doves,"* said Quan Li.

The trio was greeted with the familiar clattering of mahjong tiles, the mixed cries of jubilation, swearing and anguish from expectant gamblers and the insidious aroma of opium. Quan Li quickened his pace through the narrow alley-way realizing Cheung's fear of his son's exposure to unsavoury vices at such a tender age. The pungent odour of human excrement, opium and rancid garbage filled the air. The smell was much different from any other Wing had previously endured. Cheung watched Wing who was desperately trying to refrain from vomiting. Cheung whispered to his son,

"*Don't fight the stench just try to breathe normally, and the smell will subside just as it did on board the ship. Your mind can be your greatest ally or your biggest foe. Don't let your imagination work against you. Your mind must always control your body to endure and overcome physical hardships.*" Wing started to breathe normally allowing the odours free access to his lungs as his uneasiness dwindled.

Off the main alley were several very small narrow passageways. Wing inquired, "*What are these small openings? Where do they lead?*"

Quan Li looked at Cheung, who signified his approval. "*They are made purposely small to discourage the white demons from entering. The passages lead to social clubs, sleeping rooms and other things you may be too young yet to understand.*"

Surprised by Quan Li's change of demeanor and tone, Wing understood not to pursue further questioning. Halfway through the alley, a door opened. The fragrance of Chinese cooking filled the air. Trailing the adults, Wing halted to catch familiar fumes. "*Father, my legs can go no further. Can we stop here?*"

"*My son, your stomach can go no further. The smell of Chinese cooking is too much also for me to ignore. Shall we stop for lunch?*"

Quan Li said "*Let me take you to my favourite restaurant. Their seafood and barbecue duck is the best in chinatown. It is at the far end of the alley and across the street. I will take you there now. You can order while I quickly go back to the store and change my clothes. I cannot go like this.*"

Understanding his friend's desire to be suitably attired for the occasion, Cheung agreed. Quan Li led his friends to the front door of the restaurant and then scurried off to change his clothes.

Once inside the restaurant, the owner escorted father and son to a table. Cheung ordered the house specials recommended by a smiling young waiter. Wing looked around the restaurant. The familiar décor and furnishings made him feel comfortable.

By the time Quan Li arrived, the food was ready. One after the other the dishes came out. Cheung and Quan Li watched Wing's eyes grow larger with the arrival of each new dish.

Cheung smiled at Quan Li and turned to his son. "*My son, eat slowly. Your stomach may not have recovered from Ming's meal last night. Remember your eyes may be larger than your stomach.*" Wing's eyes grew larger.

"Father, look at the size of these scallops and prawns and the crabs are immense. They are much larger than any we see in China." Quan Li acted as the host making sure tea-cups were continuously filled and offered the choice morsels for his guests.

"Cheung, you must try this egg foo young. It is made with onion and crab roe."

Cheung sampled each dish and joyfully watched his son, while Quan Li placed healthy portions on Wing's side plate.

Wing smiled. "Uncle, thank you. Don't worry about me. You must eat. You need strength to recover from your injuries."

Cheung said "This barbecued duck is as good as any I have tasted in China. Son, have some before it gets cold and the delicate crispy skin loses its texture."

Remembering his father's words, Wing slowed the pace of his attack on the succulent fare. He looked around the ornate dining room at the other diners and turned to Quan Li. "Uncle, on the way here and even in this restaurant, I have seen no women and children. Where are they?"

"Wing, the local population of Chinese is only about seven hundred people and most all are young men sponsored by their families, clans and villagers to work and send money back home from Gum San. Only the rich merchants can afford to bring their families here. There are six women and only a few children here. The children belong to the household of merchants. The married women and their children are always escorted and rarely appear in public. Of the six women, two are soiled doves from San Francisco, sold to the tongs (brotherhood societies) for unpaid family debts."

Wing's curiosity was aroused, but noting Quan Li's altered tone at the end of his words and a glaring look of disapproval from his father, Wing discontinued further inquiry.

Cheung changed topics. "Now, my friend how is our business doing?"

A smile broadened on Quan Li's face. "Very well. This year will be our best ever and next year looks better. Your reputation for honesty, promptness and guaranteed quality has forced the other merchants to copy our lead. But the long-time residents know who started this trend. They all got tired of being cheated on weight and being given lesser quality produce intermixed with what they agreed to expect in the first place. You were right not to follow the others to increase our profits. Or even promising to deliver goods that we were not sure would arrive on time. The local merchants are following our example due to our success. But our business does not prosper as much as those involved with the selling of opium.

The two major merchants in Chinatown, Kwong Lee and Tai Soong, have made a fortune importing and selling the drug even though the tariff on opium is 50% instead of the standard 12 ½%. This year the Americans have made it illegal to manufacture opium in their country. Many of the San Francisco manufacturers are in the process of moving here. Many of our local merchants have formed partnerships with them or are planning to set up their own manufacturing plants in Chinatown. The number of opium factories in Chinatown is going to increase drasticly. The government here doesn't care. The city is making too much revenue from the sale of opium licenses to be concerned." Quan Li had written to Cheung on several occasions requesting to pursue an opium license. Cheung's only reply was always the same "Profit and conscience cannot always follow the same path."

Quan Li looked Cheung curiously expecting further clarification. Quan Li my friend, every human being has choices that can affect the lives of others for better or worse. The fact that those who will be injured by our callous pursuit of profit are strangers who we may never meet and that others will profit greatly does not matter. In our own village now, opium is sold by those who have no other means to control their own thirst but to entice the idle rich, the foolhardy and even children to sample their "doorway to enlightenment". At first they give it away at no cost or sell it very cheaply. Some even put it in candy to give to children. Then as the need grows stronger they increase the price so the life of the victim and that of their family are corrupted. After they are in control, their victims can only work for them to satisfy their hunger. Many families have been ruined. Many proud men, now slim, unwashed shadows walk our streets begging for money to feed their ever-increasing addiction. The families of these men struggle to survive. Their sons are sold as slaves to work in factories in Canton and their daughters as toys for the rich. Meanwhile, very few do the work of many. The land lies fallow. This drug has stolen the will to work. Crops are not planted, tended or harvested. When the tax collector comes and the harvest is so poor he levies a higher tax the next year. As more farmers lose their land to the tax collector they join bands of outlaws to rob the tax collectors and the rich. Tormented by guilt and the hunger for more opium, many drown themselves in the river. China is not the same as when you left." Putting his arm around Quan Li's shoulder. "Now Quan Li, please try to understand the pain and misery that this evil drug brings. No amount of profit can entice me to deal in this drug that we Chinese call "foreign mud". How would we be able to face our ancestors knowing that our hands were tarnished with such

an evil deed? How could we ever justify it to our future generations? Using the excuse of smugglers and pirates - if we had not sought to profit from this enterprise others would have - is a very poor legacy for us to pass on to future generations."

"Cheung, I will not ask again." conceded Quan Li.

Cheung queried Quan Li as they ate, "I see railway notices in search of laborers posted on buildings and walls all over town. The ship that brought us here was filled with Chinese coolies who have come to build the new railway. Surely, this new enterprise should improve the demand for our Chinese goods?"

Quan Li shook his head. "Not much since the company that hires the laborers also supplies the goods and provisions essential to the needs of our compatriots on site. They charge double and triple our prices but we cannot compete because none have the ability to communicate with the headman in his native tongue. In addition, the railway headquarters is located in Yale, which is located in the interior of the province. Safety for Chinese travelers is always laden with risk. The newly-appointed American railway contractor is only concerned with building the railway as quickly as possible. He has no time to squander over the price of essential goods for his coolies."

"There could be a great business opportunity for us, if I could speak with the head man in charge."

"Cheung, I have made sleeping arrangements for you at our brotherhood society, the Chee Kong Tong. Incidentally, where did you sleep last night?"

"We were very fortunate to find accommodation just outside of town in a western rooming house."

"It is not safe for Chinese to dwell outside of Chinatown. Anything can happen to you or Wing. Most of Chinatown has small narrow passageways, so that it is very difficult for any but the smallest lofan to enter. The stench from open sewers also discourages undesirables from entering."

When the meal was completed Quan Li gave the Dai's, a quick tour of Chinatown comprised mainly of three city blocks. The main streets of Chinatown were Cormorant Street and Fisguard Street which ran east and west. Traversing these two streets was Government Street at the east end and Store Street at the west end. The buildings were mostly two and three-storied and made either of brick or wood. Many of the storefronts had an over-hanging canopy that served as a balcony for the upper level. The sidewalks were wooden platforms raised six to eight inches above street level. On both sides of the streets ran open ditch sewers. At the end of the

tour, the trio arrived at the shop on Cormorant Street. Quan Li introduced Cheung and Wing to the staff and customers and proudly guided them around the premises. The building was a two storied brick building. Outside at the front of the store was a large selection of fresh fruits and fresh vegetables stacked in elevated metal tubs and buckets. A clerk was located at the storefront behind the cash counter to the left of the front entrance. Two rows of double-sided shelves ran along the full length of the retail area with floor to ceiling shelving along the interior and rear wall. They were filled with a vast array of imported items: sacks of rice, dried and canned goods, bottles of sauces, as well as preserved and pickled products.

Upstairs was Quan Li's living quarters which he shared with the staff. Quan Li led father and son up an open stairway along the rear wall of the building to view his living quarters. It was one very large room with brick walls and open rafters. At the top of the stairs, crates and boxes of dried and canned goods were stacked up to the rafters. A narrow pathway between the stacks led to a small cleared area which housed four double bunk beds, a small round table and eight chairs and the cooking facilities. At the front was a large window covered with rice sacks sewn together to act as a curtain. Two large calico cats looked up and ran to their feeding dishes when they saw Quan Li who introduced them as Yin and Yan. Quan Li filled their water dish then half-filled their feeding dish. He turned to Cheung. "*If I feed them too much they will become lazy and useless. Better they are always a little bit hungry like us, my friend, remember?*" Cheung smiled in return. "*Cheung, my friend, I tried to find you accommodation at some of the hotels but I had no luck. They all said go away. Your money is no good here. So I reserved a room for you and Wing at our brotherhood society, the Chee Kong Tong.*"

"*No Quan Li, we have good safe accommodation already. My good friend, I am relieved to know no serious harm has befallen you. I sincerely thank you for trying to save my son and me from serious injury. I wish you to stay at the Chee Kong Tong until you have fully recovered. You need some undisturbed rest. Your attempt to save us from harm on our arrival was a great act of friendship. Take your time to recover. Appoint someone else to manage until you have fully recovered. The employees that you have hired seem very capable. We will stay at Mary Beckham's rooming house for now.*"

"*Aiyah, nice lady. Her cook Ming Yee buys his rice and Chinese goods here. I see him two times a week. He eats very well. When his boss lady comes, I give her*

authentic Chinese antiques ……made in England." Quan Li raised his eyebrows with a big grin. All three burst into laughter at Quan Li's shrewd business acumen.

When Cheung and Wing returned to Mrs. Beckham's, Louisa was patiently sitting in a loveseat on the front veranda having tea with Mary. Before the carriage came to a halt Louisa was off the veranda and down to the sidewalk. Mary watched from the veranda with keen interest. The look in Louisa's eyes was more than just friendship. She was far more mature than her years. Hopefully this infatuation will fade with time for she was still very young. Hopefully, she will learn that only misery and tragedy can come from such a relationship.

Looking at his pocket-watch, Cheung checked the time, *"May Yun, I hope that your wait was not too long. How was your first day at your new school?"*

"Oh Uncle Cheung, Father has asked for you and Wing to come visit us at the synagogue whenever you have the time. This morning was just lessons in Hebrew at the synagogue. The local schools are not in service until autumn. Everything went well. Father wants me to improve my Hebrew and set a good example for the other children in his parish. It finished at noon. I came here right after lunch. I have been back twice."

"I am so sorry May Yun, but father and I visited Mr. Thompson at the Customs House, fetched our friend Quan Li at the city jail, had lunch in Chinatown and toured our store, then made arrangements to go on a voyage."

Surprised by the news and shocked that Wing was so casually unaffected by abandoning her, Louisa burst into tears. *"You are returning to China?"*

"No, no, no" said Wing, as he comforted Louisa, *"We are just going to the mainland to seek more business. We will return in a few days."* Wing took a handkerchief out of his pocket and handed it to Louisa.

Embarrassed by Louisa's reaction, Wing teased, *"What's the matter? Did you think that I was shirking my responsibilities to undo all your evil deeds? Don't worry, I will correct all your mischief when I return."*

Returning the handkerchief, Louisa smiled, *"I am glad that you know this. I plan to be very, very bad while you are away. I may burn down the whole town while you are gone."*

"Just leave our store alone, okay?"

"Your store was first on my list of evil deeds."

Wing and Louisa burst into laughter. Cheung laughed but the gravity hidden in his smile weighed deeply in his thoughts. Hopefully, time and common sense will resolve the problems that lie ahead.

"*When do you leave, Wing?*"

"*In four days.*"

"*And when do you return?*"

"*Father does not know for sure but he thinks three, maybe four days. He has to make contact with someone who is in charge of building a path for the iron dragon.*"

"*Uncle Cheung, may I show you and Wing where I live? We live very close by.*"

"*May Yun, there is only an hour before dinner. I have some work that must be done. Why don't you take Wing? Give your father my regards and tell him I will visit him soon. Wing, please be back before five o'clock for dinner.*"

As they departed, Cheung paused, wondering about their safety. Louisa has come to visit without accompaniment three times. Safety must not be a concern if Nathan would allow his only daughter to walk the streets without an escort. Trusting Nathan's judgment, Cheung allowed his concern to pass.

Along the path, Louisa tried to cling to Wing's arm but he pulled back in protest, "*Louisa, no touching in public. There are rules of conduct that you must not transgress.*" Concerned that his tone may have been too harsh he smiled, then added. "*Otherwise you must walk six paces behind me like all obedient females. Like this.*" Wing mimicked a quick shuffle with arms folded and his head bowed. Louisa followed trying to narrow the gap as the pace quickened. After a short pursuit through a wooded area, they collapsed on a soft mound of grass in a clearing surrounded by tall evergreens. As they lay on the grass, Wing said, "*I do not understand why there is so much hatred here for the Chinese. Maybe you should not be seen with me or the locals will treat you likewise.*"

Louisa replied, "*according to my father, most of the Europeans that live here also hate Jews. That is why our people originally moved to Kaifeng in China to escape the hatred and senseless violence. China was the only place where Jews were accepted and allowed to worship in peace. My father said that we owe the Chinese a great debt of gratitude for accepting our people to settle there and live in peace.*"

"*So if your father was happy in China, why did he bring you here?*"

"*He said China is changing forever, with the arrival of Europeans. They will bring with them the past hatred and resentment from which our people escaped. The Chinese are being exploited by foreigners. My father thought that the Chinese could not help but learn to eventually hate all foreigners. He could not bear any*"

longer, to watch the misery and growing hatred. My father thought that Canada, as a new country, would present a new opportunity for Jews to live in safety and peace."

"Your father, Louisa, is a very wise man. My father believes that China is changing forever. He is very troubled by his dreams of the future in China. He foresees great turmoil, death, destruction, and tragedy for the Middle Kingdom. He said that it is better to be hated in Canada than starving or dead in China. My father has come to find a place for our family to live. He thought that it would be here because the Chinese were treated respectfully in the past, but recent events have confused him. Now little sister, close your eyes."

Feigning anger, Louisa said, "I told you not to call me that. I forbid it. I know what you are suggesting and it is not going to work."

"Okay, okay, just close your eyes, little empress."

Louisa closed her eyes intrigued with her prospects. Wing fumbled in his trouser pockets for a small package.

"Now open your mouth," Louisa gave out an exasperated sigh of disappointment then felt a small oval object in her mouth and the sweet taste of a candied olive.

"Where did you get this from? I love them." Wing filled her lap with an assortment of individually wrapped preserved fruit. After savouring the treat and spitting out the pit, Louisa seized the opportunity to show her gratitude.

Wing pulled back, as he playfully brushed off her embrace. "Sorry, not in public. Which way to your dwelling?" She grinned with amusement.

The two stood up and straightened their garments. Louisa picked up her scattered treats. "By the way, you still owe me five favours."

Wing paused to think. "How many treats do you have in your hand?"

"Four."

"And you are eating one, right? Five treats cancels out five favours. We're even." Wing stepped away laughing.

Louisa followed giggling, "I don't think so"

When she finally caught up he said. "Now, which way to your house?"

Louisa pointed towards her home and Wing started to run. Close behind was Louisa, laughing. "Hey you're not getting away that easy. Keep the candies. You still owe me five."

Wing gave out a high-pitched laugh and shook his head in playful disgust "You are much too clever for me. Must you always win?"

"Always, don't you forget it!" An endearing, mischievous sparkle appeared in her eyes. Wing looked in her eyes and his heart was pounding. She caught his look and broadened her smile, staring even more intently into his eyes. As they near their destination, Wing recognized one of the kids from the ship, sitting on the front stairs of a nearby house. Michael Simpson returned his glance.

"Isn't that Michael from the ship"

"Yes, his family lives there but I don't think he will bother us anymore. He and his sister haven't bothered me. I think that he has learnt his lesson." Then Louisa pointed down the street. *"That is our house, over there."*

The house was a two-storied Tudor-style wood frame bungalow located on a large manicured corner lot. The residence had a basement and was elevated 6 feet above street level with a stone foundation. The exterior was covered in white plaster with wooden trim painted black.

Wing turned to Louisa. *"Very nice house. Sorry, I don't want be late for dinner. I'll come back and see the inside another time."*

After a quick look around, Wing headed home. As he rounded the corner, Michael and two older boys, much taller and very strongly built, greeted him.

The biggest one spoke. "Hey Chink, Michael here said that you can whoop me. My father said no Chink can whoop a white man ever. So I am gonna put you in your place." The bully took off his cap and gave it to his friend who watched in amusement.

Wing thought, Father said no fighting, so what can I do? They block the path to the rooming house. I can only run in the opposite direction so where do I go? I may get lost. Maybe I will just let them have their fun and perhaps they will tire of their amusement.

"Watch out. He is very devious. He let us beat him up last time. Then when we thought he was beaten, he surprised us."

Wing raised his open hands suggesting that he would not fight. The bully was unaffected by Wing's tactic. The aggressor cautiously advanced, swinging at Wing who evaded any serious contact as the other two shouted out their support. "Come on, hurry up I'll be late for dinner. Just thrash him."

A loud voice suddenly signified a new presence. "What's going on here?"

The four looked around to see Jonathan Beckham.

"If there is any fighting to be done here, it'll be done with me."

Intimidated by Jonathan's words the bully answered back cautiously. "Jonathan, we're just having some fun here. He's just a chink. Michael here said the chink can take me as he beat up three boys all at once on the ship and I don't believe him because no chink can beat any white boy in a fair fight."

Jonathan seized the boy by the collar, shook him and then tripped him over his leg. The boy landed hard on his back. "Now if I catch any of you tormenting this lad I will find you, and you will pay dearly for it. Tell the boys in the neighborhood they will have me to answer to, if I hear this boy has been bullied or harmed in any way. Do you understand?" The boys nod in unison. "Now off with you." The three scattered as Jonathan kicked out, narrowly missing the backside of the boy holding the cap.

Jonathan turned to Wing. "Are you alright? I know that you are not supposed to know how to speak English but I spoke with Mr. Thompson. He stated that Captain Anderson said you could speak English fluently. Now if we are going to be friends we must be straight with one another. It will be our secret. No one else needs to know. Can you speak English?"

Wing lowered his eyes, "Yes, I can. I attended a missionary school in China."

"Why the pretense?"

"In China, being able to speak English means your family is wealthy. My father fears that I may be kidnapped and held for ransom."

"Wing, I don't think that will be a problem here."

"Jonathan, you are not Chinese."

"Yes, you're right and your father is much more knowledgeable about this matter than I am."

"Thank you for saving me from those boys."

Jonathan offered Wing his hand in friendship and the two shook hands.

"Hey, was it true what they said about you beating up three boys on the ship?"

Wing paused momentarily. "Yes."

"Could you have handled those three?"

"My father has forbidden me to fight, unless it is to save my life.' On the ship it was a very dangerous situation and I feared for my friend's safety. A group was threatening to throw her over board. They may not have been serious, but I decided not to risk it. The boys today were bigger and stronger

than those on the ship. The element of surprise was gone. They were prepared. I was going to let them have their fun and run once the path to the house was clear."

Jonathan placed an arm around Wing, "You're a courageous lad. Let's get home for supper. We don't want to be late. Don't worry, your secret is safe with me."

When they arrived in the dining room everyone was already seated. Mary, sitting at the head of the table, peered at the grandfather clock strategically placed in the hallway entrance. When it chimed five o'clock, out came the evening meal course by course. First the lentil soup, then roast beef, Yorkshire pudding, boiled vegetables and finally apple pie.

During the meal the topics of conversation floated from the weather, upcoming civic events, the construction of the new railway, then Chinatown.

Mr. Gray spoke. "I think that Chinatown is an abomination and should be torn down and dismantled as soon as possible. It is a health hazard and if left untreated for much longer it will become a major source of disease. I cannot walk within three blocks of it without feeling noxious over the vile smells."

Realizing the attempt by Gray to antagonize the Chinese guests, Jonathan responded. "Mr. Gray, it smells down there because the honey-pot men and their wagons won't go down there so the Chinese have to empty their chamber pots into the open ditches or dump them off the Johnson Street Ravine. Chinatown is built on mud flats. The Chinese live down there because the land is cheap and the rents are very low and that is all they can afford. And it is the only place that they can live in relative safety."

Jonathan gave Gray a stern look, then grinned at Wing who smiled in return. Cheung caught the eye contact between the two. That was three times during the course of the meal that he had noticed such an occurrence. Perhaps a secret alliance has formed between the two. They did arrive back at the house at the same time. Alliances are difficult without words. But fathers should not know everything and maybe this secret should remain unquestioned for now. Wing will need friends with whom he can confide and who can advise him. Surely, he must have more than just a few friends for future support. What if something unexpected happens to me? Yes, my son, Jonathan is a wise choice to have for a friend.

Gray continued, "well, something has to be done soon to halt the possible spread of disease. I'm told that there are lepers dwelling in the ravine who only come out at night and the Chinese help to feed them."

Mary added. "Mr. Gray there are lepers everywhere even in England, Europe and the United States. There are many sanitariums that treat them now rather than forcing them to live in leper colonies."

Rossini said. "Yes, we have ma…many of these people in my country, too."

Cheung spoke, "Mr. Gray, it is a popular belief in my country that the disease was brought to China by traders from the west. It is thought that the disease originated in Africa and rapidly spread around the world by the English slave traders." Unwilling to defend English slave-traders, Gray stood up and left the table.

The next few days passed quickly. Cheung and Wing spent most of their time in Chinatown. Cheung checked his financial accounts, researched the local economic situation and met with his workers and suppliers. Cheung and Wing arranged where and when to meet with Jonathan to share his company to and from his mother's residence. Louisa appeared every day and waited for Wing to finish his piano lesson. Then they explored the neighbourhood with a newfound immunity.

On the day before their departure, Cheung and Wing decided to surprise Nathan and Louisa with a visit to the synagogue. Nathan had offered to give them a tour whenever they would drop by. Dressed as Chinese laborers, they walked the streets, avoiding contact with locals whenever possible. Cheung instructed Wing "You must now change your stride with short rapid steps and your head down as Chinese peasants all do."

After a short walk they reached their destination. Above the round-arched entrance of the two storey brick building was a sign which read "Emanu-El Synagogue". Adorning the front door of the building was a very ornate wood-inset rose-coloured window centrally located above the triple-arched front entrance. Cheung tapped on the centre door. When there was no response, he knocked more loudly. Still no response. He opened the door and the two entered. Father and son stared in awe at the opulence. A beautiful domed ceiling covered the main floor seating area with rows of wooden benches in lush red upholstery. The rows of benches were divided into three sections by two red-carpeted aisles. An ornamental platform covered the eastern wall. Above was a U-shaped gallery that surrounded the main

seating area. Nathan was pre-occupied in thought at the pulpit preparing a sermon beside a very large brass menorah. Over his shoulders was a fancy prayer shawl. As he looked up from his notes, he recognized his visitors and waved them forward, signaling them to be quiet with his forefinger against his lips. He closed a large ornamental book and laid his reading glasses on the pulpit. Then he called out "Louisa I have a surprise for you." Then he offered Cheung and Wing skullcaps to wear. "These are kippahs. They are worn as a sign of respect." Father and son put them on their heads and bowed.

Louisa peered over the railing at the back of the gallery and squealed "Wing! Uncle Cheung! I'll be right down," as she flew down the steps from the gallery. She embraced Wing who gave her a reserved smile in return.

Wing scolded her sarcastically, "Louisa, I think you better learn to behave like a young lady."

"Sorry, you're responsible. You shouldn't have saved me. You have a lot of work to undo all the bad deeds I plan to do."

"Uncle Cheung can I give Wing the grand tour?" Cheung consented.

Nathan guided Cheung into his office where the two parents discussed Cheung's journey and planned what to do if any emergencies arose.

As Louisa showed Wing the upper level, she asked. "Why are you going to the mainland?"

"I think my father wants to make a deal with the railway company to supply goods for the Chinese workers. Once we reach the mainland, we will have to take another ferry to the interior. I'm really hoping to see all of the things that my father has spoken of during his travels."

"Judging from our arrival, there are a lot of people who dislike the Chinese. I just hope that you will be careful and come back safely. I think that it would be much safer to have you stay with my father and I, or even at Mrs. Beckham's place."

"I am not sure our fathers would approve of you and I staying in the same house. And my father does not trust our fellow boarder, Mr. Gray, who may create problems for me while my father is away. So my father has decided to take me with him. It should be a great adventure."

Chapter 7

The Journey to Yale

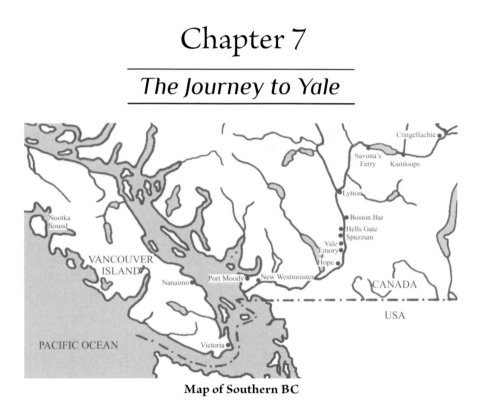

Map of Southern BC

ON THE MORNING OF DEPARTURE TO THE REGIONAL HEAD office of the Canadian Pacific Railway (CPR) in Yale, Nathan and Louisa accompanied their friends to the dock. With tears flowing from her eyes, Louisa tried to clutch Wing in public as he abruptly shrugged her off, walking away in embarrassment. When the ship left the dock Louisa saw the tears in his eyes as he waved back in apology. She understood the reason that fueled his embarrassment and waved back frantically, accepting his apology. She could sense his longing to remain close to her, rather than just

a brotherly concern for her safety and well-being. She interpreted his tears as a sign of hope.

The SS *Princess Louise* was a handsome side-wheeled paddle steamer, about 180 feet in length and with a displacement of 932 tons. From the upper deck Cheung and Wing proceeded to the dining lounge with their luggage in hand. As they walked by other passengers, Cheung could feel the tension and animosity in the air. He decided to avoid the crowded dining room. Cheung led his son to a quiet area on the promenade deck at the back of the boat.

The travelers had dressed in Chinese garments for the journey to arouse as little notice as possible. This was a good time, thought Cheung to have a serious talk with my son to prepare him for unforeseeable circumstances. *"My son, we must talk about our journey and how we must conduct ourselves. We must act and speak as peasant farmers – shuffling our feet, hanging our heads, avoiding eye contact, answering every address with "no saby" and bows of respect. If they laugh and ridicule us, laugh with them feigning ignorance but don't arouse their anger. We must stay away from drunks and young ruffians displaying their manhood. If they hit or kick at us grimace in pain and quickly scurry away. The bottom rung of every society will try to elevate themselves on the shoulders of those they consider too weak to retaliate. They only wish to win prestige by stealing the dignity of others. So the more that we amuse them, the less likely they will react with hostility. However, the lowest in any group may seek to raise their status. If they scream insults or spit at us we must just bow then quickly scurry away saying 'No saby, no saby' which means I don't understand (French derivation of savoir to know or understand – "savez"). My son, pride can cost a life – not only yours but also mine. The lives of your mother, your brothers and sister depend on ours. Our pride could cost them dearly. My life is more than half over and I have survived much more than fate should have allowed. My dreams reveal that your life will hold the key to our family's future. Do not, under any circumstances, risk your life to save mine. Your life is more valuable than mine. Please heed my words. Now let us speak no more of this matter for now."*

Cheung watched Wing's response to the sudden harshness of his demand. Thoughts sparked by his father's words cluttered Wing's thinking. Wing couldn't imagine being left by himself in a land of hatred and hostility without his father. Tears streamed from his eyes. Wing covered his face with his hands, sobbing in silence. Understanding his son's shock at their new

reality, Cheung put his arm around his son tenderly soothing him, realizing that Wing understood the gravity of what may lie ahead. This expression of his father's devotion and willingness to face the ultimate sacrifice had caught him by surprise. He understood too well his father's instructions, but could not accept the new reality. The image of watching his father die without being able to help, precipitated a flood of tears. Soon both father and son were clutching each other in a tearful embrace on the isolated lower deck.

Later father and son spent the rest of the morning talking about Cheung's prior trip to Gold Mountain and the calamities that he and his friends had experienced along their journey. *"Chinese parents are often over-protective. We hide the misery of the past and only relate joyful memories. By relating forgotten disappointments and tragedies, our young would be better prepared to deal with the future."*

"But father, I still do not understand why all this needless cruelty towards the Chinese. Why do the lofan hate us so much?"

"My son, I did not expect so much hatred for our people in Canada. I expected that there would be a reasonable period of adjustment between different cultures. I think that the inhabitants fear that they cannot compete with Chinese labour. Our people who come here are mostly farmers and laborers. They have had to compete every day of their lives in poor overpopulated villages and towns to feed their families. When they come here they are desperate to find work to repay their sponsors and send money to feed their families in China. The local employers see their urgency to work so they pay them half the normal wage. However, these wages are still 10 times more than the wages in China. With so many unemployed Chinese laborers, employers can be very selective, so those employed must work twice as hard to keep their jobs. The cheaper the labour the greater the profit for the business owner, so he hires more Chinese laborers because white laborers will not work at the same wage as the Chinese."

Wing only frowned and shook his head. Cheung continued, *"The locals don't understand that adversity and competition builds strength. They could learn so much from our work ethic, perseverance and patience. But they choose to avoid competition by making our lives miserable to encourage us to return to China. Little do they know of the misery and suffering experienced by the people in China or the future misery that will follow, as I have seen in my dreams."*

"But father why do they treat us as inferior?"

"My son, it is my belief that no man is born better than the next man. What we learn and do during our lives is what makes us better. A society's culture, philosophy and art reflect the environment of its people. When the New World was discovered western nations raced to seize the wealth, resources and land of others with their technological superiority. Knives and spears are no match for guns and cannons. Their leaders justified their conquests under the guise of civilizing savages and converting heathens to Christianity, which was only a ploy to pacify the natives. These leaders were blinded by ruthless ambition and endless greed. Wealth and power corrupt all who possess it and it can always be used to sway others with the best of intentions. Individuals with wealth and power are not always endowed with wisdom. Greed may harness human initiative but it is inherently self-destructive because those who rise, eventually fall in time, to those they have victimized. Now my son, what is better, to live in peace or to live in constant fear?"

"But father the world has changed and there is no peace in China."

"Yes, these are sad times and we must adapt to change. So we must embrace technology for now to survive."

"So father the race for bigger ships and better weapons never ends? Is this what you see?"

"Yes, weapons will become more destructive and wars will grow beyond what is now imaginable."

"Will there ever be a lasting peace?"

"I hope so, blind ambition consumes itself eventually. Any peace will only be temporary until there is a single authority that is just and fair to all people independent of biases and personal self-interest. Until then, conflict between the privileged and the exploited will continue to persist."

Wing reflected in silence on the meaning of his father's words.

"Now my son, let us talk of your dreams. Have you had any more?"

"Nothing very vivid, father."

Cheung saw a slight hint of embarrassment in his son's eyes. "Did any of these dreams include Louisa?"

"Father they were just silly flights of fantasy. No situations of danger arose in any of my recent dreams."

"My son if you do not wish to discuss them so be it, but do not disregard them. Our dreams are the window to the future. I have grave concern about your last dream where you are suspended on a rope on the side of a mountain. The only precaution that we can take to avoid this situation is to keep you away from the

mountains. Are you still practicing the secret art of the Sha-ling monks? These exercises will help build your strength and endurance under any circumstance. If we ever become separated you must send a letter addressed to Mr. Thompson at the Customs House on Wharf Street or to Nathan at the Emanu-El Synagogue in Victoria. I will always check with them to find you."

"*Yes, Father, I practice every day when I am alone. I have not thought any more of that dream. I will try to give it more thought.*"

The two sat and pondered on the isolated deck. It was mid-morning and the fog was lifting. The river was peaceful and calm. All that could be heard was the drone of the steam engine and the rhythmic thrashing of the paddle-wheel. The vessel passed by many island of various size. The larger ones were covered by dark evergreen forests. Some had hills others were flat. A large flock of seagulls quietly followed the vessel. Father and son stood watching the seagulls gracefully gliding behind the boat. Suddenly the gulls started to squawk and bunched up as the backdoor of the galley swung open and the gulls swooped closer towards the back of the boat. Cheung and Wing heard the sound of footsteps.

"*Up your mother's butt, you useless monkey, now hurry up,*" shouted someone in a sarcastic tone.

"*Shut your mouth and watch where you are going, camel dung,*" bantered back another.

Two Chinese galley members appeared dressed in white. Each carried a garbage bin of food waste from breakfast to the lower deck to be dumped. They looked up, and seeing Cheung and Wing, bowed their heads in acknowledgement, then continued on with their load down a gangway. After a couple of minutes, the high-pitch shrieking of seagulls competing for their morning meal gradually faded. The two galley members appeared again with the empty garbage buckets on their way back to the galley. Cheung waved as they stopped and lowered their buckets. Cheung recognized their dialect. "*Friends, will they serve us in the dining room if we go up there now?*"

Happy to hear strangers speaking their dialect of Chinese, one of the two responded proudly in English, "I never see Chinese eat there. Chinese always stay on low deck with pigs and cows. Trip only take half day. You important, stay here with lofan?"

"I am a merchant from Canton. My name is Dai Woo Cheung and this is my son Wing Sing."

"My name Liu, this is my friend Bing. We come from same village near Canton. You wait here, we bring you rice." Cheung accepted the offer with a nod.

Half an hour later, the two men reappeared with four large plates of stir-fried pork and mixed greens on a bed of rice. The smaller of the two ran back up the stairway and quickly returned with a thermos of hot tea, four teacups and four forks. As the four ate, Cheung asked the men the usual questions about their village, their family and how and when they came to Gold Mountain, as was the custom. The two had grown up in the same village and were childhood friends. They had left at the same time sponsored by their village. They were both married to young village girls a month prior to leaving for the West.

Cheung thought this was a familiar theme. In China the young men of small villages were always forced to marry by their families before leaving, to provide the village with greater assurance that they would return and live up to their obligations and responsibilities. These bonds that tied these men to their village and families were generally as strong as any that tied Christians to their God, perhaps stronger. It was very rare to hear of anyone who would shirk his commitments, for every individual was identified from whence he came. When one wondered whether someone was trustworthy, his family's reputation would be available at his clan organization. A man's and his family's past accompanied him across the Pacific. Every newly arrived Chinese immigrant sought out and joined an association based on kinship, district or dialect. These organizations looked after their members when they were sick, injured, unemployed, homesick or destitute. Every member paid a fee to join and the association secured lodgings for the homeless, nursed the sick, wrote and read letters for the illiterate, mediated disputes for members, disseminated news about the homeland, provided for the members' recreational needs, as well as looked after funeral services and shipping of the remains back to relatives in China. Many of the larger associations had branches or affiliates wherever there was a large enough population of Chinese. What a man and his family did in China and how it was perceived followed him to Gold Mountain, enhancing or hindering the level of co-operation that individual would receive from others.

"How did you come to be employed by this shipping line?" inquired Cheung.

Bing spoke, "when Hudson Bay Company buy ship they promise no one lose job. They keep promise. They carry mail no Chinese suppose to work on a mail-boat but we work in galley. Nobody care but we hide in galley no one see us. Everyone keep mouth shut. Captain like us very much. Crew like Captain very much. We give crew special food. I chop up all kind vegetables, chop up meat, put in wok add ginger, garlic, soya sauce. Tell them special recipe. They like it very, very much. They eat everything. Always come back for more." Cheung and Wing laughed in admiration.

When the morning meal was finished, Cheung thanked the two and asked if he could reward them for their kindness but neither would accept money. They stood up gave a short bow, gathered the dishes and utensils, and then scurried back up to the galley. Later in the afternoon the two friends reappeared with four plates of seafood and mixed greens on rice. During the lunch Cheung had gleaned information about New Westminster, its population of Chinese and the location of its Chinatown. When the lunch was completed, the two went back upstairs but returned later with two packed meals for the travelers. Turning to their compatriots, Cheung said, "*You have been very kind, my friends.*" He offered each money, which was rejected again. "*Please take this,*" he handed Liu a piece of paper. "*This is the address of my business in Victoria. If you ever need help in the future, we will be glad to return your kindness. Thank you once again.*"

Cheung knew that these were poor simple men much like himself, when he first arrived at Gold Mountain. His father had taught him to always return kindness. So it was something that he wished to teach his son. The two men thanked Cheung. The four exchanged polite bows. Then the two men returned to their duties.

It had been a warm sunny day. The water had been very calm. The side-wheeler had made good progress crossing the Strait of Georgia. The 16 miles up the Fraser River Delta to New Westminster was just as tranquil. It was now mid-afternoon as the *Princess Louise* came to dock in New Westminster on the northern bank of the Fraser River. After they disembarked, Cheung learned that the terminal ticket office was closed until early the next morning and that the steamship to Yale and Fort Hope would leave at 7 a.m.. In the meantime the two travelers would have to walk to Chinatown in search of overnight accommodations. To avoid the traffic into town, Cheung and Wing waited outside the terminal for the traffic to clear, then

followed the course described by their compatriots to Chinatown and their affiliate kinship association.

New Westminster was the old capital of British Columbia before the colony was amalgamated with Vancouver Island in 1866 to become the colony of British Columbia. When Cheung and Wing first saw the town from the lower deck of the *Princess Louise*, it appeared to be just a small settlement carved out of a riverbank of dense evergreen forest. The hillside on which the town was perched stood about two hundred feet above the shoreline with a varying average slope of 10 to 15 degrees. Towering Douglas firs stood like imposing sentries stationed at the top of the riverbank bordering the town site. The town seemed to be bustling with the activity from lumber mills, sawmills, farming and fish processing plants.

It was early evening. Cheung was surprised at the amount of heavy traffic that continued to flow through the streets as freight wagons and carriages passed by, along the dusty main road, Front Street, which ran along the river. Besides the squeaking wagon wheels, the sound of drivers barking orders and the banging of freight, the distant sound of music and merriment emanated from the local taverns. Dressed as peasants, father and son walked cautiously to Chinatown. Cheung carried some belongings in a large black leather handbag, while Wing shared the load by awkwardly balancing a bamboo rod on his shoulder with wicker baskets attached at both ends. The skies in New Westminster had been cloudless for approximately two weeks now and the town was just recovering from another day of blistering heat.

Chinatown was located very close to the government wharf on Front Street. Unlike Victoria, the population of about four hundred permanent Chinese residents was less concentrated. Chinese habitation was dispersed along Front Street and Columbia Street between Douglas Street and Mary Street occupying about three or four city blocks. The affiliate branch for their district clan was located near the heart of this area.

When they arrived in the lobby of the Hoi Sen Society they were greeted by the curious looks of young men casually reading while sitting on mahogany benches and wooden chairs. At the centre of the lobby area was a large, rectangular wooden table, on top of which were much-used Chinese periodicals, newspapers and books. The gathering whispered quietly, curious of the new visitors.

Cheung was surprised. Why do they not approach us to inquire of recent news about the homeland, as is customary whenever sojourning Chinese arrive? They must see through our disguises. Our clothes are obviously too new and Wing looks too healthy and strong to pass for one of them. Fortunately his height will hide his age. They will think him much older as long as he doesn't ask too many questions. He does carry his pole awkwardly but that skill can only come with time. Well I guess these men are our own district clan. They are not those whom we wish to deceive.

A friendly middle-aged man standing behind a large L-shaped mahogany reception counter greeted Cheung and Wing. After answering a few preliminary questions about their ancestry, what work they were involved with, where they came from and where they were going, the man disappeared through a door at the back of the room. The men, silently gathered in the room, had listened to Cheung's answers and they conferred quietly. One approached respectfully and introduced himself.

"Mr. Dai, my name is Tan Way Cheung. Are you the same Dai Woo Cheung with whom my uncle, Tan Sung Yuen, journeyed to Gum San? He told us many wonderful stories about his journey in search for gold."

Cheung turned to face the young man and smiled inquisitively, "Well, maybe. Does your uncle have a small black mole below his left eye?"

Way Cheung smiled and said, "Yes."

"Does he stutter like a silly fool when he gets mad or excited?"

Way Cheung said, "Yes."

"Does your uncle sometimes walk with a limp because of an injury to his right leg?"

Way responded, "Yes."

"No, sorry, I don't know the fool." The trio burst out in laughter.

Clutching Cheung's hand with both of his, the young man laughed. "Yes, you are the famous Dai Woo Cheung my uncle has spoken so often about. He asked my father to name me after you."

Cheung responded. "The silly fool names a nephew after me but he cannot return my letters after we both learned how to read and write together. Tell the fool that I thought he was dead. And ask him why he has such a lazy pen."

"Do not blame him. His wife is a very shy insecure woman and is so fearful of being abandoned that she hides his mail. Whenever he is angry with her, he threatens to return to Gold Mountain. He thought that maybe you had died or returned

to Gold Mountain. I know that he tried to write to you often, and he kept threatening to visit your village, but somehow my aunt always ruined his plans. She is constantly fearful that he will leave and not return, because so many never return."

"I should have visited your village. Is my old friend well? Has he many children?"

"Two children, a son and a daughter, and he is in good health. He is a wealthy man and praises your wisdom and insight for his success and good fortune. When he returned to the village with gold he bought land and built a large mansion. When his son became old enough he paid for his tuition to be educated at the American missionary school. When his son rebelled at having to learn a foreign language he sent me to the American school in his place. He spoke to us often about your dreams and visions of the future. He sponsored a few of our villagers to come to Gold Mountain to explore the possibility of finding gold. After I visit our villagers who have a mining site in the interior, I have been instructed to meet my uncle in San Francisco to help him with a mission." Smiling, Cheung thought to himself, So, his old friend had not forgotten the promise that was made so long ago.

The man reappeared behind the reception counter and signaled Cheung and Wing to follow him. Way Cheung interrupted, "Uncle, if you are looking for accommodation for the night why not stay with me tonight? I have more room than I need. This must be your son. He is most welcome, also." Cheung accepted the invitation. Wing gave Way a courteous bow.

"Way Cheung, this is my son, Wing Sing. Please excuse me while I talk to the man behind the counter."

As Cheung walked to the counter and apologized to the desk clerk for his inconvenience, Wing looked at his newfound friend. He was four or five years older, a little shorter but very strongly built with wide shoulders. His eyes were soft and his smile was gentle and kind but not condescending. Wing liked and trusted him immediately. When Cheung returned, Way picked up Wing's pole before he could protest and smiled as he carried the balanced baskets for his less practiced friend, who smiled back in relief. Two doors down from the Hoi Sen Society was Way's two-storey wooden tenement building. After a flight of stairs they walked down a narrow hallway. Way's room was the third door down. Way opened the door with his key and then stepped back to let his guests in first. When Cheung and Wing stepped into a fairly spacious single room with a double bunk bed in the right corner, a small desk bureau in the left corner, a medium-sized couch

and a small table with four chairs sitting in the centre of the room. Except for a small wooden suitcase and a few books and newspapers on the small table, the room was neat and undisturbed.

Way Cheung turned to Cheung and said, "*I can sleep on the couch tonight. The two of you can use the bunk beds. There is better accommodation available in town but it may be too dangerous to stay where we are not really welcome.*" Cheung agreed. After a fine meal in Chinatown, Way Cheung gave Cheung and Wing a quick tour of New Westminster and shared the information he had acquired since his arrival, three days prior.

As they walked through the town, Way Cheung remarked. "*This is a very busy place. Everyone in New Westminster has great anticipation of commercial prosperity now that they have finally decided the route of the railway that will connect the east and west coasts of this country. Because there are lots of employers that are in need of laborers, the Chinese in New Westminster are safer here than in Victoria and do not have to hide in disgusting hovels that discourage entry by the lofan. I have been reading some of the newspaper articles.*" Way Cheung dug in his back pocket and took out some clippings from New Westminster's local newspaper, the *British Columbian*. "*They describe us as hard working, honest, industrious, dependable and law-abiding. They praise us for our cleanliness, our willingness to adapt and our trustworthiness.*"

Cheung interrupted, "*Way Cheung, these are similar words of honey they used to describe us in 1858 when your uncle and I first arrived from San Francisco. So what they think of us depends very much on their needs at the time. During that time, we brought prosperity to the local businesses in Victoria so they spoke of us with sweet words. But the sweet words did not last. This city needs the Chinese for cheap labour at present. That may not last for long after the completion of the railway. Because thousands will ride the railway to the West in search of adventure, wealth, land, freedom or just a new life. What if there are not enough jobs for these new people? How will they treat the Chinese when that time comes? Will they be kind and fair-minded then? They may if they have good leadership. But their leaders ride the winds of popular sentiments, not what is fair, reasonable and just. They cater to the self-interest of those who can vote. The Chinese cannot vote. Our acceptance in New Westminster may not last. Please relate my sentiments to your uncle.*"

Taken by surprise, Way was shaken by Cheung's foresight. My uncle was right. This man could possibly see beyond the mist of time. "*Yes uncle,*

I will pass on your comments to him." Turning towards Cheung, Way smiled in admiration and bowed his head respectfully. Wing followed his father and Way as the tour continued. Way pointed out the major landmarks, the business locations that employed Chinese workers and any trouble spots frequented by drunks, young toughs and belligerent locals to avoid.

As they reached the top of a hill, the trio walked westward along Royal Avenue. They were followed by two boys of about nine years of age. The boys whispered insults that grew louder as the threesome ignored them. Soon a small band of five children were following and started to chant, "Chinkee, Chinkee, Chinaman,

Sitting on the fence,

Trying to make a dollar,

Out of fifty cents."

Way turned and smiled at the youthful entourage. Some of the children started to run away but Way produced a small tin of barley candy from his pants' pocket and shook the tin. He opened the tin and offered the contents to the older boys as the younger tots who had disbanded returned for a piece of candy. One by one each child received a candy. When he approached the last child, a pretty blonde-haired, six year-old girl, he squatted down and offered her a candy. After she gingerly picked one up and put it in her mouth, he secured the lid back on the tin and placed the tin in her hand. The tin was still half full. She ran home with her treasure followed by the others. Cheung smiled at Way's clever act of kindness. *Well done, Way Cheung. You may be the answer to my dilemma.*

When the three return to the lodging Cheung turned to Way as they approached the apartment door. *"Way, may I speak with you? Wing can stay here. My son, we will be back shortly."* A half an hour passed. When the pair returned, Wing looked at his father inquisitively, wondering what was being planned. His father sat down on a chair with his back to the hallway door. He beckoned his son to sit across the table as Way sat on the couch. *"My son, I have conferred with Way in privacy because I need his help. I am sorry for the mystery but I had to check with him first whether my plans would interfere with his own. I have told him of your dreams and my concern for your safety and welfare. My son, you must stay here with Way in New Westminster while I am away. I cannot risk you being anywhere near the mountains. Way has agreed to stay with you until I return; I expect to be back in two or three days."*

Cheung looked in his son's eyes for compliance. Wing responded with a nod.

The SS *William Irving* was the newest and most luxurious sternwheeler to navigate the Fraser River. It was built in New Westminster. The owner, John Irving had commissioned the construction of the vessel at the staggering sum of $75,000 in anticipation of the construction of the Canadian Pacific Railway. The steamship stood approximately 40 feet high and was about one hundred and sixty-six feet in length with a width of fifty feet. The main deck featured the engine room, the firebox and boiler, cargo storage and the kitchen. On the upper deck were the dining room, cabins, salons and observation lounge. The top level was reserved for the wheelhouse that was crowned by Irving's trademark, the gilt eagle, and the smokestack. The ship was built to impress not only her passengers but also the shipping line's rivals. Since her launching on March 18, 1880 she was the talk of the river. All the locals had lined up to sample the silver service in the dining room, lay on her patent spring mattresses and survey the exquisite carpentry and opulent furniture.

Cheung stared at the distant cottonwood trees perched on the shoreline. His mind was troubled as he listened to the rhythmic thrashing of the paddle-wheel. The more time that he spent with Wing, the more he enjoyed his companionship. When Wing revealed his recent dream, Cheung had considered bringing Wing back to Victoria to leave him in care of Quan Li , until he met Way. Even though he was confident that Way could be trusted to safeguard his son, he still felt an uneasiness with the temporary separation from his son. What else could I do? How could I risk Wing being so close to the mountains? Or so close to Louisa. They are both much too clever to be easily dissuaded by parental authority. Their bond might wane with time and distance. I should feel relieved that I have avoided the fulfillment of his dream. Or have I?

Until Way demonstrated his cleverness and resourcefulness, leaving his son with the nephew of his old friend was out of the question. But Cheung liked how Way assumed the role as a big brother to Wing. He hoped that, given more time together, they would develop a long-lasting friendship. His old friend would never have trusted anyone so young for a perilous journey alone if he was not completely confident in the ability of his nephew to face unforeseeable challenges.

Two loud blasts from the whistle of the *William Irving* alerted all the passengers on board that the steamship was nearing a rival vessel, the *SS Western Slope*. This signal by the trailing vessel was a warning to the leading vessel to move aside and let the faster vessel pass. The signal could also be construed as a challenge. For each Captain prided himself as a master of the river with an intimate knowledge of every hidden snag, sandbar, eddy and white water passage on the Fraser River and each was furiously proud of the vessel under his command. Being the fastest vessel on the river greatly enhanced ridership since supplies in demand arriving first fetched the best prices. In addition the race for jobs and gold claims was won by those who arrived the earliest and were the quickest to the desired destination. So the fastest boats won the bulk of passengers and cargo.

John Irving, the Captain of the *William Irving*, was the son of the steamship's namesake. From an early age his father, the self-proclaimed "King of the River", had schooled John Irving. When William Irving died in 1872, John took control of his father's company, the "Pioneer Line" at the tender age of 17 years. Besides nurturing his son's expertise on the Fraser, William Irving had implanted in his son his spirit of competition. John also shared his father's dream of expansion. To do this he had to annihilate the competition. His major competitor was a cantankerous old rival by the name of Bill Moore. A steamboat veteran, Moore resided in Victoria which was the headquarters for his ever-transitory corporate steamship entities. His current business was called the "People's Steamship Line". Moore and Irving, plus a few smaller independents, were locked in a bitter rivalry over control of the Fraser River between New Westminster and Yale, which was the new western headquarters for the Canadian Pacific Railway. At stake were the lucrative government contracts to transport provisions, supplies and Chinese laborers. As periodic rivalries heated up between Moore and Irving, price wars and reckless riverboat races would ensue with greater frequency resulting in reduced profits for all as well as more accidents along the route. Victoria and New Westminster had vied to be the capital of the newly-formed province. The selection of Victoria as the new capital created much bitterness and ill-will between the province's two major cities. The rivalry between the two shipping lines, with Moore's headquarters in Victoria and Irving's in New Westminster, added more fuel to a pre-existing animosity between the two cities. The respective newspapers of each city, the *British*

Colonist in Victoria, and the *British Columbian* in New Westminster helped perpetuate the feud as they hurled insults at each other's cities, each other's steamship lines and each other's most colourful and flamboyant citizens – John Irving and Bill Moore.

Trusting no one to command his newest flagship, Captain John Irving belted out to his engineer, "More steam!"

His engineer shouted back, "Captain, we're already forty pounds above regulations now. I think that she's already up to capacity."

"Listen here. I didn't build her to come in second to that hog-pen scow. If she bursts she bursts, but not without giving it her best. Now, more steam. And bring the extra sides of bacon (used by steamboat veterans for acceleration and patching temporary holes) out of the galley larder and throw them into the firebox when I give you the order," barked the Captain.

The *William Irving* had just pulled even with the *Western Slope*. The water level was low from the recent lack of rain and the river narrowed soon to a small channel wide enough for one vessel. Cheung watched the boat race with curious amusement. The passengers on the ship seemed to be exhilarated by the race. Each time one boat pulled slightly ahead, the passengers on board the rival vessel would shout "More steam." Cheung thought this race must be a friendly competition to entertain the passengers. As the river, narrowed the two riverboats drew closer together. He observed the passengers on the other steamship. What appeared to be friendly faces and gestures from afar turned into nasty looks and obscene gestures and insults when the steamships came closer together. Cheung assumed that it was he who was drawing all the adverse attention from the passengers of the *Western Slope*. He decided to grab his leather bag and looked for the stairway to the lower level. Suddenly eggs started to fly from both boats. The dining-room attendants from each boat had brought out crates of eggs from their galleys to pelt the passengers of the rival steamboat. During the mêlée, Captain Irving tried to keep the vessels dead even during the race waiting for the right time to forge ahead. He would wait until a quarter mile at the narrows before making his move. Hopefully the *Western Slope* would keep up her present pace and when the *William Irving* sped by, her rival would be caught off guard and would not be able to turn fast enough to avoid grounding on the sandbar on the portside of the channel entrance. Captain Irving had skillfully jockeyed for position, keeping the *Slope* on the portside with

his plan in mind. He smiled, thinking to himself, the longer she sits on the sandbar the better.

The non-participants in the egg fight retreated inside the dining room. They watched through the windows in great amusement. Cheung had been hit with a couple of eggs. He knew the dining room was not accessible as smiling faces laughed at him behind the glass-door entrance. When the egg-throwing passengers from the *Western Slope* saw Cheung's dilemma he became the main target for their eggs. Cheung slipped and repeatedly fell on the egg-covered surface of the promenade deck and struggled as he clutched his black leather valise. When the egg-throwing participants on board the *William Irving* recognized the main focus of amusement for the on-lookers, they turned and targeted their fellow passenger, the Chinaman. After the supply of eggs had been depleted, Cheung escaped down a companionway and found refuge in an isolated corner on the starboard side of the cargo deck. He was attired in western clothing to make a favourable impression on the big boss for the railway company. His clothes were now covered in egg slime and shell fragments. Since this was the only set of Western clothing he had brought, he would have to find a laundry service in Yale before he could make arrangements to meet with Andrew Onderdonk, the new American railway contractor.

Cheung quickly changed into Chinese clothing, wearing black silk trousers, a white cotton shirt and black cotton Chinese slippers with leather soles. He put his soiled western garments in his leather bag. Cheung heard shouting from the upper deck. The race between the two steamboats was still in progress. Some of the crew members were busy cleaning the egg fragments off the promenade deck. One of the passengers, surrounded by others, shouted out, "Hey, where's that Chink?" One of his cronies pointed around the corner and below.

The first man said. "Let's have some fun. Let's lighten our load aboard and throw him over the side. It will be like a human sacrifice to win the race."

Another laughed. "Yes, let's throw the Chink over. I hope he can swim."

Over-hearing the plan, Cheung looked for a safe place to hide. A group of four men followed the trail of egg remnants. They headed around a corner and down a companionway on the starboard side of the vessel. As the group searched for him on the cargo deck Cheung tried to hide carrying his leather bag in hand. He thought, if they throw me over, where do I want to be? It

was better to be on the side closest to shore and at the widest part of the vessel's girth to ensure maximum clearance so as to avoid being ridden over by the paddle-wheel. I will have to throw my bag off first then dive out as far as I can, instead of being thrown off by his pursuers. Cheung crept pass horses, wagons and a locked enclosure at the back of the cargo deck. He thought to himself that must be for the Chinese laborers. Maybe I can hide inside but how do I get out when we reach the destination and how do I get past the guard?

No, that was not an option. He proceeded to the front of the boat to access the fender railing along the vessel's exterior. His pursuers were getting closer, laughing in anticipation of the spectacle they would create for the gallery above. Cheung scurried between the loaded carts and wagons towards the storage area near the front of the boat. It housed a vast array of emergency items: ropes, pulleys, harnesses, and ladders, to assist a steamship in contending with every foreseeable river hazard.

"There he is at the front," called one of pursuers, pointing at their victim.

The storage facility contained an access to the ship's exterior. Once Cheung reached the storage area he crawled along the narrow outer peripheral fender rail on the starboard side of the boat. He carried his bag in front of him so that his pursuers could not grab it from him. All of his important papers were hidden in the bottom lining of his bag together with money in case of an emergency. His pursuers followed. The leader, a large, strongly built man about six feet in height shinnied along the exterior fender rail drawing closer and closer to his quarry. Cheung knew that his time was running out. He could not fight, because the consequences would be more dangerous than being thrown off the boat and he could not proceed any farther along the ship's fender because a dinghy was secured along the side of the steamship blocking his path. He was trapped. The big man was now drawing closer, within five feet. Cheung prepared to jump. He hurled his leather bag as far as he could, away from the vessel.

As the Western Slope started to draw ahead, the Captain yelled through the voice pipe from the wheelhouse to the engine room, "Now, full steam ahead!"

The *William Irving* suddenly lunged forward. The pungent smell of burnt bacon permeated the air, as Cheung and his pursuers grabbed the side of the ship. Hearing the other passengers cheering above, the lead pursuer

stopped and turned back wondering if free drinks were being offered on the upper deck. Cheung was relieved that he didn't have to jump into the water because the vessel's sudden burst forward may have drawn him into the paddlewheel. The increased speed continued for only a short distance as the vessel's passengers celebrated the victory. Meanwhile in her wake, the *Western Slope* was temporarily grounded to a halt on the pre-destined sandbar at the entrance to the narrow passage.

Cheung pondered, "What do I do now? There is very little chance that I will ever see that bag again. Now what will I do without money and identification? Even if I had jumped off to rescue the bag it would have been a silly risk to take. Who would look after Wing? There is so much yet to teach him."

After the pursuers dispersed to join the festivities on the passenger level, Cheung shinnied back to the front of the boat and collapsed on the cargo deck. He decided that he would remain on the cargo deck for the duration of the trip. Having won the race, Captain Irving slowed the boat down to regulation speed. As the steamboat approached Mission, the Captain sounded a whistle to signal the sliding bridge which blocked the narrow passageway to be removed from the path of the steamship.

Charlie was an old horse, trained to operate a sweep that controlled the opening and closing of the bridge. He worked the sweep independent of human supervision. Long past his prime, Charlie's painfully slow pace was the bane of every steamboat Captain on the Fraser River because while they waited for old Charlie, vanquished rivals would catch up and the race would start again.

Captain Irving glared out of his wheelhouse at the feeble old horse. Turning to one of his officers he remarked, "When that old nag dies, I am going to have him stuffed and mounted in my living room. So I can kick him in the arse for every time he's held me up." After the *William Irving* passed through the bridge, the whistle of the *Western Slope* sounded, signaling Charlie to leave the passage open.

Mission was a regularly scheduled stop for steamboats. The flat-bottomed stern-wheelers always docked nose first. Unlike side-wheelers, they only needed a shallow riverbank to load and unload their cargo and passengers. From past experience, Cheung knew that the cargo was always loaded in the reverse order of boarding. The cargo at the front of the boat would be unloaded at the earlier scheduled stops and the cargo at the rear of the boat

would be unloaded in Yale, the final destination. Cheung found empty space on a wagon loaded with provisions and covered by canvas. He hid there because he had left his steamboat ticket in his leather bag, and if asked to prove that he had paid for passage he could not. The consequences of such a situation could be tragic. Better to remain unseen. The other scheduled stops were Chilliwack and Hope. Both were fairly short in duration, only ten to fifteen minutes. When the *William Irving* left Chilliwack the *Western Slope* approached the dock. One of the crew had noticed what must have been a small gash on the bow of the *Western Slope* on her port side just above her waterline. They had patched it up temporarily with slabs of bacon, so the boat race would not be resumed.

It was now three o'clock. The boat trip from New Westminster to Yale was 95 nautical miles and was supposed to take ten to twelve hours depending on the stops. There were only three scheduled stops but any private wharf flying a white flag was a request for a pick up. Most of these requests for unscheduled pickups would appear on the downriver trip. The recent rivalry for river supremacy between the steamboat lines had greatly shortened the times between New Westminster and Yale. The average upriver run took approximately ten hours and the downriver run only five hours.

The water level was extremely low even for this time of the year. The Captain had to check the water level upstream. When the *William Irving* pulled into Hope, Captain Irving was told that the water level was so low that a steamboat could not make it all the way to Yale. There was a small stretch called the Douglas Slough, located 3 miles before Yale, that was currently impassable. Irving was familiar with the section. His only question was, "Does anyone know the depth of the gravel?"

One of the clerks at the shipping office spoke up. "My uncle panned that part of the river. He said that it's all sand and gravel. He went down at least five feet." Irving knew that he would have a lot of unhappy passengers on his hands if he had to drop them off at the Slough to journey the last three miles to Yale on foot towing baggage. But what about the Chinese laborers? This was only his second load for Andrew Onderdonk who complained bitterly about the first delivery when his laborers had to walk to Yale from the Slough. Onderdonk may give the sole franchise to Bill Moore or to one of the independents. He has forced us to compete against each other to bring down our cargo rates. Leaving the railway laborers and its supplies three

miles short of the intended destination would cost the railway company additional expense and it could tarnish his future prospects with the railway company. He thought to himself: delivering his human cargo to Yale would surely enhance his prospect of acquiring additional government contracts.

As Irving left the shipping office, the manager asked, "Junior, what are you going to do?"

"I'm going to Yale," replied Irving with a confident smile.

The manager shouted back, "That creek's not fit for a spawning salmon."

"My boat can float on a heavy dew."

The news was quickly relayed to the local taverns and saloons and then transmitted by telegraph to the upriver communities. Soon men women and children on horseback, buggies and carts were all heading to the troubled shallow spot to watch Junior "tread the dewdrops" with his newest flagship.

Captain Irving purposely slowed his pace to the shallow creek. He wanted as many as possible to witness the feat. He knew that "treading the dewdrops" would enhance his reputation in local folklore. When he arrived at the creek, nearly the whole population living on that stretch of the Fraser were gathered on the banks of the river to watch the spectacle. The 12-foot-wide Cariboo Road that connected Hope and Yale provided easy access for the spectators. When he reached the Slough, cargo, passengers, crew and unnecessary equipment were unloaded to make the vessel as light as possible. The crew was ordered to create a channel by dredging. Many local volunteers were recruited to assist, including the Chinese laborers. When a channel was created through the deepest portion of the creek, the Captain backed up the vessel then drove it up the channel. After a frontal attack at half speed gained only halfway through the shallows, passengers, townsfolk, crew members and the Chinese laborers were enlisted by crew members to help pull the steamship. Pulleys were secured by ropes to trees at the end of the shallows, then secured to the capstan and either side of the prow. Cheung peered out to see what was going on. The wagon that he was hiding in had been tied to a tree. Cheung observed from a safe distance. Rocks and gravel flew out behind the stern wheel as the vessel ground forward at three quarters speed. The recruited support on both sides of the riverbank pulled under the direction of crew members, keeping the vessel properly aligned. After several hours, the vessel drew close to the end of the shallows. With only a few feet from navigable water, the Captain of the *William Irving*

pulled the vessel back once more for the final assault. With the engine at full throttle, the vessel broke through the remaining shallow creek bed into deeper waters. A loud cheer erupted and all participants were jubilant at the accomplishment and the part they all played in the historic event.

Triumphantly, the Captain smiled and thought to himself, maybe now, they will stop referring to me as "Junior", or "the little prince" behind my back.

Captain Irving docked the boat on the riverbank to reload then went ashore to receive his accolades and ingratiate the witnesses with his humble words of thanks to his supporters. It was truly a historic moment in local folklore. The *William Irving* finally docked in Yale at approximately eight o'clock. The voyage had taken 12 hours. When the ship's whistle sounded, the whole population had flocked to the riverbank to greet the first steamboat to arrive at Yale in over a week. Everyone wanted to hear what incredible feat of navigational skill or reckless abandon had allowed the *William Irving* to navigate the shallowest stretch of the mighty Fraser. As the celebrants lifted their glasses to honour the local hero, the mayor of Yale offered a toast to the town's newest folklore hero: "Great job, Junior". Irving rolled his eyes in disgust.

Cheung peered out from behind the freight wagon where he had been hiding. The wagon was parked outside a tavern where the driver had joined in the town's revelry. Cheung relinquished his hiding place relatively unnoticed and walked down the main street along the waterway. The street was fairly quiet since most were celebrating. The Irving feat would be retold and embellished for the rest of the night.

Like most small towns along a waterway, Yale's main street faced the water and was aptly called Front Street. Wharfs and docks serviced by sternwheelers were located on the waterside of the main street and the town's major business outlets on the other side. The announcement of Yale as the headquarters for the British Columbia section of the CPR had turned the small outpost for prospectors into a boomtown overflowing with canvas tents and lean-to shacks. The town site was fairly level and just thirty feet above the height of the river.

The small town was crowded with men of every nationality – turbaned Sikhs, blonde Scandinavians, Irishmen, Englishmen, Scotsmen, French Canadians, Americans, and Chinese. The main source of laborers was from employment agencies in San Francisco. Most of them were disappointed

remnants from the California and Fraser River gold rushes, with no training, no profession and little or no railway experience. The availability of labour was very limited in British Columbia since construction of the Northern Pacific Railway in Oregon and the Southern Pacific Railway in California attracted most of the experienced labour on the Pacific coast with higher wages, double that offered in British Columbia. The labour force available to build the railway in British Columbia was severely limited.

Front Street was cluttered with men arriving and sitting idle, waiting for their assignments. Cargoes of grain, lumber, iron rails, tools and equipment lined both sides of the streets. Empty freight wagons arrived and loaded wagons departed, some drawn by horse, some by mules, and some by oxen. Laughter, merriment and the sound of mouth organs and fiddles emanated from shanty-styled saloons, which occupied almost every third building on the main corridor of commerce. Painted women in alluring costumes adorned their entrances. Fights and arguments along the main street were a common occurrence, as well as drunken patrons sleeping on the wooden walkway.

Cheung caught a glimpse of a young Chinese boy running down a side alley. He called out to him, "*Little brother, where are you going?*"

The boy was about 16 years of age, less than five feet tall and slight of build. He stopped and ducked under a side entrance stairway. He was slightly out of breath and trying to avoid drawing attention but responded in a whisper, "*Do you not know of the curfew, imposed on all Chinese laborers working on the iron dragon? Ah no, you must be one of the Gum San prospectors that has come long ago to search for gold.*"

Cheung whispered back in the boy's dialect, "*No, little brother, I am not a gold seeker. I am just an unfortunate stranger in search of a place to rest his weary bones and maybe a little rice for his stomach. Can you help me?*"

Cheung had also moved into the stairway shadow. The boy signaled, "*follow me, big brother, I can help you.*"

Cheung followed the boy to a huge encampment of canvas tents. There was no sentry. They entered the camp without any questions being asked. There was a sea of campfires and four or five tents for each fire. The atmosphere seemed one of anticipation. Men stopped to momentarily stare curiously at the new arrival dressed in silk. But they continued on with their previous activities once Cheung and the boy wandered past their fire. Once

they arrived at the boy's campsite the young boy called for his friends. He whispered to them in private as Cheung sat himself on the ground beside the fire. Cheung thought, they will know from my clothes and my uncalloused hands that I am not a labourer. Why should I hide anything? They are mostly simple farmers. There is no danger here.

The boy returned with a pair of chopsticks and a bowl filled with steaming rice, topped with steamed salmon. *"I am sorry sir but this is all that has been provided to us by the bosses. Please eat. There is no shortage. When you have finished I can get you more."*

Trying to control his hunger pangs, Cheung proceeded to eat slowly. He choked with the first mouthful because his mouth and throat were parched after a very hot day without water. One of the nameless faces rushed forward and gave him a cup of tea. Cheung raised the cup to his lips and slowly sipped the tea. Cheung thanked the man with a bow. He choked as he continued to eat. Another man approached with a steaming kettle of water and pointed the spout of the kettle at Cheung's bowl of food. Cheung understood the man's intent to moisten the rice with hot water, so it could be more easily swallowed. Cheung nodded to the man and offered his bowl to allow the contents of his bowl to be submerged with hot water. He thanked the man holding the kettle, then raised the bowl to his lips and slowly shoveled the soupy mixture into his mouth with the chopsticks. He smiled while spectators gathered and waited patiently for him to finish. After two more bowls of rice and salmon have been consumed, Cheung was ready to satisfy the curiosity of his hosts. He knew that there would be many questions, not only about himself, but also about his journey. He answered the customary questions about his affiliations. As the crowd gathered around the campfire, he told them about his first journey to Gum Sam in 1849 with his father in search of gold, then his journey to Canada in 1858 for the Fraser Valley Gold Rush, his return to China in 1862 and his recent journey to Yale. He simplified his story and omitted details about his business and his family that he deemed too personal. He captivated his hosts, who listened intently until he was finished. In his narration, he had hoped to answer most of the questions that he would be asked concerning his origin and family history. No one questioned the authenticity of his story for it was too incredible to be fictitious. The only questions were those of interest and curiosity for more details rather than those of doubt. No one disbelieved his story but

now the questions turned to information about this new land of endless riches and opportunities. They only knew what they were told by labour contractors back in China whose honesty was suspect especially in light of the treatment that they had received on their journey from China. Would they actually receive a dollar for one day's work when they could only make seven cents a day in China? How can they afford to pay these wages and still feed and house us as well? How cold will it get in the mountains? Are the mountains really filled with gold? Are the native people like wild savages that hunt for their food in the forests? Does the water always taste so good here? Their questions were endless and answering one question only led to others. Cheung answered to the best of his ability. He realized that his hosts were just poor simple farmers, their families' only hope for survival. He would neither build their hopes too high nor steal their aspirations and dreams but he would enlighten them of misunderstandings and potential danger. When the questioning drew to a close a new arrival called out to Cheung, "*Honourable Doctor how are you? What brings you here to the camp of the iron dragon?*"

Cheung turned his attention to the familiar voice. "Loun An, *how are you, my friend? How is your leg? Has it fully healed?*"

Loun An whispered in Cheung's ear. "*It is fully recovered but let's not talk about it. That silly fool that cut me is still doing my chores.*"

Cheung whispered back, "*How did you know that I was here? What a stroke of luck! By the way, don't call me a doctor. I have just a rudimentary knowledge in herbal medicine and only treat those close to me when no one else is available. Do you understand?*"

Loun An winked and continued to whisper. "*When you told these men what village you had come from, they sent someone over to our camp to let us know that you were here. I rushed right over as soon as they mentioned your name. Where is your little frog of a son? Is he with you?*"

Loun An saw Cheung's grimace and realized not to pursue the subject any further. One of his hosts spoke, "*Honourable guest, are you a doctor? We are in need of a doctor.*"

Cheung spoke, "*My friend is only joking. I am a simple merchant but I have some knowledge of local herbs and treatment acquired from my last journey to Gum Sam. If that can be of help to you, I will gladly be of service to repay your*

kindness to an unfortunate stranger. All I have is just advice. As long as you are content with that, I will be glad to share what I know."

Hunched over near the campfire, Cheung looked around at the men that shared the campfire. The initial 20 to 30 who had listened to him at the onset had swollen to a hundred. They were all young men from Guangdong, the southern province of China, ranging in age from 13 to maybe 30 years. He couldn't understand why but he felt a deep sense of sorrow for these smiling hopeful men who had come so far and blindly risked so much to feed and provide a future for themselves, their families and their future generations. For some unknown reason he struggled with his emotions. He felt tears welling up ready to burst. As he felt his eyes starting to cloud up, Cheung quickly stood up and stretched his arms and legs.

A nameless face approached. Loun An introduced him as one of his own camp. The man bowed to the waist with his palms pressed together. Cheung was surprised by such a deep display of respect. *"Mr. Dai I speak for all the Chinese passengers of the floating dragon that voyaged with you from China. We would like to thank you for your service to us during the voyage. We suffered many hardships but your kind intervention with the boss man of the floating dragon changed many things for us. And speaking with others in this camp that have made similar journeys, we know that we were extremely fortunate not to have suffered as much as them. Without your medicine and your extra rations of food many of our group may have become sick and died. We humbly thank you for your kindness."* As the man bowed, all who had followed him from the other campsite copied his gesture. Cheung bowed in reciprocation, trying with great difficulty to tame his eyes.

Chapter 8

Riding the Rapids

THE LEATHER BAG THROWN OFF THE *William Irving* DRIFTED down the Fraser River through three sets of mild rapids and into a young native fisherman's net just ten miles east of New Westminster. When the twelve-year-old found the valise, he ran home with it to show his father, who brought it to New Westminster to sell or barter the bag and its contents for more useable items. When the boy's father appeared in Chinatown with the items, curiosity spread throughout the Chinese community. The leather bag carried the name, Dai Woo Cheung, embossed in Chinese calligraphy on the top inner lining. The Chinese assumed that the bag had been stolen. No one could communicate well enough with the native to ask how he acquired the bag.

After lunch, as Way and Wing came out of a restaurant, they noticed a group of Chinese congregated around a big powerfully-built native trying to ascertain how he came into possession of the bag. Upon seeing the bag Wing feared the worst and broke his father's enforced silence in English, "Where did you get this bag?"

Way was surprised by Wing's ability to speak English. He smiled to himself, *I should have known.*

The native responded, "Son find in net, ten miles," then pointed upriver. Wing conferred with Way in private. Way took a bill out of his wallet and gave it to Wing.

Wing approached the native again displaying a five silver dollars, "Five dollars for everything and you show me where you found the bag, okay?" The native looked at the generous offer wondering whether to negotiate for more, then agreed and placed the money in his pocket. Wanting to spend his money immediately, he tried to negotiate to meet later but Wing agreed to give him another silver dollar if they left immediately. The native agreed and the three left New Westminster by canoe.

Based on his helpful open manner and his directness of eye, Way and Wing judged that the native was trustworthy. If there was foul play this man was not involved or he would not have tried to sell these goods so openly in the middle of New Westminster's Chinatown. The native's name was "Fears No Rapids", also known as Jim. Wing and Way told Jim that the bag belonged to his father and related their concern of possible foul play. They would search the river shores for clues, or maybe a body. Jim understood their urgency. He instructed them quickly on the use of the paddles. Jim couldn't help being amused by his passengers who alternated taking turns with the other paddle. Seeing their frustration he kept a slow regular pace to make it easier for the novice paddlers to follow. The ten-mile journey took them three and a half hours. When the party arrived at the small village, barking dogs and waving villagers greeted the arrivals. A row of loghouses made of rough hand-cut cedar planks stood along the bank of the river. They were 15 to 18 feet high on one side facing the river, sloping down to 12 feet facing the village. Cedar log canoes of assorted sizes and wooden racks of sun-dried salmon were scattered along the shoreline. Though Wing and Way were exhausted, they requested to inspect the location where the bag was found right away. Jim called for his son who quickly led the party to the location of the fishing net. Way sat down with his back leaning against a cottonwood tree. He wondered what to do. Prepare Wing for the worst or build his hopes? Wing looked out on the river, determined that his father was still alive. He turned to Way, "Big brother, I know that he is alive. Do not try to tell me otherwise. I can still feel his presence."

Way stood up and placed an arm around his friend's back, resting his hand on Wing's right shoulder. "Okay, let us hire the villagers to continue

searching for clues. We will spend the night here and tomorrow we will return to New Westminster. If your father is a.... if your father is well and able, he will send a telegram to us at the Hoi Sen Association in New Westminster." Wing agreed with Way's plan. Way saw an unexpected calmness in Wing's eyes. His uncle had told him of Cheung's gift of seeing the future in his dreams. Does his son have the same gift?

Soon Jim reappeared in a canoe on the river. His son accompanied him in the canoe. Two other canoes with tribe members accompanied them. Jim stopped and directed Wing to sit in the middle of his canoe while he directed one of the others to pick up Way. The search along the upstream shoreline took up the rest of the day. The canoes stopped at each wharf to ask if any of the residents had seen or found the body of a Chinese. They were also informed where to leave a message if they heard about the finding of the body. The search ended late. When the searchers returned to the village, the visitors were invited to a large loghouse to meet the elders. The women had prepared a feast – an assortment of fish and wild game, dried herring roe on pieces of kelp, fiddlehead greens, bannock, several berries and wild rice.

When he was much younger, Wing had listened to stories told by his father about his first encounter with the natives of the American plains. His father had told him that beyond the hatred the natives felt for those taking their land, they were a generous and compassionate people who shared many common values with the Chinese. Father believed that the natives of the West Coast may have had Chinese origins and that many tribes along the Pacific coast shared the blood of Chinese sailors. Throughout Chinese history, there were ancient legends of Chinese sailors returning to China with tales of exotic tribes, pagan customs and rituals and the skins of animals that were unknown in China.

After the feast, Jim took the visitors on a tour and gave his guests a brief history of the Sto;lo people (literal translation "the river people"- first inhabitants of the lower Fraser River region for 8000-10000 years). He led them through a jade forest of immense evergreens to a grassy knoll which overlooked the village and the valley region below. It was their ancestral burial site. He knelt at the graves of his father and mother. The natives believed that the spirit of their ancestors still roamed the earth and that they must be paid the proper homage because they still had an influence on their well-being. Their burial grounds were sacred much like that of the Chinese. After

Jim showed us around the site, they walked back to the village. Hidden from the view of the river, on the other side of the village were more loghouses and a few pithouses which were dirt mound domes standing 10 feet high with log-supported entrances facing the village. The rectangular loghouses ranged from 20 to 60 feet in width and double the width in length and were constructed of cedar planks lashed onto wooden posts and cross- beams. The loghomes could house a nuclear family or an extended family of a hundred or more people. Bulrush and cedar mats were used to separate individual families. Large wooden planks covered over with tanned hides along the exterior walls served as beds.

At the end of the evening, Wing and Way Cheung were given the choice of sleeping under the stars or sharing Jim's lodge. Jim had been so kind that Way and Wing wished neither to insult their host nor to inconvenience him. Way and Wing conferred and decided that they would accept the invitation to sleep overnight in Jim's lodge as a gesture of friendship. Jim led them to one of the pithouses. The structure was a grass-covered dome. The floor level was 2 feet below ground. The interior was circular in design. Four main poles interconnected by willow vines with flexible poles supported the interior roof of tree branches, mud and bark. In the centre was a large open fire it. It was vented by a central opening in the ceiling for the smoke to rise. Deerskin hides covered the dirt floor surrounding the central fireplace. Woven baskets containing food, cooking implements and tools hung from the rafters. Along the outer perimeter were wooden plank beds elevated on wooden poles.

Wing and Way woke up to the smell of fresh coffee and freshly baked bannock bread with fresh wild berries. Jim had already been up hunting with his oldest son. As he walked into the lodge he handed his wife the morning's catch consisting of two quail and a grouse. He asked his guests, "How you sleep? Good?"

Rubbing his back, Way spoke. "Sleep good. Thank you." Jim smiled at Way's intent to please his host.

During breakfast, Jim explained that bodies sometimes surfaced in the shallower areas of the river. He would continue to look. But in the deeper sections the body would probably never surface because this was the domain of the giant sturgeon which eventually devoured the rotting carcasses along the bottom of the river. These monsters of the Fraser grew to over 20 feet

long and could weigh over two thousand pounds. No one really knew their maximum size or age except from the huge decayed and battered carcasses that would occasionally wash up on the banks of the Fraser.

Wing and Way nodded to Jim that they understood his explanation. Wing thanked Jim and asked for the cost of yesterday's search. Jim smiled at his guests and said "We friends. No pay. Please eat. Food good? Yes? You come again. I teach you catch salmon with spear. Hunt moose, deer, elk."

Wing and Way Cheung smiled at each other realizing that their decision to sleep in the lodge the night before was the right choice. As they gathered up their clothes and belongings to leave, Wing saw his father's valise. They had left New Westminster in such a panicked state that he had never even ventured to explore the contents of the bag. Maybe there was a hidden message for him. Father had told him that there was a hidden compartment for special emergencies in the bottom lining. Wing assumed that meant money or other precious items. He decided he would open the hidden compartment when he and Way had a moment in private. He would inspect the contents of the bag now. When they opened it they found most of what Cheung had taken with him except for his extra change of clothes. Inside a cotton bag they found the Western garments that he was wearing when he had left New Westminster. They were caked in dried egg and shell fragments. His Western-style hat and shoes were also in the cotton bag and were also covered with the same egg debris. Wing and Way stared at the soiled articles trying to make sense of what they saw. Way studied the evidence and said to Wing. *"Your father was on the steamboat. Something happened that angered some of the passengers and they threw eggs at your father. I don't understand why they waste eggs. Maybe some kind of lofan ritual or custom. I must ask Jim."*

Way Cheung turned to Jim, "Why white man throw eggs? Some strange white man custom?"

Jim looked at his friends, "See many times. Two steamboats see who number one. Passengers throw eggs all the time. I get too close with canoe. They throw egg at me. Everyone laugh. No good."

Remembering his arrival in Victoria, Wing added, "Yes, the locals threw eggs at us when our ship docked in Victoria."

Jim left the two alone to prepare his canoe for the trip back to New Westminster. With the evidence at hand, Way was able to assume that there was some event, maybe a boat race, that sparked passengers to throw eggs at

Cheung and, secondly, that Cheung was wearing his second set of clothing. Since he had time to change his clothes, there was a lapse of time between the attack of eggs and when the bag ended up in the river. Now if Cheung had been badly hurt in the incident there would have been blood on his clothing. So somehow Cheung and his bag got separated during the incident. Maybe he drowned? *"Wing, can your father swim?"*

"Yes he swims very well."

"So he must be somewhere between where the bag was found and Yale. Now what should we do? We must check New Westminster for messages and someone must go to Yale to find out what happened on board the steamboat and look for Cheung." After discussing the options the two decided that they would return to New Westminster together just in case there was a message from Cheung. If there was none, Way would leave for Yale on the next steamboat.

When Wing and Way were alone, Wing seized the moment to check the hidden lining at the bottom of the leather bag that his father had told him to check if an unforeseen mishap should happen to him. Way discovered a hidden overlapping seam that he folded back to access the false bottom that snapped open with a little prying. Once opened, they discovered five small red silk bags with a gold-colored drawstring, each bag contained an American double eagle twenty dollar gold coin and all of Cheung's and Wing's identification documents, the deed to Cheung's store in Victoria and a letter to his wife in China and a letter to Wing should he have died.

Wing picked up one of the red silk bags embossed with the Chinese character for good luck. His father's words echoed in his mind – always return kindness. Turning to Way, *"Jim is a good man. He has many mouths to feed."* Wing picked up one of the silk bags. *"He is a good provider but this could help him greatly in a time of crisis. If I give this to him he may not accept it. I will leave it under the headrest on his bed."* Way smiled, in admiration of Wing's generosity and Cheung's leadership.

Jim suggested an alternative route back to New Westminster. The trio portaged for 20 minutes to another tributary which was much smaller and narrower. They travelled comfortably downstream for half an hour as Way was positioned at the front while Wing sat at the center. When they approached the long set of rapids, Way pointed his paddle towards the shore, expecting to portage. Looking at Way from the back of the vessel, Jim shook his head and pointed his paddle at the rapids and shouted "ready?" Then he

steered the canoe into the rapids as two Chinese faces suddenly lost their colour. As his life flashed before him, Way frantically paddled narrowly avoiding boulders and outcroppings. His arms ached and sweat covered his brow, as he struggled to save face in front of his host and younger companion. At the end of a half-mile of rapids Jim slowed the canoe down as they rested at the shoreline. As he turned around Way was exhausted but relieved at having survived the ordeal. Wing continued to clutch the sides of the canoe with both hands. Seeing the desperate relief on the faces of his friends Jim smiled and said. "You do good, now him", pointing his paddle at Wing. Way passed his paddle to Wing as the two friends changed seats in the canoe. Neither complained, afraid to appear fearful. They exchanged wide-eyed looks of suppressed anxiety as Way raised his eye brows as a gesture of good luck to his friend. After a few minutes they approached another set of rapids. Having watched his friend's ordeal, Wing adjusted his paddling strokes leaning into the turns and paddling from the opposite side of Jim's paddle. He had watched Jim closely during Way's ordeal and he realized that the secret was flowing with the current, not fighting against it. He knew that his job was to support the path that Jim chose. If Jim's strokes were synchronized with his from the opposite side then he was going in an acceptable direction but any sideway motion of the canoe conflicted with Jim's intended path. Using this as a guide he timed and varied the frequency and depth of his strokes around boulders and rocks, having studied Jim's mechanics. After a smooth passage through a long section of swift rapids, Jim smiled at Wing and said, "You learn fast. You like fast water. You makem skookum Sto:lo." (skookum - Chinook term meaning –strong, powerful, brave).

Way Cheung tapped Wing on the shoulder. Smiling, he asked, *"Little brother, how did you learn so fast? Now give me that paddle. Let me try again. Now share with me what you have learned. What am I doing wrong?"*

"Big brother, don't fight the current. Let Jim lead. When he matches your stroke you are on the right path. When the canoe drifts sideways he loses control of the lead. Do not try to lead, just support his intended path. Your job is only to avoid obstacles. When he quickens his pace you must quicken yours but from the other side of the canoe. When he slows by dipping his paddle you must do likewise from the other side of the boat if you want to keep the vessel straight or the same side if you want to exaggerate the turn. When you do what he does from the same side

of the vessel it exaggerates his lead. When you do it from the other side it keeps the vessel straight. Try to match him stroke for stroke. The wider and deeper out you extend the paddle the wider the turn. I will keep very low so you can read his movements."

Surprised by his younger companion's words of advice Way Cheung could only shake his head in befuddled amazement. With admiration he teased. *"How can you learn all this so fast? I truly must have been spawned by a water buffalo."* Pleased with the cloaked compliment, Wing burst into laughter.

Determined not to be outdone, Way exchanged seats once again. The trip through the next section of rapids was smooth. Jim guessed that the advice given to Way in Chinese contributed to his improvement. He raised his paddle above his head as a salute for their performance. When they reached New Westminster, it was late morning. The three checked the Hoi Sen Association for a message, but there was no word from Cheung.

Three days had passed now since Cheung had departed. The next steamboat did not leave for Yale until the next morning. After dropping off their bags, Way and Wing invited Jim for lunch in appreciation for his kindness. He had never eaten in a Chinese restaurant. Jim was a tall man, about six feet, with powerful shoulders and no excess flesh; the muscles on his body rippled with every movement. Dressed in a thinly tanned deerskin trouser and vest, Jim attracted the curiosity of other patrons.

During lunch, Jim tried everything placed in front of him. His pupils dilated with the arrival of each new dish. Wing and Way had filled his side plate with the best morsels off each new dish. As Jim sampled each course his eyes smiled with delight and he grunted "good". After the seven-course meal was complete, Jim felt a closer bond with his new friends.

Outside the restaurant, Wing told Jim. "Thank you for helping to find my father. We thought that you might not accept a reward, so we left a gift for you under your headrest. Thank for your kindness." Jim shook hands with his friends. He promised to have the villager keep watch for further signs of Wing's father.

When they returned to their lodgings Way and Wing sat across the table as they planned what to do next. With a slightly troubled look on his face, Way spoke first, *"Wing, your father made me promise not to let you out of my sight except under extreme emergencies. This is an extreme emergency. But there is much that you must still know before I leave tomorrow. First the promise*

that your father made to his father and their friends and some of these matters are contained in the letter addressed to you upon verification of his demise but you cannot open that letter until we have proof of his passing. A pact was made between your father, his father, his uncle and a few others who shared a gold claim near Marysville in California, during the early days of gold rush. In the event of the death of any member, the survivors promised to have the remains of the dead member shipped back to their villages in China. This is the main reason for my journey – to help my uncle recover the remains of your grand-father and his companions. This was one of the main reasons for your father's journey. My uncle and your father are only members to survive a massacre. If we cannot accomplish this mission, your father hopes you will one day honour his commitment. In addition, both my uncle and your father wish to find a place in Canada to relocate our families. I am here in New Westminster to assist my uncle with his search. It was just a fortunate coincidence that our paths intertwined. After I visit a local mine operated by some friends from our village, I must leave for California early next year to meet my Uncle. We must recover the remains of the pact members and accompany them back to China. Your father's letter will tell you where the bodies are located and where the remains must be sent. My uncle has given me the same information. If we should fail, your father instructed me to tell you not to attempt to fulfill his commitment until you are much older with the help of your brothers. Now you know all that I know. I was instructed not to allow you to go beyond the borders of Chinatown. Your father has asked me to remind you to be cautious and not to leave the hotel after dark and to contact your friend Nathan if you have any problems that the local Hoi Sen Association cannot help resolve for you. Any questions little brother?"

Wing responded. "Not right now, big brother. Give me some time to think." Wing thought for a few minutes, "Big brother if your uncle and my father are fulfilling the same mission, was there a date pre-arranged for them to meet to retrieve the bones together?"

Exasperated by Wing's ability to think always a step ahead Way replied. "Yes, they paid an astrologer to help select the date. If either was unable to appear, they agreed to send a blood relative to help fulfill the mission. Little brother, aiya why must you always think so much?" Begrudgingly, he admitted, "Yes, your father and my uncle were going to meet in San Francisco in the spring. Truly, you will hurt your head thinking so much all the time."

Wing chuckled at Way's sarcastic humour. He asked, "*during this mission, was I going to be included or left somewhere else?*"

Way Cheung said, "*I do not know. Your father never said what he was going to do with his clever little monkey. Hey, didn't you hear what I told you about hurting yourself thinking too much? I am the oldest here. I'm in charge. Let me do the thinking.*" Way Cheung got up and chased Wing around the table. Good, thought Way this should distract him from worrying about his father.

After a few minutes of frolicking, Way Cheung addressed Wing. "*Little brother, while I am away, here are the instructions that you must follow. Tonight after dinner we will go to the Hoi Sen Society and I will introduce you to the older gentleman that greeted you when you and your father first arrived. His name is Lee Kong. He is the secretary and treasurer of the society. You must report to him every day because I have arranged for him to keep an eye on you. If you have any problems go to him. If you or I receive any messages he will come to you right away. As soon as you receive any communication send a telegram to me at the Hoi Sen Society affiliate in Yale. I will leave you money. Do not spend anymore of your father's American gold pieces. Tonight I will show you a restaurant where men go to eat cheaply. I will introduce you to the owner and have him also keep an eye on you. Remember stay in the populated areas of Chinatown. Don't go out past dark and don't trust anyone with personal information. People may become suspicious seeing you eating alone. So I will arrange for Lee Kong to accompany you at meal times. I have paid for the room in advance. I will be back in a few days or send word to you by telegram. Do you have any more questions, little monkey?*" Wing shook his head.

Way Cheung left early the next morning. Wing walked with him carrying a small bag containing a canteen of water and some food supplies purchased the night before in Chinatown. Dressed in western-style clothing, he stood a little over five feet tall. He was pleasant looking but his most appealing feature was his broad disarming smile. His body was compact and very well muscled. Wing's father had told him that Way's uncle was trained in the forbidden art of the Sha Ling monks. Way's uncle and the Sifu that Cheung had chosen to instruct members of the Dai household were taught by the same master. Both Way and Wing assumed that each would be able defend himself, in a moment of crisis.

As the pair approached the ticket office, Way warned Wing to go no further for it was beyond the confines of Chinatown, though only a short

distance away. Wing obediently submitted. The two exchanged bows. Way further warned Wing, "*Little brother be vigilant. If anything happens to you, it will be my responsibility. So, do not stray from my instructions and remember trust no one and stay in Chinatown. Do not watch my departure. I will stay on the cargo level to avoid what may have happened to your father.*" Wing bowed, then returned to the lodgings.

Two days had passed since Way Cheung had left for Yale. Wing had explored all the streets and shops in Chinatown during that time. Often tempted, Wing continued to comply with his preset limitations. Though he missed his father, his intuition told him that Cheung was not in any imminent danger. Wing somehow knew that Way's journey would not be in vain. Wing checked in at the Hoi Sen Society three times every day, first at 8 am, then at noon and then at 8pm. Wing appeared in the lobby of the association ten minutes early and walked with Lee Kong to the local restaurant, as instructed. He filled the rest of his day exploring every corner and crevice within his constraints. Though he loved his father's company, he had never felt so free and unfettered.

On the third day, Lee Kong greeted Wing with a telegram in hand. Very excited Lee Kong said, "*Wing it just arrived ten minutes ago. Should I get someone to read it for you?*"

Wing took the message. "*No, uncle. I know someone who can read it to me. I will tell you later what it says. But thank you very much.*" Wing quickly returned home with the telegram. Once inside his suite he opened the envelope. It read:

"Dear Son,

Sorry for your needless worry. Way and I are both fine. We will be back tomorrow. Please be careful.

Dai Woo Cheung"

Wing notified Lee Kong that all was well and that Cheung and Way would be returning the next day. Elated and relieved by the news, Wing felt somewhat ambivalent, as shadows of restored constraints would soon enshroud his fleeting taste of independence. His father had been particularly overzealous with his son's security in light of Wing's recent dream. Wing decided that he would make the most of his remaining freedom before his father's return. He would extend his boundaries for the time remaining. He would see and explore as he pleased. The fulfillment of this silly

dream was an impossible reality. It was just the product of boredom. Father worries far too much. I should have never spoken of this dream. How could I have known that he would take it so seriously? That other dream during the ocean voyage foresaw Louisa's assault on the floating dragon. Maybe I should be cautious but there still is so much to see and do. I will only stay out a little later than Way prescribed.

That evening Wing had dinner with Lee Kong. After the meal, Wing walked his older companion back to the Hoi Sen Association. Once Lee Kong had returned to work, Wing looked down the empty street. It was dark now and the lamplighter was lighting the street lamps. All the shops were closed except for taverns and saloons, the only source of sound and human activity. Wing thought to himself, there is no sense going back to the hot room and sweating for another hour before it gets cool enough to sleep. I see no danger here. I will take a walk and watch the activity along Front Street.

Wing sat on an empty crate on the raised wooden walkway that bordered the dirt road. It was long past Way's curfew. Intoxicated by his remaining hours of independence, Wing envisioned Way scolding him for breaching his curfew. If Way could see him now what would he say? What would his father say or do? As Wing tried to visualize the reactions of his guardians, he laughed out loud to himself. It was much more fun to imagine Way's response than that of his beloved father. Way always had a comical or sarcastic quip to add to every situation. With father you could never say what was on your mind or do anything that exceeded the well-defined boundaries of parental respect. He always had to think before speaking or responding to his father. With Way, he spoke whatever entered his mind without forethought of consequence. Wing stared at the outline of distant mountains, enjoying his fleeting hours of unfettered independence. Behind the wharves across the street was the slow-moving river. The reflection of the moon glimmered behind the waterfront structures. Out of the corner of his eye, Wing caught a movement two blocks away. A small shadowy figure ran across the street as if being pursued. It stopped briefly looking back in the direction of a steamboat that was docked overnight at the docking facility. From the manner in which it moved Wing guessed that it was probably a young boy. Curious about the movement Wing decided to get a closer look; he continued to watch for more movement from a seemingly safe distance.

He focused more diligently. At a quick glance the figure appeared small but his movement was not like a child's. Wing suspected the figure was Chinese and he was intrigued. Suddenly, three much larger figures quickly followed him in pursuit. They spread out combing both sides of the main street. The leader of the group was the tallest of the three. He carried a foot long club in his right hand. They carefully checked all the possible hiding spots along the riverbank and then all the hidden alleyways running off the main street. They disappeared behind an unlocked door temporarily then reappeared. As they passed, Wing continued to sit and stared back with confidence. A little shocked by Wing's aggressiveness, the three men whispered in confidence, shook their heads and then glared back in return. Wing had purposely made this visual statement of defiance as a means of dealing with his growing fear. Wing knew from the manner these men acted and talked that they were a menacing presence. After the three had passed Wing remained paralyzed, afraid to make further eye contact. He listened and hoped that the sound of their footsteps would grow more distant. When he finally turned to look the three men were only a few doors away. Wing was bathed in perspiration. He was afraid to return to his room because the search party was presently between him and the hotel. So he stayed where he was. The search party seemed to have given up and started to walk back to the vessel.

A man stepped out of a tavern and sauntered down the street. He came to a stop on the walkway behind Wing. He spotted the search group and shouted in an inebriated state. "Hey you men.... what, what are you looking for?"

"A little slant-eyed bastard that jumped ship," shouted one of the searchers. "Have you seen him? Just the usual scrawny little Chink dressed in a white undershirt and black cotton trousers."

Seeing Wing sitting below him on the side of the road, the drunk called out jokingly, "There's one sitting here, but he's dressed in fine silks. Why not just take him?" The man laughed at the searchers and added, "Didn't you know? They all look alike. One Chink is just as good as another."

The searchers looked at Wing. He was sweating, breathing heavily and motionless, but alert and cursing his youthful curiosity. The men looked menacingly at Wing. One of them shook his head conversed with the other two in a whispered conference then they started to approach. Wing knew he must run but his legs suddenly felt very weak. As the search party drew

closer, Wing forced himself to stand up. He turned to run but he was surrounded. He feigned one way then quickly changed directions. He evaded one tackler only to be caught by the outstretched hand that seized his pigtail. Suddenly he saw a blinding flash of white light, as his body collapsed on the ground.

One of the searchers turned to the man with the club. "You hit him too hard. You may have killed him."

"I only said I would bring one back. I never said alive. They'll never know it's the wrong one. Now take that fancy shirt off him." The blood-soaked silken garment was discarded at the side of the road.

The drunken spectator was dumbfounded, "Hey, I was just joking. You killed that poor boy."

The man with the club waved his weapon at the spectator, "Go home and keep your mouth shut or we'll shut it for you. The law here is not going to give a damn about what happens to a worthless little chink." The three left as the biggest man slung Wing over his shoulder. Wishing that he had kept his thoughts to himself, the drunken spectator stared at the bloody garment unsure whether to report the incident to the local police.

When a Chinese worker found the bloody silken garment early the next morning, he picked it up suspecting that someone in the Chinese community had been assaulted by the locals. The news that this clothing had been found spread quickly throughout Chinatown. When Lee Kong saw the garment he automatically thought of Wing. He sent someone to check the whereabouts of his young ward. When Wing could not be found, Lee Kong concluded that it was Wing who had been assaulted. He therefore sent people to check at the hospital, the jailhouse and along the riverbank. No further evidence could be found. Realizing that the boat from Yale would return later that day, he delayed sending a telegram to Wing's father.

The expected travelers returned later that afternoon. Lee Kong was waiting for them at the dock. As the two disembarked he waved at them frantically. Cheung sensed something was terribly wrong. Lee Kong was very anxious and appeared in a state of panic, "Mr. Dai your son is missing. We have searched everywhere for him but he can not be found. We have searched throughout Chinatown and the neighbouring areas as well as the hospital and jail. We even searched along the riverbank and under the wharves. No sign has

appeared except a bloody silk shirt that I think he was wearing when we had dinner together last night."

Cheung queried, *"Where can I see this silk shirt?"*

Lee Kong answered, *"It is at my office. Shall we go there now?"* Cheung and Way increased their pace in the direction of the Hoi Sen Association. When they entered the lobby the men seated on the reading chairs looked up and gave a nod of concern. They all realized that Cheung was the father of the missing boy. Once inside Lee Kong's office, Cheung inspected the garment.

Yes, he thought, this is a shirt that I had made for him in Canton. He asked, *"Who found this shirt? And where and when was it found?"*

Lee Kong lifted a finger signaling for Cheung to wait momentarily. He disappeared into the lobby and returned with another man, *"This is the man who found your son's shirt. It is your son's shirt is it not?"*

"Yes it is," answered Cheung. *"Can this man show us where he found the shirt?"* Lee Kong looked at the man, who beckoned them to follow.

Remembering that Wing had his key for the lodging, Way asked Lee Kong, *"Can I leave my bag here in your office until we return?"* Lee Kong nods.

The four headed to the site to try to piece together what had happened to Wing. When they arrived at the spot, Way and Cheung walked around to see if there was any evidence of a struggle. It was mid-afternoon and the investigators tried to discern possible clues amidst the wagon tracks and hoof prints. Near the side of the road was a large patch of fresh blood. There was a lot of blood, thought Cheung, hopefully it didn't all belong to Wing. The clues seemed to indicate a struggle or fight. There were three, maybe even four, sets of different shoeprints left on the dusty roadside. One set was much smaller than the others. These must have been those of his son. Yes there were possibly three others. It could not be clearly discerned through the foot-prints of other pedestrian. All that Cheung could deduce was that from the size and depth of the prints these others were men of considerable size. In addition after the confrontation one set of footprints the largest became heavier. He must have been carrying something maybe Wing. These prints were the easiest to follow. Walking down the middle of the roadway Cheung followed the heaviest prints, oblivious to the abusive shouting from passing passengers and drivers. Although intermittently distorted by other traffic, Cheung could see now that there were three sets of footprints.

Trying not to draw any further attention than was necessary, Way and the two others followed and watched Cheung from the wooden walkway.

Cheung thought, if these men walked down the middle of the road the incident must have occurred fairly late at night. The footprints led down the street and turned into the main docking area. The four men conferred as Cheung offered them his theory, based on the clues. Lee Kong and the other man departed. Cheung had sent Lee Kong on a mission to the local newspaper to offer a twenty-dollar reward from the Hoi Sen Association for information leading to the whereabouts of his son. Cheung and Way descended down the causeway of the boat terminal. At the ticket office, they asked for information from a reluctant ticket agent, who tried to dismiss them with a 'come back later.' comment. There was no one else in the office. Cheung realized that he needed the man's immediate co-operation. He took a silver dollar out of his pocket, placed it on the ticket counter and moved it in the direction of the young ticket agent. The agent accepted the coin and gestured a hesitant thank you. Cheung asked, "Sir, can you please tell me about the steamship that docked here overnight its cargo, its scheduled stops and its final destination?"

The agent arrogantly said, "The ship was the *Western Slope*. It was contracted to carry laborers directly from Victoria to Yale. It docked here overnight to pick up some construction material for the railway. Now, I am sorry, but you'll have to leave. I have lots of paperwork to do." He then quickly ushered Cheung and Way out the door, then placed a sign marked 'Closed' on the outside of the door, barring any further questions.

For the rest of the day Cheung and Way were preoccupied with solving the clues to Wing's disappearance. What they concluded was that Wing for some reason had been kidnapped to work on the railway. How ironic thought Cheung that I should go to such great lengths to avoid this fate for my son only to have it happen anyway. I guess dreams can prepare us but not help us avoid what lies ahead.

By the time Way acquired another key for his room it was late evening. When they finally arrived back at the lodging with their bags, Way collapsed on the couch while Cheung lay on the bed. Emotionally spent, both were asleep in a matter of minutes.

Cheung woke up first the next morning. He was dressed and planning another trip to Yale on the next steamship heading upriver, which didn't

leave for another two days. Cheung knew that time was of the utmost importance but the steamboat was by far the fastest mode of transportation. He would have to wait. After Way woke up and dressed the two men went out for breakfast. Way was unusually quiet during breakfast, not knowing how much blame he must shoulder for Wing's disappearance. He could not eat until he knew Cheung's feelings. When the jook (rice gruel) arrived, Way just stared at the steaming bowl, mixing the contents with his soupspoon. Cheung understood Way Cheung's discomfort. "*Way, please do not blame yourself for my son's disappearance. I do not hold you responsible. Please eat up. Otherwise I will have to account for your loss of health to your uncle.*" Way relaxed a bit and started to eat with trepidation.

Still blaming himself Way said, "*Uncle, did I act with too much haste? I do not know what other choices I could have made.*"

Cheung put a hand on his shoulder in a gesture of friendship, "*The past cannot be changed. Under the circumstances, I would have made the same decision. Your decision was sound and well-intended. I thank you again for your concern and your attempt to rescue me. Who would know that losing my leather bag would result in so many mishaps? I am not sure, but I suspect my son may have violated his curfew.*"

Way Cheung asked, "*What do you mean? How can he be blamed?*"

Cheung looked at Way Cheung, "*Did you not tell me that he was instructed to stay in populated areas and not to stay out past dark?*"

Way said, "*How do you know that he did otherwise?*" Way thought for a moment his eyes widened upon reflection, then nods calmly at Cheung's reasoning. "*Yes, you are right. This must have undoubtedly happened late at night for all the footsteps located at the center of the road.*"

"Also in retrospect," added Cheung, "*my strict enforcement of rules to impede his freedom caused him to rebel. Maybe the blame is mine. It matters not at this point. My only concern now is to find him. You have plans of your own. None of this is your responsibility. It is all mine.*"

"*Uncle, how can I leave you with the task of finding him by yourself? How could I face my uncle? What would you do if it were I that was lost in the same manner?*"

Cheung smiled at Way. "*Okay we will leave for Yale tomorrow. Thank you, my friend.*"

When Cheung and Way checked for messages at the Hoi Sen Association, Lee Kong greeted them with the name and address of a respondent who

read the reward article in the morning newspaper and wanted to claim the reward.

Cheung and Way quickly headed for the address of the respondent. It was located on the outskirts of town just four blocks away at the top of the hill overlooking the town. When they reached the residence, a middle-aged man of average size greeted them. His first question was, "Did you bring the reward?"

Cheung nodded and patted his pocket.

The man asked, "What do you want to know?"

Cheung said, "Can you first describe my son?"

The man said, "He was quite young, slender but stood quite tall, compared to other Chin... Chinese. Almost as tall as you," pointing to Cheung.

Cheung asked, "What was he wearing?"

The man continued, "Dark silk trousers, a dark silk jacket and a light-coloured silk shirt."

Scrutinizing the man's eyes closely throughout his responses, Cheung was satisfied that the man was at the scene but was unsure whether the man was involved. Cheung looked closely at the man's eyes and then asked. "Can you tell me what happened?"

"How do I know that you really have the money?"

Cheung took a small red pouch out of his pocket, and then revealed the contents - a gold twenty-dollar piece.

The man related the story of last night's sequence of events. He added that he was drunk and incapable of stopping the three culprits, but he was going to the constabulary office today to report the crime, so that justice could be done and the boy could be rescued if he were still alive. At the end of the conversation, Cheung put the twenty-dollar piece in the palm of the man's hand.

Cheung judged the man to be loud and blustery and probably a coward but not mean or evil enough to be involved with the crime. His shoe size was smaller than the footprints found at the scene of the attack and he did say that he was standing on the walkway during the assault.

The corroboration of Cheung's theory only confirmed his planned course of action. He had to leave on the next available steamboat excursion to Yale. He thought about his most recent journey and its lack of success. He was never able to meet with the American railway contractor in Yale. He

was told at the Chinese encampment that the company operated its own stores on site. The extra days that he spent in Yale were used only to treat men at the campsite in need of medical advice and those with medical problems that were easily treated. He wondered whether Loun An and the men from his own village had left for another campsite yet. Apparently the newly arrived laborers would stay a short duration while they waited to be assigned to various locations, along the proposed route of the railway. Cheung knew that Wing would remain in Yale for at least a week. What he could not understand was taking someone against his will because in Yale all the workers came and went as they pleased except for the curfew. Why would they kidnap someone to work on the railway when a worker could leave whenever he wished?

Walking back to their lodging Cheung discussed his plans with Way. *"Tomorrow I shall leave for Yale. Until I find my son the trip to California must be delayed."*

"Uncle, what do you wish me to do? Shall I wait here for a message from your son?"

"No, it would seem that he is badly hurt and probably in Yale. You can return to Yale with me if you wish. But please feel no obligation to interrupt your plans. This problem may take a long time to resolve. While I appreciate your concern and your eagerness to help me, I feel that my taking up any more than a week of your time would extend beyond the reasonable bounds of friendship. If you come with me to Yale you must agree after a seven day search that you will continue with your own plans. Is it agreed?" Way complied with a nod.

That evening during dinner at their usual restaurant, Way and Cheung overheard loud talk at a distant table. A small group of men were crowded around a new face. Way and Cheung asked who the new man was. A man stated, *"He was the one that escaped from the steamboat last night."*

Cheung and Way introduced themselves to the man. Cheung asked in the man's dialect, *"Why did you leave the boat? Did you not come to work to earn money and return to your village rich like all the others?"*

The man spoke, *"Of course I did but the company cook trapped me into playing fantan on board the ship. I lost so much that he said that he would take all my wages for the next three years. All the others that were gambling with us told me afterwards that he cheated me but what could I do? I didn't even want to play. He gave me no choice because he controlled the food. He would not feed me*

unless I played and he was a close friend of the labour contractor. If he took my wages my family back home will starve. Our village is very poor. I had no choice but to escape. The contractor gets paid for each labourer that arrives safely at the end of the destination. It will cost him dearly for having the cook for a friend. Up his mother's butt." Hearing the explanation, Cheung finally understood the sequence of events leading to his son's disappearance. He returned to his table to eat his dinner.

Way followed, puzzled by Cheung's calm response to the man's explanation. Was this man not responsible for Cheung's present troubles? Once seated across the table from Cheung, he asked."Uncle, you told that man nothing of the misfortune and problems that he has caused you. Why did you not?"

"Way Cheung, this man did not intend to hurt my son. He only wishes to feed his family. How can I think ill of him when I may have done likewise in a similar situation? I bear him no malice and wish him only good fortune. I will not relate my injury to him to curry from him a favour for the present or in the future. Let this man seek his fortune with a clear conscience." Way smiled in admiration at the wisdom of his uncle in choosing such a man for his best friend.

Early the next morning Cheung and Way caught the sternwheeler to Yale. Once again it was the *William Irving*. This time the trip upriver was smooth and uneventful because the earlier shallow sections which were first conquered by the William Irving had been deepened by rain. Having remained on the cargo deck the whole trip the two men arrived in Yale during the early evening. Quickly they proceeded to the CPR campsite. When they reached the site they were shocked to find it vacant. The tents were all gone. They hunted for someone to find out what had happened.

When they arrived at the local branch of the Hoi Sen Association in Yale they asked a man at the front reception desk. "Honorable sir, *what has happened to the campsite for the Chinese laborers? Where did they all go so quickly?*"

The man replied. "*Aiya, the work has started in earnest. Instructions came quickly from the big boss that the workers would be transported and distributed along the route of the railway over the last two days. No more resting.*"

Cheung inquired. "*Is there a list of names or a map of the campsites?*" The man shook his head. Cheung continued, "*Do you know where the head office is?*" The man pointed at a building. Cheung and Way walked up the street towards a one-storey wooden structure in the middle of town. Over

the front entrance was a sign marked, "Railway Office". They entered the building.

Sitting behind large wooden desks, two men are pre-occupied with paperwork. One with a moustache and glasses looked up and asked, "Are you looking for work?" then added, "You speakee English?"

Cheung responded, "Yes, I speak English, sir. Do you have a list of names and a map of your campsites?"

The man was surprised by Cheung's fluency in English, "Oh, you speak English. We have a map of the proposed route but the campsites may be distributed anywhere along the route. Most of the crews left last night. There is no list of names. The labour contractors may have that. Anything else?"

"Do you know in what direction they went and how they left?"asked Cheung.

"They went mostly by wagon in both directions, East and West. Some had to walk because we don't have enough wagons to transport them, as well as our equipment and supplies."

"Did you notice an injured boy in the campsite who arrived in the last two days?"

"No, any of the sick or injured were transported with their crew."

Just then the other man who was clean-shaven and very tall approached the counter and addressed Cheung "I have seen you before. Weren't you the Chinese doctor that treated some of our workers in the campsite a few days ago?" Cheung responded with a nod.

"The Chinese High Commissioner appointed a Dr. Mclean to attend to the Chinese working on our railway, but he disappeared a couple of weeks ago. So we need someone to replace him. Do you want the job? We'll pay you a very good wage. How about it? None of the celestials trust white doctors. They won't let a white doctor touch them. From what I observed, they seem to trust you."

Cheung quickly thought, "How many doctors do you have?"

The second man answered, "Right now only one, but there should be more on the way, but none who the Chinese will trust. So what do you say?"

Cheung and Way walked outside the office to confer in private. "*Way, my path seems clear. I must find my son and this may be the best way for me to search for him. Our paths must separate here.*"

Cheung entered the office again and approached the office counter. "What are your terms? May I leave whenever I wish?"

The tall man offering the job smiled. "There is no contract of employment so you can leave whenever you like. The pay is two dollars a day. We will provide you with room and board. When can you get started?"

Cheung said, "I can start tomorrow morning."

The man responded. "Good, our doctor was planning to leave early tomorrow. You can leave with him. I don't know your medical background but I assume from the respect that you received in camp you know what to do. Anything you don't know, you can ask the doctor who will be travelling with you. We will expect you at eight o'clock tomorrow morning. By the way, what is your name?"

Cheung answered. "Dai Woo Cheung."

The man responded."Doctor Dai, that name will not do. The Chinese are very superstitious about names. Why don't we call you Doctor Cheung or Doctor Woo? Is that okay? Do you have a preference? How about Doctor Woo?" The two men nodded then shook hands with Cheung to seal the agreement.

After Cheung and Way left, the second man said to the first man, "Those men are looking for that injured boy that we had dropped off at George Keefer's residence. Let's make sure he doesn't find him until we have no further use for his services. Let him continue looking while we keep them apart. When the boy recovers, maybe we can give him a job which will resolve our problem, and keep them apart permanently. We never told our new doctor that we would transport him back to civilization if he decides to leave, did we?" Both men roar with laughter.

Overhearing the laughter from outside the office, Way turned to Cheung, "these men are not worthy of trust."

Cheung replied, "You are right. I could sense no kindness in their voices. That is why I omitted to ask anymore about Wing. I might have continued to inquire before they expressed a need for a Chinese doctor. When I realized they needed my services, I knew that I could not trust them with information that could be used to enslave me. I will find Wing without their assistance. Now we must find a place to eat. And we may have to adjust the arrangements for our journey to California. You and my old friend must wait for me. It may be too dangerous for you both to proceed without me."

After dinner, arrangements for sleeping accommodations were made for Way and Cheung by the Toi San Society. In the overcrowded room that they shared with six others, Cheung wrote letters to Nathan and his store manager Quan Li disclosing his present dilemma. He requested Nathan to ask Mrs. Beckham to store his belongings until he and Wing returned to Victoria. He would not alarm his wife since there was nothing that she could do but worry about circumstances over which she had no means to control.

Chapter 9

Louisa's Anguish

NATHAN BEILIHIS STUDIED HIS DAUGHTER'S FACE AS HE PUT ON his overcoat. The last letter from Cheung had robbed Louisa of her natural joy for living. She had languished in a state of despair since the arrival of the letter a month ago. As concerned as he was with Wing's disappearance, Nathan was distressed even more by his daughter's reaction. She was withdrawn and had isolated herself from all those around her. Most of her time was spent alone in her room. Even her teachers at the new school remarked that she seemed preoccupied during class, always staring out the window. When she appeared for her evening meals, her eyes were reddened and swollen from endless bouts of crying. She had no appetite and she was starting to lose weight.

Today the mail ship was scheduled to arrive. Louisa had risen early and had patiently waited for her father to complete his morning ritual of praying, reading, then eating breakfast. They would wait for Mrs. Beckham's cook Ming to arrive and walk to town altogether. Ming now journeyed to town almost every day without Jonathan. He would pick up the mail for Mrs. Beckham and her residents whenever the mail ship arrived but it was only after the line-ups had subsided, to circumvent any unpleasantness from the locals. When he accompanied Ming, Nathan would pick up the mail for

Mrs. Beckham's residents leaving Ming more time to shop and visit with his friends.

Today was the first time that Louisa would accompany Nathan and Ming. Listening for footsteps on the stairway up to the porch, Louisa called out in a restrained tone."Ming is here. Are you ready, father? "She opened the door just as Ming reached the top of the front stairs.

"*Good morning Moksi (priest – or revered one). Good morning, May Yun. How are you on this beautiful sunny morning?*"Louisa returned a courteous smile.

Nathan responded, "*We are as good as can be expected, Ming. Nice day for a walk. I love the colours of fall. I do hope there is mail for us today.*" It was late October and leaves cluttered the road. As the three walked, both adults tried to include Louisa in their conversation but Louisa rejected any attempts to be drawn into their discussions by remaining distant and preoccupied with her own thoughts. The adults yielded to her ambivalence. When they reached the post office at the Customs House on Wharf Street, the three saw only a small lineup of mostly remittance men waiting for money from home. Nathan politely offered. "Ming, why don't you proceed to Chinatown and make your regular stops while Louisa and I wait for the mail. I will pick up your household mail for you."

Ming concurs but after walking a few steps, he turned around. He raised his index finger to signify a suggestion to Nathan, "*Would May Yun like to come with me today? Chinatown is full of lonely men, stranded from their families and communities. The only children in Chinatown belong to the wealthy merchants who guard them closely as their wives. May Yun will certainly be a very welcome sight for these homesick men, especially when they learn that she can speak their language. Regardless of what you may have heard, Moksi, the dangers have been greatly exaggerated. Chinatown has been designed to discourage the entry of local ruffians and local authorities. May Yun will be completely safe with me and we will only visit areas that smell that smell the least offensive.*" Nathan smiled at Ming's inspiration. Perhaps this will put some colour back into those cheeks. Far better that, than a long sulking walk back home if no letter has arrived today. Nathan welcomed the suggestion, then searched his trouser pockets. He tried to offer Ming money.

"Ming, please take her for a fine lunch. She hasn't had a good Chinese meal since we left Hong Kong."

Ming rejected Nathan's money, "*Sorry, Moksi, it will be my pleasure to treat your daughter to a meal fit for the Dowager Empress herself. I will escort May Yun to your church after we have finished.*"

Louisa smiled broadly at her father for the first time since the arrival of Cheung's letter. Nathan watched as the two departed for Chinatown. He detected a glimmer of youthful enthusiasm in his daughter's walk. He bowed his head in hope that Ming could restore her lost vitality.

When Ming and Louisa arrived at the Emanu-El Synagogue on Blanshard Steet, it was mid-afternoon. Nathan was delighted to find the sadness that had enshrouded his daughter had been finally lifted. Louisa excitedly ran towards her father. He caught her in his arms and embraced her. Tears of relief trickled down his cheeks. "Father, I had so much fun today. At first, the smell was very difficult to adjust to, but Wing told me how he just breathed it in normally until he got use to it. I'm glad it worked. Everyone was so kind to me. I don't think that I ever ate so much in my life. They all just kept trying to feed me, offering me treats and giving me lycee money (a gift of money in red envelopes usually given to the young during special occasions). Father, can I go back with Ming next Saturday?"

Father brushed away his tears. Patting Ming thankfully on the shoulders he replied. "If it is not an inconvenience to Ming, you have my approval."

Ming responded, "*Moksi, she is such a joy to be with. It would be my pleasure. The restaurant owner would not let me pay for lunch. When people found out that she spoke Chinese the word got out so fast that the restaurant filled up with men all curious to gaze at her. The restaurant owner said to bring her back anytime no charge. I introduced her to all the men that I knew. Each one gave her a treat or gift. Oh, this is yours.*" Ming passed Louisa a cotton rice sack filled with red envelopes and assorted Chinese treats. Ming added, "*The only children in Chinatown belong to merchants who keep them locked up in their residences above their stores. Women and children are a rare sight in Chinatown. Your daughter has brought a great deal of pleasure to many lonely men homesick for their families in China. Thank you May Yun. I must leave now, or dinner will be late. Mrs. Beckham's guests must be served promptly when the hallway clock chimes five times or the world would surely come to an end. Oh Moksi, was there any mail for us?*"

Nathan reached inside his jacket pocket then handed Ming the mail for the Beckham household. With a broad smile Nathan turned to his daughter. He pulled out an envelope from the inner pocket of his jacket. Louisa

squealed with delight and reached for the envelope. Nathan spoke, "My daughter, you will have to wait until after dinner. It's a long letter. Let's hope it's good news."

After Louise had cleared away and washed the dinner dishes she rushed to the parlour to join her father beside the fireplace. Nathan sat on his favourite armchair with his feet resting on a settee. The smell of burning cedar logs permeated the room as the fire crackled and hissed. Nathan saw the hopeful anticipation building in Louisa's eyes. Next time, he thought to himself, I will read the letter first so I can prepare her for disappointment. He looked at his hopeful daughter, "Louisa it has been a wonderful day. If you find disappointment with the contents of Cheung's letter, you must promise me that you will not isolate yourself in your room for countless hours crying. Do you agree?"

"But Father I cannot control my feelings. Wing may be dying or seriously injured. How can I control my concern for him? If I only knew where he was I would go to find him. I cannot stop thinking of him. Father, he saved my life -- do you expect me to forget that?"

Nathan conciliated. "Cry, if you must, my daughter, but not locked up in your room. Agreed?" Louisa nodded. Smiling at his small victory, Nathan tore open the letter and started to read:

October 15th, 1880

Dear Nathan,

I hope that this letter finds you and May Yun in good health. It has been two months of searching without any sign of Wing. I am sure that he is still alive, or I would have felt the passing of his spirit, as I experienced during the passing of my father. I am determined to find him, regardless of how long it takes.

My new job with the railway requires endless hours of travel by rail, wagon and horseback. I am called a Chinese doctor but in reality I am an assistant to Dr. Sweat, presently the only medical officer for the western section of the railway. There was a doctor hired by the railway company, as requested by the Chinese High Commission, to look after the Chinese but he disappeared and was never seen again. Worksites have been dispersed all along the proposed route, with apparently 32 teams of Chinese workers. We are constantly on tour visiting as many worksites as possible. Certain sites are too remote or too small for us to visit them because our services

are always in great demand at the larger sites. I cannot believe the callous disregard for human safety. Continuous and repeated warnings and criticisms of the way that the railway company is operating fall on deaf ears as Chinese labour contractors send more and more of their compatriots to sacrifice their lives and limbs, to perform hazardous tasks without adequate instructions, training or protection. The company has set up a new 30-bed hospital in Yale, but only for white laborers injured on the job. Injured Chinese workers are considered expendable. The railway company and their labour contractors will bear no responsibility for injured or dead Chinese. The individual crews make up their own private agreements concerning injuries, sickness and death since the composition of crews is based on clan affiliations. No accounts are being reported of Chinese fatalities because the less the Chinese and their labour contractors know the easier it will be to recruit. Poverty and starvation are the tools used to bend the will of men to fulfill the ambition of others. The desperate need of Chinese workers to feed their families in China has replaced the whip and chain that shackle slaves of poverty. The coolie laborers are mostly farmers from the southern provinces of China. As soon as they arrive by steamboat they are forced to march to a worksite. A walk of twenty miles and longer is not uncommon. Some die of sheer exhaustion and dehydration along the way to the campsite. Without knowledge of the area and the ability to communicate, the sick and injured are abandoned to die at the side of the road, sometimes with a bowl of rice. For no man will jeopardize the needs of his family for the sake of friendship and no friend would ask another to make such a sacrifice. Brothers of poverty accept the reality of their fate with dignity.

They arrive dressed in baggy cotton trousers fastened by rope, wide-sleeved quilted coolie jackets and straw sandals or cloth slippers with leather soles without any warning of weather or working conditions. Unlike the locals who are accustomed to the cold, the coolies from southern China suffer as their bones and joints ache while adjusting to the cold. Many suffer from dizziness and headaches due to the thinner air at the higher altitudes. The nights and mornings are very cold and blankets are supplied at a high cost. After a few weeks in the cold mountains, the labourer replaces his cotton garments with woolens purchased through the company store. Many use newspaper inside their garments and under their bed covers to protect themselves from the cold. The cloth shoes are replaced with work boots

after their footwear is torn to shreds. Once again the cost is docked from their salary at the end of each month. The price of the items in the company store is generally twice as much as the cost of the same item in Yale but the laborers have no choice but to pay the price or suffer without the item. Anyone caught purchasing their items through any suppliers other than the company store is penalized with a reduction from his one dollar a day wage to eighty cents. All provisions must be supplied by the company. Though many complain of the lack of fresh vegetables, the contractors will provide only rice and dried salmon at this time of the year because the cost of freight is so dear. Any freighted vegetables are generally reserved for the white laborers who receive a dollar and a half for unskilled labour with all food and board, equipment and provisions included, basically twice the wage of a Chinese labourer. Salmon is supplied and acquired by the company from the local natives who deliver it to the camp. Rice comes by wagon in dried cakes weighing 30 lbs.. The rice is pre-cooked, compressed into a mash then dried – when it is cooked it has the consistency of paste with no resemblance to rice. The workers complain bitterly to no avail. Each man is supplied with one 30 lb cake each month. The labour contractors have been warned unless they provide some fresh vegetables soon for their men, the danger of disease is imminent. With deductions and levies for clothing, shoes, tools, food, tea, lamp-oil, tobacco which is needed to repel mosquitoes , drugs, provincial tax, religious fees and repayment of debt to labour contractors, most workers can save very little from their monthly pay to send home to their families in China. The dream of returning home financially secure with $300 in savings will be attained by very few. I was notified at the head office that there is a strong possibility that many men will be laid off during the winter months. How any of these men will survive winter during a layoff is beyond my ability to comprehend. Most of these men send off what remains of their earnings after deductions as soon as they are received, to their families through their labour agency. Each man lives in mortal fear of being laid off so they become easy pawns for some of the less scrupulous labour contractors to manipulate. Empowered with their ability to speak English, the contractors guard this skill from others to protect their jobs by discouraging communication between whites and Chinese. As the contractors and their friends drink tea and play cards they need only to lift a finger, or raise an eyebrow to have the laborers run to light their pipes or pour their drinks. It defies my ability

to understand how Chinese can treat their own people in such a frivolous manner. The beauty of this chain of command is that the railway owners can absolve themselves of moral liability. They can blame their American railway contractor who, in turn, can blame their labour contractors, who are Chinese. So the Chinese are blamed for the inhumane treatment of their own people. The less anyone knows the better for those who have ultimate responsibility. In this way, anyone of significance can claim ignorance of any wrongdoings or acts of immorality. I wonder how history will treat the characters of this historical grand opera. Will the Chinese be portrayed as brave desperate men struggling to feed their families back in China or just some mindless pigs to the slaughter? Will the railway owners be villains or national heroes exalted by future generations for an amazing accomplishment with only the expenditure of insignificant Chinese lives? What think you my friend? How will they be remembered?

In closing I would like to ask a favour of you. If you are able, could you please save for me any articles in the local newspaper that relate to the Chinese situation in Victoria? I hope to move my family to Victoria in the near future and I wish to stay aware of public sentiment towards the Chinese. Please give my warmest regards to May Yun and assure her that I will find Wing and I will inform you as soon as this task has been accomplished.

Your loyal friend

Dai Woo Cheung

Nathan had been so absorbed in reading that he did not notice his daughter's reaction to the letter. Tears were streaming from her eyes as she visualized the scenes Cheung had painted in his letter. As she sobbed, Nathan thought quickly. What can I do to divert her from endless weeks of tears? Suddenly he stood up and walked towards the basement door into the central hallway. The abruptness of his action surprised Louisa who expected to be comforted by her loving father. She walked to the hallway just in time to catch a glance of her father descending the stairs into the dimly lit basement. She listened as he briefly rattled around below. After a few minutes, the sound of his footsteps drew louder as he ascended the stairs. Her father re-appeared with his hands clutching the sides of a large wooden box. Confused by her father's reaction, she brushed back her tears for a moment to determine what her father was doing. As he laid the box on the dining room floor she saw that it was filled with newspapers. Looking

into his daughter's swollen eyes Nathan smiled. "Now that you are finished crying shall we get started searching for those articles requested by Uncle Cheung. I have no idea who left all these newspapers in the basement. I discovered them a few days ago and planned to use them in the fireplace. There are a few more boxes in the basement. I think we almost have a complete collection of the British Colonist. Why don't we cut out all the articles relating to the Chinese that might be of interest to Uncle Cheung and paste them into an album? We can provide Cheung with a history of articles about the Chinese presence in the city. You can give the album to Uncle Cheung when he returns to Victoria. Do you like my idea, little princess?"

"Oh yes, Father, and I will start right away, but I will need scissors and a large photo album. Do we have an unused album?"

Nathan shook his head, "I don't think so, princess. I will buy one."

"Oh father can I come and choose it myself? I will hurry home right after school. I promise not to keep you waiting. This album must be a very special one. Do you think we can look for one in Chinatown? I want to find a pretty red one with Chinese calligraphy at the front."

"Why don't you shop for one with Ming on Saturday? I'll give you the money, but if we don't find one with calligraphy on the front, I will get my calligraphy set out and honour your album with my artistry. Did I ever tell you how my Sifu Lin Yu said that my calligraphy was the best that he had ever seen by a foreign hand? He said that I was probably Chinese in a past life."

In a submissive tone, Louisa said, "Yes, father, I think that I may have heard you talk about this more than once."

Glancing sideways at Louisa through his spectacles, Nathan burst out in laughter, "Yes, my daughter, perhaps a hundred times."

Nathan strolled back to the parlour. "I will check for relevant articles that I find in today's newspaper. If there are any that may be of interest to Uncle Cheung I will circle them and you can cut them out. The articles can go in your album. Now be sure you don't miss any important articles. We have to be very thorough."

Intently sorting the pile of newspapers, Louisa responded, "Don't worry father. I'll be very careful not to miss a single article."

Relieved that he circumvented a catastrophe Nathan retreated to his armchair with his reading glasses and the daily newspaper. He rested his feet on a settee, and soon the sound of snoring resonated throughout the house.

• • • • •

When Wing was carried back to the steamboat in New Westminster, the labour contractor realized that the unconscious boy was not the same as the one who was missing but did nothing, since the ferry to Yale was to leave in the morning. The unconscious victim would probably not survive with his severe loss of blood. The body was deposited in a corner on the cargo deck with the Chinese laborers who presumed that he was either dead or dying. When the vessel reached Yale the next day the laborers were unloaded and Wing's body was left behind. A crew member noticed the body and summoned the Captain. When the Captain arrived he decided that this was a problem for the railway company. He sent a message to the CPR office to take care of the body. The CPR sent a wagon to load the body and transport it to a burial site. When two deckhands pick up the body Wing gave out a faint groan. Realizing the boy was still alive, the wagon driver took him to the local doctor who examined the gash at the back of Wing's head, which was extensive. The doctor removed the pigtail and shaved the back of Wing's head to clean and suture the gash. Later, a wagon arrived and transferred Wing to the home of Mrs. George Keefer, the wife of an engineer who on occasion cared for the sick and injured. After three weeks, Wing recovered but had lost the ability to speak and had no memory of the past. The head office was informed of Wing's recovery. Realizing that he was the son of their newly-acquired Chinese doctor, the company officials had Wing delivered to a very remote work site with instructions for the site supervisor to guard the boy from any possible contact with the Chinese doctor.

As the sky-monkeys passed by, Loun An looked up to watch the procession. The tall boy at the front looked very much like his friend, the little frog, but he was as dark as a siwash (refers to native people, derived from French word "sauvage") but had no queue. He made eye contact but there was no acknowledgement.

Loun An called out "Little frog, is that you?" No response. How could it be him? His father would never allow this. But the likeness was remarkable.

Suddenly he was jarred back to reality by the herder "Chop, chop, come on, back to work, you lazy little bastard."

The herder assigned to overseeing his group of thirty laborers walked up to Samuel Harper. "You arrived here three weeks ago with no railroad experience and now you're a foreman. I've been here for three months and not even a sniff of a promotion. Tell me what I am doing wrong? Who did you bribe to get the foreman's job?"

"What do you have to complain about? The Chinks are doing all the manual labour and taking all the risks. You just have to make sure the work is done. Are you happy with that?"

"I just don't understand how a herder can advance to a foreman's position in such a short time. Come on, tell me how you did it?"

"Well if you really want to know I'll tell you. Do you remember two weeks back when work was halted for three days? Because of the heavy rain there was a fear of mud slides. My crew was the only one that worked during those three days."

"How did you get them to do that?"

"They see others dying from exhaustion and lack of nutrition. I promised them fresh vegetables if they worked through the downpour. They were so desperate they agreed."

"How did you manage to get the vegetables? They are reserved only for white workers?"

" Unfortunately, keeping promises to John Chinamen was not a promise I needed to keep. The mosquitoes swarmed all around them whenever the rains stopped but they continued working even through the evening. They all smoked pipes and I think the smell of tobacco kept the mosquitoes at bay. So my crew got the scheduled work done while the rest of you snoozed. Construction has progressed so slowly, when the superintendent heard about my work, he decided that I should be rewarded, so he promoted me. Just work your crew harder, promise them anything. It doe not matter as long as you get a promotion"

Harper continued his inspection tour of the worksite. He decided to check the blasting on the north wall. He watched a labourer quickly scramble up a ladder just in time to avoid the impact from an explosion. A small rock sailed pass Harper. He yelled, "hey, you brainless fools, a rock almost hit me." He climbed up the rock embankment. The herder in charge yelled

orders for his bookman to translate to the blasting crew. "Tell them too much powder not safe. Less powder deeper hole. Okay?"

"Okay boss." barked the bookman as he relayed the message in Chinese.

As the angry foreman approached, the herder waved and yelled out, "Harper, sorry about that. Just about got you? These Chinamen are new and aren't broken in yet. We keep losing them. Glad I don't have to do what they do."

Still angry at the near mishap, Harper stormed up the slope to reprimand the perpetrators. When he arrived at the blasting site, he looked down and studied the rock wall. A face popped up over the ledge. He looked at the face in stunned silence. As the boy stood up, Harper stared directly into the boy's eyes. No, it can't be the little bastard from the ship, not here. He's about the same height, but no ponytail. He shook his head and thought - these Chinese do all look alike. The boy passed by with a distant look. Harper discerned no response from the boy in return. The herder said, "That's my best man, he's bigger and stronger than the rest. He's totally fearless and can perform feats only an acrobat could do. It is a strange thing that he seems to understand everything I say, but he cannot speak a word, even in Chinese. It seems like his mind is always elsewhere else. I was given orders by the site supervisor to keep him away from the Chinese doctor."

"What Chinese doctor? I didn't know we had one," asked Harper, as he remembered overhearing about Dai's medical visits on board the Strathearn.

"There is one, according to management, but our campsite is too remote for visits."

So it must be the little bastard from the ship and his father must be searching for him. This information could be very profitable. "Well, keep him safe from harm. I may be able to use him later. Do you know what happened to him? His mind appears pre-occupied."

"I don't know anything about his accident but he has a very large scar at the back of his head. He does whatever I request. Best worker I've ever had."

"Well keep him dangling, but don't let him set any charges. Okay? I don't want anything to happen to him. Is that clear?"

The herder complied with a nod.

Wing hammered the chisel held in place by his cohort. He thought to himself. Why can I not remember? Who am I? Why can I not speak? He hammered harder and harder, scaring his partner who shook his head in

disapproval and signaled to ease up, during Wing's backstroke. Wing relaxed momentarily, then continued with less intensity.

· · · · ·

Dinner had just been completed, the dining room table cleared and dishes washed and stacked. The smell of burning pine lingered throughout the house as a small stack of logs hissed and burned in the massive stone fireplace. Sitting comfortably in his armchair beside the fireplace, Nathan calmly announced, "Louisa I picked up the mail today."

Racing to the parlor with excitement, Louisa cried out, "Is there anything from Uncle Cheung?"

"Yes Louisa, but it is a long letter. So go upstairs and change into your nightgown before we read the letter." Louisa rushed upstairs and returned minutes later.

"So please, let's not get our hopes up, and try not to get upset. Okay, my dear?" Louisa waited impatiently. Having read the letter beforehand in preparation for Louisa's emotional response Nathan unfolded the letter:

November 25, 1880

Dear Nathan,

I hope that this letter finds you and May Yun both safe and in good health. Sorry, I have no news on the whereabouts of Wing as yet. I am still hopeful that I will find him.

I have made many friends during my work with the railway. The conditions are dreadful and fraught with danger. Many are still dying and getting injured due to callousness, lack of safety precautions and sheer stupidity.

I have gained a deep admiration for my colleague Dr. Sweat who is a veteran physician experienced in all facets of medicine. He is firm but very fair and is very good at treating injuries. People say that he served as a medical officer in the American Civil War. At first he was very formal and abrupt with me and very dubious of my abilities. As we worked together on some treatments and conferred with others we developed a friendly relationship and an understanding of mutual trust. The kind doctor has been very generous with his knowledge and has even adopted some treatments and cures from eastern medicine. My services are in constant demand but we cannot be everywhere that we are needed. When I am free in the evenings I visit as many camps as possible. I teach the workers how to treat

injuries and illnesses and also how to maintain good health through personal hygiene and proper sanitation within the individual campsites. With such a plentiful supply of clean water so close by, the workers enjoy the luxury of taking baths at the end of the day. Using good drinking water in this manner would have been reserved for the rich in China. Many have died of dehydration after being over-worked to exhaustion without water by their ignorant white herders. The doctor and I have argued with foremen and site supervisors to provide tea or water at each work site that we visit. Most comply since removing the dying and the dead cause more wasted time than water breaks. Medical problems are discussed during these gatherings and many teams have elected a representative to acquire basic knowledge of treatments and local remedies. A select group follows me during my camp tours. The more that I can teach them, the better chance of their survival and their ability to help others survive. Hopefully they will share their knowledge with others. I have selected a few of the brightest students for more intensive training. Should a mishap affect my ability to perform maybe one of these men can serve as my replacement. The main pre-requisite is some ability or motivation to speak English so they can communicate with the physician in charge when they are in doubt of how to proceed. A quick mind and a sense of compassion are the only other qualities that I look for but if they gamble or smoke opium I will waste no time with them since they cannot be entrusted with the lives of others.

The process for construction has three stages. The first is carried out by the surveyors who lead the way by staking the pre-determined path for construction. This has been done years in advance by a corps of engineers, who sometimes must however alter the course if they discover an overlooked obstacle or find a better route. The graders and bridge builders are called navvies, (an English term first used to refer to construction laborers working on "navi"gational projects). They are assigned to clear bush, rock and trees, in preparation for a 18 meter wide path for the railway. To prevent future rock-slides and avalanches, mountainsides are demolished with dynamite to form a gallery along the path of the railway. Boulders are removed and crushed to create grading material and fill. Ancient forests that have never seen an axe are sacrificed to produce ties and lumber to build bridges and trestles over rivers, deep canyons and along steep mountainsides. Tunnels are blasted and drilled through mountains. Swamps are drained and filled as well as

gorges, with blasted rock and debris removed from tunnels and mountain-sides. Then the path must be leveled and graded with crushed rock, sand and gravel. Wooden railway ties called sleepers are placed across the graded path half a meter apart, center to center. Flat cars powered by a locomotive arrive at the end of the rail line with wooden ties, iron rails, fish-plates and boxes of metal spikes. Wooden ties are loaded on horse-drawn wagons and distributed over half a kilometer in advance in a repetitive process. Iron rails are unloaded from each side of ox carts by the track-layers. The six hundred pound rails are carried and aligned by teams of workers. They are checked by levelers and the distance between them measured by gaugers and then spikes are hammered in place to secure the rails to the ties. Crushed rock is tamped in place between the ties as ballast for additional stability. So far this year, very little track has been laid. The past months have been primarily focused on clearing, blasting, tunneling, and building trestles and bridges.

Avalanches, mudslides, cave-ins, falling boulders, flying debris and explosions claim many lives and limbs. After experiencing constant danger for a short duration many white workers and natives quit to seek safer employment elsewhere. Tied by contractual obligations, the Chinese have no choice but to do as the railway company has instructed. If contracts are not fulfilled, family members in China may be indentured into servitude, even their unborn. Some workers die from sheer exhaustion, some from dehydration, some from sun stroke, some by falling off bridges and trestles. The ground quakes day and night. The sound of blasting resonates off the distant mountainsides, constantly echoing through canyons and valleys at every visited campsite. Blasting loosens the foundation of every mountainside which can give way at any time without warning. At one campsite, the blasting caused a landslide which destroyed a very large Indian burial ground. A shout of "look out below" forces all to run for safety, away from falling boulders, an avalanche or a cave-in.

Chinese work crews are created based on their regional dialect and village affiliations. They consist of groups of thirty workers, a bookman who keeps accounts of hours worked, and a white boss called a herder. The majority of herders are inexperienced roughnecks and hoodlums from the slums and saloons of San Francisco; many have never performed an honest day's work in their lives. Many display a blatant contempt for the Chinese workers under their supervision. The bookmen are Chinese. They

can generally speak and understand English and translate orders from the herder to the laborers. The bookman are fastidious accountants, docking laborers for lost and broken equipment, lunch breaks, travel time, sick time, they even deduct pay when laborers stop to bury or help injured and dying co-workers. Chinese newcomers are given the manual work of clearing rocks, boulders, debris and tree stumps. Later as their strength improves, they are assigned to more strenuous tasks like building tunnels and trestles, handling explosives and blasting. The most dangerous is related to blasting. Some of the blasters are called sky-monkeys because they work suspended from a rope, like a monkey swinging on a vine. These men are often mistaken for natives because they become very muscular and tanned since they work dressed only in a loincloth. They work in pairs -- one man holds a chisel in place while the other hammers to create a hole to house explosives which are stored inside a basket attached to the life-line. Once the fuse is lit by one of the pair the two quickly scramble up a ladder to safety. Sometimes the fuse burns too rapidly, and sometimes too slowly. Sometimes the burning fuse stalls then re-ignites with fatal consequences when the worker is sent back down to check it.

The agents for the Chinese labour contractors visit the campsites occasionally and are a privileged group who often eat and socialize with the white laborers. Most have come from Chinatown in San Francisco. Some have had previous experience as manual laborers on the Central Pacific Railroad, the first transcontinental railway connecting the eastern states and California. These men understand the dangers and hardship for those they advise and control but they are in turn controlled by their companies in San Francisco whose major concern seems only to be profit. I often join these men who congregate at a separate table during mealtime. I have tried to rally support for ideas to improve the safety and health of their workers. I have warned them that fresh vegetables and fruit are needed to prevent an outbreak of scurvy and beri beri. I recommended crews to be allowed portable garden boxes and seeds to grow their own vegetables but the request has been denied by management without explanation. I am sure this idea would conflict with profits for the company stores located at every major campsite.

Opinions about the future for our countrymen in Canada vary. I queried many as to their views on the future of the Chinese in the United States

as well as Canada. Most did not care since their ambition has always been to return to China. Special representatives for the labour contractors sometimes visit the campsites to praise the workers for their contribution and promote the significance of the railway for Canadian unity. They preach how thankful and indebted Canada will be to the Chinese for their contribution to this great national endeavor. A small minority who desire to remain in Canada after completion of the railway are united in the belief that the construction of the railway will enhance the image of all Chinese and that our contribution will undoubtedly endear us to all Canadians once they understand how many Chinese lives will have been sacrificed and how much danger, suffering and hardship will have been endured to build their transcontinental railway. I am hopeful that this vision of Canadian gratitude will become a reality.

Although my primary goal is to find Wing, my experience here has been very rewarding. I feel a great sense of accomplishment at the end of the day in being able to help others who are in such dire need. Nathan, I hope that your work at the synagogue is progressing well and that May Yun is studying hard at school and making many new friends. May Yun, please be assured that I will find Wing. Please give my regards to Mrs. Beckham, Ming, Thomas and Mr. Thompson.

Yours sincerely,

Dai Woo Cheung

Tears started to flow from Louisa's eyes. Nathan looked at his daughter in earnest. "Shall we write a letter to Uncle Cheung tomorrow? Let us send some articles from your scrapbook that you have collected? He will be very concerned about how his business will be affected with what is happening to the Chinese locally."

"Father, we can go through my book tomorrow. Good night, father."

Nathan thought to himself, she is going to her bedroom to cry. As she approached to kiss him good-night he embraced her and cradled her in his lap. She sobbed quietly until she fell asleep. Nathan carried her upstairs and deposited her on her bed, removed her house coat and slippers, tucked the pillow under her head, and placed the blanket over his daughter. As he walked down the staircase Nathan pondered, would it be better to leave out some contents of Cheung's letters or read it all? He decided that reading

everything would better prepare her for the disappointment. Writing a long letter with many articles may keep her busy enough to curb her sadness.

Chapter 10

Winter Vissitudes

ALL ACTIVITY AT RAILWAY CAMPSITES WAS SUSPENDED AT THE
beginning of December due to heavy snow. Temperatures reached minus
30 degrees Fahrenheit. The danger of avalanches and the inability of steamboats to deliver supplies and provisions, while the Fraser River was covered
with ice, made railway construction impossible.

The main street of Yale was idle. Mounds of snow were piled up beside
the canopied wooden walkways along Front Street. The empty road was
covered with freshly-fallen snow. Many shops were closed for the winter.
The wooden plank shacks on the main thoroughfare housed many gambling houses, saloons, and brothels. They catered to whims and emptied the
pockets of anyone who dared to enter their doors. Fiddle music, clapping
and laughter could be heard from the street.

The CPR office was closed for the winter. Their office employees, labour
contractors and higher-paid help had departed to Victoria and New
Westminster for the winter. Cheung stayed behind, hoping to find Wing
or information about his whereabouts amongst the laborers in Yale. He
became well-known and recognized by the laborers, but was afraid to trust
anyone to help him search for his son. Dr. Sweat had forewarned Cheung
that Yale was not adequately prepared for the winter. The town stores were

ill-prepared to support the winter onslaught of Chinese workers on the outskirts of town. Due to weather conditions, very limited provisions and supplies would reach Yale over the winter months. There would be severe shortages and the price of food and supplies would rise greatly. Starvation and disease were unavoidable consequences facing the Chinese laborers. As Cheung visited the encampments in search of his son he gave his routine campfire talks about how to maintain good health and also how to prepare for the imminent approach of scurvy and beriberi.

Thousands of Chinese laborers had been laid off and were dwelling in a gigantic encampment of canvas tents on the northern outskirts of town. Jobs in town were scarce. An appeal by Cheung to the community for food, relief, and jobs was mostly ignored by the locals who were perturbed by petty thefts and beggars as well as the fear of infectious diseases. Cheung made friends with the Sto;lo band near Yale. They guided him on frequent occasions to their nearby village to treat victims of foreign diseases which their traditional remedies could not cure. The Sto:lo were thankful and very generous but their supplies were limited and Cheung would not endanger their survival by over-imposing on their generosity. They repaid his services with dried salmon, dried berries and ooligan oil. Cheung also treated many local residents, mostly Chinese miners and merchants at the Toi San Society, where he was boarding at the CPR's expense. For those who could not afford to pay for his services, he would only ask for contributions to a relief fund for the worker's camp. But it never seemed enough. Though some residents were very generous there were far too many laborers to feed. All were hungry and many were already dying of scurvy and beriberi, which they called black leg. Those with scurvy always looked pale and tired. Spots would appear on their body, bleeding from their nose and mouth would occur, teeth would fall out, followed by jaundice, fever and death. Victims of beriberi would first experience fatigue and lethargy, difficulty walking, then tingling and loss of feeling in hands and feet, paralysis of the lower legs which appeared to turn black in the cold, followed by mental confusion, difficulty with speech, and vomiting, resulting in heart failure and death. Yale was not prepared for the winter hordes of Chinese laborers. Fresh vegetables, food and medical supplies were scarce. Steamboat service would not resume until spring and only the occasional delivery of supplies arrived by sleigh. The locals were relieved only after Dr. Sweat, at Cheung's request, informed

them that the laborers were not suffering from smallpox, but had scurvy and beriberi which were not infectious diseases. Cheung bartered for as much food and necessities as he could acquire with donations he received and his own savings. Awaiting transfer to Victoria's Chinatown bone house in the spring heaps of dead dream-seekers inundated the Toi San Society storage facility. The vivid reality of Yale's winter surpassed Cheung's greatest fears which he foresaw in his dreams. Who was responsible for this? Couldn't the town's leaders or the railway company foresee the shortage of food and supplies? Did they care?

Firewood was plentiful, so gigantic campfires burned day and night, surrounded by sick ghostly figures wrapped in coats stuffed with crumpled newspaper for insulation. They clutched make-shift blankets over their heads, gunny sack remnants covered their hands and feet as they huddled together for warmth. Some had survived by begging, some by foraging through garbage, some by fishing through holes in the ice while others resorted to stealing chickens, pigs, or anything that could be sold or traded for food.

One day, Cheung was approached in town by a sickly man shivering and covered in rags. He cleared his throat with a hacking cough, and then called out in a weak voice, "*Mr. Dai, it's me Loun An. Are you searching for Wing?*"

"*Loun An, you are not well. Come with me, you need food and medicine.*"

Cheung escorted the youth to an eating place nearby. Once they were seated, Cheung analyzed his guest's medical condition then ordered food. "*I think that I saw Wing working as a sky-monkey. I called out to him. He saw me but he did not recognize me. He lost his queue and has grown bigger and looks much stronger. His skin has been darkened by the sun. He appears as a native. I have looked for him in camp but I have not seen him again. When others told me that you were making visits to our encampment and working for the railway as a doctor, I knew that you must be searching for him.*"

The food arrived. "*Don't talk, just eat. I will go to find you some medicine. You are not well. Just keep eating, but very slowly with small sips of tea. I will be right back.*"

A few minutes passed by. When Cheung returned to the restaurant, Loun An was hunched over the table, dead.

• • • • •

Some company personnel remained behind to guard equipment and supplies stored at the various railway worksites. Samuel Harper had been given instructions from the head office in Yale to keep Wing at the worksite. Instead of delegating the role off to a subordinate, he decided to fulfill the task himself.

Samuel and Wing remained in the log bunkhouse during the heavy snow. The single-room bunkhouse was long and narrow with bunks on both sides, and a narrow aisle down the middle. Near the entrance was the kitchen , then an eating area, followed by the sleeping area. Sam knew Wing could understand his words even though he had lost the ability to speak. The bunkhouse larder was well-supplied with all types of foodstuff: sacks of flour and sugar, tins of coffee and beans, crates of eggs, canned vegetables and fruits, sides of pork, beef, and venison, slabs of smoked bacon and fish. Out of necessity, Sam taught Wing what he knew about cooking and baking which Wing grasped very quickly. They experimented on occasion with the cuisine. Out of boredom, Sam taught Wing how to play checkers and various card games. Wing's mind seemed to become more focused and less distant as time progressed. The two played cards and checkers to see who would cook, who would wash the dishes, who would clean up the cabin, who would clear the pathway from the cabin to the outhouse, who would chop the kindling, etc. A friendship was developing out of the need for human companionship. Sam had always been a loner, never trusting or confiding in other human beings since growing up in the slums of Newcastle as an orphan. He had little experience with human warmth or kindness. Growing up on the streets was a perpetual struggle for survival. Everyone competed for their own needs. No one could be trusted and if you did, it always ended in disappointment. As a consequence, he never appreciated the use of having friends.

During the good weather, Sam and Wing would pack a lunch and go on exploratory outings into the wilderness. In the supply shed they found all the clothing and equipment that they needed for their winter excursions. The pair outfitted themselves in the railway's finest winter attire – long johns, jeans, sealskin mukluks and mitts, woolen toques, and the traditional white Hudson Bay jackets with the horizontal red, green and black stripes. They each attached a holster with a hunting knife on their belts secured around their jackets.. Sam carried a rifle strapped across his back and a pair

of binoculars hung around his neck. Wing carried the provisions on his back in a heavy canvas knapsack. They ventured out of the cabin on snowshoes sometimes to hunt for fresh game but mostly to counteract the misery of confinement. On one occasion the two found the tracks of a herd of elk. As they followed the tracks, they also encountered the tracks of a pack of timber wolves, stalking the herd. Wolves were not generally a problem during railway construction since the constant explosions and noise of construction kept them at bay. When construction ceased, they became progressively bolder and wandered closer to the vacant campsites. To avoid an encounter with the wolves the two friends decided to return to the cabin. As they turned to head back a loud howling of wolves could be heard in the valley below, but tall evergreens blocked their view. Curious to observe what might be happening, Sam shed his rifle and his snowshoes and crawled to a snowy ledge to get a better view of the valley below. Wing lagged behind to remove his snowshoes and the knapsack as Sam urged him to follow. From his elevated vantage point 200 yards away, Sam watched the wolf pack as they cautiously stocked the herd before selecting their quarry. Cautiously hesitant, Wing remained a safe distance back from the ledge.

The elk were massive in size, a single kick could kill a wolf, but the lighter wolves had much better traction in deep snow and could run all day. Finally, a mother elk and her calf had been singled out from the herd. They were surrounded by six large grey wolves while three others kept a large bull and the rest of the herd at bay. Sam crawled farther out the ledge with his binoculars to watch the final kill. Suddenly, he heard a loud crack below him, and he tumbled down a steep embankment. He shrieked loudly. The branch of a protruding pine tree perched on the lower lip of the embankment broke his fall, 10 feet below the ledge. Sam became tangled in the branches; he was badly hurt and felt light-headed. He assessed his situation - a mile from the cabin in heavy snow, with limited supplies, no rescue equipment and an inexperienced adolescent. As he lost consciousness, Sam realized the situation was hopeless.

The wolves were temporarily distracted by Sam's distant cry. A bull elk seized the opportunity to charge the distracted wolves and rescued the mother elk and her calf. Once they rejoined the herd, the bulls united to form a barrier around the herd. The frustrated wolves decided to abandon their pursuit of elk.

Wing returned to the cabin to fetch ropes, a pulley, a blanket, and a sled. The wolf pack ventured uphill to the ledge in hopes of finding easy prey but realized Sam's carcass was unattainable. When they detected Wing's scent they returned and watched the rescue effort as Wing secured a rope with a pulley to a nearby tree, removed his jacket then lowered himself to where Sam lay precariously suspended. He tied the rope around Sam's torso and under both arms. Some overhanging limbs of the tree blocked the way up. Before hoisting Sam back up the slope, Wing realized that he would have to clear some branches to avoid entanglements. He needed a knife but he had left his coat and knife at the top of the slope. He thought momentarily, then remembered that Sam had one attached to his belt. After he cleared the obstacles, he tucked the knife inside his trouser behind his back, then climbed back up the cliff. After reaching the top of the slope he used the pulley to hoist Sam up. Wing then put on his coat and secured Sam on the sled with a blanket and proceeded to tow him back to the cabin. From a safe distance, the wolf pack followed the pair. They crept closer and closer as Wing struggled through the snow with Sam and a heavy knapsack. The pack impeded Wing's path with flurries of menacing attacks, in an attempt to tire him out before launching an assault. Woken by the growling wolves, Sam was jarred back to a dangerous new reality. A snarling flurry mass of grey and white flashed around him as Sam was shaken abruptly by Wing. They were in a small wind-swept clearing a quarter mile from the worksite. Sam's left arm was painfully sore as he struggled to unwrap himself from the blanket and reached for his knife to help defend from the rear. His knife was missing. The wolves watched closely as Wing removed the knife attached to his jacket and handed it to Sam. The wolf pack became more aggressive, and eventually separated the two men forming a wall between Sam and Wing. They forced a wider and wider separation between the two. Even though his left arm was broken Sam pushed himself off the sled and awkwardly stood up, swinging the knife side to side, wondering what to do next. The pack of timber wolves consisted of 6 large adults and 3 adolescents. The adults ranged from 80 to 120 pounds in size, standing 3 to 4 feet high. The largest were 6 to 7 feet nose to tail. Wing took the rifle which was slung over his shoulder. He pointed the rifle but nothing happened when he pressed the trigger. It was too heavy to use as a club so he heaved it over to Sam. Wing detached one of the snowshoes hanging over the knapsack on his back and

swung it at the 5 large grayish predators as they surrounded and distanced him farther from Sam who was being kept at bay by the others. Sam reached for the gun but it was not loaded and the shells were in the knapsack. Sam yelled, "The shells are in the knapsack." Wing released the knapsack from his back one arm at a time while he fended off the wolves swinging the snowshoe with his free hand. The knapsack contained the ropes, pulley and provisions and weighed too much to reach Sam with a throw. Sam and Wing were now 20 feet apart. Wing held out the wrapped meat sandwiches so the wolves could smell them, then he hurled them as far as he could in the opposite direction. While the wolves were temporarily distracted, Wing quickly emptied the contents of the knapsack in the snow except for the shells. Only the adolescents broke formation to retrieve the sandwiches. The adults held their stations but watched the fledglings quickly devour the sandwiches. As the adults growled disdainfully at the adolescents Wing picked up the knapsack, rotated it in a circular motion, and flung it towards his friend. It landed a few feet short with the wolves in between. Sam moved towards the knapsack, struggling to retrieve it, while threatening the wolves with the knife in his usable hand. Wing watched Sam, wondering how he would fend off the predators and load the rifle with just one hand. Expecting the final assault was imminent, Wing pondered his fate while a voice inside his head echoed, "against superior opposition, feign weakness and eliminate the leader". Wing dropped the snowshoe out of his hand and slowly approached the dominant aggressor and bowed submissively in a Chinese kowtow. The leader backed up, confused. Sam thought to himself, is he going to sacrifice himself? He shouted, "No! No! Don't!" The pack stood back but remained at bay surrounding Wing waiting for their leader to initiate the final assault. The lead wolf growled menancingly, circling its prey to determine the point of greatest vulnerability. Wing heard the quickened rush of parting snow. The wolf lunged high in the air towards his helpless victim from the rear. Sensing an impact Wing suddenly flipped from his knees onto his feet, turning to his left in a single motion. He extended his left arm up to fend off the attack. The wolf seized his left wrist in his jaw. Wing raised his left arm high as the wolf elevated to maintain his hold. Wing reached behind his back under his coat with his right hand for Sam's knife then plunged it deep into the wolf's chest. Wing twisted the blade until a weak whimper of anguish sealed its fate. The canine body went limp, and fell over on the

blood-stained snow. Without showing any sign of fear, Wing rose up with the bloodied knife in his right hand. Shocked by the sudden change in circumstance, the wolves cleared a path as Wing approached. They faded back, confused and dismayed. With the blood-stained knife in one hand, Wing calmly collected the contents dropped from the knapsack with the other hand and walked confidently towards his friend without looking back. The pack surrounded their fallen leader. Sam shook his head in disbelief and admiration wondering, will his friend recover his memory? When? Would they remain friends? He owed this boy his life.

• • • • •

The CPR office re-opened during the first week in March but hiring was delayed due the threat of avalanche. A letter addressed to Dai Woo Cheung arrived in care of the CPR and was delivered to the Toi San Society. The envelope was very thick. Many homesick onlookers gathered in the lobby, hoping the fortunate recipient would share any news concerning recent events in China. Cheung explained that the letter was from a friend in Victoria and went up to his room to read it in privacy.

Dear Cheung,

Louisa sends you her warmest regards. She has shed countless tears and has read your letters many times and sympathizes with the Chinese laborers who must face so much suffering and hardship to keep their families from starvation in China. I am very pleased with how well she has adapted to her new school and how conscientiously she has applied herself to her schoolwork. Mary Beckham and Louisa have become very close friends. Mary advises and treats Louisa as the daughter that she has always wanted. I cannot express how relieved I am that Louisa has found a female confidante who is so kind, wise and trustworthy enough to advise her on matters a man may find difficult to counsel. Louisa has worked diligently on a scrapbook to catalogue newspaper articles that relate to the local Chinese situation. When Mary and her best friend, Mrs. Florence Baillie Grohman, discovered Louisa working on her scrapbook project, they decided to assist her by contributing articles from other locally-available sources. Mrs. Grohman has a Chinese servant named Gee whom she accompanies to town to guard him from rocks thrown by local ruffians. Here are some of the articles that Louisa has collected for you. We found a collection of newspapers in our

basement. Louisa has allowed me to borrow them from her scrapbook, would you please keep them and bring them back when you return to town. In addition, I have included some comments expressed by our friends: Mary, Mrs. Grohman, Thomas, Ming, Jonathan and others such as James Fell, a local businessman, and Walter Moberly, the major contractor for the Cariboo Road and surveyor for the CPR.

There seems to be a pattern of acceptance and praise for the Chinese during boom years, demonization by politicians and news agencies during times of economic despair, especially during elections; and then ambivalence during periods of prosperity. Here are the articles collected:

-CHRISTIAN GUARDIAN, FEB.15, 1860

Reverend Edward White, a Methodist missionary – "Although the popular cry of California and with many here is 'Stop them! Drive them back,' I say, let them come! While we are trying to get their country open to our commerce and our Christianity, it is right that we should treat them kindly who come to our shores, even though they may carry off a large portion of our precious dirt. And they seem bound to do it; for while others are grumbling and hesitating, or in too many instances drinking and gambling, the Chinese go at once to the mines, work hard, and spend as little as possible. I have not seen one of them either drinking or gambling since I came to this coast."

-COLONIST, MAY 10, 1860

Amor de Cosmos reported that the Chinese were "pioneers of the great work that lies before us – the uniting of the commerce of the Atlantic and the western shores of the old world with the East by railway enterprise across the continent....It now assumes a more tangible form by the initiative taken by native Chinese merchants themselves in consigning vessels laden with laborers and Chinese produce to our port."

-COLONIST, JULY 1, 1861

Amor de Cosmos reverses his support "Chinamen are not the most desirable population...social evils...their inferior civilization, their language, their religion, their habits of living – all so hostile to the customs and prejudices of the higher and dominant race"

-COLONIST, MAR.8, 1862

Amor de Cosmos "Our policy should be shaped so as to invite a Chinese immigration without being overwhelmed by an excessive number, and check their immigration gradually without oppressing them."

-COLONIST, MAY19, 1865

Dr. J.S.Helmcken "glad to see Chinamen come into the country, and thought them a valuable addition to the population." And felt white society should "elevate the Chinamen to our own standard, not to place them in a lower position."

-Assembly of Vancouver Island in 1865, first anti-Chinese motion

G.E.Dennes, member for Salt Spring Island, proposed the House to tax incoming Chinese ten dollars each

-CARIBOO SENTINEL, JUNE 1, 1868

"Chinamen are a curse in a mining country. It is an uncontroverted fact that the Chinamen are a curse to any country they inhabit and the blight they have caused by their presence here is every day more apparent."

-COLONIST, JAN. 27, 1871

Colonial legislature debated a fifty dollar poll tax on the Chinese in the colony

-First Legislative Assembly Sept. 2 & 5, 1871

John Robson, member from Nanaimo, asked the legislature to impose a yearly poll tax of $50 on all Chinese residents and to forbid them employment on all public works.

-*Victoria Standard* published by Amor De Cosmos, protests Robson's motion as a bid for cheap and nasty popularity that might win the admiration of the unwashed and "catering to an unreasonable prejudice existing against the Chinese population"

-Robson in the *Colonist*, "The Chinese do not contribute their fair quota towards public revenue.......The Mongolian labourer emerges from his sardine box in the morning, consumes his pound of rice and puts in his days work, baiting naught from his earnings, save the veriest pittance he subsists on. No wife and children to feed and clothe and educate, no church to maintain, no Sunday clothes to buy, he saves nearly all he earns, is a useless member of society and finally carries with him all his hoardings home to China"– the motion was voted down by those who understood federal constitutional constraints and the shortage of labour for the construction of the railway

- many *Colonist* articles appear in the following months – Chinese are portrayed as "chinks", "almond-eyed peddlers", "Celestials from the flowery kingdom", "moon-eyed Orientals", "John Chinaman", "Heathen Chinee"; "disciples of Confucius"– or portrayed as stupid and inept - a runaway wagon incident - "John always buys the cheapest animal and he either gets "sold" with a broken-winded, spavined brute or a tricky one that is sold because of its failings: and

secondly, because Chinamen, as a rule, know as little of managing a horse as elephants do of climbing trees."

-COLONIST, FEB.27, 1872

The House approved, without dissent or debate, a bill which excluded all Chinese from the right to vote in provincial elections. All Chinese are exempted from registering vital statistics with provincial officials, thereby subordinating their role in west coast society.

-COLONIST, MAY 16, 1873

Anti-Chinese society called for revision of the Sino-British treaty which permitted Chinese immigration to Canada.

-many attempts to impose a Chinese poll tax, including four in 1876

-COLONIST, JAN.26, 1875

First Nanaimo Municipal Election "Chinese were not permitted to approach the Ballot-box. True, the Act does not exclude these people: but so sensible were the Freemen of Nanaimo of the impropriety, the degradation of allowing these heathen slaves (as the great bulk of them undoubtedly are) to stand side by side with themselves at the Ballot-box and have an equal voice in the management of affairs which they little understand and in which they have still less interest or sympathy in common, that they, with one accord, decided to exclude them."

- several Colonist Anti-Chinese articles start to appear – "The Chinese Question"; "The Chinese Evil"; "Mongolian Slave Labour"; "Heathen Chinee"; "John Chinaman"; "Anti-Chinese Meeting", etc.

-COLONIST, APRIL 5, 1876

On Chinese labour: "No greater evil could be inflicted upon a nation than that the labouring class should be drawn from a people animated with no desire or capacity to be welded with the homogeneous mass; with tastes and habits that are barbarous; with a belief that is pagan; and the chief aim of whose existence is to send all their earnings out of the country to enrich another State.... They have no sympathy or interest in common with the rest of the population. Their very food is exceptional, and they worship strange gods beneath the shadow of Christian temples. ...... Give John five cents of licee and a pair of chopsticks and he will make a full meal. How can white labour hope to compete with such a class? And is it any wonder that with white workingmen and their families starving, and Chinese labour everywhere in excess of the demand, a movement should have been started to prevent further immigration from China to California?"

-COLONIST, MAY 1, 1876

Anti-Chinese Meeting at the Royal Theatre – "to deal with the injurious effect of Chinese labour in our midst."...."the majority of Chinese imported to this country are slaves purchased in China, and that while men are degraded by the laws that permit slavery to exist here in any shape"

Mr. James Fell spoke in sympathy of Chinese immigrants ""Mr. Fell disputed the fact that slavery existed on these shores and said that the last speaker had failed to produce any evidence to corroborate their statements. He maintained that England had first sought trade with China and forced that deadly drug – opium -- upon the Chinese; they must remember too that Hong Kong today was a British colony and that many Chinamen were just as good British subjects as many present. (cries of No! No! hisses

and groans) If they did not like to hear facts why had they asked him to address them? Where was their intelligence? (Groans) They were cowards if they said that they could not compete with Chinamen. (Groans) In spite of all their protests they would find Chinamen overrunning the country and penetrating every nook and corner of the habitable globe (No! No!) They had thrown down the barriers of China and now expected that Mongolian to remain at home. (Cries of Time! Time! Put him out.) If the Chinamen were a law abiding industrious and sober race he would tell them to "go and be likewise "and protect themselves by indomitable perseverance and industry. (No! No! groans) he regretted the meeting appeared to lack organization but he had merely spoken to keep the ball rolling. (Sit down! Get somebody else! Pass the rice around! And other confusion) The mayor took a vote to ask if the audience wanted to hear any more from Mr. Fell. The ayes had it. Mr. Fell resumed, saying he could understand the feeling of jealousy against the Chinamen; But they must bear in mind it was their duty, by thrift and industry, to rise to the occasion and live the feeling down. He had heard the same expressions and arguments against the coloured race here in 1862, and the men who advocated that line of argument were not as a rule industrious, solid men. (Confusion and groans. Put him out! And continued hisses.) Afterwards, 380 people signed a petition urging the government to pass an act to tax Chinamen intending to mine in the Cassiar district, $30 each.

-Apparently, Mary Beckham, Mrs. Grohman and a few of their friends attended this event in the hopes of supporting Mr. Fell but they said the crowd consisted mostly of disenchanted miners and unemployable barflies who could only view reality through a glass of ale.

-COLONIST, JULY 22, 1875 & MAY 2, 1876

Victoria Councilor, Noah Shakespeare, urged city to forbid the employment of Chinese on all local public works

-COLONIST, MAY 8, 9, &10, 1878

Nearly all candidates for provincial election promise to restrict Chinese immigration. Some suggestions include – annual poll tax, more restrictions on employment, license fees for trades, future legislation patterned on measures enforced in Australia. Premier A.C. Elliott supports opposition to Chinese.

-COLONIST, AUG. 6 & 8, 1878

Newly-elected Premier George A. Walkem introduces the Chinese Tax Act –Chinese are exempted from other provincial taxes but all Chinese residents over 12 years of age must pay a quarterly fee of $10. Any Chinese without the license would be liable in a $100 fine and, if in default of immediate payment of the fine, the tax would be levied by sale and distress of his goods and chattels. Noah Shakespeare is appointed collector of the "head tax" after assent from the Lieutenant Governor on Aug. 12th, 1878. The goods of Sam Gee on Yates, On Hing on Johnson and Tai Yune on Cormorant Streets were seized. Hearings of the seizures, all Chinese business put up their shutters and lock their doors. A general strike by Chinese workers ensues. On September 17th, 1878, no Chinese workers - cooks, maids , servants, washmen, farm laborers, shoemakers, market gardeners, tailors, cannery workers, shopkeepers- appeared for work.

-COLONIST, SEPT. 18, 1878

"John imagines the white community cannot get along without him. He will shortly discover, to his cost, that such is not the case." Restaurants and hotels, rooming houses, housewives complained bitterly. Shoe and boot manufacturers threatened to close down because they could not compete with San Franciscan manufactures. Fishing boats remained docked, with full cargoes of rotting salmon. Canneries, which also employed hundreds of whites and natives, could no longer buy fishermen's catch and threatened closure due to the lack of labour to process their supply of fish. The strike lasted only 5 days. The provincial government compromised. They agreed to return the seized goods and await the action of the Dominion government which later declared the Act unconstitutional and therefore unenforceable."

According to Mr. James Fell, there is no Constitution existing in Canada, but the British North America Act forbids discriminatory taxes and gives the Dominion government the power to control immigration.

-COLONIST, AUG. 23, 1878

2nd Separation Memorial addressed to the Queen, by way of Ottawa, - it stated that unless the railway was started by the end of April 1879, British Columbia would withdraw from confederation. -*Colonist*, Sept.3, Nov.1&5, Dec.11, 1878

The Workingmen's Protective Association, the first trade union in B.C., is formed in Victoria, for "the mutual protection of the working classes of B.C. against the great influx of Chinese "and the use of "all legitimate means for the suppression of their immigration." It required all members to pledge "neither aid nor abet or patronize Chinamen in any way whatever or patronize those employing them" and "use all legitimate means for their expulsion from the country."

It also had an anti-Chinese petition widely signed by locals, took a census of the Chinese and advertised names of their employers, to encourage a boycott. A new branch was formed in New Westminster in December.

-COLONIST, JAN.7, 1879

Noah Shakespeare, the new WPA chairman, produces a queue shorn from a Chinese prisoner at the local jail and boasts that all long-term prisoners, especially Chinese, were to be shaved in future. The queue was going to be kept as a family heirloom.

-COLONIST, OCT. 10&13, 1879

Anti-Chinese Association led by Noah Shakespeare replaces the short-lived WPA. Shakespeare condemns employment of Chinese on railway construction, criticizes government failure to discourage their immigration and promotes legislation emulating Australia's Queensland's Act.

-COLONIST, APRIL 20. 1880

Mr. Beaven- "Whereas the Legislature of Queensland passed an Act entitled the "Chinese Immigrant Regulation Act," which has received the assent of the Imperial Government, the principles of which if made law by the Parliament of Canada would beneficially regulate the immigration of Chinese into the Province; be it therefore resolved, that the Government of the Dominion of Canada be requested by this Legislature by telegram to cause a similar act to become law during the present session of the

Parliament of Canada."

Finance Minister, Robert Beaven, during 3rd session of the Provincial Legislature moved to pass an act similar to the Queensland Act in Australia which levied a 15 pound tax per year on Chinese for a free miner's license and doubled the cost of licenses for Chinese businesses. Any Chinese found mining or carrying on business without a license or any person employing an unlicensed Chinamen will be liable to a fine not exceeding 25 pounds or 3 months in prison. No Chinese shall be entitled to be naturalized.

-Journals of the House of Commons 1879, app.4

A federal select committee reported that Chinese labour should not be employed on Dominion public works and Chinese immigration should be discouraged – however no action was taken

-COLONIST, APRIL 3, 1880

Arrival of Mr. Onderdonk, the Railway Contractor for Yale to Savona, aggregating 127 miles and requiring of upwards of $9,000,000.....Between 3000 and 4000 men will be employed on the works steadily. The contractors are prepared to pay fair wages, and to do all in their power to encourage white labour and foster industries of the Province

-COLONIST, APRIL 13, 1880

The Anti-Chinese Association sent a delegation to meet Andrew Onderdonk, to ascertain his ideas as to the class of labour he will employ. Mr.Onderdonk assured the deputation that it is his intention to give white labour the preference in all cases, then fall back on French Canadians of Eastern Canada. Should he be unable to obtain a

sufficiency of white labour he will, with reluctance, engage Indians and Chinese.

Mrs. Beckham, Mrs. Grohman, James Fell, Mr. Thompson, Jonathan, and I as well as other invited guests, have met, socially, for tea quite regularly. The current Chinese situation seems to be our major topic of discussion. The consensus seems to be that the Chinese have contributed, immeasurably, in helping to build this new province.

Kwong Lee was the first Chinese company established in Victoria on Cormorant Street in 1858. It was a subsidiary of a company established in San Francisco just a few years earlier. Although Kwong Lee was mainly known for the importation of goods from China, the company and Tai Soong, were also labour contractors who aided and sponsored much of the early Chinese immigration along the west coast of North America. Of the 11 Chinese companies taxed under the new Trade Ordinance, Kwong Lee was the largest company, second only to the Hudson Bay Co., in tax contribution according to 1862 records. Kwong Lee and later Tai Soong were also involved in freighting business. They transported cargo up the Fraser on the Cariboo Road with mule-driven wagons and into the gold fields. Just what proportion of the transport trade they controlled is unknown, but it is evident that they made a major contribution to the provisioning and development of British Columbia.

In 1863, Governor Douglas commissioned the construction of the Cariboo Wagon Road between Fort Yale and Barkerville to provide easier access to the gold fields. According to Mr. Thompson's friend, Walter Moberly, who was the contractor of the Cariboo Road between Lytton and Spence's Bridge, the Chinese were the most satisfactory laborers available, since white laborers, once paid immediately absconded to the gold fields, leaving only their debts in their wake. A thousand Chinese are estimated to have worked on the Cariboo Road and a thousand more building dikes and ditches in Victoria and New Westminster. Mr. Moberly states "all the other contractors on this road experienced the same treatment from their white laborers that befell me. I found all the Chinese employed worked most industriously and faithfully and gave me no trouble." In addition, 200 Chinese worked on the road between Quesnel and Cottonwood, and 500 Chinese helped to string the Western Union telegraph wires from New

Westminster to Quesnel. Construction of many of the major roads, canals, ditches, bridges, tunnels were achieved only with the help of Chinese labour. Many Chinese risked their lives building the early infrastructure for this province. These are but a few of the accomplishments achieved with the help of Chinese labour -- there are many others which have been forgotten and ignored.

During the various district gold rushes, many Chinese claims were challenged by brutality and nefarious legal means. The Chinese generally moved in only after the easy gold had already been mined to avoid unnecessary confrontations with white miners and the loss of lives. They purchased claims at exorbitant prices from departing white miners and gleaned only what was left behind and overlooked.

Prior to the discovery of gold, the main industries in the colony were the fur trade and coal mining in Nanaimo. The primary goal of new immigrants was to search for gold which was the road to easy riches. As gold became more scarce, the people most willing and desperate for employment were the Chinese, who could not wait for the next big gold strike and who would work at wages most white men would rather starve than work for. Logging, fishing and farming, the major industries of our province were all established and built on cheap labour, most of which was supplied by the Chinese. Once businesses were established and flourishing, whites demanded the jobs occupied by the Chinese but at double the wages since the Chinese received only half that of a white worker in Oregon and California. Subjected to public ridicule, employers had no choice but to surrender. Many could only afford to pay their white workers double because their Chinese co-workers worked at half their wage. Chinese labour was subsidizing the higher wages paid to white laborers. Many businesses went broke after hiring all white staff. In the majority of the businesses that survived, the Chinese were forced out and replaced by whites. In the collieries of Nanaimo, the Chinese are used by owners and management to break strikes which arouse the wrath of white workers, their families and friends, who in turn abuse the Chinese, but they never abuse the employers who hire them.

In conclusion, most of our friends feel that what is happening to the Chinese is an unforgiveable travesty of justice and an insult to common decency. If and when the railway is completed, it will be the only impediment that will have prevented British Columbia from becoming a part of

the United States. If the railway fails, our province will undoubtedly fall under American control and the fragmentation of other provinces would eventually follow until the American dream of Manifest Destiny is complete, at the cost of Canadian sovereignty. Once the Chinese have been recognized for helping to save Canada from this fate, we are hopeful that the lies and distortions perpetuated by the newspapers and local politicians for their personal gain will subside, but presently the voices for truth and justice are drowning in a sea of ignorance, fear and hatred.

Louisa asked me to send you her love and request you find Wing and bring him back as soon as possible.

Your loyal friend,

Nathan Beilihis

A letter from Way was also delivered to the Toi San Society:

Dear Uncle,

I hope that you are well and that your mission to find your son has met with success. I did send a telegram back to my uncle in China. Fortunately, it somehow escaped the scrutiny of his wife; he is planning to meet us in San Francisco at the end of March. He hopes that you will have found your son by that time. If not, then he and I must attempt the mission without you. He has requested that you address any further correspondence to the local school where his children attend, to avoid any problems with his wife. His heart is filled with joy to know that you are alive and have produced a daughter and three fine sons. He deeply regrets the loss in communication, since the distance between our villages are so insignificant compared to the distances that you and he have travelled together in the past. He said that he planned to visit you on several occasions but he has a very clever wife who can doom the plans of any man. The less his wife knows the better.

My Uncle requested that I not proceed, until I receive a telegram informing us of his travel plans. According to those who have recently returned from California, he thinks that it is very dangerous there right now for all Chinese and that the mission must be carefully planned to avoid failure. He said that you have the best chance of finding your son alone and that I will only get in the way since railway work is very dangerous and you must focus on finding Wing without worrying about my safety. I hope that he is right because I cannot help feeling responsible for Wing's disappearance. Please keep me informed of your progress.

Our villagers are panning for gold north of Yale. They left a message at the brotherhood society for me to meet with them in Yale. Their claim has not been filed because they fear the claim would be stolen. They wish to keep the location a secret because they are fearful of bandits and thieves. I look forward to seeing how the tears from the sun are harvested from the earth.

I will check for any communications from you at the Toi San Society.

Tan Way Cheung

Cheung left a message for Way at the brotherhood society:

Way,

I have not found Wing but in my dreams he is alive and in good health. I find it strange that I cannot find him among the other laborers. I have won many friends while performing my duties. Even though I could trust many of them to help me find Wing, revealing my search may endanger Wing even more. There are those who would use this information to their advantage.

Please ask for me at the labour encampment, on the northern outskirts of town when you return.

Dai Woo Cheung

Cheung struggled with the decision whether to continue searching for Wing or accompanying Way to California. Wing had been working somewhere on the railway when work had been halted. Why wasn't he present in the encampment with the other Chinese laborers? Cheung trusted his dreams and was confident that he would see his son again. Cheung's dreams were only fragmentary glimpses of the future and easy to misinterpret. The question was always when would the event occur and how to prepare wisely. When would his path and that of his son's intertwine?

Chapter 11

The Arrival of Hope

ON THE EVENING OF MARCH 5TH WAY ARRIVED IN YALE. HE WAS accompanied by 5 men in a horse-drawn wagon and dropped off just outside of town to avoid the curiosity of strangers. He and another man strolled cautiously through the backstreets each laden with heavy knapsacks. Four others followed and watched from a safe distance. Way checked for messages at the brotherhood society. He quickly read Cheung's message. He rented two lockers to store the contents of the knapsacks and paid for overnight accommodation for all six men. Once unpacked the groups met at a Chinese restaurant nearby and shared dinner. After the meal the group returned to the brotherhood society to sleep. Early the next morning the group found the local Chinese bath-house, each member enjoyed a long hot bath and a shave. After changing into clean clothes, two of the men visited the Chinese mercantile to buy supplies. The men separated but re-united on the outskirts of town where the wagon had been hidden. Way bid his companions farewell and trudged through the melting snow north toward the Chinese encampment.

As he approached the camp, he could see the rising columns of smoke from innumerable campfires. The heavy scent of cedar and pine permeated the air. The campfires crackled and hissed from the burning of unseasoned

firewood. It was mid-morning and there was very little activity stirring. Sickly thin faces with sunken eyes peered at him beneath head-cloaked blankets as winter survivors listlessly huddled around campfires. Two ghostly figures wrapped in ragged garments passed by, dragging a corpse through Snow-covered maze of tents, lean-to's and patchwork shacks.

As Way wandered through the encampment searching for Cheung, he was bombarded with the same questions.

"Who are you?"

"What district are you from?"

"Do you have food?"

"Do you have any medicine?"

"Do you have any news?"

A growing crowd surrounded him. Shocked by the desperate conditions, Way removed the food articles from his knapsack and handed them out. After answering questions he asked.*"Do you know where I can find Dai Woo Cheung?"* Fingers in ragged cloth pointed the way.

Way walked towards the far side on the encampment repeatedly shouting *"Dai Woo Cheung"*. One after another, more haggard figures directed him onward.

Finally, a familiar voice replied, *"Way, over here."*

The two men embraced. Cheung tried to restrain his emotion, as he brushed back a flood of tears.

"Uncle, was it that bad?"

Cheung gave a nod pausing to think how to describe the horror that he had witnessed, but he was at a loss for words. Finally,he shook his head in tearful frustration.

When they were alone inside Cheung's tent Way smiled than tucked a hand inside his jacket, pulled something out and slipped a small pouch into Cheung's hand. The weight of the pouch was immediately recognized. *"Uncle, heaven has embraced me with kindness. Please accept this gift. Heaven smiles on those who share."*

"Way I cannot accept this. You could find a wife, raise a family, buy a home and live comfortably in China with this much gold. It is far too generous a gift, even though I could use it here to restore hope."

"Uncle, I have more in storage at our brotherhood society. Our villagers cannot sell their gold without arousing suspicion so they have entrusted me to store it for

them. *In your hands is only half of my share. I gladly share it all with you. I feel obligated to help you find Wing but I have been forbidden by my uncle. Please accept this gift and do with it whatever you like. No one will know where you found it."* Way smiled and acknowledged the inference for secrecy. A fit of laughter erupted between the two.

"*Uncle I must now return to town and make plans for my trip to San Francisco. I will buy you dinner in town tonight. We can meet at the society hall at dinner time. I have much to tell you about my experience harvesting the tears of the sun. There are enormous opportunities and many hidden riches in these mountains."*

After Way departed, Cheung wondered how to best use the gold. He decided to visit On Lee, the Chinese merchant who had been the most generous benefactor in town, during his winter campaign for donations. The merchant arranged to exchange the gold for cash with no questions asked. Cheung sent for representatives from each clan. Tents in the encampment wereassembled according to regional dialect, village ties and ancestry. He instructed representatives not to disclose where the money was acquired then he distributed money for food and supplies, based on the size and needs of each represented group. Fish and meat were purchased from the natives so as not to arouse suspicion in town with the sudden appearance of cash. The representatives were instructed to buy all their rice and sundries from On Lee, who exchanged the gold. Medical supplies were acquired with the help of Dr. Sweat. When the supplies arrived in the afternoon the anticipation of food lifted the spirit within the encampment. Wary faces smiled again, woeful eyes brightened, the silence of misery was broken. Hope was renewed, some even joked about their past misery and suffering.

Fearful of wasting resources, Cheung warned that eating too much too soon after long periods of starvation would lead to nausea and vomiting. To prevent wasting food, the cooks were instructed to make rice porridge with the addition of eggs, finely chopped pieces of fresh meat and fresh vegetables. No one was to receive more than one bowl on the first day, one in the morning and one at dinner on the second, then normal meals afterwards. Rice porridge was generally served at breakfast time, it combined cooked rice and leftovers in a soup. This style of cuisine would be easier for the long-deprived survivors to digest. The hungry workers had been delighted with the prospect of finally eating proper rice acquired from town instead of the mush supplied by the railway company. At first, many were disheartened to

receive proper rice in the form of porridge but their stomachs were thankful to be filled after months of deprivation.

As evening approached Cheung entered the huiguan (brotherhood society). A large rectangular table occupies the center of the front lobby. On top of the table were a scattered pile of Chinese books and old newspapers. Chairs and benches lined the front and side walls. The reception desk occupied the back wall. Smoke and the stale odour of tobacco lingered throughout the room. A few men were seated at the table, as a literate member of the group read a magazine article for the rest. Cheung was greeted cordially by the receptionist. Activity ceased momentarily as others got up to greet the doctor. Across the room Way quietly watched the homage of respect paid to his friend by the locals. With a slight tilt of the head, he acknowledged Cheung, walked past him, out the front door to avoid any unnecessary questions about their relationship, or the reason for his presence in Yale.

Cheung lagged behind. Way was not outside, so Cheung headed for the nearest Chinese restaurant. He greeted a couple of ragged men on the walkway who were peering inside the restaurant window. In an isolated corner of the restaurant Way sat at a small table. "*Uncle I have already ordered. They have very limited provisions.*"

"*No whatever you have ordered will be fine. I must thank you again for your generosity. You have restored the hopes of the whole encampment.*"

"*Uncle do you need more?*"

"*No I still have some left. Hope has been restored. The more I distribute the faster it will be spent. Their needs are endless your funds are not. Learning self-restraint and moderation is the key for survival. Overfilling their cup benefits no one. The river banks are thawing so supplies and provisions will arrive shortly. Work on the railway will resume very soon.*"

Way had ordered the dishes available. After all the dishes had arrived. "*Uncle I am sorry for the poor selection of dishes. Please eat.*"

"*Way, I understand. This meal is better than anything I have eaten in 3 or 4 months. I ate mostly to maintain my health no more. The natives always fed me in return for my service. I ate sparingly because I had to beg the locals for food and supplies to support the sick and starving. If I appeared over-nourished it would have been a problem because no one gives to a fat beggar. I needed to pace my spending based on my savings available in Yale. I ran out of funds two weeks ago since I underestimated the duration of winter. By the way, if you need any of*

gold exchanged for cash my friend the merchant On Lee can do it for you without asking any questions. He has supported us generously throughout the winter ordeal and can be trusted to keep all business affairs confidential."

"Uncle, I will leave a message for my friends to contact this man. The miners will be very pleased to receive this information. They dearly need someone that can be trusted to exchange their gold for cash without arousing curiosity. I have told them that I was leaving to meet my Uncle in California, but that I will return in 2 or 3 months. Uncle, please eat and enjoy the meal."

"Way, tell me about your mining."

" Nearly all of the miners are from our village. They are friends that I have grown up with. Our families have known each other for countless generations. Many of us are related by marriage and have common ancestry. The original group arrived in Gum San at the same time on the same ship. Once they found gold, they sent for more workers from the village to participate. They became successful because they could build immense water-wheels and wing dams to detour creeks and rivers to access the gold lying on the river bottom. Water-wheels have been used in southern China for centuries. Most white miners do not have this knowledge, the skill or the same cohesiveness to work together since their past have no common foundation. So lacking the manpower and skill to fully access the gold, most white miners quit when they think the gold is too difficult to reach. So we can profit from claims which white miners abandon."

"Will this cause resentment towards your group?"

"Not if they don't know, that is why we operate in secrecy and deal only with merchants that we trust. We buy in small volumes, using different members of our group to cloak our success. Big purchases like horses, wagons and mining equipment must be made through intermediaries. I think your friend On Lee will be very useful to us."

As the two ate Way reached into his coat pocket and took out a hand-sized object wrapped in cloth. Sliding it under the table, he placed it on Cheung's lap. It was a heavy stone cut in half. Cheung pushed back in his chair to gain more light. As he gazed down at the polished interior of the stone the dark greenish interior was exposed. Cheung was shocked. He whispered "Is this jade?"

"Yes uncle, I think so. A mountain near our campsite is full of these rocks. I have found boulders the size of an ox. The others don't know yet but I intend to share the secret with them once I confirm it is jade in San Francisco. Having it confirmed

here would raise too much curiosity and could endanger us. The message that I will leave for the miners will include a description of your work for our countrymen and your assistance in resolving our biggest problem which is exchanging their gold for cash. Some of the miners are runaways from railway camps. I am sure they will accept you as a partner if you wish to join us."

"I am overwhelmed by your generosity but I do not know if I can accept your offer until I find Wing and complete the mission in California. I have decided to accompany you to California. It will be very dangerous and I cannot bear the thought of others risking their life to fulfill a promise that I have made. I will trust my son's instinct to survive until I return. I know our paths will cross in the future. I have seen it in my dreams."

Once the meal was finished Way paid the bill. As the waiters approached to clear the table Cheung waved them back. He turned to Way *"I will be back shortly."* He walked towards the entrance. Opening the front door, he ushered in the two ragged men that he passed earlier. They followed him to the table. He said to them. *"Please fill your stomachs."* Way bowed, acknowledging the breadth of his friend's humanity..

As the river thawed the paddle-wheelers returned to service. Cheung notified the CPR head office in Yale that he was leaving but hoped to return in a few months to resume his duties.

The head office is shocked. In mocking tone, one of the two executives said "What about your son? Don't you want to find him?"

As the executives exchanged looks of mutual humour, Cheung instantly grasped why the search for his son had been so futile. These men were taunting him, so they obviously knew where Wing could be located but weren't going to disclose it. He concluded these men were probably hiding his son. He looked back disdainfully and decided that no deals could be made with men without morals,. He replied "I will return."

The men smiled at each other and laughed, "we are sure you will."

Before his departure, Cheung arranged to provide Dr. Sweat with his best trainee, as his replacement.

The next day, Cheung and Way left on board the William Irving for New Westminster. They spent the night at the Hoi Sen Society. The next day, they boarded the Princess Louise from New Westminster to Victoria. When the two arrived in Victoria, Cheung and Way headed immediately to

Chinatown. It was mid-afternoon and the sky was overcast with light clouds. Chinatown was quiet and the streets were nearly empty.

As the pair arrived at the store, Quan Li greeted his boss *"Cheung my friend how are you? I did not expect to see you so soon. Have you found Wing?"*

"I am fine, Quan Li. Wing is still missing."

" May Yun has visited our store several times in hopes of finding news about Wing? I told her that you know that I cannot read, so you will probably not write to me directly, but she is a very determined young girl. All the men in Chinatown love talking to her because they are so thrilled that she will speak with them."

" It looks like you have fully recovered. Do you feel well?" asked Cheung.

"I am as well as can be expected but very happy to see you. Business is so slow I laid off many of our staff. Most of the locals have left town to work on the railway. Have you found out any more information about Wing?"

"I know that he is alive but I do not know where he is."

"You are sure that he is alive?"

"Yes, I must trust my dreams and his instinct to survive until I return from my mission to California. Oh Quan Li, this is Tan Way Cheung, the nephew of our friend, Tan Sung Yuen."

"I am very honoured to meet you, little brother. Your uncle and I are old friends. Is my old friend here in Gum San or still in China?"

"He is in China but he plans to meet us in San Francisco."

"Quan Li, Yuen and I made a promise to my father and his friends in California long before we met you. I did not plan to postpone my search for Wing, but this may be our best chance to accomplish the task. I will tell you all about it after the mission has been completed. May Yun must not know that I was in town. She would grieve needlessly and not understand how I could delay the search for my son."

Understanding his friend's wish not to query any further Quan Li said. *"As you wish, my friend. Should I find you accommodations for the night?"*

"No I wish to be seen by no one. Can we sleep on the floor at the back room? We will leave for San Francisco as soon as possible. Can you give me the keys to my locker at the back?"

Quan Li handed Cheung the key. *"There are blankets and beds at the back that I rent out but for the past few weeks, there has been no one to rent to. Should I fetch some dinner for you while you get settled? My friends you must be hungry."*

Quan Li locked up and quickly disappeared out the front door. Twenty minutes later he returned with food and a pot of hot jasmine tea in a large wicker basket. As the three men ate Quan Li recounted some issues of interest. *"Cheung, things are getting worse for us. The city government wants to reduce the age for paying the school tax because they realize most of Chinese immigrants in Chinatown are very young. They will force us to pay it even though we have no children that use their schools. Who can afford to bring a wife or children unless they are wealthy? They tried to enforce a Chinese Tax in 1878. When we would not pay, they seized our goods and sold them off. When the national government declared that the confiscation of goods was unlawful, the province was forced to pay for the goods taken, but we received only a fraction of the value of our goods. Now they want to levy a special import tax solely on rice, and the local Anti-Chinese Society want to stop the railway company from hiring Chinese laborers. How can they hate us so much? We treat them with kindness and respect, and they treat us like dogs."*

Cheung paused momentarily to drink. He grimaced from the taste of cold tea. *"For us this land is like bitter tea. It quenches the thirst but not the soul. Liberty and justice in Gum San is only for others who share common ancestry with those that rule."*

After the meal was finished Cheung collected and repacked the dishes that have been provided by the restaurant. Lining the interior of the wicker food basket was a page from the "Daily British Colonist" a few days old, dated March 12th. As Cheung picked it up to discard his curiosity was aroused by an article on page two entitled "Anti-Chinese Society". Hmmm, just as Quan Li had related. Right below was another article "The Chinese in New York" It described the experiences of some Chinese families in San Francisco who are fleeing to other cities New York in particular because of the threat of violence and the possibility of a general massacre. The long article concluded: "The California movement is spreading terror among Chinamen. They are arriving at a rate of twenty a day." Cheung folded the paper and tucked it in his pocket.

When they were alone Cheung handed the paper to Way who read it carefully. With a puzzled look Way eyed his friend. *"At least we know now what to expect. It is as my uncle described to me in his recent letter."*

"This mission is not your promise to fulfill, but mine and your uncle's. It may be a very dangerous mission to complete. Your future is filled with great promise, do

not undertake foolish risks. Forget this mission and please return to mining with your friends."

With a defiant grin, Way responded. *"Uncle, you forget. You made a promise to your father, but I made a promise to my uncle. I must keep my promise too."*

Cheung smiled, shaking his head in mock frustration. *"Often, Way, all that separates courage from foolishness is profound ignorance."* Both men laugh.

Chapter 12

The Journey to California

ON MARCH 21ST, CHEUNG AND WAY BOARDED A SIDE-WHEEL steamship the SS *Idaho* (Idaho state was supposedly named after this vessel). To avoid unwanted confrontations with fellow passengers, the two men decided it would be wiser to travel on a less populated cargo vessel rather than a passenger vessel to San Francisco. Before heading south, the ship was on its way to the settlement at Nootka Sound to pick up a cargo of lumber. As the sole passengers on board, Cheung and Way strolled the deck of the *Idaho*. Along the shoreline near the settlement Cheung noticed a group of tall carved poles decorated with bright coloured animal figures. He pointed out the objects *"Way, look over there. Do you recognize those poles?"*

"They look like huabiao, the traditional poles standing at the entrance of villages in southern China. These poles told visitors about the ancestry and customs of the village."

"I remember being told of an English explorer who abandoned 50 or more Chinese artisans and laborers a hundred years ago on the west coast of Vancouver Island. This must be the area where the Chinese were left. I suspect these huabiao were erected along the shoreline facing the ocean to act as a rescue beacon for Chinese vessels passing by, to pick up their stranded and shipwrecked countrymen. It seems logical because the development of this art-form would have been very

difficult to achieve without the use of metal tools and the knowledge of making dyes. The bright red dye used is easy to recognize. It is called vermilion made from the henna plant which only grows in tropical climates. Buddhist monks make this dye using a formula that they kept secret for many centuries. The work on these individual poles must have taken years to complete. Constructing these poles would seem impractical for hunters and gatherers, who follow the annual migration of fish and game and the seasonal harvest of wild plants and berries."

"Uncle, I agree. The designs on the poles appear very similar to our pai lau (Chinese monuments) and Chinese artwork such as ceremonial masked and statues. During our search for you, Wing and I stayed overnight in a native village, I noticed that the natives also worship their ancestors. The links between our peoples are many. These people and ours once shared the same path."

Once docked the cargo of lumber was quickly loaded. Some of the natives helping to load the lumber had Chinese facial features but were strongly built, larger in stature and much darker in complexion than the men from Guangdong province. Cheung waved and called out to the laborers in Chinese.

"Little brothers, where are your fathers from?" The natives were temporarily bewildered. Cheung repeated his query several times. Work came to a halt, as a few gathered to parley in their native tongue. When the dock foreman noticed the stoppage he barked out "Come on you lot, we haven't time to tarry."

The natives smiled and waved back in response to Cheung and Way, then resumed loading.

"Uncle, our thoughts about their past may be correct. They must share our ancestry. It will be interesting to explore how our people may have influenced the native communities over time. I would think that our early countrymen made a greater impact here, than elsewhere in this land of ignorance and hostility."

The *Idaho* departed as soon as the cargo had been fully loaded. On the shore, a small group of native workers lined the wharf, waving to their brethren from the past. During the voyage to San Francisco the weather was pleasant and the sea was calm. The galley was solely staffed by Chinese. Inquisitive as to the dangers that laid ahead in San Francisco, the two travelers requested to eat all their meals with the galley staff. Cheung and Way cautiously responded to queries relating to their journey. The four galley members were fascinated with the adventures of their two dinner guests

and each revealed his family history and his personal account of his journey to Gum San.

Cheung addressed the chief cook. "Honourable sir, the individual crew members on board seem very kind and polite compared to most lofan that we have encountered."

The head cook Chiu responded. "We feed these men very well. They like the food that we cook for them. Some took time to adjust to our cooking, but now they all flock to the dining room in anticipation. They are easily pleased with very basic Chinese dishes. They will eat almost anything stirred-fried with oyster or soya sauce, I surprise them occasionally with our traditional dishes on special occasions, depending on whether the ingredients are available. When new crew members arrive, their disposition may be crude and abrupt like the locals on shore but they gradually soften due to pressure exerted by the rest of the crew, especially the Captain, boatswain and first mate whose table get special treatment. Our galley members have nurtured many friendships with white crew members. Our Captain is a good leader and commands great respect from his crew."

Cheung smiled "Mr.Chiu, I applaud your course of action. Common sense and good leadership will always overcome ignorance. Can you tell us about any dangers in San Francisco?"

"Mr. Dai, my staff and I have no problems. Captain Alexander always sends two crew members to escort us to Chinatown. We always leave later when the streets are sparsely inhabited. It is a very short walk to Chinatown. The mood of locals is very hateful towards our people. The white workers hate us because of the lack of jobs. They cannot compete with Chinese labour because we work twice as hard for half the pay. We are peasant farmers accustomed to working from dawn to dusk. They are miners and adventurers who have dreamt only of easy wealth and many have never worked a single day as hard as we have worked each and every day of our lives. We never drink and are therefore always more reliable. We follow orders without complaints or questioning authority. Also we won't band together to form a union to demand higher wages or better working conditions. So employers always prefer to hire us while white workers prefer to blame us instead of improving their self-discipline and work habits. They will not blame the employers who hire us as strike-breakers for fear of loss of future job opportunities. In return they taunt us with name-calling, threats and occasional acts of violence to make our working here as unbearable as possible. We cannot leave. Even at the cost of losing our lives we must stay and work because our families in China will

otherwise starve. Some families must sell a child into slavery in order for the rest of the family to survive. We cannot even afford to die, or our families must pay our unpaid debts according to our labour contracts. The only way my family can repay my debts is to indenture my son or daughter into slavery. The fear of my daughter becoming a prostitute is unbearable and haunts me every day. I work as hard as I can, so this will not happen. Each man in the galley is from my village and has a family to feed, otherwise I would not have chosen him as a member of my galley crew. We all share similar fears." Cheung gave the galley crew a token bow of respect. Way did likewise.

Chiu continued. "An agitator by the name of Dennis Kearney is promoting our expulsion from California as well as the United States. Many Chinese who can afford it are returning home to China, some are leaving for the eastern states, some north to Canada, because of the mounting violence that he has promoted. The Captain and various members of the crew have kept us informed on issues dealing with our safety. Many laws are being changed for Chinese arriving in Gum San. Officers from the Customs Service greet every ship that arrives in San Francisco Bay. You must talk with the Captain so you will be prepared for their arrival. Come, let us talk with him." Chiu led the pair to the Captain's table.

As the chief cook, Cheung and Way approached the Captain's table. "Chiu, thank you for the exceptional meal. Mr. Dai, Mr. Tan, I hope you are enjoying the voyage."

Chiu acknowledged the Captain's compliment with a smile of acknowledgement and a polite nod. He bowed, and then returned to join his table. The Captain offered his hand to the two passengers, and the two senior officers followed suit.

Cheung inquired, "Captain, we are concerned with safety issues in California and seek advice on how best to avoid unnecessary conflicts with customs officials. The galley crew has warned us to stay within the borders of Chinatown to ensure our personal safety, but our journey takes us outside these boundaries."

"As far as your safety Mr. Dai, let me get you some recent articles published on the topic." The Captain departed from the dining room and returned with a mixed stack of tattered newspapers and periodicals. "The welfare and safety of my crew is of utmost importance to me, on as well as off my ship. I have collected these articles so I can alert Chiu and his staff about the dangers awaiting them on shore. I have been to the courthouse

on several occasions to rescue them and I don't relish the thought of repeating the experience too often. Mr. Dai, let me read some of these articles for you. Here is a quote from an article from a magazine called *Our New West* by Samuel Bowles –"To abuse and cheat a Chinaman; to rob him; to kick and cuff him; even to kill him have been things done not only with impunity by mean and wicked men but by respectable citizens as well with vain glory." Here is another article written by the editor of *The Montanian*. "We don't mind hearing about a Chinaman being killed now and then, but it's been coming too thick of late. Don't kill them unless they deserve it, but when they do, why kill'em, lots." Mr. Dai, you should also be advised that California law prohibits Chinese from appearing in court to confront a white citizen. Here's an article from our local newspaper, Judge Roy Bean in Texas recently dismissed a murder case against a man, stating "I can't find nothing where it said it's against the law to kill a Chinaman." Many of our cities have passed laws prohibiting Chinese living within city limits, buying or owning property, voting or even walking on sidewalks. A town in Montana even prohibits whites from dining in Chinese restaurants. In 1879 the constitution of California was rewritten forbidding anyone of Chinese or Mongolian ancestry from earning a living by working for a white man. Last year the Governor of California announced on March 4,1880 a public holiday for anti-Chinese demonstrations. I've heard and read of stories of Chinamen in California being scalped, their pigtails and ears cut off and branded with hot irons; the genitals of a Chinese miner were sliced off by a mob and displayed as a trophy at a bar; in Nevada a laundryman was tied to the wagon wheel of a buckboard which was repeatedly driven through town until his head fell off; in Chico on March 13, 1877, five Chinese farm workers were shot, douse with oil and set ablaze. On the evening of October 24th in 1871 the Chinese Massacre took place in Los Angeles: when a white man was accidently killed caught in a crossfire between 2 rival Chinese gangs in Chinatown, it sparked a riot in which over twenty innocent Chinese including women and children were killed. Some were lynched or burned alive by angry mobs of several hundred white men. Homes throughout Chinatown were looted and burned. A well-respected Chinese doctor was found dangling in his home, his money taken and his ring finger was hacked off for the sake of his ring. During the looting of his residence the mob found a 12-year-old boy paralyzed with fear who just arrived one month earlier and couldn't

speak a word of English. They hung him too. About fifty Chinese were also beaten and found hanging by their pigtails after the riot. In July 1877 ten thousand agitators marched through Chinatown in San Francisco destroying Chinese laundries, burning Chinese buildings and shooting Chinese bystanders. The National Guard and several hundred volunteers were summoned to stop the violence. The mob tried to burn the docks and ships of the Pacific Mail Steamship Company, the primary transporter of Chinese laborers. The mob even attacked the firemen trying to extinguish the fires. The riot lasted 3 days and was quelled with the help of the US Navy and four thousand volunteers. I suspect that many more acts of brutality occurred that have not been reported because the law prefers to look the other way. Does this answer your question about safety Mr. Dai? There is no protection for you or Mr. Tan in California or anywhere on the west coast. I hear rumblings that there is trouble afoot again in Chinatown. I have warned our Chinese crew members that some of our deckhands have overheard of attacks being planned in Chinatown very soon. Please proceed with utmost caution if you plan to disembark in San Francisco. Now as far as those pirates from the customs department, they will board us as soon as we drop anchor, unless the fog is too thick for them to see us arrive through their spyglasses. Steerage passengers and their belongings would have been sent directly to their detention facilities. Since you are cabin-class passengers they will inspect your belongings on board. They may relieve you of some or all of your cash as well as your valuables as contraband. Then a tug called the "Inspector" will arrive with the Quarantine Officer from the Board of Health to check you over with a medical examination to protect the country from diseases coming from abroad. At the discretion of this official they may allow you ashore or send you to one of two places. Currently there is an outbreak of small pox in California. If the Quarantine officer suspects you have small pox or any other disease you will be confined to steerage on their quarantine facility, an obsolete Pacific Mail vessel that sits in the harbour. Otherwise you will be sent ashore to their wooden warehouse compound known to as the "shed" at the Pacific Mail Steamship Company dock for quarantine purposes which could be very lengthy, depending on who may come to your rescue, and how much they can squeeze from you or your sponsors. Both facilities are filled with hundreds of detainees awaiting authorization or deportation. Neither facility could entice a starving

bilge rat from a sinking ship. Mr. Dai, Mr. Tan please remember that I tried to discourage you from buying passage to San Francisco but you insisted without an explanation. I would have delved deeper but I was perplexed by your silence. Do you remember?"

The pair responded by nodding simultaneously.

"Well, this is why I asked about your need to go San Francisco. The motive of my passengers is generally never any of my business unless they disclose it. If you wish I can transport you to the Sandwich Islands, our next port of call. It is a tropical paradise and the Chinese inhabitants receive better treatment there. If you decide that you must venture into California, we may be able to avoid interference from the customs inspectors by saying that you and Mr. Tan are en route to Honolulu. This may curtail a full inspection. Then if you still wish to disembark in San Francisco we can row you ashore under the cover of darkness or fog. I suggest that you consider changing into more modest clothing. If you appear too wealthy, the inspectors can always justify a search and seizure for contraband. Leave your cash and valuable belongings with a member of our galley crew. You need not worry about their honesty – Chiu chooses his staff with great discretion. Jobs are very scarce; no one will risk losing his job. Everyone is aware that we treat and pay the Chinese better than any other shipping line."

"Thank you very much Captain, for your kind offer and thoughtful advice. We will consider the options that you have presented to us and will disclose our course of action before we reach San Francisco."

Handshakes were exchanged with the Captain and his officers. They returned to their table and then proceeded to their sleeping quarters. Cheung reflected on his past experience in California. The animosity and irrational violence that he thought would soften with time had only intensified; the seeds of ignorance had blossomed into blind hatred.

"Way, the violence and danger is much worse than I expected. We have no other choice than to proceed because your uncle is on his way and will be expecting us to meet him in San Francisco. Hopefully, he has been informed of the customs officials and the danger that await him in California." Heeding the Captain's advice, Cheung and Way spent the next days planning how to best proceed with their mission.

The *Idaho* arrived in San Francisco harbour on the evening of March the 26th. The voyage from Victoria to San Francisco was completed in 5 days.

Once the dense morning fog had dissipated, the Customs Service vessel appeared early the next morning. The uniformed customs officers made a cursory search, looking for prohibited and dutiable goods. Another vessel arrived, and members of the Public Health Service checked passengers and crew for contagious diseases. Officers of the Immigration Service arrived in a third vessel. As required by the 1820 Steerage Act, the Captain presented the ship's passenger manifest, which listed all persons taken aboard at any given foreign port or place. During the inspection, a large passenger vessel arrived in the harbour. Enticed by the prospect of more lucrative quarry, the officials quickly rushed through their examination of the *Idaho*'s cargo, passengers and crew.

Later in the evening, Cheung and Way accompanied by Chiu were rowed ashore by two deckhands. Once the rowboat docked, the group walked to Chinatown. When they arrived on the outskirts of Chinatown, the deckhands departed to a local tavern, while Chiu remained behind to assist Cheung and Way in finding suitable accommodation. He recommended the International Hotel on Kearney Street between Washington and Jackson Street. The travelers secured a room on the top floor and deposited their luggage. Cheung and Way offered to treat Chiu to dinner in appreciation for his kindness.

The men requested a table on the unoccupied upper mezzanine which extended above the main dining room. During the meal Chiu advised the visitors on the location of the brotherhood society for their clan, criminal activity in Chinatown, local Chinese leadership, health issues, police enforcement, rules pertaining to Chinese immigrants, etc.. *"Chiu, during our walk to Chinatown I noticed some overhead ropes suspended above one of the streets and metal rails set in the paved road. What is that?"*

"Mr. Dai, the cables and tracks are used by horseless carts called cable cars, They were invented here in San Francisco in 1873. Right now there are 3 streets that have these horseless carriages: Clay Street, California Street and Geary Street. Chinese do not use them so as to avoid confrontation with hoodlums. If you see men wearing hats with Chinese queues wrapped around the top, you better distance yourself from them quickly because they have taken the queue from one of our people and are probably members of the Workingmen's Party of California, the Knights of Labour or the Anti-Coolie Club who want to force all Chinese out of the United States. They wear their trophies with pride. Some of them also use

our queues as belts. Also, beware of children who may throw stones when you are not looking. They may spit on us and call us names like chink, celestials, rat-eaters, rice bunchers, slant-eyes while their parents watch in amusement. Chinatown is our only safe haven unless a riot occurs. If that happens, head towards the opposite side of Chinatown from wherever the noise is coming."

"How is business in the city? Is there much prosperity?"

"Too many people and not enough jobs. The major authority in Chinatown is called the Six Companies under the leadership of Chun Ti Chu, who is the main spokesman for Chinatown. The Six Companies has been sending notices back to China to tell our people not to come because the gold is gone, there are no jobs, nowhere to sleep, the voyage is dangerous, locals abuse us with violence, etc.. The shipping lines and labour contractors say lots of gold, lots of jobs, lots of food, everyone will return home rich. The misery of famine, floods, bandits, civil war, and corrupt government officials in China has caused so much desperation and hopelessness; our people will not believe the messages sent by the Six Companies. So boatloads of our countrymen keep arriving, all hoping to find work to feed their families in China. The more who arrive, the greater the competition for jobs, the lower the wages offered by employers and the more we are hated by the locals."

"Does the Kong Chow huiguan (brotherhood society) still exist? Do triad organizations exist here?" asked Cheung.

"The Kong Chow Association was one of the first Chinese organizations formed in America. It still exists but because of clan disputes and problems with district dialects within the organization, the original company split in two then later into six, but they banded together to form the Six Companies, tying all the major brotherhood societies under one banner. The common cause is to legally represent and protect the welfare and interests of their members by representing the Chinese community in dealing with government agencies, resolving disputes between members and assisting those victimized by anti-Chinese activities. In addition, the Six Companies help new arrivals find food, lodging and work, as well as lend money to those in need, and care for members who are injured or sick. They maintain schools, hospitals, and joss temples, organize funerals, return bones of the dead and send money back to China for their members. When a new immigrant arrives, he is solicited by a representative of the Six Company and encouraged to join a brotherhood society, based on his district dialect and clan association. The Six Companies building is located on Clay Street. Most of the residents in Chinatown are registered members under the Six Companies framework. There are a few tongs,

or secret societies, made up of outcasts who lack clan ties or who were expelled from their associations. They follow the same practices as the underground triads who hope to overthrow the Manchu government, but they have no motive other than profiting through prostitution, opium dens and gambling houses. Well, I think I better leave. The deckhands are probably waiting for me at our usual location, to take me back to the ship. Thank you, Mr. Dai, Mr. Tan for the wonderful meal. If there is anything more that I can do for you, please leave me a message at our shipping line office in the harbour. The galley crew and I enjoyed listening to your adventures and those of Mr. Tan's. I wish both of you a safe journey."

"Thank you Chiu, you have been very kind. Your information has been very helpful to us. Please accept our token of appreciation for your kindness."

Cheung handed Chiu a small leather pouch. From the weight of the pouch, Chiu realized that inside the pouch could only be gold. Chiu exhaled slowly, closing his eyes to envision the benefit his hosts had bestowed on the lives of his children. He struggled to fight back tears to avoid embarrassing his benefactors. Unable to speak, he quickly dropped to his knees and performed the kowtow lowering his forehead to the wooden floor, three times.

"Please Chiu, this is not necessary." Cheung and Way approached, and helped Chiu back to his feet. Once Chiu had regained his composure, bows were exchanged between the three men, and Chiu departed.

Cheung rose early the next morning to survey the city from his hotel suite window. The city he once visited with his father and uncle had undergone massive development. When he had first arrived in 1849 the settlement was set in a background of lush green hills, gently sloping down towards shore. The settlement was nothing more than a city of canvas tents with a few adobe huts and lean-to shacks scattered over a series of barren hills. Over the span of thirty years, the muddy wagon trails had given way to streets paved all the way from the harbour to the distant hills. Now banks, hotels and offices lined streets of commerce. There were stately buildings erected of bricks and granite blocks, imported from China and designed in European architectural styles. In the past, dirty ragged miners dressed in canvas trousers and plaid shirts wandered the dirt streets. Now businessmen marched purposefully to the beat of commerce dressed smartly in fine suits, shirts, ties and top-hats. Streets and side-walks were paved and gas street lamps adorn every street. Instead of wagons drawn by horses, mules and oxen, the streets were filled with fancy single horse carriages.

The harbour area had also undergone a massive transformation. Ships of all shapes and sizes filled the harbour, including clippers, paddle-wheelers, and steamers. In the early days of the gold rush, many ships were abandoned by their crew members in search of gold, so deserted ships filled the harbour. The rolling hills were devoid of harvestable timber so the abandoned ships were used for housing, hospitals, taverns, storage facilities and even as prisons. Their canvas sails were used to make tents. Now steamships of every size and type filled the bay and wooden wharves covered the foreshore. Numerous piers extended outward into the harbour. Freighting facilities and equipment littered the docks. Commercial establishments with warehouse facilities lined the harbour shore. Cheung was astounded with the industrial progress in just thirty-two years.

Way quietly washed and dressed while Cheung gazed through the suite window at the city below. "*Good morning Uncle. You must see many changes from when you were last here.*"

"*Yes Way, so many astounding changes in such a short time. After breakfast we will search for your uncle.*"

Someone knocked at the door. Cheung opened the door to find a young Chinese dressed in western attire. "*Mr. Dai, Mr. Tan, I am Lee Sam Ko.*" Bows are exchanged. "*I represent the Six Companies. We have been informed of your arrival by one of our members who works at the hotel. Your associate Tan Sun Yuen arrived a week ago and is being held by the customs service at Pier 40 the Pacific Mail detention barracks. His letter was smuggled out and delivered to us recently. In it, he requested us to contact you as soon as you arrived.*"

"*Mr. Lee, what is the procedure to free our friend? We realize that we should first register with our local society. But what is the next step?*"

"*No need to be formal. Please just call me Ko. I would guess that Yuen's money and valuables have been confiscated as contraband. So I would think that a reasonable bribe or posting a bond will secure his release, but too much too soon will often cost you more. I will not ask how you arrived without being detained by customs, but if you proceed to the detention centre, prepare to be interrogated. You will have to provide evidence of financial support, date of arrival, proof of identity, where you are residing, how long you plan to stay, purpose for coming, etc.. If you cannot prove legal entry, you will be imprisoned and deported.*"

"*What do you suggest, Ko?*"

"Mr. Dai, Mr. Tan you do not know me. I am just a stranger who has knocked on your door. Please come to the Six Companies office after you have breakfast and we can talk there."

"Ko, please join us for breakfast? We have no issue with your identity. Your appearance, knowledge and abilities are proof enough." Ko consented with a bow.

Along the way to the hotel dining room, Ko was greeted by Chinese hotel staff with a bow of recognition in passing. Cheung could see that Ko was known and well-respected. The trio selected a table in a quiet corner of the dining room. Once seated a waiter took their orders. Way sat back quietly, allowing Cheung to address their guest. *"Ko, what do you suggest as the best way to rescue our friend?"*

"You have 3 options. You can hire a lawyer which will be very expensive because the lawyers will prolong the legal process to bleed you for legal fees. If you select this path the customs people will know that you are wealthy and will prolong internment so they can collect the maximum for your friend's room and board. Second option you can hire our association as intermediaries so you will not have to disclose your identities or be interrogated. We will act to post a bond and pay any necessary squeeze (bribes) through our members who are employed as bonding agents, labour contractors and interpreters. The last option you can go to one of the independent tongs (brotherhood societies – literal meaning "meeting hall") that will take your money and promise to perform but may or may not be able to fulfill their obligation. You will have little recourse if they decide to just keep your money and do nothing. If you select us, we will check first to see if the task can be accomplished. If the task is beyond our ability to perform no fee will be charged. Any profit made by our association services support the needs of our whole community in the way of legal fees, medical costs, food and shelter for our homeless, ..."

Cheung interjected, *"Ko we are aware of your organization's work and reputation. We will use your company's services. How do we get started and how much will it cost us?"*

"We will not know the fee until our contacts within the detention facilities inform us. On November 17, 1880 the federal government negotiated the Angell Treaty in Peking to regulate and restrict immigration from China. This is the very first treaty to impose restrictions on immigration of any race into the United States. Enforcement may have increased the risk for anyone who violates or helps others to violate the newly imposed restrictions, so the cost may have risen. So the

fee for service is vague but the more our connections think you have, the more they will charge. That is why squeeze must always be negotiated in earnest, so funds appear limited."

Cheung turned to his companion, "Way, do you have any questions?"

"Have you or anyone seen my uncle? Is he healthy and safe?"

"No, we have not seen him. We only received his message a few days after he arrived. It was smuggled out and passed onto us through one of our members who interprets for the immigration service. That was two days ago. The authorities will not permit visitors because they are afraid visitors will pass information to detainees who will aid them to corroborate statements made by their sponsors during the interrogation process. There are hundreds awaiting their fate at what the locals call "the shed." The more money the detainees have, the longer they will be held. The Pacific Mail Company will charge each guest 40 cents a day for room and board. The conditions there are absolutely deplorable. I have never been there but from what has been described to me, it is still better than the floating snake pits in the harbour which hold hundreds of detainees. Getting your associate out as soon as possible would be your best course of action. If he gets sick or injured he will be sent to a detainee ship in the harbour because the city hospitals refuse to treat Chinese. If this happens, communication may be completely lost."

Way asked, "Thank you Ko. If the Chinese are hated so much here, why do they not leave?"

"Many have left California but most can not afford to gamble on the future of their families to search for better opportunities elsewhere. All the money that they earn has been sent home to China or used to pay debts associated with their labour contracts. Jobs are hard to find even though there are many jobs being advertised in the eastern states and promoted by labour contractors. These jobs are generally only temporary to help employers break strikes. Once the striking workers have yielded to the demands of the employer, the Chinese workers are jobless again and stranded in an even more hostile environment from which they departed. In addition they are deeper in debt, less familiar with the new location, and farther away from access to their home in China."

Ko took out a pocket watch to check the time, "I am sorry but I am late for my next appointment. I must leave now. As soon as I have more information about your associate, I will return to let you know whether or not we can help your friend. Thank you for breakfast. If you drop by our headquarters at 917 Clay

Street they will direct you to your tong. You can pay for your membership there."
Bows are exchanged and Ko departed.

Chapter 13

Internment in San Francisco

TWO DAYS PASSED BY QUICKLY AS CHEUNG AND WAY EXPLORED the wonders of San Francisco Chinatown and its neighbouring areas. On the third morning someone knocked on the door of the suite. Cheung opened the door to find Ko smiling. *"Good morning Mr. Dai, Mr. Tan, I have good news. Your friend is in good health. He can be freed in two to three days once a bond of $500 is posted. When he receives formal authorization to enter the country the bond will be returned. The paperwork for authorization will generally take three to four weeks to process. With so many new arrivals the process may be delayed."*

"That is great news. Can we post the bond without identification? And how much do we owe your company for the service?"

"Without identification, you must trust me to post the bond for you. I can meet with the bonding agent, Joe Tape, and post the bond. Our company will charge a fee of $100 for service. The $500 bond will be returned once an approval has been rendered by the immigration service, or will be forfeited if Mr. Tan does not return."

Cheung left the room and returned holding a small leather pouch. He passed it to Ko. *"I think this should take care of the bond and your company fee. Please keep any excess for yourself. When can we expect to see our friend?"*

"Hopefully he will be released in a few days, I must go to the bank to convert your gold into cash then meet up with the bonding agent. I will inform you as soon as I know when your associate will be released. Thank you for your generosity."

After Ko departed, Cheung and Way visited their *huiguan* in search of advice concerning their trip to Sacramento. Known as the "Canton Company", the Sam Yup Benevolent Association was located on Dupont Street, just a couple of blocks away from the International Hotel. Founded in 1850 during the early gold rush by the Chinatown merchants from the Sam Yup district, it was one of the six original *huiguan* that eventually helped to form the Six Companies. It was the major influence affecting the commercial, social and political affairs of the Chinese in North America.

When Cheung and Way arrived at the Sam Yup Association, they were greeted by a reception clerk, who asked them to fill out application forms. After completing the applications and paying a fee, the pair returned to their hotel. Later in the day a message arrived from the Sam Yup Association, requesting a meeting. When Cheung and Way returned to the Sam Yup building that afternoon, the reception clerk informed them that one of the directors would like to meet with them.

Puzzled by the request, Cheung and Way followed the clerk upstairs to the executive office, *"Mr. Chun will be here, shortly."*

A minute later, a slender middle-aged man dressed in a suit and tie appeared. Short of breath, he bowed with clasped hands, *"Mr. Dai, Mr. Tan, my name is Chun Ti Chu. I am very pleased to meet you. Mr. Dai, your registration stated that you were recently employed by the CPR as a medical assistant, so we asked one of our labour agents about you. He has just returned from Canada. He has informed us of your service in providing medical aid to our contract laborers in Canada. If there is anything we can do for you, it will be our pleasure to assist you. Please sit down. I have ordered dim sum (literal meaning "touch the heart – meat-filled gourmet pastries generally served during lunch) to be served here. What can we do to help you while you are here?"*

Cheung paused for a moment to reflect. With cloaked anger, he spoke, *"Have you been informed about the working and living conditions of the contract laborers in Canada?"*

"Mr. Dai, the organization knows the conditions are very harsh and sometimes deplorable but the conditions are worse in China. The individual labour agents that oversee the contract workers may be members of our brotherhood, but do not

necessarily represent us or our policies. We hire those who are available on location at the opportune time who can speak some semblance of English. We have very little choice in most cases since we only have ex-railway workers and miners who were once peasant farmers to choose from. Most cannot read or write and their virtues can be easily swayed by their pursuit to enrich themselves or to save their own families from starvation. We are sending messages back to China to try to stem the tide of immigration but to no avail. I realize that some of the labour contractors are causing our people misery, suffering and deaths but our resources are limited and our control of the situation in Canada is tenuous. Some in our organization may profit, but our overall objective is to survive so we can serve the needs of the Chinese community."

Appeased by Ti Chu's explanation, *"I apologize for pointing the blame at your organization"* said Cheung more calmly, *"but this winter at the tent camp in Yale has been very severe. I witnessed enough pain, sickness, death and suffering to last a lifetime. These memories still haunt me every night."* Ti Chu bowed his head in sympathy.

The reception clerk arrived with stacked wicker baskets. Ti Chu directed his visitors to a table overlooking the street, *"I understand, please have a seat."* An assortment of seafood and meat pastries are placed on the table, Ti Chu said, *"please help yourself."*

An hour passed quickly as the three men relaxed and related their personal journeys. Then Cheung asked Ti Chu, *"What do you think of the future of the Chinese in America? What can we expect will happen?"*

"Do you mind if I give you a short history lesson on the Chinese in America while you eat?"

Cheung and Way concurred with a nod.

"As you know the legal punishment for emigration from imperial China was death by decapitation. An imperial edict in 1712 requested foreign governments to send back expatriates so that they might be executed. Yet many tens of thousands of Chinese defied the law to seek their fortunes in other lands. They knew the punishment was rarely enforced because officials could be easily bribed. The saying in the south was "The mountain is high, and the Emperor is far away". At the end of the eighteenth century the infrastructure of China was starting to collapse from wasteful extravagance and political corruption. The booming population created massive shortages which led to higher prices, a catastrophe for the poor. Under the pressure of overpopulation, the Opium wars, civil unrest, and economic crisis the

Qing dynasty attempted to maintain its extravagance and ineptness by increasing taxes, sometimes many years in advance. Desperate peasants traveled overseas seeking jobs to earn enough to feed their families. The early Chinese immigrants to America were mostly all from Guangdong.

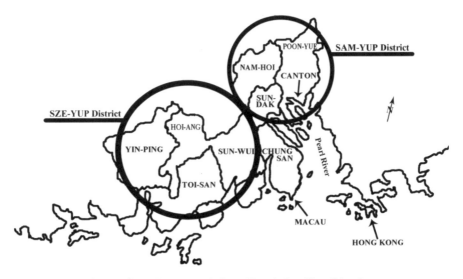

Guangdong Province & Sam Yup & Sze Yup Districts.

They came mainly from three neighbouring districts of Chung-san, Sam-yup and Sze-yup. Eighty percent came from Sze Yup which includes the counties of Toi-san, Hoi-ping, Yin-ping and Sun-wui. Fifty percent of those came from Toi-san. Over the years the local Chinese have learned many painful lessons concerning false promises, western politicians and labour movements. The British needed cheap labour to develop their colonial enterprises after they abolished slavery in 1833. They decided to replace their slaves with coolies. For plantation owners this was found to be even better than slavery because employers were relieved of housing, feeding and caring for their workers. As a result the colonies prospered, as well as the British and American shipping lines, that converted their slave ships to transport these slaves of poverty. They commissioned labour contractors to recruit illiterate peasants who signed five to seven contracts. In China we called their recruitment enterprise, the pig trade, because the victims were caged like pigs. Many were kidnapped from the ports of Hong Kong, Shanghai, Macao, Canton, Amoy, Ningpo, etc.. No man could leave home to travel on public roads without fear of being taken. Under false pretences of debt or delinquency, they could be carried off

by armed thugs, to be sold to the pig traders at so much a head, never to be seen again. Many individuals such as Shanghai Brown, Shanghai Kelly, Mother Brown and Miss Piggot became quite notorious for their harvest of piglets. Once locked up in the shipping line's barracoons or "pigpens," they were starved, whipped and beaten into submission with little chance to escape from servitude. From 1847 to 1855, over 10,000 Chinese coolies were imported into Cuba. An edict announced by the Chinese Emperor, forbidding coolie emigration was being brazenly violated by British, American and French shipmasters. Many mutinies were reported. When the Chinese discovered they had been tricked into slavery some ships were burned at sea by Chinese mutineers who preferred death to enslavement. Many captives committed suicide en route. During the early days of contract labour which started in 1845 the mortality rate on these floating hell-holes across the Pacific to South America was about three out of each ten laborers due to overcrowding, filthy living conditions, disease, malnutrition and dehydration. Murder and riots were common occurrences during these voyages. After observing the success of coolie labour in Peru, Cuba, Hawaii, Trinidad, British Guiana, Jamaica, Malay, British Borneo and other countries, the plantation owners of America emulated their British counterparts, but to a greater extent, after the civil war when slavery was abolished. The Qing government lodged several protests with the American government after many years of reported scandals. The American ambassador John E. Ward (1858-1861), claimed although the vessels carrying the Chinese were American, the recruiters were foreign nationals over whom he had no jurisdiction. In need of cheap labour to complete railway construction, the railway companies petitioned the government to encourage more Chinese immigration. The US government negotiated the Burlingame Treaty in 1868 with China to allow Chinese citizens easier emigration access to America, granting them most favoured nation status (special privileges granted to foreigners of a specified nation to encourage trade) but denying them the right to naturalization. At the peak of construction, the Central Pacific had more than 10,000 Chinese workers under contract. In 1867, two thousand Chinese working for the Central Pacific, performing the most dangerous work of blasting tunnels, went on strike. Their main demands were for equal pay and an equal work day comparable to white workers; to no longer to be whipped or beaten; and not to be restrained from seeking employment elsewhere. The head of construction for the Central Pacific, Charles Crocker, quickly terminated the strike by denying the Chinese food and water until they went back to work. When the railway was completed, many of the Chinese turned to farming.

Some traveled to the Sacramento region working to drain swampland. Most of the agricultural labour force in California is Chinese. Some farmers who hire Chinese laborers are being threatened and harassed by angry whites. Many large ranchers and farmers watched their farms, factories and vineyards mysteriously go up in flames forcing them to replace their Chinese workers with whites.

Many ex-railway workers were once fishermen in China. After the gold rush and the completion of the railway, some workers banded together in small fishing villages to form the first commercial fishery in California. They harvested, salted, dried, boxed and shipped all kinds of fish such as flounder, mackerel, shark, bluefish, salmon, cod, sardines, and shellfish such as crabs, lobster, shrimp, clams, oysters and abalone, to China, Japan, and the Sandwich Islands. They introduced and popularized the eating of shellfish in the West. All the fishing fleets from Southern California to Washington State were once totally owned by the Chinese. Afterwards the Greeks, Italians and Slavs from the Balkans started to move in. They organized and banded together to petition the California legislature for a tax on Chinese fisherman. The Chinese Fisherman Tax was passed in 1860. The government restricted the mesh size of Chinese fishing nets used to catch shrimp in the 70s and withheld fishing licenses from aliens ineligible for naturalization, which affected only the Chinese; now they want to restrict the type of vessel allowed in American waters because the Chinese use junks. While the federal government debates the constitutionality of these state laws, local enforcement of these regulations devastates Chinese fisheries. Almost all manufacturing industries in California of clothing, shoes, boots, woollens, cigars, canneries, lumber mills, vineyards etc., started and flourished with the use of Chinese labour and Chinese ingenuity but once these industries become established, the Chinese are eliminated by organized labour supported by government legislation. There are some Chinese who have had reasonable success operating their own businesses as long as they do not compete with white businesses. Chinese cigar factories were once very successful here because their products were similar in quality but lower-priced than American cigars. The public could not distinguish between Chinese and American-made cigars until a union leader named Samuel Gompers came up with the idea of putting a ring around American-made cigars so the public could distinguish between manufacturers. This put all the Chinese cigar factories out of business. The labour situation will only get worse for us in California. When the civil war and railway construction came to an end, it left thousands unemployed. The railways and shipping lines grow rich selling hopes and dreams to unemployed

veterans, freed slaves, adventurers, and hopeful immigrants from Europe. As a result, trainloads from the east and shiploads from Asia arrive almost daily. California realizes something must be done to curb the growing threat of disaster. So they appeal for help from the federal government, who protect their mandate by passing laws recommended by the local authorities to limit Chinese immigration. The Civil Rights Act and the Page Act of 1875 eliminated the right of Chinese immigrants to ever become naturalized citizens of the United States and then banned the immigration of Chinese women. As a consequence, the Chinese cannot vote, so politicians solicit the support of the working man, by blaming the Chinese for all the problems with the state's economy. The newspapers profit since hate-mongering helps to sell their product. The candidate who mongers the most hate against the Chinese always wins the election. Once elected, they pass discriminatory bills and ordinances aimed at the Chinese to inhibit our livelihood and lifestyle to appease their supporters such as The Sidewalk Ordinance in 1870 which restricts Chinese pole-carriers from using sidewalks; The Cubic Air Ordinance in 1871 restricting crowded living quarters and requiring each individual to have 500 cubic feet of living space; The Queue Ordinance in 1873 mandating that prisoners must have short hair; and The Laundry Ordinance in 1873 and 1876 requiring Chinese pole-carriers delivering laundry to pay a higher license fee. The Chinese do the work most white laborers will not or cannot do. We build their railways, levees, irrigation systems, roads, rock walls, bridges, tunnels, we mine their abandoned claims, we create new crops and new industries, we supply new ideas and expertise, in return they threaten us with hate and physical violence. Now they want us to leave a country that they took from a people who had no understanding of fences and borders. The natives only knew that land was plentiful enough for all. The early settlers befriended the natives then slaughtered them when they wanted their land. When we first arrived the locals praised us for our industry, ingenuity, dedication, efficiency, reliability and sobriety now they demonize us for these same qualities. The Declaration of Independence and the right to life, liberty and the pursuit of happiness does not apply to the Chinese. Sorry for my lengthy analysis, but you asked about the future for our people in America. I thought you should realize what has happened in the past to understand what may occur in the future."

Cheung spoke, "Differences between people can be accepted and tolerated, or rejected and disdained. Cultural and racial differences within a society always subside in time, unless leadership sways people otherwise. Politicians, radicals,

reporters, writers of periodicals and magazines with personal biases must not be permitted to promote hatred and violence. The key to justice and equality in society is having leaders who understand and have been trained in the wisdom of the past. The Declaration of Independence was written by great men who were students of philosophy and history. Their concepts and ideals have been corrupted by lesser men."

"This country has been tainted with the thirst for power and wealth. Their Declaration of Independence is being corrupted by political self-interest."

"I think you are right. By the way, may I ask the purpose of your visit to San Francisco?"

"We have come on a mission to fulfill a promise to my father and my uncle, which was made during the gold rush."

"Mission?" Ti Chu paused momentarily, "Are you returning the bones of your kin to the land of their ancestors?"

Surprised by Ti Chu's deduction, Cheung hesitated then admitted, "Yes, that is correct."

"Have you been to California before?"

"This is the first visit for Way but I came once before with my father in 1849 at the start of the gold rush. Can you advise us on the best way for us to reach Sacramento and then Marysville?"

"I recommend passage on the riverboat that charges the highest fare. This will ensure your safety. Since the working class poses the biggest threat, you will be able to avoid them because they can only afford to patronize the cheaper steamboat service. The passengers on the luxurious vessels are wealthy and are familiar with Chinese servants and employees. I suggest you use the Chrysopolis (Greek word meaning Golden City), which has been refitted, lengthened and renamed the Oakland. The trip will take 6 to 7 hours to reach Sacramento. The boat leaves at 4pm daily. From Sacramento, you can take the California and Oregon Railroad, or you can take the three-hour riverboat ride to Marysville which is 40 miles up the Feather River. The train is faster but I recommend the riverboat which is less travelled now and therefore safer. Is there anything else I can do for you?"

"No, that's all we need. Do you have any questions, Way?"

"How safe are Sacramento and Marysville? Are there many Chinese there? Is there a Chinatown situated in either town?"

"During the gold rush, Sacramento was just a boomtown filled with newly-rich single men all looking for a good time. Gambling halls, hotels, restaurants, opium

dens and houses with soiled doves lined the street. Now, Sacramento's Chinatown is much more tame. The easy gold has been harvested and now farming is the major industry. After the gold rush, many Chinese went to work on the Central Pacific Railroad. When railway construction ended in 1869, many of the Chinese railway workers turned to farming. The agricultural industry in California started to blossom. Since farm labour is very hard work with low wages it appeals to very few white workers. Most of the agricultural labour force is composed of Chinese workers. There are a few anti-Chinese societies in Sacramento such as the Order of Caucasians and the Workingmen's Party which model their activities after similar anti-Chinese groups here. In 1876 a telegram was sent to the US President supported by 25,000 residents of Sacramento to limit Chinese immigration. In the past, fires seemed to start mysteriously in Sacramento's Chinatown with delayed response from the fire department, as long as the wind was blowing away from the rest of town. Afterwards, the city demanded that buildings be reconstructed in brick, because the city thought it was more expensive than the Chinese business owners could afford. They were mistaken. So I think as long as you do not stray too far from Chinatown, you will be reasonably safe. The situation for Chinese in Marysville will be fairly similar. Will you be returning to China once the remains of your kin have been recovered?"

"No, we plan to return to Canada. We would appreciate your assistance in shipping the bones of our group members back to their villages in China."

"We will be honoured to help you. Mr. Dai, will you return to work for the railway company?"

"Yes, my work there is not complete. Thank you for dim sum and your advice. It has been a long time since I have enjoyed such fine food. We are very grateful for the time you have spent with us."

Ti Chu addressed Cheung discreetly, "Mr. Dai, we know that you are searching for your son. Our affiliate, Lee Kong, in New Westminster informed us. Considering the danger of the triads or others holding him for ransom, we understand why you would hesitate asking for any assistance. Your contributions have been recognized by all those you have helped on your journey, the passengers on your voyage from China as well as our countrymen, who are building the railway in Canada. We will be greatly honoured to help you with your search. Please trust that we will use our utmost discretion. Any information we gain will be sent to the last affiliate office at which you register."

Cheung was shaken by Ti Chu's resourcefulness. Feeling remorseful over delaying the search for his missing son, his eyes started to cloud up with tears. Standing beside him, Way placed a hand on his friend's shoulder to distract the onset of tears. Ti Chu rose from the dinner table, walked back to his desk, searched in a side drawer and took out two cards. He picked up a stone chop, or Chinese ink seal, with his right hand, removed the lid of a small round ink holder with his left, dipped the chop on a sponge compress, and stamped the back of his cards in red ink. After waving the cards back and forth to allow the ink to dry, he presented each guest with his business card. The recipients looked at the card. It was embossed with a red dragon on one side and stamped at the back by the most influential man in San Francisco's Chinatown.

The host accompanied his guests down the stairs to the front reception. *"Please present my card to any of our affiliates whenever you require assistance. I will send word to our Sacramento and Marysville affiliates to expect your arrival. Ko has kept me informed of the progress of the work that he has been doing for you. Good luck on your mission."*

It was a pleasant and sunny afternoon. Pre-occupied with Ti Chu's revelation, Cheung wondered how his search for Wing would be affected. He suggested an alternate route back to the hotel. Walking along Washington Street the pair decided to enter Fah Yuen Gok (literal translation - park corner) or Portsmouth Square. It was mid-afternoon and the square was quiet and peaceful. Cheung reflected back to an earlier time, when this square was a cow pen, surrounded by tents and adobe huts with drinking saloons occupying every corner. Now it was surrounded by brick and stone buildings, hotels, offices, shops and restaurants. As the pair approached the pillars at the entrance to the gated square, they observed groups of men gathered around others playing Jook Kay (Chinese chess or capture the flag) and Tien Gow (Chinese dominoes). The clacking of dominoes was broken by the distant clanging of an approaching street car. Cheung and Way wandered towards the far side of the park to watch the passing cable cars. *"Way, this invention is quite a marvelous achievement. I am sure it will be copied elsewhere."*

"Uncle, this country has made so much progress. This land has so much potential."

"There have so many resources, but their government leaders are self-serving and lack foresight. In China our leaders are chosen based on scholarship. They study

the wisdom of the past to achieve a government post, then rise according to the merits of their performance. American leaders are elected, based on promises that echo the need of voters. The needs of today may conflict with the needs of tomorrow. Hasty solutions may often create bad karma in the future. The government befriends those that benefit them until their needs change, so their loyalties are often printed in sand. Allies of one political party may share no loyalties with the next."

"Yes uncle, I think I understand. Today's joy may be tomorrow's regret. Elected leaders must look for immediate solutions to preserve their mandate, while Chinese focus on long-term solutions, but are less apt to make quick decisions."

"While the world was changing, China did not. Now China will be forced to change. Will they follow the example of their oppressors, or devise their own solution for change? In our society leaders were trained in philosophy, western leaders are driven by the pursuit of power and wealth. Most are trained in the art of war. Who should lead the world - philosophers or warriors? My dreams reveal that radical change is imminent and the Chinese must be prepared for more misery and hardship."

"Yes Uncle, so it is just a choice of war or peace."

Cheung nods at his friend's insight, "By the way, what do you think of Ti Chu?"

"He is very clever and knowledgeable. I think he will represent the Chinese well."

"Yes, he is dedicated and very well-spoken. He will stand tall in the wind, but the tallest tree is always the first to fall in the storm. He questions inequality and injustice, while we accept it because we have worn the yoke of oppression too long. But this is not China, maybe he is right. In my dreams I think it may be too soon for equality and justice for us, only history will reveal what might have been the best course."

"I agree with you. Ti Chu is very dedicated. I can only wish him well. Did you notice he did not have a queue? I was afraid to ask him about it because I did not want to embarrass him. I think that he will tell us, when and if he wishes us to know."

"Shall we walk along to end of the street, to see how these cable cars turn about?"

Upon their return to the hotel, the clerk at the reception desk greeted them: "Mr. Ko is waiting for you."

In a solemn manner, Ko greeted his clients. "Shall we go to the dining room to talk?"

Puzzled by Ko's composure, both expected bad news until they saw a familiar face at a nearby table. *"Uncle, how are you? I feared the worst when I heard of your internment. You have lost so much weight. Are you sick?"*

"Nephew, I am fine, just very hungry and very tired."

With a broad smile Cheung embraced his friend. *"Yuen, my dear old friend I am very glad to see you again. I knew they couldn't kill you. I only hoped that you would not try to escape. Are you in good health?"*

"Yes, I lost some of my fat but I am well. I just had a bath at the hotel and was given some clothes while all my garments are being washed. My luggage is in their repository. Everything has been charged to your room. But I haven't had a palatable meal for over a week so let us eat. I wish to fill every tiny pocket of my soul with sweet, fagrant rice. I already ordered the dishes. It should not take long to cook. Ko, please join us."

Ko gently shook his head. *"Sorry, I cannot join you. I have more clients that I must see but I will see you all again, before you leave. I will retrieve your $500 bond, when Yuen receives authorization, then I will deposit it at the Six Companies office repository. If your authorization has been rejected, you must return for interment at the Shed within 15 days, to await deportation or the bond will be forfeited. If you wish to remain without authorization, I doubt if they will sacrifice much time or money searching for you. They will be happy just to keep your bond."*

After Ko departed, the food arrived. Yuen savoured the arrival of each dish to the delight of his eyes and his nose - chopped white chickenl, beef and gai lan (Chinese broccoli), barbecue duck, shrimp egg foo yung, and cracked crab in black bean garlic sauce. Recognizing the hunger in his Uncle's eyes, Way quickly helped to fill Yuen's bowl with rice and urged him to eat. Without hesitation, Yuen attacked each dish ravenously, stopping occasionally to say. *"Oh, this is very good".*

Way assisted his uncle, selecting choice morsels from each dish and placing them on his uncle's side plate. From the other side of the dining room a couple of waiters watched the onslaught. Ten bowls of rice later, Yuen came to a rest. The waiters looked at each other and shook their heads in disbelief. Cheung and Way only laughed. *"Uncle, shall we order more?"*

"No, my hunger has subsided. Hopefully, my stomach will survive without spilling its cargo. Now, I just wish for a soft clean bed, a firm pillow, clean sheets and a quiet room with no roommates and no guards. I have not had a good night's rest for a long, long time. If I sleep for a week don't wake me up. I am so tired that I

cannot think clearly. I will share the details of my experience with you both, when my mind and my body meet again as one."

"*As you wish my friend, can you make it upstairs on your own after that feast? We are on the top floor. It's the first room on the top floor.*" Shaking his head in humour, Cheung quipped, "*Way, you must go with him. He may not survive the climb. I'll pay the bill, get his luggage and check with the reception desk to accommodate him in our suite.*"

Yuen slept for two days. When he awoke mid-morning, he noticed packed bags and three tickets for the riverboat laying on top of the table. He quickly got dressed to look for his companions. He found them in the dining room. "*Am I still in prison dreaming or am I really free of that filthy rat-hole?*"

"*You miserable old dog, I should have left you in there longer for having such a lazy pen. Even if you did not receive my letters, you might have written to see if I was alive.*"

"*I was hoping that you had passed on, so I would not have to write.*" The three joined in common laughter.

"*I name a son after you. And you insult me, by just naming a nephew after me.*"

"*Aiyah, you have not met my demon of a wife. I tried to name my son after you, but she refused because she thought the name would remind me too much of travelling abroad. I have no control over her insolence or her parents who live with us. My body may be strong but my resolve is weak when it comes to family matters. I just want to be left in peace.*"

"*Alright, but we have arrived at a time of great turmoil. There will be no peace for us here.*" Yuen sat down. He ordered breakfast.

"*So, uncle, tell us about your recent experience in the detention barracks.*"

Yuen paused to gather his thoughts. "*The so-called Shed is a two-storey building constructed of wood. It appears windowless because the windows have been boarded up, whitewashed and are covered with wire netting to prevent and discourage escape. Shrouded in darkness, the interior is filthy, overcrowded and infested with rats, fleas and lice. There is very little sanitation and the odour of human sewage and bilge from the wharves permeate the building. Uniformed men wearing perfumed masks stand guard at the single entrance. Upon arrival at the barracks all must undergo an embarrassing physical examination standing naked in line to wait their turn to be examined by the doctor. Even the women who have never undressed in front of Chinese doctors are treated in this manner. After passing the physical examination you must wait for the interrogation officer to*

verify your identity. The interrogation may last for days. They will ask you petty details about your family, your friends, your village, your travels, people that you met, things that you saw. They will repeat the same questioned in different ways to trick you into making a mistake. All answers are recorded and corroborated with those of your sponsor, spouse or references that have been recorded from previous interviews. Any conflicts or mistakes serve as justification for deportation. This interrogation process could have been easily performed in China, but the shipping company would not profit from selling passage and the customs officers could not collect bribes. The living quarters are divided into barracks. Each barrack is a large bare room with long rows of bunks without tables and chairs. The bunks are stacked, three and four high with minimal headspace. At the side are open buckets that serve as toilets. Most of the men pass their time playing chess, dominoes or gambling. The few who are literate, read books and newspapers. There were a couple of female detainees but they were kept in separate quarters so none could see or hear them. Detainees are treated no better than pigs. The guards beat and bully you without cause or for their personal amusement. We all witnessed others being beaten but no one will risk the future of their families in China to help. When someone breaks the rules, disobeys orders, falls into a depression, a panic or hysteria, the guards throw the detainee into a coffin-like closet which is used for solitary confinement sometimes for weeks. Meals are served in a large dining hall. Men and women have separate meal times so they cannot meet and talk. Even husbands and wives are kept apart. Food is sometimes in short supply so it is rationed or denied. The officials claim that Chinese are accustomed to only two meals a day. Most Chinese are kept for three or four weeks. Some are kept much longer. Suicide is not an uncommon occurrence."

A waiter arrived with Yuen's breakfast of jook (rice porridge) with mixed meats and a couple of barbecue pork bao (steamed bun made of rice flour) "Yuen please eat, we are packed and ready to leave today for Sacramento if you feel strong enough. If not, we can wait until you are. The tickets can be used whenever we wish."

"Cheung, what about your son? I did not expect you to postpone the search for your son. Recovery of these bones could have been performed without you."

"I do not expect others to fulfill a promise that I made. California is much more dangerous than when we visited it 30 years ago. This mission will be dangerous. I trust my son to be able to survive on his own. He possesses many gifts beyond his

years. I know that he and I will meet again in the future because I have seen it in my dreams. The vision was too vivid to ignore."

Yuen turned towards his nephew and laughed. "Way, we can never be sure if these dreams are going to help us, or take us to visit our ancestors."

Cheung continued, "Yuen, have you been informed of the current hatred and violence being directed at our people, or the threat of expulsion of all Chinese from America?"

"Yes, it was a common topic at the detention compound. Violence, murders, lootings, fire-bombings, massacres, etc. by hoodlums demanding jobs. Yes I am aware."

"The federal government may close the door to immigration from China at anytime. Our visit to the astrologer was worthwhile. It is fortunate that we did not wait any longer. This may be our only chance to perform this mission. Yuen, do you feel strong enough to travel?"

"Yes, I am. I've finished eating. Let's go."

As they walked past a few restaurants, Yuen looked at the signs in their windows, "Do you know what is this Chop Suey? Nearly all the Chinese restaurants have signs in their windows and on their front doors advertising it now."

"I asked the manager of the hotel restaurant about it. He told me the story of how it was invented," replied Cheung. "Apparently, Chen Lan Pin, the first resident Chinese Ambassador to the United States, travelled with an entourage throughout the eastern states. He visited many remote communities to promote international goodwill and understanding. On September 28, 1878 after a prolonged meeting with President Hayes, his Cabinet members and local dignitaries, he invited them to stay and enjoy a Chinese banquet. When the head chef received the news he rushed in a panic to see the Ambassador. Kowtowing before the Ambassador and banging his head on the floor, the chef told the Ambassador "Please forgive me, Your Excellency, but during the recent tour all our food supplies have been used up. I have been ill and have not yet been able to replenish our supplies, since we have returned. There are not enough provisions left in our larder to serve a banquet for such a large gathering. And it is too late to shop for more food supplies."

Angry at his predicament, the Ambassador shouted, "How dare you make me lose face to these barbarians. It is too late to cancel, they are assembled in the dining room." As the chef continued banging his head on the floor the

Ambassador indignantly shouted, *"Get up you silly fool. Now tell me what supplies are left?"*

The cook replied *"Very little, Your Excellency, the cupboard is almost bare."*

"Almost bare? How were you going to feed the staff tonight?"

"Leftovers, that's all we have. The route of our recent tour has not allowed us to replenish our provisions. I was going to do it tomorrow morning."

The Ambassador reflected for awhile. *"Is there enough to feed the staff?"*

The cook gestured with a nod.

"Most of these barbarians have never tasted our food, so chop up the leftovers, add soya sauce and anything else you have left in the larder, fry it up all together and serve it on rice. They won't know the difference. You better do a good job! If you cause me to lose face, I swear that I will have you cut up, boiled in oil and served to the barbarians."

In fear for his life the head chef scurried off to the kitchen.

Later that evening the banquet was a great success. The Ambassador received a flood of compliments about the delicious cuisine. One of the guests asked to know the name of the wonderful dish.

The Ambassador paused to summon an attendant. "What is the name of that stupid head cook?"

The attendant answered. "Su Yee."

Remembering his earlier threat, the Ambassador whimsically responded. "It is called chopped Su Yee."

The next day the newspapers gave the Chinese cuisine a raving review. The Ambassador's staff laughed at how the barbarians have been duped. They related the story to the local Chinese communities. Within months, every Chinese restaurant in North America was promoting their authentic recipe of "Chop Suey".

Laughing hysterically, Way remarked. *"This may be our greatest triumph."*

Chapter 14

The Journey to Marysville

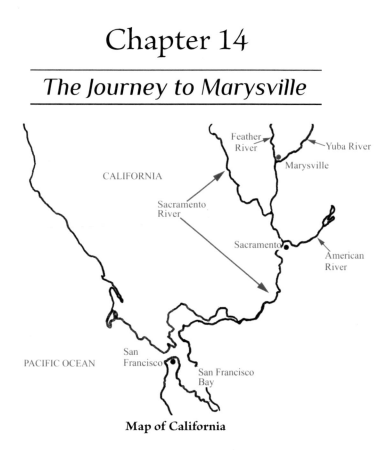

Map of California

THE MOST FAMOUS AND MOST POPULAR STEAMBOAT EVER TO ply the waters of the Sacramento River was the *Chrysopolis*. The 245-foot long *Chrysopolis* was built by John G. North of San Francisco in 1860. The ship's beam was forty feet with a depth of ten feet and had a 1,357 horse-power steam engine with side-paddle wheels thirty-six feet in diameter. The *"Chryssie,"* as it was known to locals, held the fastest speed record between

San Francisco to Sacramento of 5 hours and 19 minutes and could cruise at a speed of almost twenty knots. The Chrysopolis was the most luxurious steamboat built ever to ply the waterways of California. The interior was adorned with red plush upholstery, rosewood paneling, and crystal chandeliers. In 1875, the Central Pacific owners converted the *Chrysopolis* into a double-ended ferryboat, removing her paddle wheels and twin stacks and extending her hull from 245 feet to 283 feet. After the transformation, the vessel was renamed the *Oakland*.

At 4 pm the *Oakland* cast off the dock. It was a pleasant day, so the trio spent most of the time sitting on the sparsely-populated promenade deck. The great majority of the passengers were patronizing the famous all-you-can-eat for a dollar venue in the dining room. Way sat back to listen as his companions recounted memories about their early journey to Gum San. Yuen reminisced. *"My father was a revolutionary who belonged to a secret society sworn to oppose the Qing government. Their motto was "resist Qing and restore Ming." When the society was revealed by an informant, our family left the village of our ancestors to hide in the countryside. We had many narrow escapes. Fearing my life was in jeopardy my father sent me to live with my older brother in a neighbouring village. I never saw my parents again and I assume they did not survive. We never found their bodies. My brother had a wife and two boys to care for. When a flood wiped out his crops after I arrived, I knew that he could not feed me as well as his family. His children were starving and his rent was overdue so I borrowed some money from a friend to help my brother feed his family. A Chinese merchant in San Francisco named Chun Ming wrote to one of our friends in Canton that gold had been discovered in California and that he had struck it rich. When I heard the news I decided to unburden my brother. I signed a labour contract to pay for my passage to California. During the voyage I met Cheung, his father and his uncle. They knew that I was alone. Cheung and I were the youngest on board and about the same age, so we played together and became good friends. I guess Cheung's father and uncle felt sorry for me so they protected me and treated me as a son."*

"Uncle, I think that I have heard some parts of this story before but only in small bits. Too many details of your journey have not been revealed and my father would not permit me to ask questions."

"Way, I promised your father never to discuss anything with you that would encourage you to leave home after he lost his first wife and sons during the Taiping Rebellion."

"Yuen, let me add my portion. The report about the discovery of gold in America spread very quickly throughout Sam Yup district. My father and uncle were merchants who lost their family business. Their store was plundered by rebels and then also by the government forces that followed, so they had no means to support their families. Our family also included my mother and my five-year-old-sister. My uncle had a wife and a four-year-old-daughter. My father had recurring dreams of riches in a land of savages. My uncle believed in my father's dream, based on past childhood experiences they shared growing up. They asked relatives to look after their families and promised to send back money as soon as they were able to find work. They signed contracts with labour agents to pay for their passage to California. They brought me along, not to over-burden our relatives. I was also to help earn more money and pay back their debts faster. When my father, uncle and I boarded a large clipper in Hong Kong we were lowered into the steerage compartment with hundreds of others. When the iron grate was locked over the hatch, we finally understood the gravity of our situation. The ship stopped in Macao to pick up more passengers, until the hold was so overcrowded that we could hardly breathe. The air was foul with the stench of human waste and vomit. All the passengers were young males, there were no women and I was one of the youngest on board. To break our spirits they used whips, and rationed our food and water. There were no tables and no chairs. The ceiling in steerage was less than eight feet high, and bunks were stacked in three tiers. They were 6 feet long, 2 feet wide with about a foot and a half of head space. There were insufficient bunks for all passengers, so we took turns and slept in shifts. During the third week of the voyage the weather was hot and humid. The sea grew calm and the winds stopped blowing, many passengers died from the unbearable heat because there was inadequate drinking water, and the crew hoarded it for their own needs. Riots, murders and suicides occurred as a consequence, until clouds appeared and it rained."

"Cheung, we survived because your father and uncle were trained in the ancient art of the Sha-Ling monks," added Yuen. "They fought a group of bullies who stole the food and water rations of the weak and the sick. They brought order and leadership to the chaos in steerage. Bodies were raised to the upper deck and dumped in the sea to prevent the spread of cholera, duties were assigned based on skill and ability, they created equality regardless of age, and regardless of

whether you were weak or strong, they set rules for sleeping, eating, cleaning, etc.. They led by example and everyone respected them and came to them with their problems for advice. Without them many more may have died on board that wooden piss-bucket."

Cheung continued. "After 62 days at sea, we arrived at San Francisco one morning in early January of 1849. The steerage passengers were all filled with joy at having survived the ordeal. The feeling was indescribable. We rolled up our bedding, loaded our baskets, put on our best clothes and waited. My father and uncle could not bear to abandon Yuen, so we asked him to join us. We were one of the first ships from China to arrive in San Francisco. Of the original 500 plus emigrants who left from the port of Macao, less than 400 survived the voyage. Many of the crew members fled the ship in search of gold as soon as the ship docked. We learned later kidnapping, or being shanghai-ed, was a practice used to procure crew as well as laborers in the pig trade within Chinese ports such as Shanghai, Amoy, Hong Kong and Macao. We were met on the wharf by an associate for the labour contractor who registered and grouped workers together, based on relationships, dialects and district associations. Deals were haggled and agreements were signed by the contractor and employers in need of laborers. Many of these men carried guns and whips. We were assigned to two tall heavily-bearded lofan dressed in jeans, cotton work shirts, and heavy work boots. They wore knives on their belts and carried rifles. By mid-afternoon, they picked up ten of us in a horse-drawn wagon. As the wagon climbed through the hills a steady flow of men on horseback, wagons and carriages passed by. The town was a cauldron of human enterprise, composed of dreamers, schemers and thrill-seekers from every part of the globe. It was a clash of cultures as I had never seen. The harbour was overflowing with the daily arrival of ships of every shape and size, displaying flags from every nation on the Pacific Rim. Abandoned by their crews with the lure of gold, the skeletal remains of ships laid along the shoreline. Their timber and sails were salvaged to construct shacks and tents for gold-seekers. Strange music, singing and laughter flowed out of countless taverns. The streets were filled with natives dressed in animal skins and woven cedar, darkly-tanned Mexicans in sombreros and fancy clothes, bearded Hindus in turbaned headdress, tattooed Kanakas from the Sandwich Islands, French trappers in Hudson Bay jackets and big heavily-bearded Americans in canvas pants, plaid shirts and heavy boots. Chinese merchants were dressed in clothes made of embroidered silks. The great majority of our countrymen were dressed in blue quilted jackets and vests made of cotton, wide collarless

knee-length shirts, and short crow-coloured ankle-length cotton pants. Our people, appearing so much smaller in stature, shuffled along with the tide of humanity in straw sandals carrying bamboo poles loaded at both ends with all their worldly possessions. Their queues hung at the back to the hip or were wrapped around the top of their head in a circular fashion under a wide-rimmed umbrella-shaped hat made of split bamboo. Puzzled by the swarm of activity, my father shouted out to a countrymen, "little brother, why is everyone rushing?." He shouted back. "Gold, the mountains are filled with gold." We camped overnight on the outskirts of town. Our new bosses cooked a very large pot of beans mixed with big pieces of pork and gave us plates and utensils to help ourselves. Unlike the meager portions on board the ship we all ate beyond our capacity to digest. Our bosses attempted to communicate using hand signals and seemed amused by our mannerisms and our responses to them and our new surroundings. They supplied us with blankets and directed us to sleep around the campfire. The next morning we headed back to the harbour and boarded a steamboat to Sacramento then another to Marysville. When we reached Marysville, the bosses loaded up the wagon with more provisions and equipment. We journeyed on narrow trails along the riverbank. Miners were working claims all along the way on both sides of the Feather River, but the number of sites grew less numerous the farther we travelled upriver. Four days later, we reached our destination which was an isolated campsite on a tributary of the Feather River. We were very fortunate to have been contracted by these two men. Paul was the older of the two partners, thirty-five years of age and over six feet tall. He was slender, with pale skin and curly red hair. Paul was originally a school teacher. The junior partner was named William. He was in his early twenties, just under six feet tall, average build, darker complexioned, with light sandy hair. William had been a seminary student. Both were from the east coast and came out west to seek their fortunes. We stayed and worked with them for two years. They treated all of their workers with respect and dignity which was a rarity during the gold rush. They taught us how to mine for gold and learnt to trust us enough to carry on mining while they explored more sites and staked more claims. They made more money selling new claims than mining our site even though ours was fairly profitable. Paul and Will hid their success wisely, never buying too much and always using credit whenever possible. They also taught us about horses and mules and also showed some of us how to shoot a rifle in case of bandits, thieves and wild beasts. As time passed, my father developed a close bond with the bosses. He became their foreman and was also given the responsibility of delegating duties

like cooking, washing, feeding and caring for the horses and mules, cleaning the stable, cutting firewood, etc.. I may never forgive my father for giving me the duty of maintaining the outhouse."

"Hey, try being chased by a grizzly, carrying a bucket of huckleberries? It was at least 10 feet tall and must have weighed over 1000 pounds." added Yuen.

"You should have just dropped the berries."

"I did. That was the only thing that saved me. Will shot that bear the next day."

"My father, my uncle, Yuen and I accompanied the bosses every 2 weeks into town to help load supplies. They taught us how to drive the wagon. We took turns. Paul and Will were admired and respected by the townsfolk and their fellow miners. We received similar respect from the townsfolk who were inspired by our association with the bosses. During our trips into town we travelled in an armed caravan with other miners for protection against bandits. We became familiar with most of the other local miners. There was a spirit of co-operation and communication among many of the resident miners. Paul came up with a simple warning system based on the Morse code. A pause and three rapid shots stood for "B" or bandits, four rapid shots stood for "H" or help. Many of the miners came by to visit our campsite, for my uncle's cooking, out of boredom and loneliness or to have one of our bosses write letters for them. In the evening, Paul taught any workers willing to learn how to speak, write and read English. My father and uncle were determined to learn, and they also forced Yuen and me to join them. The four of us seemed to be the only workers interested in learning the local tongue. Many topics arose during our nightly sessions around the campfire. Will joined the gatherings later as our language skills improved. Many heated discussions arose as a result. Paul was a man of science. Will was a man of God. We gained a great deal of knowledge and insight about the Christian religion and the opposing theories of science from debates which sometimes lasted all night. We sparked many discussions with our questioning but we were instructed by my father to always remain neutral. One of my questions that brought the most heated debate was how absolution opened the door to heaven? Why would an individual live according to the Bible if he could be forgiven for all of his transgressions on his death-bed? It did not make sense that anyone could be freed of accountability after a lifetime of transgressions. The argument over this topic would rage till dawn. No one ever won the debate concerning religion and science because neither Paul nor Will would ever admit defeat. It seemed amazing how a book written by countless men so long ago could transcend almost two thousand years of endeavour to find the truth about human

existence. We enjoyed watching our bosses argue, so we often asked questions that would prompt the debate. Anyway, the mining operation was very successful, and we were able to pay off our labour contracts during the first year of employment. Paul and Will shared their success with their workers. They paid us well and they appreciated our loyalty, as well as my uncle's cooking. During the early gold rush many contract laborers were badly mistreated, and abandoned their employers to find work elsewhere or to find their own diggings. After only two years of mining, Paul and Will had grown very wealthy and one day they announced that they had made a decision to return to their homes on the east coast. My father tried to convince them to continue mining because they were going to sell their claim. He wanted to continue mining the claim for them in their absence because he was sure there was much more gold to be found. The next day Paul and Will conferred with my father in the privacy of their tent. My father returned with tears in his eyes. He gathered my uncle, Yuen and myself. "They are giving the four of us their claim, the horses, the mules, the wagon and the equipment as a reward for our service and loyalty. The others can stay to work for us if they wish. On their departure, the four of us drove Paul and Will to Marysville and thanked them for the years of kindness and for their generosity. Too bad men like these are so rare in this land of hopeful dreamers. After they left we found more gold as well as a 10 pound gold nugget!"

"Way, there is still much more to tell you, but we are nearing Sacramento. Cheung can continue the story later."

Located at the confluence of the Sacramento River and American River, Sacramento was a thriving port and a major corridor to the northern goldfields. It was called Yeefow, "second port," by the Chinese because it was the second stop after reaching San Francisco, which was known as Daifow, or "big port." Located 80 miles to the northeast of San Francisco, Sacramento was a thriving distribution center for goods and services for all those involved with early mining activity. After the gold rush the future of Sacramento was further enhanced by two factors: the regional reclamation of swampland into rich farmland, and secondly, being named the western terminal for the transcontinental railway.

The Chinese were among the first to arrive in Sacramento at the start of the California Gold Rush. Tong yun gai (Chinatown literally "Chinese street") was located along the shores of the Sacramento River on First Street and included four blocks between Second and Sixth Street. First Street was

a levee road built on a low bank riverfront prone to flooding. Even though it was considered the least desirable part of town, the location facilitated easy access to the harbour and the business section of town.

When the *Oakland* docked, the three men waited patiently to avoid the rush to disembark. As the cargo was being unloaded on the lower deck they stepped off the ferry on to First Street. They walked for two blocks to the shelter located adjacent to the Sze Yup Association building between Fifth and Sixth Street. Cheung decided to show Ti Chu's card to the receptionist. "*Mr. Chun has informed us to expect your arrival, Mr. Dai. We have prepared a room for your group. You are to be his guests as long as you are in Sacramento. Your money will be of no use here. Our establishment here is just an overnight shelter to serve people in transit but we will try to accommodate you as best we can.*"

"*I am sure your accommodation will be adequate. Is there a restaurant still open nearby?*"

"*Food will be brought up to your room. Do you have any special requests?*"

"*No, whatever you bring will be fine.*"

"*Your room is at the top of the stairs, first door on the right. Here are your keys.*"

As they proceeded upstairs, Way said "*Uncle, this stamped card carries face (prestige) it signifies - treat me as the owner of the chop (stamp).*"

Cheung turned to Way, "*Don't lose yours!*" both laughed as Yuen remained puzzled.

Way took out his card and showed it to Yuen who smiled. "*I must borrow this card on my next visit to that shithouse detention facility they call the shed.*" Laughter erupted as the visitors climbed the stairs.

The next day the three boarded a riverboat to Marysville. They found a vacant corner on the promenade deck. Way anxiously waited to hear more about Cheung's story.

"*Uncle, now tell me about the rest of your journey. I wish to hear about the gold nugget.*"

"*Has your uncle not told you this story a hundred times?*"

"*No, I was warned by my brother not to encourage dreams of adventure and easy wealth. But my brother has reconsidered after hearing of the success of our villagers. So Cheung, go on with the story.*"

"*In the early days of the gold rush miners could find seven to eight ounces of gold daily just picking it out of the earth. Many Americans hired natives to find the gold nuggets for them. A single pan washed from the river could yield hundreds*

of dollars in gold. In the Yuba River district, a huge nugget weighing 240 lbs was found by two of our countrymen who had just arrived from China. They had no previous experience in mining. Just a mile downstream from our site, a 40 lb nugget was said to have been found. Both nuggets were found by Chinese miners on claims that were thought to be mined out and abandoned. When my father and uncle heard about the 40 lb nugget they visited the nearby camp to see if it was just a rumour. After seeing it, they warned the miners about the danger of the discovery for the whole area if word got out about the find. So they agreed to chisel it down to smaller pieces and sold it in smaller pieces. Then they denied ever finding it afterwards. It was later accepted as a rumour. After seeing the large nugget and the wing dams which were built at the other camps to divert the river to mine the river bottom, my father and uncle discussed the idea of building a wing dam for days. There were only 10 of us while there were over 100 miners in the other camp. It would take us years to build a wing dam at our site. Should we hire more workers? Could we produce enough gold to support more workers? Will there be enough gold to share? Or will we just use up our savings in vain searching for gold that is not there? On a day too hot to work, Yuen and I went to a small uninhabited lake for a swim and discovered beavers living there. Since we had been warned by our former bosses about the danger of beaver fever we decided to return home. When I told my father about the beaver it aroused his curiosity. My father and uncle went out to watch the beaver the next day. They saw only two adult beaver but assumed they had some young. When they returned they decided to trap the beaver and place them upstream from our mining site. Hopefully, the beaver would build a dam for us and then all we had to do was build a trench to divert the river around the area that we wished to mine. The next day we built a large wire cage to hold the beaver. We hid downwind waiting for the adults to come onto dry land. Once they were both sufficiently far enough from the lake we threw blankets over top of them bundled them and placed them in the cage. Then we opened up their lodge to check for their young so we could keep the family united. There was a litter of six which we placed in the cage with them. Once we relocated the family at a chosen site we released the adults so they could build a new lodge for their family. We kept the young in the cage and left the door of the cage open. The adult female came back to feed her young accompanied by the male. We covered the cage with branches and leaves to resemble a beaver lodge. The adults returned to the cage at night but worked incessantly during the day to build a new lodge. At night Yuen and I took turns guarding the young. We

set up our tent next to the cage. Yuen and I decided to build a dome-shaped cage similar to the interior of a beaver lodge. We placed it on top of the pile of material and debris assembled by the adults on the riverbank. After cutting down some small trees and a pile of twigs and branches we placed the young beaver inside the cage and threw some of the trees and branches over top of the cage. We watched the beaver at work for the next few days while my father, uncle and the rest of the work team started to build a trench to redirect the course of the river. The beaver adapted to the domed cage residence. We cut down trees and laid them across the location that we wished the beaver to build a dam. They followed our lead so we cut and placed more building material close by, to help them speed up the process. Six weeks later the beaver had finished building a dam which blocked the river. When we opened the trench that connected the ends of a sizeable loop in the river the water poured in filling the trench in seconds rushing forth to join both ends of the loop. We had changed the course of the river in just six weeks with only 10 men and 2 unpaid beaver. The crew members all rushed to check what lay on the river bottom. There were gold nuggets everywhere. My uncle shouted to my father. Come quickly and look at this!'. As we all approached he hoisted up a huge nugget for all to see. Later we found it weighed just over 10 lbs. That was the biggest one that we found. I'll let Yuen continue from here."

"The boat is nearing Marysville, Way, there is much more but we still have a long journey ahead. We can tell you the rest on our journey to the mine. It will be worth your patience." said Yuen as Way frowned.

In the 1850s Marysville was a gold rush boomtown and the major distribution center of mining equipment, food and supplies for gold miners working in the mountains to the east. After arriving in San Francisco or daifow, early Chinese migrants headed upriver by steamboat to Sacramento or yeefow, then to Marysville which was then called sanfow or third port. Situated 40 miles north of Sacramento in the Sacramento Valley, Marysville was known as the "Gateway to the Goldfields" and was located at the confluence of two rivers. It was bordered on the south and east, by the Yuba River and on the west, by the Feather River. After the gold rush, the settlement of mostly tents and adobe huts was gradually replaced by brick buildings and the population had grown into one of the largest cities in California with mills, iron works, factories, machine shops, schools, churches, two daily newspapers and a population of approximately 10,000. The center of

Chinatown was located at First and C Streets. The Suey Sing Tong, and the Hop Sing Tong were the earliest Chinese associations established there.

The riverboat arrived at the Marysville docking facility just as the heavy tule fog lifted (tule – 10 foot high bulrush found in marshland). When they arrived at Chinatown the group wandered down First Street to find the Suey Sing Tong. A group of mischievous youngsters gathered to follow. They started to chant.

"Chinkee, Chinkee, Chinamen
Sitting on the fence,
Trying to make a dollar,
Out of fifty cents."

The walkway was crowded, Cheung and Yuen led as Way followed. One of the youngsters pulled at Way's queue. Way stopped, turned and searched in his pocket for his pacifiers to disarm the young mob. As the children watched Way, a youth called out, "Here comes Jack!" They all flocked across the street towards a diminutive Chinese pole-carrier. The man was dressed in western-style clothing and shoes. He stopped to greet the children and offered them fruit and candy from one of his baskets.

Dumbfounded by the event the travelers watched a display of mutual affection between the tiny man and the children. Cheung stopped a passing laundryman, shouldering a pole of laundry, and pointed. *"Little brother, who is that man?"*

"He called Jack Ellis, real name Yuen Yeck Bow." Said the laundryman.

"Is he a wealthy merchant?"

"No he cook for Mr. Ellis, big man in town. Boss has big store near ferry on Yuba. He sell everything for mine, hunt, farm, ranch."

"The cook gives away his groceries. Will his boss not be angry?"

"No, boss very good man, very wealthy, very generous. My friend hit with stone by his boy. Boy run home. Friend follow. Father stop friend. Give him dollar then whip son. Now boy very nice to Chinese. Very wise man."

"Thank you very much, little brother. Oh, can you show us how to get to the Suey Sing Tong?" The man pointed across the street to a corner building at 305 First Street then quickly shuffled away with his baskets of laundry.

More children arrived. Once the supply of fruit and candies were depleted, the mob of children dissipated. Way chuckled at being upstaged and offered his friends fruit lozenges from his tin of sweet appeasements.

When Ti Chu's card was presented at the Suey Sing Tong, the receptionist bowed. *"Mr. Dai our head office in San Francisco informed us to expect your arrival. A room will be vacated for you as soon as we discharge the occupants upon their return today."*

"There is no need to move anyone. We will take any space that is available. Can we just leave our bags in your storage facility?" The receptionist took the bags.

"Can you send a courier with a message to Yuen Yeck Bow? We wish to invite him for dinner. Tell him that we have just arrived in town and enjoyed watching him today on the street with the children. As a long-time resident, we hope that perhaps he could provide some information for us. We can meet him whenever it is convenient and at any restaurant that he chooses."

Way and Yuen were puzzled by Cheung's request but remained silent. As they strolled through Chinatown, Cheung decided to calm their curiosity. *"We will need advice from someone who is familiar with the locals and the town to insure our safety and our success. There are many things that can go wrong travelling along secluded wagon trails. Where should we secure a wagon and horses? What do we know about buying them? Can we still access the burial site or is someone mining it? In the past, we always travelled in caravans with others who carried guns. Will we need guns or do we hire others with guns? Who can be trusted? Yuen Yeck Bow is well-accepted and understands this community and his boss sounds like a good man. If we can win his friendship perhaps he can introduce us to his boss who may advise us. I prefer to seek advice from those who are part of the community rather than those who are isolated from it."*

Yuen turned towards his nephew, *"See what I told you? Cheung always has a plan. His ideas make me feel like my mother gave birth to an ox."* Way chuckled.

When the party returned to the tong, they were greeted by the receptionist, *"Mr. Dai, Yuen Yeck Bow is glad to accept your invitation and would be honoured to meet with you at the restaurant across the street at six o'clock tonight."*

Cheung visited the restaurant to order the food in advance, then returned to the tong. He researched the latest newspapers available at the tong. Later the men, dressed in western attire, proceeded to the restaurant at the designated time. Yuen Yeck Bow had already arrived and was talking to the restaurant owner when they appeared. Instead of greeting his countrymen with a traditional bow and palms clasped together, seeing the men in western clothes, Yuen Yeck Bow shook their hands. *"I am always glad to meet any of my countrymen. Do you have any news from our homeland?"*

"Yes, a new treaty with the US government was signed for the Chinese government to regulate and limit our countrymen from coming here. Because of the possible threat of excluding Chinese immigration by the American government, shiploads of our countrymen are pouring into San Francisco before any legislation on exclusion is formally passed. Meanwhile, anti-Chinese activity is occurring everywhere in California. The Chinese residents of San Francisco are leaving for the north, the east and back to China."

"Yes, Dennis Kearny has been here too," remarked Yeck Bow. "Many of the Chinese in Marysville are armed and ready to protect ourselves and our property. We have taken in residents from neighbouring communities who have been expelled from other towns. The receptionist here told me that you have a card with the chop of Ti Chu. Are you an associate of his?"

Showing his card Cheung said. "No, Way and I met him once while we tried to rescue Yuen from the immigration service in San Francisco. He had heard of my work with the Canadian Pacific Railway and wished to help us with our mission."

"May I ask what your mission is?"

"Yes, we are planning to retrieve the bones of my father and friends who died during the early days of the gold rush. Yuen and I have been here before but this is Way's first visit."

"When were you here last?"

"We arrived in January of 1849. We worked for a couple of American miners four days north of here on a tributary off the Feather River."

"Are you the beaver dam miners?"

Surprised by Yuen Yeck Bow's comment, Cheung was unsure how to respond. Yuen and Cheung looked at each other and reluctantly nodded response.

"How did you come to know about this? Is this common knowledge?"

"The story was told to me by an old miner in town who returned to China over 10 years ago. No one believed the story but me. Apparently, he heard about it through a friend who caught a glimpse of two young miners helping the beaver build a lodge while he was searching for his lost dog. He thought nothing of it until he returned a few years later and noticed the wing dam and the graves."

Cheung and Yuen looked at each other, wondering just how much was observed by the interloper.

"Do you know if the claim has been re-staked? Are the graves still there?"

"I have never been there. I have only heard that the area has been mined out and now sits vacant. So I imagine that the graves are still there. Can you tell me what happened? Was there lots of gold?"

"Yes, we found lots of gold. One nugget weighed over 10 lbs. There were nuggets everywhere. After a couple of months, some of the workers were stricken with beaver fever so we had to make a decision about the beaver. After all the work they did to help us find the gold, we decided to move the beaver back to their original home. Trapping them again was easy because they had become very tame; we visited them often when we had nothing to do so they had become pets. One day after they had been transported, we decided to check the beaver's progress in building their new lodge. Yuen and I packed a lunch and hiked to the pond. After spending several hours watching the beaver, we heard three gunshots, the signal for bandits. Four more shots followed – the signal for help. We rushed back to camp but we were more than an hour away. On the way back, I was overwhelmed with sadness and felt a deep sense of loss. Tears started to flow from my eyes. I ran faster and faster. When we reached the campsite, Yuen and I approached cautiously. Everyone was dead and everything of value was gone. They had all been beaten and tortured to find where our gold was hidden. We found them tied together by their queues with their throats slit which was the trademark practice of Joaquin Murieta. Some of our neighbours arrived to help but it was too late. Yuen and I dug graves and buried the bodies, with the understanding that we would eventually return once the flesh had decomposed so we could clean the bones. It was a pact made by all in our group that any survivors of an attack would retrieve the bones of the dead and send them back to their relatives in China. We stayed in Marysville for a few months. The attitude of the townsfolk had changed towards us. My father knew that the local situation was getting worse for Chinese worker and warned us to always stay in the shadows. He had read in the newspaper, that on May 8, 1852 a mass meeting in Tuolumne County was held, condemning ship-owners, capitalists and merchants for flooding the mining industry with Asians. The outcry of "California for Americans!" went out throughout the state. The mining district in Marysville took immediate action, staging their own mass meeting at which they declared "no Chinaman shall henceforth be allowed on any mining claim in the neighbourhood." Along the American River over 300 Chinese were expelled by bands of white miners. At Horseshoe Bar 400, Chinese were removed. So for the two of us, it was time to move on."

The food arrived and the four started to eat.

"That is quite a story, Mr. Dai."

"Please call me Cheung. Also this is my friend, Yuen and his nephew Way."

"Please call me Jack."

"Well Jack, how about your journey?"

"I came from Gum San to find gold to help support my family back in China. My father was a poor farmer in the Sze Yup district. He struggled to feed the family and could not pay his taxes. A very good friend of mine had just returned to our village from Gum San. We use to attend the same missionary school together. He had come back very rich and told me about the easy wealth in California. He offered to sponsor me. So we made an agreement and he loaned me a generous sum of money. I gave most of it to my father to help him pay his taxes so he could feed the family and keep his land. With the rest I paid for my passage to Gum San. When I arrived in California the gold rush was over so I went to work helping to build the Central Pacific Railway. Chinese wages started at $26 a month with a minimum of 26 working days but we had to supply all our own food, equipment and tents while the white workers got $35 a month with all meals and board included. An American foreman was put in charge of our team of 20 workers. He kept track of our hours and distributed all the wages. We worked from sunrise to sunset with an hour for lunch and dinner and lived in tents and dugouts in the earth. We ate very well: rice, noodles, fish, pork, chicken, beef, cuttlefish, bamboo shoots, dried oysters, mushrooms, a variety of vegetables, etc.. A Chinese merchant contractor in a separate rail car always followed behind us to supply all our needs. As well as foodstuffs, he supplied clothing, shoes, lamps, bowls, chopsticks, pipes, tobacco, etc. On Sundays we rested, did our washing and gambled. The bosses preferred to hire Chinese laborers over others such as Irishmen, German, Englishmen and Italians because we did not drink, fight or strike. We enjoyed the luxury of bathing every day after dinner because water was so plentiful here while in China we dare not waste good drinking water on a bath. Constructing the first 23 miles of railway from Newcastle to Colfax was easy. When we reached the Sierra Nevada and the Rockies the work became much more dangerous. After reaching Cisco, the mountains were 7000 feet high and made of solid granite. Dynamite had just been invented in 1863 and was not in common use yet. At first we had to use hammers, crowbars, picks and shovels to construct tunnels through unyielding walls of granite. Using black powder on granite walls made for very slow progress and at times we only managed only a foot a day. However, we became experts in grading, drilling,and blasting. Avalanches and cave-ins became more frequent and

many more died once they started using dynamite. At Cape Horn, a three-mile long gorge above the American River, three miles east of Colfax, the engineers were baffled on how to carve a roadbed along a steep cliff 2000 feet above the American River. One of our countrymen recommended an age-old technique used in China to build fortresses along the Yangtze River gorges. Wicker baskets were made out of reeds and workers were lowered in the baskets to drill holes and tamp in dynamite. Once they lit the fuse, the workers were hoisted up quickly; many did not make it up on time. Sprayed by shards of granite, many fell 2000 feet into the canyon below. Eventually, at the cost of countless lives, rail beds were carved on the vertical face of sheer rock. The winter of 1865-1866 was extremely severe. Snow storm after snow storm blanketed our campsite. The ground was frozen solid and snowdrifts sixty feet thick had to be cleared before we could grade the roadbed. The agonizing cold was almost unbearable for our countrymen who had never seen snow. Tunnels were dug beneath the snowdrifts and for months we lived like moles travelling through snow tunnels from worksite to campsite. Members on my crew were constantly being replaced due to deaths and injuries. I knew that if I didn't leave soon my death was just a matter of time. One day I heard that powerful new explosive called nitroglycerine had been delivered. It was being tested at our site for first time. I arrived just in time to watch the explosion. I thought that I was a safe distance away but the explosion was enormous and I tried to duck quickly to avoid falling debris. That is all I remember because I was hit on the back of the head by a rock. I didn't wake for two days. When I received my pay at the end of that month I decided to leave. The bosses employed natives to track down and return runaway workers. Those brought back by the natives were beaten and whipped severely afterwards to discourage others from leaving. I was fortunate to escape but I had always been kind to the natives and I enjoyed playing games with their children who frequented the campsite. The relationship between the natives and the whites is one of buried anger. The tracker that they sent after me remembered my kindness so he escorted me safely to the nearest town. The natives have no love for the white man or his railway. Many natives work on Chinese crews because the white workers will not accept them on their crews. We gained information about this land and the native culture when they ate with us during mealtimes."

"Jack, you were very lucky. The natives in Canada have been very friendly towards us as well," said Way.

"Yes many Chinese have married native women and live in the mountains. Some of our countrymen live with the natives and have adapted to their way of life.

They ride horses, shoot guns and hunt buffalo just like the natives but you may not be able to recognize them as our countryman."

"It would be interesting to meet one of these men."

"Anyway, I kept track of the progress of the railway even after I departed because I left many friends behind. The transcontinental railway was completed on May 10, 1869, when the Union and Central Pacific joined at Promontory Point, Utah. Before this railway, it took four to six months to cross the country from East to West by horse and wagon, now it takes only six days by train. Thousands of Chinese died during the construction of the railway. Over 20,000 pounds of bones were returned to China. The railway never kept track of the dead Chinese. Many bodies were hidden, some abandoned in deep river canyons and caved-in tunnels, others buried in unmarked graves, all along the path of the iron horse. Without our sacrifices and dedication, this railway would have never been completed. In 1866 when the first train swept down the eastern slopes of the Sierra we were caught up in the spirit of the epic accomplishment, cheering and waving our hats. I felt that I had been a part of something that was worthy of historical significance, after helping to lay many miles of track over the most difficult terrain in the world. To me, it was a great source of pride until I saw the newspaper photograph celebrating the last spike. There was not a single Chinese face in that monumental photo. I heard afterwards that all the Chinese workers who attended the celebration were ushered out of the background before the photo was taken. After the celebration completed, the Central Pacific immediately laid off their Chinese workers. Some who had even been promised return passages to China by their recruiters, were stranded and abandoned in Utah. Some still remain in small towns along the route of the railway, and a few still live in abandoned boxcars. After the success of the first transcontinental, all new railway projects sought to hire Chinese laborers. It is a tragedy how we sell our lives so cheaply to others, who take all the credit for our toil, then leave us behind like garbage. Then they open their doors to new immigrants with offers of free land while they try to restrict and expel us from a country that we helped to build. Any contributions that we have made have been ignored. Will the Chinese ever receive any recognition for their service and contribution to this country?"

**Last Spike Ceremony at Promontory Summit, Utah on May
10,1869 – The Central Pacific & Union Pacific Railways join to
form the First Transcontinental Railway in North America**

"Not in our life time, Jack," stated Cheung.

"After leaving the railway I worked in many small towns and settlements along
the route of the railway until I reached Sacramento. I later found work helping to
reclaim the swampland at the delta junction of the Sacramento and San Joaquin
Rivers. The swamp was so heavily-infested with mosquitoes; no white workers
would do this kind of work. The soil was rich but it was covered with water and
marshes where the tule grass grows ten feet high. We drained the water by building
endless miles of levees, ditches, dams and canals. We toiled with tule knives from
sunrise to sunset, waist deep in slimy mud, under a burning sun and a swarm of
mosquitoes. Many workers died of malaria, infections and sheer exhaustion. Most
of the laborers were farmers from the Pearl River Delta who possessed expertise
in drainage, reclamation and flood prevention that had been developed in China
over many centuries. These worthless swamplands had been given to the state by
Congress and the state had given the land away, on the condition that the land
would be reclaimed within three years. After reclamation these once worthless
swamplands were sold as farmland for $20 to $30 per acre. By 1877, 5 million acres
had been reclaimed and the land was selling for $100 an acre."

Way inquired, "The land owners must have become very wealthy. Were any of the owners of these lands, Chinese?"

"No, free land was never offered to the Chinese but some became small farmers, renting land as share-croppers who agreed to give the landowner half their profits for vegetables and grain, and three fifths for fruit. Over the past 10 years our people have contributed many innovations in the field of agriculture: they created the tule shoe for horses to work in the swamps, they were the first to hatch eggs using artificial heat, and they produced a new peanut in Tehama County, a new superior variety of rice, and the new Bing cherry. We enrich the farmers with our cheap labor. Many ranchers cease to be profitable after they were forced to replace the Chinese with white workers. Some went broke and others had to sell their land."

Cheung answered, "Jack, this new transcontinental railway has made the jobless situation worst. Hordes of white workers have come west to find jobs. The new railway sells false hopes for a $40 fare. The shipping lines are using similar tactics in China. Cheaper transport of manufactured goods by rail from east to west has lowered the price of goods made in the west closing down many western factories. The stock market has severely declined and mineral deposits are being depleted adding failed investors and jobless miners to the ranks of the unemployed. The politicians have decided to direct the blame on the Chinese for all the misery, instead of admitting that they have created these problems by supporting private enterprises with their legislation. Apparently, it is our fault because we choose to work for low wages."

"These politicians, railway and shipping line owners and newspaper men have no morals or conscience. There are good men who support us, like my boss, but in a sea of ignorance, they are like grains of sand standing against the tide. So, we must prepare for more suffering. When prosperity returns maybe things will change. Thank you for a fine dinner, I haven't eaten like this since I left China."

"Please, enjoy the meal. Jack, the extent of your knowledge and understanding is very impressive. After we recover the bones of my father and friends, I will return to Canada to work for the railway. Our countrymen are dying in great numbers. Their situation is comparable to your railway experience but worse. Their wages are lower, they have more expenses deducted, their food is like garbage, their supplies must be purchased at company stores at two to three times town prices. Any laborers caught buying elsewhere have their wages reduced by 20%. In addition, hatred towards the Chinese is greater now than before, even in Canada. I serve

as a medical assistant for the only doctor on the western portion of the railway. I must return as soon as possible."

"Some men from my village may be working on the railway in Canada. So, what I can do to help you?"

"We need advice and the right contacts to secure what we need to complete our mission quickly, without arousing local curiosity. Do you have any suggestions for us or any people we can contact to help us?"

"You obviously need help from my boss, right? Okay, that is no problem. He is a good man. I am sure he will help you."

Yuen spoke. "Jack, how did you get a job as a cook?"

"A local banker needed to replace his cook who was a friend of mine who was returning to China. I said that I could cook so they hired me, mostly because I could speak English. We all took turns cooking on the railway crew and anyone who complained had to take over the position. The cook that I was replacing stayed for a couple of weeks to show me what to do. These lofan eat very boring tasteless food which is very easy to cook. They don't like much variety either, same thing all the time. Mr. Ellis hired me when the banker and his wife moved back east."

"He owns a store?" Asked Yuen.

"He owns a few properties. His store is a two- storey brick building located on First Street between D and High Street. He also has a stable on High Street and a private residence."

"Is he involved with the local government?" asked Cheung.

"He is on city council and has served as Treasurer for Yuba County helping with state taxes and delivering them to Sacramento."

"Can you tell us the best store in town to find Chinese goods?" asked Yuen.

"The best place to shop is Hong Wo Sun Kee. It is the largest Chinese store in town and is located close by, on First Street."

"Is there anything else I can do or help you with?"

"No, Jack, thank you very much for joining us tonight."

"I will talk to Mr. Ellis as soon as I return to the residence. I will leave you a message at the Suey Sing tong. Thank you again for the fine meal, it reminds me of home." Jack rose from the table, shook hands with each of his hosts, then departed from the restaurant.

"Well, what do you think?"

"Cheung, I like him. I think that he will be very helpful."

"Yes, Uncle I agree. Will we all go to meet his boss? Or just Cheung?"

"I want all of us to attend because anything I overlook may affect us all, and I do not want to be solely responsible for all the decisions. I prefer to share the blame."

Yuen wrinkled his left eye at Cheung and quipped. *"By the way, the fish that you ordered, was over-cooked."*

Chapter 15

Fulfilling The Promise

A MESSAGE WAS LEFT THE NEXT DAY AT THE SUEY SING Association by Jack. It was delivered to the men upon their return from lunch. Cheung opened the message:

Please come to my residence on the northwest corner of D and 8th Street tomorrow evening at 7 o'clock.

Sincerely,

William Ellis

The next evening, the three men arrived at the Ellis residence promptly at 7 o'clock. They were escorted inside by a native woman. Mr. Ellis cordially greeted each man with a handshake as they were introduced then offered his guests a chair at his dining room table. He called out to the woman, "Rosie, can you please have Jack make us some tea? Now gentlemen how can I help you? Jack has told me that you wish to retrieve the bones of some miners who died here many years ago. He said that you were miners who once worked at a claim a few days north of here during the gold rush."

"Yes, a group of us worked here in 1849 for a couple of American gold miners. A pact was made by all members of our group that the bones of anyone who died would be sent back to relatives in China by the survivors. This is our mission. We just need advice on how best to accomplish this task.

We have been away for a long time. We are unaware of changes relating to the natives, road access, river conditions, bandits, etc."

"The roads have been maintained better since hydraulic and hardcore mining equipment has to be transported on them but they may be soft this time of the year. Almost all traces of the native villages that populated the riverbanks of the Feather and Yuba River have disappeared. The survivors are scattered in the hills and mountains. My maid, Rosie, is the last of her tribe. I purchased her for $150 from a miner who was down on his luck in a poker game. He and his friends had kidnapped her when she was just a child. I told her that she was free, but she has nowhere to go, now that all her people are gone, so she chose to work for me. A lot of snow has fallen in the mountains this winter and our weather has remained fairly cool for this time of year. When it warms up, there will be some flooding in the foothills and avalanches higher up in the mountains. Bandits should not be too much of a problem but we do have a gentleman bandit named Black Bart who appears to be harmless. He patterns himself after a romantic figure out of a Beadle's Dime Novel. He is very polite to his victims, never harms them and sometimes leaves a poem after taking their money. As far as I know, he has never fired a bullet. He carries a shotgun which I doubt is even loaded and wears a flour sack over his head with two slits for his eyes. In one of his holdups he said that he had men in the bush with rifles pointed at the driver. Later it was discovered that the rifles were just sticks of wood. He always treats his victims cordially, so they are almost delighted to be robbed by such a famous celebrity. He has developed quite a following amongst the ladies and the children. The newspapers love him because their sales always rise whenever he commits a robbery. At least he has inspired an interest in poetry. All the children can recite his poems. My son has a copy of one of his poems in his room. I'll get it for you."

Ellis left and returned with a newspaper clipping. He read it :

"Here I lay me down to sleep
To wait the coming morrow,
Perhaps success, perhaps defeat,
And everlasting sorrow.
Let come what will, I'll try it on,
My condition can't be worse;
And if there's money in that box

'Tis munny in my purse."

Black Bart

"Does this sound like a killer? I do not think bandits will be a problem for you. Other miners who envy the success of Chinese miners may pose a bigger danger. Many Chinese mining camps have been attacked by white miners who loot the dwellings, force the resident miners to leave or just murder them, then take over the mining site while the law looks the other way. There have been some small communities of Chinese established in isolated areas. Unless they are armed and willing to defend themselves, white gangs will eventually attack them. The law offers you little protection. I cannot remember hearing of white men ever being prosecuted in Court for robbing or killing a person of your race in California but a few towns have stood in support their Chinese miners. The citizens of Bangor, Butte County took a different view of anti-Chinese activities. Four white men who escaped the sheriff of Butte County while being held for murdering a Chinese miner were pursued by the citizens of Bangor. Three of them were instantly hanged. Your group must be well-armed and know how to use a gun if you plan to travel here. Do any of you know how to use a rifle?"

"Yes, Yuen and I know how to shoot a rifle but that was a long ago and I think guns have changed."

"If you cannot find anyone else to teach you about rifles I will have one of the clerks at my store instruct you. How do you plan to reach your destination? Will you be using a buckboard? Are you familiar with horses and mules? If you need to rent horses, mules, wagons, etc., my stable can supply whatever you need. If you have to travel over mountainous terrain you should use mules but they are more temperamental to deal with. I have maps at my store. If you drop by the store I may be able to show you which camps are friendly and which may be dangerous. The Chinese miners arrive and depart from town in a caravan. There is safety in numbers. It might be a good idea to get to know them so you can leave with them. When they come into town they stay overnight in Chinatown."

"Mr. Ellis, thank you that is a very good idea."

"Mr. Dai, Jack told me that you were working as a medical assistant for the railway company in Canada?"

"Yes, the Canadian government is attempting to join the East with the West as your country has done. They have seen the growth and development

created by your transcontinental railway so they hope to do the same in Canada."

"There are many facts about our railway that the great majority of Americans are not aware of. The four entrepreneurs who started the Central Pacific Railway Company almost went broke a few times building the railway. These men were inspired by Theodore Judah, an eastern engineer. I met with him at a hotel in Sacramento when he was promoting his ideas. Judah conducted a preliminary survey establishing a feasible route through the Sierra Nevada Mountains. He tried to persuade the wealthy elite in Sacramento to support his plans. Four storekeepers who are now referred to as the 'Big Four' stole his ideas then excluded him. Judah died of yellow fever crossing the Isthmus of Panama in a frantic attempt to find new backers in New York. He left the fruits of his labour with the four men in Sacramento who knew absolutely nothing about railways but risked everything on a wild-ass gamble. The Central Pacific Railway Company was formed by four partners. They were Leland Stanford, the president, Collis Huntington the vice-president, Mark Hopkins the treasurer, and Charles Crocker who was in charge of construction. Two were dry goods merchants and two were hardware dealers. When they started out, laborers were hard to find because mining jobs were much more lucrative. When the Comstock Silver Mine in Nevada opened up, the Central Pacific lost sixty percent of their labour force. They were in desperate trouble. By 1864, the company had only 600 men working on the line when they had advertised for 5000. Only white laborers had been hired up to then, and only fifty miles of track had been laid. Chinese workers were used successfully on the Central California Railroad in 1858 and the San Jose Railway in 1860. Despite the objection of James Strobridge, the Central Pacific's superintendant of construction, Charles Crocker hired fifty Chinese. It worked out so well they decided to recruit more, to the chagrin of their president. Stanford suffered the embarrassment of reversing his previous stance on advocating the expulsion of Chinese from California. He had once described the Chinese as the 'dregs of Asia' and a degraded people. The company executives then lobbied the government to open the doors to Chinese immigration, which resulted in the Burlingame Treaty in 1868. The Central Pacific imported labour from China using Crocker's brother's company, Sisson & Wallace, and a Dutch merchant Cornelius Koopmanschap of San Francisco to recruit workers from China.

The company dispatched recruiters to China with callous promotion and promises. They negotiated for discount rates with shipping lines. By 1867, of the 13,500 workers on the Central Pacific payroll, over 12,000 were Chinese. The arrival of the Chinese averted corporate disaster for the Central Pacific that could not have otherwise made the deadlines set in their government contracts. These contracts implemented a checkerboard pattern of land grants in which every second square was awarded to the contractor. In 1862, the federal government offered these land grants for the building of a transcontinental railroad. The land would encompass 10 miles of land on each side of the laid track and in 1864 was later extended to 20 miles. Mineral and timber rights were included and if completion deadlines were not made, the land grants would be forfeited. Speed in construction was essential for two rivals. A race for land grants resulted between the Central Pacific which was awarded the contract to lay tracks eastward from Sacramento, and their rivals, the Union Pacific which was awarded the path westward from Omaha, Nebraska. The idea was for both to meet somewhere in the middle. The faster each company built tracks the more land they would accumulate. Under the terms of the government contract, the railway companies would be paid from $16,000 to $48,000 for each mile of track laid depending on the terrain. The Central Pacific also finagled funds from other public sources through subsidies, loans, bonds and gifts from federal, state, county and city governments. Congress awarded them a cash bonus of $18,000 that soared to $48,000 for each mile of track for mountain construction. When the two lines finally met in Utah, the Central Pacific had laid 690 miles of track and the Union Pacific 1,086 miles of track. A congressional investigation later revealed that the Union Pacific received $73 million but could only justify $50 million in true costs while the Central Pacific gained approximately $63 million. In addition, the Big Four was in ownership of most of their Central Pacific stock which rose in value to approximately $100 million based on their success. They had also received 9 million acres of land grants. With their newborn wealth and power the Big Four could control the fate of every business enterprise, every town, and every city in the western states."

Cheung said, "This strategy worked so well here in California the railway owners in Canada will surely try to adopt the same strategy."

"Is the Canadian railway project going to succeed?" asked Ellis.

"I have no doubt it will. Chinese lives carry little concern for the politicians and the railway owners in Canada, they seem to lack humanality."

"What is that?"

"A sense of human compassion."

"The word does not exist."

"Mr. Ellis, you are right, the word seems meaningless here."

"A young radical named Denis Kearney is stirring up a lot of hatred and violence among the masses of disenchanted workers. He is a former seaman who owns a small delivery business in San Francisco. He was a member of the pick handle brigade that caused the 1877 San Francisco riots. Supported by the Anti-Chinese Union, the Knights of Labour and the United Brothers of California, he has been attacking the big railroad companies for making millions through land grants by corrupting government officials. When he became leader of the Workingmen's Party he focused his attack on Chinese immigrants for working for starvation wages and robbing Americans of jobs. You must beware of his influence which runs rampant among many of our local community."

Cheung said, "Well, it is getting late, my friends and I would like to thank you for your time and advice, Mr. Ellis. We will come by your store very soon."

"Gentlemen, our country is guilty of great hypocrisy. What we promote abroad is seldom practiced at home. One day I hope that our people will recognize how they have used and abused the natives, the blacks, the Irish, the Mexicans, and the Chinese. Hopefully, attitudes will change in time but I feel doubtful that it will occur in our lifetime. Please do not hesitate to call me whenever you need information or advice. I will be glad to help."

The group remained in Marysville for two months in preparation for their mission. They met with Ellis and Jack on Saturday afternoons for tea. They learned how to use the Winchester repeating rifle. Twice a week a clerk from the Ellis store was assigned to take the three men into the woods to practice shooting targets. When the Chinese miners came into town, Jack introduced the visitors to the miners. A date was set during the beginning of June when the three men would join the Chinese caravan. Ellis outfitted the men with guns, supplies, camping equipment, and tools and leased them a wagon with two horses. Jack introduced Cheung to the owner of Hong Wo

Sun Kee, the Chinese merchandise store where special food supplies and all the items necessary to conduct the ritual of bone-cleaning were purchased.

The day before departure, Jack arrived to bid farewell. The group was given a gift with a note from Ellis:

My friends, I wish you success on your mission and a safe journey. Our time together has been very enjoyable and enlightening. Foreseeing what lies ahead may help to safely guide you.

Best of luck,

William Ellis

Inside a long black leather case was a nautical spyglass telescope.

Eight wagons left Marysville with 28 passengers aboard. All were well-armed, proudly displaying rifles for the benefit of local observers. As the morning sun rose above the mountains in the east, the early mist dissipated revealing the grassy foothills below the Sierra Nevada Mountains. The valley trail meandered alongside the riverbank. Grooves created by wagon wheels led the journey to the northern gold fields. When the caravan stopped to camp on the first night, the horses were watered and fed. A campfire was started, a schedule for cooking duties was set up. A communal cache of food was gathered for the four-day journey and each wagon contributed supplies based on the size of their group. After a meal of vegetables, cured meat and rice, Cheung could feel the growing curiosity amongst his fellow travellers towards them, as the caravan gathered around the campfire. Realizing the necessity for support during unforeseeable circumstances, he decided to relate his previous experience in California to alleviate any concerns of their fellow travelers and to allow for a more open exchange during the evening campfire. As the evening progressed, many of the others shared accounts of their personal journey.

Near the end of the evening, Way asked the gathering, "*Are there any hidden dangers that we should be aware of?*"

A miner responded, "*Returning to our campsites is fairly safe but you may be at a greater risk of being robbed on your return trip into town. Chinese are always suspected of having hidden caches of gold when they depart from the gold fields. Gangs of white miners may also attack Chinese campsites. Some will just loot, force you to leave then steal your claim, others will torture and kill, to find where your gold is hidden. Also beware of the tax collectors, they will use physical abuse and have been known to kill Chinese miners. They may travel in groups and*

often they are just bandits disguised as tax collectors. We cannot tell the difference. So when one arrives we show that we are well-armed then we agree to meet with them and pay our taxes in Marysville on a specified date. So far none have ever appeared. So we don't bother to go anymore." Laughter erupted.

Cheung spoke. *"Jack told us about Chinese who live with the natives. Have you met any of these men?"*

Another miner responded. *"Yes, there are a few of these men with native wives in the foothills. They sometimes come to our campsite to join us for meals. They often bring us salmon and venison. We exchange their fish and game for supplies."*

Conversations and friendly banter continued until midnight as the gathering gradually dwindled. The visitors laid their blankets and bedding at the back of their wagon. The moon was so bright no other light was necessary to read a book. They fell asleep listening to the rushing river, the chirping of crickets and the distant serenade of coyotes.

Early the next morning the caravan was awakened by the sound of ravens and the tapping of woodpeckers. The cook for the day had breakfast prepared by the time the campers had risen. Extra rice had been cooked the night before in preparation for breakfast. Water was added to the leftover rice to make jook, or rice porridge. Leftover meats from the previous night's dinner were cut up and thrown in. Dried mushrooms, dried shrimp and onions were added to enhance the flavor.

The day passed quickly. As the wagon sauntered along, Way was fascinated by the rugged beauty and amazing abundance of wildlife in the Sacramento Valley. *"There is so much here to see and enjoy. This land goes on forever without a single farm. The soil is so rich, many crops would flourish here. The weather is similar to ours in Guangdong. It is like the land of milk and honey described in the bible."*

Yuen responded, *"The only problem is the owners of the hives and the cows want us to do their work without sharing the harvest. Cheung, is it time to tell Way the rest of the story?"*

"Go ahead you do it, he's your nephew."

"No you do it. I'm driving. I'd rather listen."

"Okay. Months before my father died, he had a dream about being robbed by bandits. The dream was not very vivid but he became fearful and believed it might eventually occur. His dreams were just like mine. The more vivid and detailed the

dream, the more likely they may occur in the future, but we never know when these events will occur. The less vivid ones may just be flights of fancy, so we are never sure whether or not they will occur. In order to prevent the loss of our gold, my father decided to keep the hiding place a secret so none could reveal it under torture except himself. The others in the camp protested but eventually agreed to his proposal. My father documented the name of each member and his home in China. Survivors of a massacre were obligated to send a share of any gold recovered to the families of the dead members in China. A small amount of gold had been hidden nearby to satisfy bandits, but the main cache was hidden elsewhere. My father never disclosed any more about the location of the gold, except that it was buried very deep. After we buried the dead, Yuen and I searched for the gold without success so we decided to return to Marysville, convinced the gold was lost forever. Whenever we arrived in town, my father and uncle always took Yuen and me with them to collect the mail at our local tong. It became a habit to do this first. So upon our arrival in town, we checked for mail. There were letters addressed to each member of the group from my father. Yuen and I each retrieved a letter. In the letter, my father was cautious and used secret riddles, just in case the letters fell into the wrong hands." Cheung took an envelope from his bag and gave it to Way. It was addressed to Dai Woo Cheung. Way read it out loud:

"My son, if you are in possession of this letter, then my journey has ended. My greatest joy has come from watching you mature and my deepest regret is no longer being able to participate in your quest for wisdom. I am so thankful and proud to have fathered the fine young man you have become. You have experienced and suffered many challenges, hardships and tragedies at such an early age without bitterness or complaint, but with an open mind and a level of understanding well beyond your years. In a sea of ignorance and despair you must continue to never abandon hope and optimism for the future. Hatred, violence and revenge only serve to divide humanity, and we are all members of the same family in the same universe. There is but one earth so we should all strive for one common goal – peaceful co-existence. The greatest obstacle is greed. Please remember, your life is also a reflection of my own life, your life flows through mine, as that of your children will flow through yours. When I see my father again I will be able to stand before him with pride and honour at what I have left behind. I have no doubt you will do the same when your time comes. Please give my love to your mother and your sister and ask them to forgive me for being so far away and for not having

held them in my arms as often as I had wished. I leave them in your care. I am confident that you will guide them wisely.

Near your family of friends at the base of the tallest tree the harvest awaits.
Dai Him Kwok

Cheung brushed back tears as Way handed the letter back. The others remained silent as they waited for Cheung's sadness to subside. After Cheung's eyes have dried, Yuen added. *"The letter that I received ended with the same comment."*

"Uncle, I do not ever remember you mentioning any family of friends in your stories of the past?" asked Way.

Yuen smiled and winked at Cheung. *"Yes, we did."* Way was puzzled.

Yuen smiled at his nephew and winked, *"The beavers!"*

On the second night, the caravan received visitors as they set up camp. A group of four greeted them, three were bronze-skinned natives, scantily clothed in leather loincloth. They were muscular and stood a head higher than the miners. The fourth was much shorter and slightly-built. Unlike the rest, he wore short cotton pants and a leather vest with his hair pulled back and tied behind his head in a short ponytail. The miners greeted them with familiarity and invited them for dinner. One of the natives carried the carcass of antelope which he dropped beside the campfire. The youngest member in the group stretched and rubbed his shoulders and neck after unburdening himself. The carcass was quickly butchered into smaller portions by a couple of the miners. Fresh game was a prized commodity shared by the miners, and each group took a portion of meat. They offered gifts which they thought the natives would want, in exchange for the meat. Some of the meat was prepared with Chinese spices and served for dinner. After the meal, a miner brought out an *erhu*, a Chinese stringed instrument played with a bow, and played a few traditional Chinese ballads. Some were drawn to tears by the melodies of home. Others applauded loudly to thwart the spread of melancholy. Later, Cheung was introduced to the head of the native group, the shortest man. When the other man returned the customary bow, Cheung queried, *"Very glad to meet you. Please call me Cheung. You are Chinese?"*

"Yes, please call me Wong. I am glad to meet you."

"You must have had a very interesting journey. May I ask how you came to California and how you came to live with the natives?"

Wong sat on a log near the campfire as the trio of friends waited to hear his story. He paused awhile to think. *"I never knew my parents. As far back as I can remember I was an orphan begging for food on the streets of Hong Kong. Strangers gave me food and shelter if I would agree to go away and leave them alone. I wandered all over the city so as never to annoy any area too long with my presence. I do not know how I survived. Each day was a struggle until I joined a group of older orphans who begged and stole to survive. I later found work in a garment factory. When others that I knew came back from Gum San wealthy, I decided to try my luck by signing a labour contract. When I arrived the labour agent sent me to work on a cattle ranch. One day while herding the cattle, we were attacked by the natives. We were badly outnumbered so we decided to abandon the herd. I fell off my horse attempting to escape. When the others turned, they noticed that I had fallen and was scrambling to retrieve my horse. The foreman sent a rider back to help me. After the rider retrieved my horse, he just smiled and then abandoned me, returning with just the horse. When the natives arrived I sat with folded arms and legs, offering no resistance, preparing to die. They had never encountered a Chinese before and seemed surprised by my appearance and behavior. They bound my hands. One of the men got off his horse and doubled up with another rider. They put me on the horse and led me back to their village in the foothills. I served as a slave to the chief and his family. I learned their language and their customs. The chief came to trust me. My status in the tribe grew as I introduced many new ideas. I set up communication with Chinese miners and organized an exchange of goods and herbal medicines for fresh game and fish. I introduced new spices to enhance the flavour of their foods and different techniques for preparing their food. I tried to teach them to grow crops. As time passed, the tribe allowed me to join their hunting parties. I became accepted by the tribe as one of their own. I fell in love with one of the Chief's daughters, whom I married, and the boy that carried the antelope to the camp is my son."*

"Do you wish to one day return to China?"

"I have no ties there. This is now my home."

Beside the campfire, Yuen and Way have listened to Wong's journey. Way asked, *"Are you safe from the white miners?"*

"No, but our village is well-positioned, high in the foothills so we can watch for the early approach of strangers. Finding our village would be a difficult challenge for strangers."

As his son approached Wong placed an arm around his shoulders. "This is my son. His name is Yuba, the same name as the river and the name of this county."

"Yuba, I am Cheung and this is Way and Yuen."

"Hello I am glad to meet you." Yuba bowed in the Chinese tradition.

Standing near their wagon, Yuen noticed Yuba staring at their new Winchester rifles.

"Are those the new Winchester repeating rifles?"

Yuen handed a rifle to Yuba, "Yes, here have a close look at the rifle. It is the newest model that we could find in Marysville. Do you know how to use it? If you do, you are welcome to try it out."

"May I, father?"

"I think it is too dark to test it now. Maybe we can return tomorrow morning and you can try it out before breakfast?"

Cheung replied, "Perhaps, we can set up some targets for you to test your marksmenship if that is fine with you?"

Yuba smiled and nodded.

Early the next morning the native group arrived to watch Yuba test the new rifle. The whole caravan gathered to watch Yuba's marksmanship. Three tin cans were placed at fifty yards and three more at 100 yards. Bets were made by the miners. Cheung bet $10 that Yuba would hit all the targets and received 10 to 1 odds from the other miners. Yuba balanced the rifle in his hand then checked the lever-action reloading mechanism of the rifle. He said, "it holds 15 shots, right?" Way and Yuen confirmed. Yuba stood looking at the targets for a minute. Cocking the rifle he aimed, and fired, hitting the first tin. The spectators cheered. He carefully reloaded, fired, hitting the second tin, and then reloaded swiftly, fired, hitting the third tin. More cheering erupted. Yuba turned to smile at his father. Then he turned back to look at the more distant targets, firing and reloading, hitting all three tins in rapid succession. Temporarily stunned by what they had witnessed, the spectators broke out in a cheer and crowded around the marksman, congratulating him on his performance. Yuba raised the rifle in triumph.

Cheung collected on his bet, then he conferred with Yuen and Way. After the crowd dispersed, Cheung approached Wong and his son. Yuba handed back the rifle. Cheung rejected it, as he displayed his winnings. "The gun is yours. I can buy another one in Marysville. That was great shooting."

Incredulously, Yuba looked at the gun. "This is mine? I cannot believe it. This gun is amazing. I felt like it was a part of my body."

Way joked, "Just don't sleep with it or you may blow off a very precious limb. By the way, you will need bullets. We have a few extra boxes of ammunition to go with the gun. I'll get them for you."

Wong turned to Cheung. "That was very generous of you. You have made my son very happy. Thank you very much. If there is anything we can do for you, please do not hesitate to ask. We hunt throughout the valley and foothills. We will visit you, once you have settled. Is your claim much further?"

"Only half a day away but we are not here to mine. We have come to retrieve the bones of my father and associates who were massacred many years ago during the early gold rush."

"How many were in the party?"

"Eight died. Yuen and I were the only survivors."

"I know the site of eight graves. Is that the one? Our village is not far from that location."

"Yes, probably, but there was no native village nearby when we were mining there. Have you been at your location for a long time?"

"No, the tribe only moved ten years ago. We must yield our hunting grounds with the approach of others. Your site sits vacant."

"We will look forward to your visit but we hope to stay only as long as it takes to retrieve the bones and join the next caravan returning to Marysville."

"There is a large group of white miners one half mile west of your site, so be careful. They may be dangerous. Our village is located above the valley. There is always a tribe member on watch to check for danger. Our sentry will be able to see them turning off the main trail, towards your campsite from our lookout. One shot, a pause then three shots in rapid succession means they are heading your way. You'd better prepare an escape route just in case."

"Thank you Wong. That rifle may be the best investment I have ever made."

"Can I send members of the tribe to help you dig up the bones?"

"No we need to perform the ritual ourselves."

"I thought so."

Cheung reflected for a moment. "I think I have something else that may be of use to you."

Cheung went to the wagon and returned with a long black leather case which he gave to Wong. Opening the case, Wong discovered the spyglass telescope. *"What a marvelous instrument, I will never be able to reciprocate your kindness. Our tribe will treasure this wonderful gift. This will enhance our tracking game and alert us from impending danger. Our people will be forever in your debt. My friends, you will always be welcome at our village."*

After the natives left, the group joined the others for breakfast. As the three packed up, Yuen said, *"Cheung, you never cease to amaze me with your talent to win allies. How did you know Yuba could shoot like that? Giving Wong the telescope was brilliant. Now you owe Way and me a new telescope."*

Cheung laughed, *"Hunters must rely on good vision. His recognition of the gun suggested that he was familiar with guns and possibly a marksman. His father's request for his son to demonstrate his skill under better lighting was a hint to me that Wong wanted his son to put on a good show for us. I didn't know that he was that extraordinary, but the odds were so good, I could not pass up the wager."*

Yuen remarked. *"Way, how can I be so blind, not to see something so obvious?"* The three laugh.

One by one, the wagons separated along the main trail to their various campsites. The group covered their tracks leading off the main trail to avoid detection by neighboring miners. When they reached the campsite, it was vacant. Overgrown with vegetation, it did not appear to have been occupied since Cheung and Yuen had departed almost thirty years before. The men quickly unloaded and set up camp.

After lunch, the group trekked to the beaver's lake. They brought one of the horses to carry guns and shovels and also to carry back the gold. They cautiously scouted the area and circled the small lake, checking to see if anyone could see them. Only small remnants of the old beaver lodge remained but all the beaver were gone. 100 feet from the shore of the lake, elevated on a small bluff, a massive pine tree casted a shadow over the former beaver site. Smaller trees surrounded the large pine but directly below it laid a grassy patch. The men dug until they found a bottle with Cheung's father's name written in Chinese. It was a marker. Cheung's father realized others would stop digging after a reasonable depth. Remembering his father said that he buried the gold deep they continued to dig deeper until they hit something solid, a large flat stone. When the rock was lifted, they discovered a gunny

sack. The men tried to lift it, but the rotting fabric tore. Another bag was enclosed inside the first. Cheung took out a knife and carefully sliced the bag open. Inside were leather pouches. He picked one up. The weight was recognizable. They opened one. It was filled with nuggets of different sizes. They opened another, filled with gold dust. They counted more than 20 pouches each weighing approximately 10 to 15 pounds. They distributed them into 4 large sacks, tying the sacks in pairs with a rope in between, and then laid the rope across the back of their horse.

On the way back to camp, Cheung said, *"Way, Yuen and I have already discussed the sharing of the gold. We feel that with the risks that you have undertaken to help us, that you should receive a full share. There is even more than I expected. My father never was very good at spending money."* They all laughed.

When they returned to camp, they hid the gold. After dinner, they discussed their plans. Cheung said. *"Tomorrow we will dig up the remains of my father, my uncles and the rest. I am very happy with what we have accomplished today, but we are in great danger with this much gold, if anyone has been watching us. Do either of you have any ideas on how to get this gold back to San Francisco safely? Or even Marysville?"*

Yuen replied. *"Now I see the problem your father had. This gold is so vital to the survival of our families that no one wanted to take the risk of transporting it. This may be our only chance."*

"Do we take it out in small pieces or all at once? Time and politicians are not our allies. More and more restrictions are being placed on Chinese immigration. We may not be able to return to remove the gold and each visit may become more dangerous. And I must return to Canada to find my son. I think the gold must be removed all at once and as soon as possible. But how?"

"Cheung, I know you will come up with a plan, you always do."

"Yuen, too bad my ideas don't always turn out as planned. I will need time to think of a strategy."

In Chinese culture, rituals associated with death are linked to the belief that the spirit of the dead remain among the living and must be remembered and honoured to ensure the prosperity of those they left behind. Customs and rituals vary with the individual's position, his clan and his district.

The next morning the men constructed a portable canopy of tree limbs and canvas to prevent sunlight from entering the grave site and disturbing the spirit of the dead. The men then changed their garments. Cheung

dressed in a black robe to express the deepest sorrow for departure of family members. Yuen and Way dressed in white out of respect, but reflecting no blood tie. Offerings were made to appease the spirit of the deceased; joss sticks of incense were lit; a platter of food and wild flowers were placed near the grave; and hell money or fake money were spread over the gravesite. A wash basin was filled with water and rice wine to clean each bone. Each bone was removed and cleaned individually, starting at the feet ending with the head. During the ceremony of his father and uncle, Cheung sang songs of filial piety, recited rhymes and related joyful memories of the past. During the process Yuen honoured his benefactors, expressing his gratitude and praising each member for their kindness and generosity. The bones were neatly arranged then wrapped in a yellow cloth and placed in large urns. The process took three days to complete the eight individual ceremonies.

On the fourth day, Yuen stated, *"With these eight urns, we will surely be a target for robbery. Any non-Chinese that see these urns is going to suspect that we are carrying gold in them. If we cover them up, it will arouse even more suspicion. This may be as dangerous as transporting strongboxes of gold for all to see because they may shoot us over disappointment that the urns only contain bones."*

"Yuen I think I have a solution."

"You always do, but is it going to get us killed?" Cheung and Way chuckled.

Cheung smiled, *"Death awaits us all. Hopefully we can delay it as long as possible. Tomorrow I will visit Wong. I have an idea but without his co-operation my idea is useless."*

The next day, Cheung and Way set out on foot to find Wong's village. Yuen remained behind to guard the gold. Cheung carried a knapsack on his back as the two trekked up a winding trail. After two hours, they approached the foothills. From a nearby elevated location came a voice.. "Hello my friends." Yuba climbed down grassy bluff. "We saw you leave your campsite. My father sent me to invite you to honour us with a visit. Will you follow me to our village?"

Cheung and Way agreed.

"There is a shortcut but it is a steep climb. It may be a difficult journey with that load on your back."

Yuba gestured to Cheung, offering to relieve him of his backpack and also Way's rifle. Cheung and Way obliged. Yuba took the knapsack and placed it on his back then strapped the rifle across the top. Cheung and Way

followed Yuba up a hidden labyrinth of narrow pathways along rock ledges, clinging to rails of braided vines. They crossed a short bridge made of vines and wooden slats. They continued to climb until they reached a dead end on a small plateau just below a steep embankment. Yuba imitated the sound of a coyote. A vine ladder was dropped from above. When they reached the top of the embankment, Yuba was greeted by a tribe member holding the telescope. After allowing the visitors a few minutes to rest, the visitors were led along a path towards the exposed face of the embankment. The path ended at a small cluster of pine trees. Camouflaged in the branches of the largest tree was a log platform. When Cheung reached the platform, the sentry offered him the telescope. Way followed behind. Cheung had an unobstructed view of the Sacramento Valley but he was curious as to how much of their activity was hidden from the vantage point. The undulating hills in shades of green and yellow appeared in long chains, broken by rivers and streams. The waterways supported the growth of pine and oak along their riverbanks. The main trail leading up the foothills was clearly visible. Smoke stacks marked several mining sites along the Feather River and its tributaries. Through the telescope, Cheung located their campsite and the place where the gold was buried near the beaver lake. Trees blocked the view of their activity at both sites. Relieved, he passed the telescope to Way.

Yuba stated that a sentry was always posted at the lookout from dawn to dusk. Yuba led the pair towards the village, a half-mile away. Curious scantily-clad and naked children gathered around the new arrivals. Yuba returned the knapsack and rifle then departed.

The village was located beside a slow-moving river, and oak trees surrounded the perimeter of the village. The dwellings were large dome-shaped mounds 10 to 15 feet in diameter covered by reeds and mud. Only half of the dwellings appeared above the ground with the other half dug into the earth.

Yuba returned with Wong and a tall white-haired native. Wong introduced the guests. "Cheung, Way we are honoured by your presence. This is our chief Sun Eagle. When we saw you approaching I sent Yuba to invite you to visit our village." The Chief greeted the pair with a smile, nodding his head and raising his right hand with open palm. Cheung and Way reciprocated the gesture.

Cheung turned to Wong, "We were coming to see you."

"Good, so you will stay with us tonight. The chief cannot speak our tongue so I will have to translate."

Sun Eagle spoke to Wong who translated, "The Chief would like to thank you for the gifts to our tribe and wishes to express his appreciation by inviting you to a feast tonight in your honour."

Cheung and Way accepted the invitation, as the Chief continued speaking.

"The Chief would like you to know that this was not always our home. The village was once much larger and occupied much of the valley below. We are just one of a few remaining fragments of the Maidu tribe. We call our people the 'Nisenan' which means the people."

"Wong, how large is the tribe?"

"There are just over 150 people in our village. The Chief says that their people were once as countless as the stars. There were once 74 Maidu villages distributed in the valley, foothills and the mountains. Some villages had a population of over 500 but many have died from diseases such as smallpox, measles, cholera, and syphilis, brought by the fur traders and trappers. The natives believe the fur traders wanted control of the hunting grounds so they bartered goods infected with disease in exchange for our furs and hides. The Chief said 9 out of 10 of his tribe died of disease. Many were massacred later by miners in search of gold. Contact has been lost with the remaining tribes who are now scattered and hiding in the hills and mountains, far away from the expanding villages of the white man."

"Wong, does the Chief know that our people once came for gold too?"

"Yes, he knows, but he bears us no malice. We never killed, raped or harmed his people. We never fenced the land of his ancestors. Anyways, allies are hard to find. Would you and Way like a tour of the village?"

"Gladly. Let's go."

A band of giggling children followed the men. Way turned and took his tin of peace-makers from his pocket and offered them to the flock. The children screamed with excitement at their first taste of sugar. After each has received one, he gestured to the eldest that the remaining sweets were to be shared by all, and relinquished the tin. The leader ran off with the prize, as the band scurried after him.

The first stop was Wong's abode. The entrances to all dwellings faced south to capture maximum sunlight. They walked down a narrow path and through a door made of tule reeds into an open living area, approximately 15

feet in diameter. A stream of light from a vent in the ceiling illuminated the interior. Sunlight also penetrated through the open door. The ceiling stood 12 feet high in the middle of the dome's interior. A collection of intricately woven baskets lay on a deerskin covering the dirt floor along the right wall. One contained bows, quivers, arrows and others contain tools and utensils. A bed was located to the left of the entrance. Yuba's Winchester rifle hung on a solitary pole near the centre of the domed structure. The pole served as the main support for the ceiling joists. Mud and vegetation blanketed a lattice work of tule reeds on the domed ceiling. A fire simmered as smoke escaped through the ceiling vent. Wong introduced a pretty middle-aged woman as his wife. She wore only a bark apron and a shell necklace. She smiled then continued grinding acorns in a stone mortar with a stone pestle. Wong said. "That is our rice."

As they continued the tour, Way pointed to large standing structures made of reeds, some were suspended from poles, others from trees, "What are those?"

"Those are storage bins for acorns. They come in different shapes and sizes. Acorns are our main food source. Each adult eats almost a ton of acorns each year. But they have to be processed. Our women pound them into flour. They leach out the bitterness with boiling water. Raw cakes can be formed by leaving them to bake in the sun. The cakes can then be eaten, broken down to make a soup, or cooked in boiling water to make porridge."

Way watched men standing very still knee deep in the river, bent over with their hands lowered in the water. "Wong, what are they doing?"

"Watch closely."

They watched for a few minutes and then one of the natives in one swift scooping motion tossed a fish on to the shore.

"That is incredible. No net, no spear, no rod."

As they walked through a grove of oak trees, Cheung said. "The soil is good here. Why do they not grow crops?"

"I tried to grow corn but the deer ate it all. There is plenty of game and other food sources so there is no need to plant crops. But some years the acorn harvest is poor but that is why we always store more than we need."

Close to the river is a large dwelling without a vent. Way inquired, "What is that?"

"That is the 'temescal,' the sweathouse. It is very hot inside and the fire inside burns perpetually. It is reserved only for men who lay on mats inside to cleanse and purify the spirit. It is always used before and after a hunt or battle. It removes the scent of the hunter to avoid detection by the prey. Sometimes special herbs are used to conjure visions and speak with the Creator. The heat inside is only bearable for a short duration. When a man can bear the heat no longer, he exits and dives into the nearby river to cool. Would you like to try it?"

To foster rapport with the Nisenan Cheung realized that he needed to experience their cultural traditions. Cheung and Way agreed. The men removed their garments and entered the sweathouse. Two natives welcomed the guests as Wong introduced them and chatted to them in their native tongue. Cheung and Way started to sweat profusely as soon as they entered the lodge. After ten minutes, Way felt dizzy and light-headed. Fearful that he might faint and appear weak, Way calmly exited and dove into the river. Wong and Cheung followed closely behind.

Wong said. "You both did very well. Most cannot endure as long as you have done, on their first visit to the temescal."

As they bathed in the river Cheung spoke, "I have never felt so refreshed in my life as I do right now.. This feels amazing. My whole body feels completely relaxed. I feel full of energy, strong and alert. My skin tingles."

"Yes, me also. I have never felt so alive," said Way, then he asked Wong, "How much longer will the other two remain?"

"They have a wager about who will remain the longest. I do not know what they are gambling, probably their turn at the lookout station. But on rare occasions, some fools have even lost their wives."

As Cheung and Way rested under a large oak tree, Wong returned to his abode to help his wife prepare for the feast. Cheung and Way sat beside the river. *"Cheung what do you think of Wong's choice of living like a native?"*

"Wong has no commitments. He suffered in China and he was betrayed by his boss and co-workers. So for him his life here offers what he found lacking elsewhere. In this village he has a wife, family, friends, and the respect of people whom he can trust. Until the government decides to take it away his decision is sound. But it may not be safe for his children. For his sake I hope that this way of life survives the test of time."

"But you have some doubts that it will last?"

"Ours never did. What has occurred in China will change us forever. Restoration of the past is futile. Only adaptation to present circumstances will ensure survival of our future generations. Isolation from the rest of the world is temporary and serves only the present, not the future."

The beating of log drums, the sound of bone whistles and a chorus of chanting natives woke the guests. The pair quickly dressed and proceeded to a large campfire at the centre of the village. Many of the adults were more formally clothed in buckskin and adorned with feathers, beads and shell necklaces and headbands. Loin-clothed dancers with painted bodies and feathered spears followed the beat of the drum as the tribe chants. Outside the circle of adults children imitated the dancers who moved in synchronized sequence.

Wong beckoned and offered the guest a place beside the Chief. "The songs being sung are acted out by the dancers. Each song tells a story which the dancers interpret through their movements. Some dances are done in unison, others are random. All the children are taught these traditional songs and dances which have been passed down through many generations."

When the dancing stopped, food was served by young women. The guests and the Chief were served first. Wooden bowls of acorn mush, trays of acorn pancakes infused with berries and grasshoppers, grilled trout, roasted fowl and venison, and a pots of cider made from the berries of the Manzanita tree were served in a communal manner, each individual taking as much as they wanted from the trays, bowls or baskets that were offered to them.

After the feast the Chief gave a speech to his tribe, formally thanking Cheung and Way for the rifle and the telescope. He presented them with deerskin moccasins as a token of appreciation. As the celebration drew to a close, Wong approached the guests. "Would you like to sleep in my lodge tonight? My wife will stay with her sister tonight."

Cheung replied. "Thank you for your kind offer. We will be glad to join you. Where was Yuba tonight? I didn't see him at the feast. Will he join us later tonight?"

"Yes you did. He approached you many times," laughed Wong. "He was one of the painted dancers. He is in the sweathouse washing off the paint. We shall be asleep by the time he returns."

As they settled for the night, Cheung spoke, "Wong, we have recovered the bones and wish to return to Marysville soon. We are afraid that the urns

containing the bones of our deceased may be mistaken for containers of gold. We may need protection to ensure that the urns arrive at Marysville safely."

"We will happy to escort you back to Marysville, whenever you wish."

"Thank you very much for the kind offer, and also for all your hospitality. We have had a wonderful day."

"Yes, today was a wonderful experience that I will never forget," added Way. "Thank you very much Wong."

The next morning the pair bid farewell to the village as Yuba led the way back. At the lookout Cheung showed Yuba where to look for a white flag which would be hoisted, as a signal when their group was ready to travel.

Yuba offered to unburden Cheung of his knapsack and Way's rifle for the descent. Both graciously complied. Yuba was surprised by the light weight of Cheung's knapsack. Once his guests reached the bottom of the hidden pathway. Yuba returned to the village.

Back at the campsite, Yuen greeted them. *"Welcome back, I was afraid you got lost when you did not return last night. Did you find the village?"*

"Yes, Yuba found us first and led us to the village. They have agreed to escort us back to Marysville. So we must start packing as soon as possible."

"The urns are already packed on the wagon. We only have to pack the tent, the food, the cooking equipment, and the gold. I thought we were leaving with a caravan?"

"No, I didn't want to wait and the caravan members may ask questions that we may not wish to answer, and this may affect the gold arriving safely in China. Leaving without the caravan is a better idea. Let's just bring what we need for a four day journey back and leave everything else for Wong and his tribe. We can leave the tent and cooking equipment. I am sure the Nisenan will find a use for them. We can sleep under the stars and I am sure the natives can provide game that we can cook over an open fire. Let's just pack the gold."

In a couple of hours the wagon was loaded and the group hoisted a white flag at the specified location.

The next day Wong, Yuba, and three other men from the village appeared on horseback. Cheung showed Wong and his group their campsite. Wong and their other travelling companions were pleased to receive the tools, equipment and provisions.

As they departed, Cheung exchanged their Winchesters with rifles borne by Wong and another native. Wong hitched his horse to the back of the

wagon and sat beside Cheung at the front while Yuen and Way sat at the back of wagon displaying their rifles. Yuba and a fellow native on horseback led the way. Two natives rode behind. Wong said, *"I doubt if anyone will attack. The two Winchesters displayed at the front is a powerful show of force against an attack. The miners know that if any natives are attacked that we will retaliate, which will disturb their mining operation. A gang of bandits must have time to organize enough men to plan an attack on an outfit as well-armed as ours. Large gangs take months to organize. Generally, only gold shipments and stage-coaches are worthwhile for them."*

Unencumbered by other wagons, the party covered half the distance on the first day, travelling till midnight with very few stops. At the campfire after dinner, Wong said, *"The local tribes are being summoned to a big pow-wow. They want to confront the white man's government leaders with a combined show of force before we are all annihilated. I may not be able to hold back Yuba during a time of conflict. He has too much of his mother in his blood."*

"Has he ever killed?" Asked Cheung.

"No never, I have told him to always fire a warning first so that the victim understands the danger of further aggression. He has removed several hats on occasion but nothing more."

"Wong, massive numbers of new immigrants arrive in California every day from all over the world. They are like locust. The best route for survival is learning how to live with them in peace, and the sooner the better. Create friendships with worthy and influential allies. There are many whites who disagree with the current treatment of the natives. You must find these people and nurture a relationship. The people of your tribe must adopt new ways and open your minds to new ideas. As the Chinese must do. Conflict will only invite disaster."

"Contact Jack Ellis in Marysville at the Suey Sing Association whenever you need any advice. His Chinese name is Yuen Yeck Bow. He has many powerful friends. I will tell him about you when I reach Marysville."

Next evening on the outskirts of Marysville the group bid farewell to the natives. Wong and another native attempted to return and exchange rifles. Cheung resisted. *"We don't need them anymore. Please keep them and take your own rifles back as well. I know that you will use them wisely. Wong, please think about what we discussed yesterday. I left a small gift for you under the bed I slept on after the feast. I hope that it may someday be useful to you and your tribe."*

Raising their rifles in a salute Wong, Yuba and natives rode off in haste. Way queried Cheung. *"You left a pouch of gold under the bed last night, right?"*

Cheung smiled at Yuen and Way.

"I wondered why you didn't let me carry the knapsack?"

"Way, I brought the gold to offer it for protection, but Wong volunteered it before I could ask. It was too heavy to carry back to the campsite, anyways."

"Nephew, he always comes up with a plan. What do we do next?"

"We'll head into town. Drop me off at Mr. Ellis' home. I will meet you in front of the Suey Sing Association."

Yuen and Way waited for an hour in front of the Suey Sing building. Cheung arrived. *"We will leave the urns at the association. I'll request a private room."*

Cheung quickly entered and returned. *"Yes, they will provide us with a private room. Ti Chu's card still works well. Let's bring the urns upstairs to the second room on the left."* Cheung turned to Yuen, *"Here's the key. You and Way can transport the urns and I will stay with the wagon."*

After the urns were transported, Cheung directed Yuen to drive to Ellis's shop. Ellis and Jack were waiting with the door open. The wagon was driven inside and the door was locked behind them. Ellis greeted the travelers, *"Welcome back gentlemen, and congratulations on completing your mission."*

Cheung talked with Ellis and Jack for a while in his private office. They came out and exchanged handshakes. Cheung led his friends outside towards the closest Chinese restaurant. They found a secluded corner to talk. *"Mr. Ellis has a friend who will exchange the gold for cash tomorrow. I am giving half of a pouch to Ellis, and the other half to Jack for their help on our mission. Once we receive the money we will distribute each deceased member's share inside their urn with the bones. We should probably acquire a few more urns to send home our own shares. Then we will have the association transport them for us to Ti Chu in San Francisco for safe-keeping until we arrive."*

"Shall we give Ti Chu a reward for his help as well?" asked Way.

"Yes, I think so but only after we have received notification that the urns have arrived at their destinations intact. His card has served us well. If we give him a reward too soon it may stir suspicion of what is contained in the urns. I am sure that he can be trusted but I will not risk what belongs to others. Do you have any questions?"

In profound admiration, Yuen sighed, "*An ignorant man shows his wisdom by remaining silent. Way, don't bother asking him how he came up with this plan? You'll get a headache. Let's just eat.*" The men join in laughter.

Jack arrived with the cash the next day. He was very grateful for his reward and told the group that the money would be sent to his family back in China. Ellis invited the group for dinner the next night. During the evening, Cheung related the details of his journey to his hosts. Jack decided to continue to work with the Ellis family and if Wong contacted him, he would do whatever he could to assist him and his tribe. After Jack departed, the money was apportioned and wax sealed in the urns together with the bones of the deceased and addressed to Chun Ti Chu who would receive delivery through his association's courier service. A message from Cheung was attached to the shipment of urns to wait until the three men arrived in San Francisco before sending off the urns to China.

Chapter 16

Return to San Francisco

A FEW DAYS LATER THE GROUP ARRIVED IN SAN FRANCISCO AND checked in once again at the International Hotel. Over dinner they discussed their upcoming meeting with Ti Chu. Cheung spoke first. *"I asked Ti Chu to store the urns until we arrive because I was hoping one of you would travel with the urns."*

Way chuckled. *"Uncle, your plan sounds good to me. Uncle Yuen should return to China with the urns. It is becoming far too dangerous in California."*

"Nephew, it is too dangerous for me, but not for you. I am still capable of defending myself when the need arises. No, I am going to Canada to help Cheung find his son, just as he would do for me."

"But Yuen, it is of utmost importance to each member's family that the urns arrive safely at the proper destination," said Cheung. *"They should be personally delivered by someone who knew the deceased, to ensure the proper relatives receive the urns. Our mission is not complete until their arrival is confirmed. You must deliver the urns and then notify us by telegram when they have reached their rightful destination. Way has commitments to fulfill for your villagers mining in Canada. He and I will remain in San Francisco until we receive your confirmation. If anything goes wrong, Ti Chu will have the authority to correct any problems regarding the shipment of the urns."*

Yuen surrendered, *"Okay, I'll go but I'll return to help find Wing."*

Later in private, Way turned to Cheung smiling, *"Once he arrives home, his wife will never let him leave."* The two erupted with laughter.

When the three men arrived at the Sam Yup Association they were escorted to Ti Chu's office. They saw their urns sitting in a far corner of the office. Their wax seals were still intact. Ti Chu greeted them. *"My friends, congratulations. Sorry, Cheung we have no information concerning your son yet, but I am glad to see you all arrived back safely. Your urns are in the corner. Can I send them off now?"*

Cheung spoke, *"Thank you very much Chu for all your help with our mission. Your card served us very well and made our mission much easier to accomplish. Yuen is returning to China so he thought that he would travel home with the urns. So he is ready to leave whenever the urns are ready to be shipped."*

"The Pacific Mail Steamship Company services all our shipping needs. They leave for Hong Kong twice a week; the next ship will be leaving in two days. We must place all the urns in a single crate to minimize the new Disinterment Ordinance Tax of $150 for each body. They torment us while we are alive now they pass new laws to torment us after we die. Once these urns reach Hong Kong, our agency will pick up the crate and transfer it to another Pacific Mail vessel headed to Canton. Once they reach Canton, Yuen can unpack the crate to send the urns off to their individual destinations. I will inform our Pacific Mail agents that Yuen will be travelling with the crate so he can take charge or have access to the urns whenever he wishes. Yuen will need an exit visa authorized by our agency before he can buy passage aboard the ship. We have an agreement with the steamship companies for them not to allow passage to any Chinese person without an exit visa approved by the Six Companies, which confirms that the passenger has paid all his personal debts before departure. Ko retrieved Yuen's bond of $500 from the immigration department. Let me get it for you and issue an exit visa for Yuen now."

Ti Chu approached an ornate rosewood cabinet. Opening the folding doors, he pulled open a drawer, removed $500 from a small strong box, removed a document from another drawer, filled in Yuen's name, stamped and signed it and handed the cash and the document to Yuen. *"You have to present this document to the ticket agent at the shipping terminal before he will allow you to buy a ticket. Are the rest of you staying for a while?"*

"Yes, Way and I have a few things to do before we leave for Canada. So we will be here for a while. Can we pay you for the Disinterment Ordinance now?" Ti Chu agreed.

"Did you say it was $150?" Ti Chu nodded. Yuen stepped forward and gave $150 to Ti Chu who deposited it back in the small metal strong box in a desk drawer.

"Cheung, you must not carry that much cash. It is too easy to be a target for robbery. Things are changing here in Chinatown. You must be vigilant at all times of your surroundings. Some of the tongs outside of our control are fighting amongst themselves. Many new splinter organizations have been recently formed such as The Society of Pure Upright Spirits, Society for Maintaining Justice, Society for Peace and Benevolence and Society for Broadening Human Life. They were originally formed to protect their members from rival tongs and the lofan. In their efforts to survive, they have forgotten their reason to exist and have adopted the ways of the west, that is profiting at the expense of others. They now control the brothels, the gambling houses, the opium dens, and the shipment of little sisters from China, as well as extorting funds from our own people through blackmail, protection rackets, and kidnapping. They corrupt the police with bribes who look the other way as long as whites are not affected by their activities. These tongs have grown very wealthy and powerful. Recently they have imported many boo how doy (hatchet men or paid assassins) from China to do their fighting and killing. Many are soldiers from the failed Taiping Rebellion. These men have very little respect for human life, even their own since their families are compensated if they die in battle. They only fear being the last to join in any conflict. They are sworn to secrecy and will kill their own brothers if requested to do so by their leaders. Our organization has tried to remain neutral but our members have occasionally become entangled in their futile web of madness over honour and revenge. If we do not protect our members they will join other tongs. We not only have to fear the lofan, now we have to fear our own people. There is no safety in Chinatown for anyone. One of our members, an elderly man named Yee Foo, was scolding his pet cats in Stout's Alley when two of these highbinders (originally, assassins wore belts or binders high on their waist to carry their weapons, usually hatchets) who thought he was scolding them. Without hesitation they drew their guns and killed him as he sat holding the cats in his arms. It may be wise to avoid Stout's Alley and Waverly Place; they seem to be the favoured locations for confrontations between rival tongs. Be careful, these men are very dangerous and they will approach

unfamiliar faces just to instill fear and respect. It would be wise for you to act fearful when they approach. They wear their weapons openly so they can be easily recognized. If you offer any resistance you may go on a journey from which there is no return. It looks like more restriction of Chinese immigration is close at hand. Your timing for performing this mission seems incredibly auspicious. The door for Chinese immigrants may close very soon. We're fighting it but the politicians will do whatever wins favour with voters. They care for nothing except maintaining their seat at the subsidized pigfest."

"Thank very much Ti Chu. We will heed your advice. Would you like to join us for dinner at the hotel? We would like to show our gratitude for your assistance."

"I am busy tonight but not tomorrow. Lunch or dinner is fine with me."

"Okay tomorrow evening at 6 o'clock at the International Hotel dining room, we look forward to seeing you."

The group exchanged bows and the visitors departed. Once outside the men proceeded towards the hotel. Cheung turned to Yuen. "We had better go to the Pacific Mail Steamship office to buy your passage to Hong Kong."

As the three men wandered towards the harbour two men with colt revolvers tucked under their belts passed them, then turned to follow. Cheung signaled to Yuen and Way with his hands that they were being followed. Cheung covertly took out his wallet and withdrew most of the cash and tucked it inside his underwear. Yuen and Way continued at a regular pace. The streets were empty. Just before they passed a dark alley the two men passed, then they turned to block the path. Both men were slender and wiry. One was about five feet tall and the other slightly taller. Both were in their late-thirties and well-dressed in western attire. Each rested a hand on his pistol and the shorter of the two spoke in a sarcastic tone "Brothers, we are members of the Kwong Dock Tong (Society for Broadening Human Life). You must be new arrivals. We have never seen you before. You are very well-dressed in western garments. You must be very rich merchants. We would like to ask you for a donation to our tong for the cause of broadening human horizons. We can talk in there." He directed the group into a blind alley.

Heeding Ti Chu's advice, Cheung feinted fear and nervously fumbled for his wallet. "Yes, how much would you like? We have just returned from Sacramento. We wish not to cause anyone any trouble."

"We would like all the cash in your wallets and any jewelry."

Cheung handed them his wallet. The first man remarked. "*These men are well-connected. There is a card stamped by Chun Ti Chu.*"

The second man searched Yuen and Way for wallets without luck. The first man took Cheung's wallet. He smiled at the meager amount left in the wallet. He searched Cheung pockets for more, drawing his gun and then said in a more affirmative voice. "*Now all of you, drop your pants before you hear our puppies bark* (euphemisms - puppy-gun)."

The second man drew his gun. He noticed something tied around Yuen's neck. He went to remove it. Yuen pulled back to protect his piece of precious jade. "*This was my father's. You can have anything but not that.*"

The second man raised his gun to pistol-whip Yuen. Way leaped out, knocked the man over, disarming him. The first man was shocked and pointed his gun at Way. Cheung blocked the pistol with his left hand and elbowed him in the throat, then removed his pistol. The man dropped to his knees clutching his throat with both hands and coughing to clear his throat. Cheung forced the first man to lay on his stomach with his hands behind his head and stood above him with a gun. He gestured to Way to do the same with the second man. "*We can kill you both and no one will care or know who did it. Or you can swear not to bother us again, and we will leave your guns somewhere close by, so you can recover them. You will not lose face by having to explain how your guns were lost. The choice is yours. Do you wish to live?*" They agreed. Cheung wondered what to do next. Yuen whispered in Cheung's ear to talk in private. Way guarded both prisoners as Cheung and Yuen planned their next move. After a brief discussion they reached a consensus, Cheung said, "*Okay, go to the nearest store and buy what we need. My money and wallet is still in his pocket.*" pointing to the shorter highbinder.

A few minutes passed, Yuen returned with a brush pen, a small jar of ink and a few pages of letter-sized paper, Cheung and Yuen composed a letter in private while Way continued to guard the prisoners. Once the ink was dry, they folded the letter in half, so that the written portion was folded back and hidden.

Cheung and Yuen approached the prisoners. Cheung said to Way and Yuen, pointing to the second man. "*Keep him over there and make sure he cannot hear us.*" Way made the man cover his ears.

Cheung got a gun from Yuen and took the first man, "*now tell me your name and the name of your friend. If it differs from what your friend says, you will pay an early visit with your ancestors.*"

"I am Yen Mah Sin, my friend is called Cho Yan Chi."

Cheung signaled Yuen to hand over the pen. "*Now sign your name on this paper.*"

Cheung allowed the ink to dry then folded the paper again, hiding the signature of the first man. Way and Cheung exchanged captives. As Yuen held the gun, Cheung asked the second man. "*Your friend has signed his name on this paper and has told me your name. I have folded it back so it does not reveal his name. Now sign the paper, if your name does not match with what he has told me, your plans for the future will be sadly interrupted.*"

The second man signed Cho Yan Chi. Cheung smiled as he showed the paper to Yuen. They signaled for Way to bring the first man back to reveal what they have signed. Cheung unfolded the letter:

To Chun Ti Chu,

We swear allegiance to the Sam Yup Tong and forsake our allegiance to the Kwong Dock Tong. If we dishonour this agreement, may we die a slow and agonizing death.

Both men looked in horror, realizing that they have just signed their own death warrants.

"*To insure you keep your promise, this letter will remain with Chun Ti Chu in a sealed envelope until we leave San Francisco. Chun Ti Chu will not know the contents of the letter. We will leave your guns with the bullets removed, in one of the garbage cans at the far side of Portsmouth Square.*"

As they departed for Portsmouth Square, Cheung said, "*That was a close call. I am glad they believed we would shoot them. That was a great idea, Yuen.*"

Way said, "*Uncle, maybe you should hide the jade just in case we get robbed again before you leave for China. We may not be so lucky next time.*"

"*This is all I have to remember my father by. I couldn't bear to part with it.*"

"*But we could have bought it back for you through Ti Chu's contacts.*"

"*Sorry, I did not think of that.*"

"*Oh I forgot about the jade that I need to check out. It's still in the locker at the hotel. I better get it confirmed,*" said Way.

"*What jade are you talking about?*"

"I think there is jade near our gold mine. No one knows yet. I have a large piece of it at the hotel. I will show it to you once we return to the hotel."

The three stopped to buy a bag of oranges. They emptied the bag and left the oranges on a vacant bench. They found a secluded area, took out the guns, removed the bullets, placed the guns inside the empty bag, and then deposited the bag inside a garbage container at the opposite side of the park. The two highbinders waited patiently and watched at the entrance. As the three walked pass the highbinders, Cheung stopped to speak, "*We are going to Sam Yup Tong to drop off this letter to Ti Chu now. The envelope will only be opened by Ti Chu if anything happens to us. On our departure, an envelope containing this letter will be couriered and addressed to you at your tong. We bear you no malice.*" Both sides bowed, acknowledging mutual consent.

The three stopped at the entrance to the Sam Yup building. Cheung peered back. The two highbinders had not followed, so the trio continued past and walked towards the harbour to secure passage for Yuen and then they returned to the hotel. Way retrieved a small bag from the hotel storage facility. When he opened the bag, Yuen inspected the stone carefully. "*I have a friend in our village who showed me how to test for jade. Yu (jade) is the stone of heaven; it generally feels cool to the touch, and also soft, but it is stronger than steel. It should feel heavy compared to glass. Here run it across your cheek. Does it feel cool?*"

Way placed the stone against his cheek, and then nodded.

"*Now get a knife and try to scratch it. Jade is stronger than steel so you will not be able to scratch it with a steel blade.*"

Way took out a pen knife and tried to scratch it. The point of the blade slipped off.

"*Another quality of jade is its depth. You can generally see into the stone. The best test is to tie a hair around the stone and pass a flame beneath it. Real jade will absorb the heat and keep the hair from burning. We can try it if you would like to provide a hair from your queue.*"

Way loosened the binding on his queue and pulled out a hair. Yuen wrapped the hair around the stone. Cheung handed Yuen a match. Yuen lit the match and passed it under the hair wrapped around the stone. It did not burn.

Yuen said, "*Yes it's jade. Where did you find this stone?*"

"Uncle, a mountain near our gold mining site is covered with these stones. Some are huge."

"Do the other villagers know of your discovery?"

"No I didn't want to create false excitement so I kept it quiet until I had proof."

"Maybe you should keep it a secret for now, Way, until we can plan how best to use the discovery. What do you think Cheung?"

"This is your village's discovery; I do not think that they would appreciate someone from another village sharing in their good fortune. And I would not blame them for this sentiment."

"Cheung if not for you, your father and your uncle, I doubt that I would be standing here now. These villagers who are mining were funded with my money which I originally acquired with your help. I am sure these villagers will gladly accept whomever I recommend."

"Thank you, my friend, but I better just concentrate on finding my son when I return to Canada."

The next evening the story of the highbinders was related to Ti Chu, without identifying the men by name. "You were very fortunate not to have been killed or marked for death. The Kwong Docks are the most dangerous tong in Chinatown. But I must commend you for how you handled the situation. Those two men may have to guard your safety to prevent me from opening your letter and revealing their identity. Your strategy was brilliant. Who came up with this idea?"

With a big grin, Cheung looked at Yuen, "Yuen came up with the plan. It's about time he shared some of the blame." Laughter ensued.

Yuen said, "I have dealt with triad people before. Saving face is almost as important to them as the air they breathe. We knew if they were released that they would eventually try to kill us to save face. We were not going to kill them, so our only option was to appease their need for revenge by creating a threat on their lives. So we created the letter and tricked them into signing it before they understood what we were doing."

"Too bad you men are planning to leave; I could really use your help to restore peace in Chinatown."

"Ti Chu, we understand and appreciate what you are trying to do for our people here, but we really don't want to be involved with local disputes. We have enough problems of our own. I hope you understand?"

"I understand. I only wished we could provide more information about your son. He seems to be very well-hidden."

"The head office knows that I am searching for him. They want me to continue to work for them. So they are hiding him from me. I am sure that I will find him but I don't know how or when." The food arrived. Cheung urged the others. "Let's eat. The seafood here is so abundant and fresh. Ti Chu, were you able to improve the working conditions for our Chinese laborers on the Canadian Railway?"

"I had our labour agents make several requests for better food, more food, more training, more safety, but the company will not listen. They simply don't care how many Chinese lives are lost to build their railway. They just keep sending for more workers. They have hired their own recruiters to canvass the villages as well as the cities. Our people are mostly illiterate and cannot read our notices. I cannot forewarn our people of the danger before they arrive in Victoria. By then it is too late, they have signed a labour agreement that they or their family must honour. I am sorry, Cheung, I do not know what else I can do. If you have any ideas, please let me know."

"Ti Chu, thank you for your efforts. Maybe I can write an article for the Chinese newspapers about my personal experiences working on the railway in Canada? It may stop some of your locals from going to Canada to work on the railway. I can also include some information on maintaining good health, avoiding disease and treatment for injuries."

"Cheung, the Chinese newspapers such as the Chinese Daily News, the Golden Hills News and the Chinese Free Press that start up in California never last long. They are not financially feasible because so few Chinese here can read. The overwhelming majority are uneducated peasant farmers. Labour to produce a newspaper written in Chinese is many times more costly than a western newspaper. Typesetting in Chinese with 11000 characters requires far more labour than in English, with only 26 letters and 10 numbers. Even if the characters are well systemized, an expert Chinese typesetter can only arrange 4000 characters a day."

"Ti Chu, a written language with a 26-letter alphabet based on sound is a monumental achievement. The major flaw with our culture is reluctance to change. I remember how much time I spent learning to write in Chinese. How much time and energy have countless Chinese scholars wasted, learning to read and write our antiquated language with over 10,000 characters?"

"Cheung, please write your articles anyways and I will have copies printed and they will be posted on the Chinatown bulletin wall at Dupont and Clay Street,

and also on bulletin boards throughout our network of affiliated tongs in America and Guangdong. Anyways it is getting late. Are you going to give me that letter for safe-keeping?"

"No, it was just an idle threat that we won't need to execute. I thought that they would follow us after they got their guns back but they didn't, so I'm sure they believe the letter is already in your possession. If anything happens to us everything in our suite is yours, including the letter. I will leave those instructions with the front desk."

"Well thank you all for the fine dinner. Good-bye, Yuen, I wish you a safe journey. Cheung, once you finish your article come by my office. We can go over it together and maybe have lunch."

Bows were exchanged as Ti Chu departed.

Yuen said, "I am glad to be leaving California. This country is so beautiful and filled with endless possibilities but the politicians have created so much bad karma. Remaining too long is an invitation for disaster."

The next morning Cheung and Way accompanied Yuen to the pier. When they arrived, Yuen said "I hope to see you in Canada. I know that you both think my wife will prevent me from coming back but these past months have been one of the best times of my life. Waiting to die is boring. Your plan to send me to safety has failed. I will return as soon as I can, to help find Wing."

Cheung placed his arm around Yuen's shoulder and said, "okay my friend, thank you. Take care and have a safe journey."

Way bowed to Yuen, "Uncle, I put that piece of jade in your bag. Please contact your friend to check the value and find out how we can best profit from importing it to China. It may not be the best jade but it must have some value. I hope you were not offended by our well-meaning roost to send you to safety. Uncle, please tell my family that I miss them very much and I hope to see them soon. Have a peaceful and safe voyage. You have always been like a father to me."

"Way, you have no idea how often I have wished you were my son."

Way smiled with misty eyes as he surrendered his uncle's bag. Yuen extended his arm around Way's shoulder momentarily and then walked up the passenger ramp onto the steamship.

Once on board, Yuen proceeded to the promenade deck. He looked out and found the faces of his friends, then waved good-bye.

Cheung and Wing watched the ship depart. Cheung smiled and turned to Way, "The road to hell does not seem so bad when you have such good friends who wish to share the journey."

Chapter 17

San Francisco Tong War

OVER THE NEXT WEEKS, CHEUNG WROTE A FEW SHORT ARTICLES concerning his experience on the Canadian railway. It was recommended that they remain short, since the few who would read it for others would only do so if they were not too cumbersome to read. Too lengthy an article would lose the audience.

At a lunch with Cheung and Way, Ti Chu praised the articles. *"Cheung, your articles have proven to be very effective. I was able to also have your articles posted in China. Even though our people are fleeing California due to anti-Chinese attacks, local recruitment for workers to help build the Canadian railway has fallen off, according to our labour agents. But in Hong Kong recruitment has risen because the situation in China grows worst with famines, droughts, floods, disease and civil unrest."*

"We may not save our countrymen who are extremely desperate in China. At least they are now better informed about the hardship and danger involved with working on the railway in Canada."

"I think your articles have served the intended purpose. I don't think any more articles are necessary. The information will now be passed on by word of mouth throughout the Six Companies network. By the way, it may not be safe to walk the streets of Chinatown over the next few days. Two tongs are fighting over a mui

jeh (slang for prostitute). A woman was taken from a brothel without payment of redemption money. I know that both tongs have gone into war council so a big battle is anticipated. I will let you know as soon as I get more details. One tong will challenge the other to meet for battle at a certain time and place. Both tongs will agree in advance on what weapons will be used, which will probably be knives and hatchets. They will then gather their boo how doy and fight until there is a victor. The defeated party will be liable to pay reparations to the victors. It must be negotiated by a third party. Since we have remained neutral, I may be elected to serve as a mediator. If no settlement is mutually agreed upon, the madness will continue."

"Ti Chu, it sounds like a dangerous job. Will you do it?"

"I must try to restore peace in Chinatown at every opportunity. The government is trying to expel all Chinese from this country. The more violence and criminal acts that are reported about the Chinese, the more justification they will have for our expulsion. Every petty detail about Chinese activity which may appear negative is blown out of proportion by the press who profit by printing whatever they think will appeal to their readers. The Six Companies organization will try to neutralize the negative reports as best we can, but a tong war creates a problem that is difficult to nullify. We must try to pacify the opposing tongs as soon as possible."

"Okay, be careful Ti Chu, it's a thankless job and too easy to be accused of being biased. Good luck."

After midnight, Cheung and Way were awakened by volleys of gunfire. The sound of gunshots gradually drew closer as they watched from the window. A running gun battle between two groups could be seen below their suite. Across the street an injured man was left behind as the battle continued past the front of the hotel. Minutes later the gunfire ended.

The injured man across the street struggled to his feet but fell again, and lay sitting against the wall in a pool of blood. Cheung and Way quickly dressed and went downstairs to check the aftermath of the gun battle. On the main level they saw that the front door had been barred shut and was now being re-opened. Except for a few broken windows along the street, the area had incurred very little damage. Cheung and Way heard a groan from the injured man. They surveyed the area, before cautiously crossing the street. They approached the man who was lying unconscious face down. His shirt was soaked in blood. Way turned him over. *"Hey, this is one of the men who tried to rob us. Let's just leave him for the police. He'll probably bleed to death by the time they arrive."*

Cheung said, *"No, go and get some bandages and a couple of towels from the hotel. There is good and bad in everyone. Let's help him."*

Way rolled his eyes then ran back to the hotel. He returned shortly with supplies. Cheung had already removed the victim's shirt and used it to apply pressure on the wound. He replaced the shirt with a towel and secured it by wrapping the bandage around the victim's torso, then the two carried the man to the hotel. In the hotel lobby, they were aided by hotel staff. The hotel manager protested, but he was ignored by Cheung who instructed the workers to bring the victim upstairs. Cheung offered the manager a fistful of bills. In the living room, they covered the sofa with towels before placing the injured man there. Cheung gave the helpers a generous tip as they departed, then treated the gash in the unconscious man's chest. *"He is very fortunate that no major organs have been damaged, but he has lost a lot of blood so it will take time for him to recover."*

The next day, as Cheung was cleaning the victim's wound, the man woke up and stared at him in silence. *"Yen Mah Sin, you are going to need stitches to close this wound. You are fortunate, the gash was deep but did not pierce any organs or major blood vessels. I can stitch you up. But if you would rather be taken to a hospital you will end up in jail. Do you wish for me to stitch you up?"*

Sin asked. *"Why do you help me? I tried to rob you."*

"I will not judge you for what you do. We are all victims in this country during these times. I am sure you have your reasons for the path you have chosen."

"The hospitals do not treat Chinese, so stitch me up."

Way watched as Cheung sewed the stitches. The man accepted the pain without flinching or uttering a sound. Way and Cheung were surprised at his tolerance for pain. The scars on his body revealed a history of pain. *"I'm finished now,"* said Cheung. *"These stitches will have to be removed in a few weeks. Get some rest now."*

When the victim awoke, Cheung checked the bandages. *"I noticed many scars. Have you been tortured?"*

"Yes, I served as a soldier and was captured during the Taiping Rebellion. The government troops wanted me to reveal the location and size of our army. They gave me only water and tortured me for three days. I was rescued on the fourth day."

Surprised by his revelation, Cheung continued, *"Why did you join the rebels?"*

"In 1855 my parents sent me north to visit my older brother in Hunan. A new Viceroy Yeh Ming Shen had just been appointed to deal with the rebellion. His personal estate in Central China was attacked by rebel forces composed of troops, mostly from Guangdong. My parents feared retaliation was forthcoming. In June, July and August, Yeh Ming Shen ordered the decapitation of 75,000 people in Guangdong. The majority, like my parents were innocent victims. I was only ten years old at that time. When my uncle brought me home to my village, both sides of the main street were lined with the heads of our villagers. The heads of my parents were among them. I joined the rebels two years later."

"How did you become a highbinder?"

"Our rebellion was defeated by the Manchu with the aid of French and British forces in 1864. After our defeat, rebels were being hunted by government troops, so I joined the army of a warlord who had a friendly alliance with corrupt government officials. Over the passing of many years I heard many wonderful stories of Gum San from those who had returned with great wealth. When a recruiter for the Kwong Dock Tong offered me a job and free passage to work as a soldier in America I decided to go."

"Did you know what you would have to do?"

"When you become a soldier you do not have to think, you just follow orders. I am bound by the terms of my contract. If you hand me my jacket I will show you. I always carry it with me."

Way brought him the jacket. Sin took out his contract from an inside pocket. He handed it to Cheung to read:

To Yen Mah Sin, Salaried soldier:

The plans and schemes of our organization, as denoted by seal, is the work of the leaders; the work of the soldier is to fight battles and oppose foes from within and from without. You, Yen Mah Sin, together with all other salaried soldiers, shall act only when orders are given; and without orders you shall not act, except in the case of emergency when our members are threatened or attacked. When orders are given you shall advance valiantly without hesitation to your assigned duty, striving to be first, never shrinking or turning your back upon the battle-field.

You shall always follow the orders from our director at all times. You will strive to always be punctual, work for the good of the organization, and serve us to the best of your ability. If, in fulfilling your duties, you are slain, the organization will undertake to pay $500.00 sympathy money to your

heirs. If you are wounded, a surgeon shall be engaged to heal your wounds; and if you are incapacitated for any length of time, you shall receive $10.00 per month. If you are maimed for life, and incapacitated for service, you shall receive the additional sum of $250.00; and a subscription shall be opened to defray the expenses of your passage home.

This document is given as proof of our agreement, as an oral promise is devoid of validity.

It is further stipulated that you, in common with your comrades, shall exert yourself to kill, or wound, anyone at the direction of this organization. If, in so doing you are arrested and have to endure the miseries of imprisonment, this organization will undertake to send $100.00 every year, to your family, during the term of your imprisonment

Seal of the San Francisco branch of the Kwong Dock Tong.

Dated March 20th, 1878

"Sin, this document is very clear concerning your duties. What if the leaders tell you to kill your brother or your uncle? Would you do it?"

"That is very unlikely. The leaders are Chinese and understand family ties come before all else."

"Not according to what is stated in your labour agreement."

"Will you kill your best friend, or innocent woman and children?"

"Our leaders would never order us to do these acts."

"Well, I hope you are right but your leaders profit from the misery of others through prostitution, blackmail, kidnapping, extortion and murder. These are evil pursuits and evil men cannot be trusted. When you meet with your father and mother in the next realm, will they praise you or blame you for honouring an evil agreement? Now remember you only follow orders, you are not suppose to think."

Way smiled at Cheung. Sin grew quiet and peevish as his anger simmered. Then he tried to reach for his jacket in an attempt to leave, but he lacked enough strength and started to fall. Way caught him under the arms. Cheung helped Way as they laid him back on the sofa. *"You have lost too much blood. It will take a few days of rest for you to walk the streets. Just lay still and rest. We will return with some food."*

When Cheung and Way entered the lobby of the hotel the police were questioning the staff members. More fearful of the tong than the police, each one interviewed ended with "No saby". Every resident in Chinatown knew the answers to the questions being asked, but all knew a closed mouth

ensured survival. Consequently, the cause of the tong war, who was involved and who escaped remained a mystery to the police. When Cheung and Way were stopped by a young constable they responded, "No saby", as they continued towards the dining room.

As they entered the dining room, the diners stopped to watch as they passed. Cheung asked a waiter, "Why are they watching us?"

"*They know that you have the boo how doy in your suite which may endanger their safety. Many guests will leave our hotel unless peace is restored very soon.*"

As breakfast arrived, Ti Chu entered the dining room. He approached the table, pulled out a chair and sat down, "*You said that you didn't want to get involved with our tong wars, and now I hear from some of the employees that you rescued one of the boo how doys. Cheung, you should not have interfered last night. You and Way may be marked for death by the rival tong. Fortunately, I have been selected to mediate a truce. I have negotiated a temporary cease in hostilities because both tongs want time to recover and bring in more soldiers. The man that you house helped a mui jeh to escape from a brothel run by their rivals, without permission from his tong. Unless their rivals receive her back or compensation, the war will continue. They may even have their lawyers file a false claim against your guest. Chinese cannot testify in court, so they can buy witnesses and bribe officials to have their victims sent to prison or deported back to China.*"

Cheung asked Ti Chu."*Do you know how much compensation the rivals are asking for?*"

"*No, but I must talk to your guest to find out where he is hiding the girl, so I can talk with her.*"

"*Okay, let's have breakfast and discuss our options. Helping others has its pitfalls.*"

After the meal, the group proceeded upstairs. Way carried breakfast for Sin who was awakened with their arrival. Sin bowed his head as he is introduced to Ti Chu, "*I know who you are. I am deeply honoured.*"

Sin addressed his hosts. "*The two of you have very powerful friends. By the way, what are your names?*"

"*Just call us Cheung and Way. There is no need for formality.*"

"*Sin, I have been elected to restore peace, but to do so I need to find where you are hiding the mui jeh. Please tell me where I can find her.*"

"*That mui jeh is my niece. I received a letter from my Uncle informing me that she had been kidnapped and sold. So I searched every brothel in San Francisco to*

find her. The brothel owner was waiting for higher bids, to be the first to violate her virtue. The tongs do not know of our relationship. I want to send her home to my uncle before she dies of disease. She was never sold by her parents. She was kidnapped against her will. My tong thinks that I am in love with her, I prefer that they not know my secret. Tell my tong that I will agree to pay her redemption money, but I need time to acquire it. Do you know the death toll from last night?"

"Two deaths, one from each tong, many injured but none critically, except you. Your assailants believe you have joined your ancestors. Very few reparations will be necessary since neither tong won nor lost face. If you die, your tong may demand compensation as part of any settlement to balance their loss. So please try not to make my job any more difficult."

"I do not understand why you need to talk with her?"

"I need to know the terms of her labour contract."

"Can you give me my jacket" Way picked it up and handed it to Sin.*"I have her contract. I was studying it to find what I needed to pay for her freedom, but the challenge to fight was accepted by our leaders before I had a chance to negotiate the terms of redeeming Ling Yee's contract. Here is the contract that she was forced to sign."*

Ti Chu looks:

To Ling Yee, an indentured prostitute,

This agreement confirms that Ming Chee Wong has paid the sum of $300 to secure the contract of Ling Yee who agrees to give her body to Mr. Wong Ming for the service of prostitution for a term of four years. Ling Yee will receive no wages. At the expiration of four years, Ling Yee will become her own master and Mr. Ming shall not hinder or trouble her. If Ling Yee runs away before her time is up, her mistress shall find her and return her, and whatever expense is incurred in finding and returning her, shall be paid by her by the addition of days to her term. If Ling Yee shall be sick at any time for more than ten days, she shall make up by an extra month of service for every ten days' sickness. This document is written proof of this agreement, as witnessed by Ling Yee's personal mark.

Dated September 5th, 1881

Ming Wong

Ling Yee's finger print signifies her acceptance.

"She has only recently arrived so the whole amount would usually be due because her term has only just started, but I will see what I can negotiate. Both

sides want peace. Every business in Chinatown is controlled by these tongs. Wars are costly and will disrupt their profits from their victims but neither wants to lose face by appearing weak. Once it is revealed that she was kidnapped into servitude, the amount for compensation demanded by the rival tong should be greatly compromised since her family is an unwilling participant in her present circumstance. Sin, you must swear that what you have told me is the truth. Your life and that of your niece are at stake, if any portion of your story is discovered to be false."

Without hesitation, Sin said, "I swear it."

Ti Chu offered an explanation. "Girls like this are often kidnapped or sold to compensate for debts created by their family members from gambling, smoking opium or unpaid loans. They are offered in Canton for a little as $5 each. Many laborers mortgage their families for passage to foreign lands to find work. The Qing has given full sanction to these brokers of misery. It is not unusual for enslaved families to be held in bondage for generations before a descendant can purchase their freedom."

"What can we do to help him or the girl?" asked Cheung.

"If the girl was kidnapped we may be able to negotiate a settlement. If she had been sold by her family it would have been a different matter. The practice of selling women in California started around 1854. From 1848 to 1854 over 45,000 Chinese had arrived in San Francisco, only 16 were women. One of first women was Ah Toy, an exotic beauty, who enslaved men wherever she went. Her domicile was on the south side of Clay Street between Dupont and Kearney Streets. Men flocked from the gullies and ravines of the high Sierras, just to gaze on the countenance of this mystic beauty during her daily appearance in Portsmouth Square. It cost one ounce of gold for each patron to satisfy their curiosity. She even took two white men to court for mixing brass filings in their gold. The judge dismissed the case, after which Ah Toy decided to retire. She left for China only to return with a boatload of Chinese maidens of easy virtue. Prostitution in San Francisco Chinatown was started by this woman. According to most men, the sins of the prostitute could not be any worse then those of their customers. Anyway, let me meet with the rival factions to find out what appears acceptable." Ti Chu left with Ling Yee's contract in hand.

Cheung addressed Sin. "So I am glad to see your family comes before your duty to the Tong? It is good to know that you would risk everything for your niece."

"Yes, but I have done many things I regret. You torment my soul with your suppositions."

"Then change your occupation."

"This is the only life I know. I was consumed with hate and anger after the death of my parents. I only wanted revenge and to taste the blood of government troops. I have committed acts of violence that will not allow me to sleep. I did not care whether I lived or died. Being like this makes it easy to be blind to fear and death. Saving my niece was to be my sole act of kindness in this life. I rescued her before they harvested her innocence."

"Why do you persist in being a soldier?"

"I know no other life."

"Any man can be a labourer. Nothing is required except a strong back."

"My employers will not allow me to leave unless I pay my redemption money which is an impossible amount to acquire."

"Everyone thinks you are dying. It is a good opportunity for you to start a new life. Let me think of a plan."

There was a knock on the door. Cheung said, *"Act gravely injured."*

Way answered the door. Two highbinders stood at the doorway.

"We are here to take our friend away."

"He is gravely injured and cannot be moved. He will probably die if you move him. I have just cleaned his wound and changed his bandages."

The men entered and inspected the blood soaked bandages. Pretending to be unconscious, Sin took laboured breaths. The men shook their heads in solemn respect, then turned and left.

"Good job, Sin. Now let me think what to do about your niece. Way and I must stop Ti Chu before he speaks with your tong. He must tell them you are mortally wounded and will probably not recover. Eat your breakfast but don't answer the door. Way and I must go to Ti Chu's office."

Ti Chu greeted the men when they arrived at his office. Cheung said *"We need to discuss a plan to help Sin before you visit either tong. Sin wants to stop working as a highbinder and terminate his relationship with his tong."*

"The Kwong Docks will wash his body (euphemism – kill him). Highbinders cannot quit because his tong will fear that he will join a rival. He would be marked for death, right away."

"What if he dies of his wounds first?"

"You want to fake his death? They will want to honour him with a funeral. How do you plan to avoid his burial?"

"What if he requests no funeral and to be buried at sea?"

"That would be a very unusual request and arouse a lot of suspicion, but it would save his tong the expense of a costly funeral, so they may go for it. You may need credible witnesses."

"We can try to get some of his fellow tong members to witness his dying requests."

"What about his niece?"

"We can fake her death as well. Only we know that she is Sin's niece. Everybody else thinks they are lovers. Maybe someone can witness her killing herself, after she hears that he is dying. Okay, Way and I can do that."

"Sin's death may cause a problem for me to mediate with two dead for one tong against only one for the other. Perhaps not, the death of Sin may be balanced against the loss of a mui jeh. I will have to think on how to resolve the inequity. Sin's heirs will also receive legacy money from his tong."

"Do you know where I can find a good herbalist? I heard that there was a drug that a person could use to appear being dead. Hopefully, I can find some at a herbalist shop in Chinatown."

"There are many herbalists in Chinatown. I have a friend who is very knowledgeable about Chinese medicines. He has a shop nearby. We can go there now."

They walked only a few blocks than stopped at a small shop. Inside Ti Chu introduced Cheung and Way to a herbalist named Dr. Li Sam Cho, a small man with a loosely-cropped mustache and goatee, wearing glasses and well-dressed in silk. His shop walls were meticulously lined with hundreds of small drawers, each containing a remedy to treat different medical problems. Medicinal substances were dried, peeled, pulverized, distilled and mixed by workers under the supervision of the herbalist. They were obtained from the twigs, bark, flowers, roots, berries, and leaves of known trees and plants locally and from the east. An expert Chinese pharmacist could recognize the nature and name of every compound in his shop just by smell. Over countless centuries, Chinese,herbalists have explored the medicinal qualities of anything that flew, walked, crawled, swam or burrowed. The skin, glands, organs, horns, teeth, shell, bones, hairs, claws and eyes of every known creature had been studied to create powders, creams, ointments and elixirs for every known medical affliction. Based on philosophical Buddhist beliefs, however, experimentation on other living creatures was forbidden in researching drug effectiveness. The underlying principle of Chinese medicines was one based on similarities and opposites. One theory was "like cures like" or that a venomous creature was immune

to its own poison; another was "like becomes like" or that the qualities that an animal or plant exhibits can be reproduced in a patient by processing the essence of the animal or plant. A new land with different plants and animal-life offered a new world of possibilities for Chinese herbalists.

Cheung asked, "*Dr. Cho, may we talk to you in private?*"

Dr. Cho directed the group to his office upstairs. Cheung asked, "*we need a drug that makes a person appear to be dead. Do you have something like that?*"

"*Yes, it comes from Cuba. It was brought to me by Chinese contract laborers who worked in the sugar cane plantations there. It is very powerful and if too large a dose is taken, the symptoms become permanent. It works very quickly. I would experiment with the dosage to find the correct amount for the duration you feel will be necessary.*" The herbalist handed Cheung a small bottle.

"*Thank you, Dr. Cho. That is exactly what I need.*"

"*With the recent tong war and your need for secrecy, I can guess how you plan to use this compound. Ti Chu and I are old friends from the same village. The workers who saw you come in are my wife, my sons and my brother. Your secret is safe with us. I have no love for the rival tongs. I have to pay three of them for protection. They steal from everyone and control every business in Chinatown.*"

When Cheung and Way returned to their suite they discussed their plans with Sin who readily agreed with the plot. After a couple days of experiments with the drug, the dosage was determined for Sin's niece. Sin signed two letters written by Cheung: one addressed to his comrades at his tong and another to his niece. Way delivered the first letter to the Kwong Dock Tong. The second letter was to be delivered to his niece.

The desire to enhance the imagination or to drown cares and sorrows through the use of narcotics is a human foible shared by every society. The Chinese smoked opium to find temporary solace. Over 200 opium dens were located in the nine city blocks that comprised Chinatown since 1876. It was estimated that 40% of the Chinese in California were using opium. To avoid possible conflict with the tongs, Cheung and Way decided to approach the opium den in Stout's Alley during the early dawn. The cobble-stone streets were quiet. Vendors prepared their displays. Workers walked hurriedly en route to their local café for breakfast. The pair wandered past many low class brothels, single 12 by 10 feet rooms with open doors facing the dim narrow alley furnished only with a washbowl, a bamboo chair and a mattress. The scantily-clothed loungei (literal – woman with open legs) laid

in provocative poses, luring their prey *"two bittee lookee, flo bittee feelee, six bittee doee!".*. The opium den was located in the basement of a small grocery store midway along Stout's Alley. As the pair entered the dimly-lit room their noses and eyes were assaulted by a numbing cloud of vapor and the pungent flowery odour of opium. In varying degrees of transcendent bliss, human skeletons languished in the futility of illusion. They laid in contorted postures on bunk beds covered with straw mats, desperately clinging to pipes like castaways with a life preserver. The bunks were arranged for two smokers to lay face to face, their heads resting on blocks of wood or a tin can. In between was a tray containing a nut-oil lamp, a bamboo pipe with an ivory mouthpiece, a round earthenware bowl, a few slender wire pokers, a cup of water, a sponge to wipe the bowl and a pill box of opium. The dim light from the low-flamed opium lamps flickered to penetrate the hazy veil of vapour. Not a word was spoken. The walls and ceiling were blackened by years of smoke. The only sound was the deep sucking of opium pipes and the fizzle of opium being readied for use. The opium den was a crypt for lost souls, broken dreams and hopeless aspirations.

Cheung and Way passed through the room unnoticed. They presented Sin's letter to the proprietor who directed them to follow him to a backroom. They waited for a few minutes, then the niece arrived. She was very petite, extremely attractive girl, 14 or 15 years old dressed in pink silk gown embroidered with plum blossoms. *"Hello, I am Ling Yee. According to my friend who read the letter, Sin said that I am to follow your instructions."* Cheung explained his plans and gave Ling Yee a vial containing the drug. Cheung and Way returned to the hotel. Sin greeted them. *"Did you see Ling Yee? Is she well?"* *"Yes she is fine,"* said Cheung. *"Are you prepared for tonight?"* *"Yes, I may join a group of actors in my next life."* *"Well you'd better do a good job or we will all be marked with death by your tong. Way has a small container of fresh chicken blood for you. Smear it on your bandages just before the company arrives."* *"I feel sorry that you have gotten involved with my problem. I will always be in your debt."* *"Okay, we are going to lunch. We will bring you back some food."*

At 6 o'clock, there was a knock at the door. Three men were greeted by the residents. Sin laid back and appeared to be sleeping in discomfort, his breathing was very laboured and shallow. One of them was Cho Yan Chi, Sin's partner in the failed robbery who lowered his eyes and stared at the floor, hiding his recognition of the hosts.

The man in charge, dressed in embroidered Chinese silks, introduced himself: "*I am Ching Quan Dow, director of the Kwong Dock Tong. These are my associates, Cho Yan Chi and Qwok Ting Min. We would like to thank you both for helping our member. May we please see our associate?*"

During the visit, Way slipped away unnoticed, to warn Ling Yee.

Sin was gently prodded awake by Cheung. He was covered in sweat, appeared groggy, his eyes were distant and rolled back. He struggled to speak, pausing frequently to catch his breath. "*Mr. Ching, thank you for coming. I hope that I have not caused you too much inconvenience.*"

"*Rest easy, Sin. We need to know where to find the mui jeh. Can you tell us where she is? We wish to keep her safe from our rivals for now but she may have to be returned. You should have consulted us before taking her. A war is bad for business.*"

"*Yes, she can be found at my friend's opium den at Stout's Alley where Yan Chi and I have often visited before.*"

Yan Chi interjected, "*Yes, I am familiar with the opium den. The owner is one of our clients.*"

"*Please be aware that Ling Yee was kidnapped. Neither she nor her family agreed for her to become a loungei (prostitute, literally woman with open legs),*" said Sin.

Quan Dow said, "*That may be helpful in negotiating reparations but we must first find her. Your taking her served as a good reason to resolve disputes that have been brewing for a long time.*"

Sin uncovered his torso to reveal the blood soaked bandages. He continued, "*if I die, I would like to request being buried quietly at sea without a funeral like my early ancestors who were sea merchants.*"

"*You have been a good soldier and have served us well. If you die it shall be done as you have requested. My hope is that you recover and continue to serve us.*" The three guests then bowed and left quickly.

When the tong members arrived Ling Yee was found dead. The proprietor told the tong men that she heard that Sin was dying and decided to meet with him in their next life and took poison only minutes ago. Sin conveniently died the next day.

Ti Chu negotiated a peaceful settlement. The death of Sin was the second suffered by the Kwong Dock Tong which was balanced by the rival tong paying the $500 compensation to Sin's heirs in China. Since the girl had been

kidnapped, the brothel owner would not be reimbursed by the Kwong Dock Tong but he could seek reimbursement from whom he purchased the girl, with the support of the rival tong. Neither tong had lost face. Cheung and Way volunteered to bury both bodies at sea together in a single private ceremony; Ti Chu accepted their kind offer on behalf of both parties. Sin and Ling Yee were secretly issued exit visas and left for home on a Pacific Mail Steamship, two days after their burial at sea. Cheung and Way donated the funds for their passage home. Ti Chu was commended by all of Chinatown for ending the war and for his dedication in serving the community.

A week later a telegram arrived for Cheung:

To Dai Woo Cheung,

Mission is completed. Will contact your store to find you.

Tan Sing Yuen

Cheung and Way celebrated by inviting Ti Chu out for dinner at their hotel restaurant. Over dinner the pair disclosed the full details of their journey.

Ti Chu was greatly impressed and congratulated them on their brilliant planning and successful execution. At the end of the night, Cheung said, "*Ti Chu, we could never have accomplished our mission without your help and advice. We leave tomorrow for Victoria, please accept this as a token of our friendship and appreciation for the service you rendered us.*" Cheung slipped a leather valise under the table onto Ti Chu's lap.

Ti Chu opened the valise to see stacks of bills. "*This is a very generous gift. I could return to China, buy a home and never work again. Thank you my friends, I am overwhelmed by your generosity.*"

Cheung said, "*We know that your work here is too important to abandon. Please remember a good leader must choose the right time to oppose his adversaries. I feel that the Chinese must be very patient. Our children's children will reap the benefit of our patience, tolerance and wisdom. Hopefully, they will remember our sacrifices and your battle for justice.*"

"*You may be right,*" said Ti Chu, "*but we must try to maintain what we have gained so far, or none of us will be able to remain here to work. Our families cannot survive without the money we send home.*"

"*My friend, if there is ever anything I can do to help you please do not hesitate to let me know.*"

"Only if you do likewise. Can I supply transportation to the dock for you tomorrow?"

"If you wish, we will be leaving the hotel at 8 o'clock. But please don't spend that hard-earned money on us."

At 7:30 the next morning, Ti Chu arrived at the entrance of the hotel in a horse-drawn carriage. The driver loaded the luggage then drove towards the dock. Onlookers stopped to gawk at the three Chinese passengers riding in a carriage, dressed in western attire. When they reached the docking facility, the luggage was unloaded and brought aboard by the ship's deckhands. Ti Chu bade them farewell: "Have a safe journey and good luck with your search. Please know that I will continue to do everything I can to help you find your son. Please use my card whenever you need help. Our contacts in Canada have read your articles, and will be notified of your arrival. The merchant that you use in Yale, On Lee, is one of our affiliates. With some of your money, I will supply him with more stock and tell him to sell to our railway laborers at discount prices, over the winter months. Since the workers will be laid off they cannot be penalized for buying from him during the winter months instead of the company store. It has been my pleasure and a great honour to have met you both. I have learned so much from the experiences we have shared. I hope, one day, our paths will cross once again. Thank you for your generosity, but most of all, for your friendship."

Cheung said, "Ti Chu, we have also learned from you. We share a bond that will not be broken by time or distance. I will write to you to let you know of our progress. It has been a great honour to have a friend like you. May I ask you to please have this envelope delivered to Cho Yan Chi at the Kwong Dock Tong, on our behalf?" Ti Chu consented with a nod.

Way passed him the envelope and added, "Ti Chu, I wish you prosperity, good health and success in all your endeavors. Thank you for your comradeship."

The three men exchanged bows.

As Cheung and Way walked up the gangplank of the SS Idaho, they were cordially greeted by Captain Thomas Huntington. They exchanged handshakes, then the pair walked to the back of the vessel as it cast off, to wave farewell to Ti Chu.

Chiu approached and greeted the pair with a deep bow. He looked towards shore, "I am very happy to see you both again. Isn't that Chun Ti Chu? You have very powerful friends. He carries more face than anyone in Chinatown. Your mission must have been successful."

Cheung responded, *"Yes, our mission was accomplished with the help of Ti Chu. He is very dedicated and has the leadership qualities needed to help represent the Chinese. Hopefully, he will be given enough support by the community but there may be too many factions in Chinatown for him to overcome."*

"Yes, you may be right."

"Chiu, you have a new Captain. Is he temporary or permanent?"

"Captain Alexander is just on leave. The change is just temporary, but Captain Huntington is familiar working with Chinese galley members so I do not anticipate any problems. I can hardly wait to hear about your mission."

Chapter 18

Return to Victoria

THE *Idaho* ARRIVED OUTSIDE VICTORIA IN ESQUIMALT HARBOUR at 3:30 pm November 14th, 1881. The voyage took four days with a short layover due to stormy conditions at Cape Flattery. Upon their arrival in Victoria, Cheung and Way proceeded to the store. Quan Li was surprised to see them. *"I am glad that you both have returned safely. Cheung, your stories about working on the railway were posted all over Chinatown. None of the locals will seek employment on the railway. Many have stopped by our store to ask about you and to thank you for your stories. The Chee Kong Tong wanted to be informed when you arrive. I think they want you to talk at their association. More locals are patronizing our store in appreciation of your service to the railway workers."*

"How did people know that I own a store in Victoria? I never mentioned it in my articles."

"It was mentioned in the articles posted here by the director of the Six Companies, Chun Ti Chu."

Acknowledging the free promotion, Cheung laughed and shook his head.

"May Yun stops by every week," said Quan, *"to check information about where you are and why she has not been receiving letters from you. She has been informed of your articles by the men in Chinatown, who adore her. They all buy treats for her and always look forward to her weekend visits."*

"So business has been good?"

"Yes, we have been very busy. All the businesses in Chinatown are booming with shiploads of Chinese immigrants arriving in port."

"Have you received any messages from Yuen?"

"Yes, May Yun read it for me. She was distressed that you were in California and that you required more help to search for Wing. Yuen sent a telegram, saying that he expects to arrive in Victoria early in January. Should I tell the Chee Kong Tong that you are in town?"

"No, Way and I will go to see them now."

The lobby of the Chee Kong Association was occupied by a half dozen men sitting around a table. One man read for the gathering. A clerk behind the front desk greeted the pair. When he asked for their names, the room grew silent while the reader paused.

"*Dai Woo Cheung and Tan Way Cheung*" said Cheung quietly.

"All the people of Chinatown have been awaiting your arrival. Our director wanted to be informed as soon as you arrived." Smiling, he opened the door behind him to access a staircase. "I will go to inform him of your arrival."

The reader for the group approached Cheung, "Mr. Dai, my name is Li Tong Sun. I have read your articles concerning your work on the railway on numerous occasions for those who cannot read. I would like to thank you for all the information you have provided. Many of our local workers who were desperately seeking employment have decided to find work elsewhere rather than the railway. The bodies of dead railway workers are piling up at the wooden bonehouse on Store Street. Your articles have saved many local men from a terrible fate." The others assembled at the table, having listened to Li Tong Sun's address, stood up and bowed respectfully. Cheung reciprocated in kind. The clerk returned with the director, who greeted the pair cordially and escorted them upstairs. Once in his office, the director stated, "My name is Wang Sing Tung and if there is anything that you need, please let us know. We have been instructed to comply with whatever you request. May I ask how long you plan to stay in Victoria?"

"We have not decided yet," responded Cheung. "Do you know if the steamboat to Yale has shut down for the winter yet?"

"Not yet, but it could close down anytime now, depending on how much the river has been frozen. Anyone planning to go into the interior should leave very soon."

"Are there any safety concerns locally that we should be aware of?" asked Way.

"There is some agitation over importing Chinese workers to build the railway, but it seems to have died down because there has been so little progress with the railway. They need all the labour they can find. If you stay for the winter it would be a great honour for us, if you both could attend one of our meetings and give us a small talk about your experience on the railway? Ti Chu advised me to enclose your affiliation with the store in town in all the local postings."

"Please thank Ti Chu for his thoughtfulness. We do not know how long we will be in Victoria. Our plans have not been set. We will let you know, once our path is determined. Thank you very much."

During the short walk to Nathan's synagogue, Cheung and Way discussed their journey ahead. Way had not communicated to his fellow villagers since none could read. Way spoke, *"Uncle, I think that I should return to the mining site before the river freezes up completely. The villagers must think I have died, since I told them that I would be away for only a couple of months and it has been over eight months now."*

"I will send Yuen a telegram and ask him to delay his trip until March, when the steamboat service resumes. I will wait for him to arrive, then we will go to Yale."

As they continued to walk up Pandora Avenue, Cheung's mind weighed heavily on how best to explain his excursion to California to Louisa. He contemplated how he should justify his recent journey.

When they knocked on the door of the Emanu-el synagogue on Blanshard Street, no one answered. The door was open. The pair walked inside. They found Nathan in his office preparing a sermon. Surprised, he got up and bowed in the Chinese fashion, then shook Chueng's hand. "Cheung! Welcome back! Any news on Wing?"

"I am sure he is alive. I just don't know where he is. The railway company is hiding him because they want me to continue working for them."

"I see you brought a friend," Nathan said as he shook Way's hand.

"This is my very good friend, Tan Way Cheung. I have told him all about you and your wonderful daughter. He is only here for a short while."

Cheung related his journey to California to Nathan. After he had finished, Nathan gave Cheung an update on Louisa's emotional state. *"She seems distant and has been isolating herself in her room since she recently heard that you were in California. She thought that you had given up the search for Wing. Since she had received no letters from you, she feared any news would be bad. She has no interest in making new friends at her school. I often find her in tears. She*

has lost her enthusiasm for schoolwork. Her only moments of temporary joy come from visiting Mrs. Beckham's house and accompanying Ming to visit her friends in Chinatown."

"I will try to restore her hope that I will find Wing, to help revitalize her. I am sure that he is alive. I have a plan to bring him back but it cannot be done before the spring when the railway head office opens up again. The head men will have probably departed for the winter. When they open up again I will retrieve my son."

"Please come tomorrow night for dinner. You and Way will be a very welcome surprise for Louisa. I will only tell her that we have very special guests for dinner. Will six o'clock be convenient?"

"Yes that will be fine. We will see you at six tomorrow evening."

When door bell rang Louisa answered the door. "Uncle Cheung, you're back! Why haven't you written to me? I thought you may have d --- I mean, been seriously injured in an accident. Why did you go to California? Do you know where Wing is?" Cheung grimaced.

"No, May Yun but I shall go to fetch him in the spring." Cheung picked her up and embraced her. "I want you to meet my very good friend Tan Way Cheung."

Louisa bowed than curtseyed, "I am very happy to meet you Mr. Tan. Please just call me May Yun."

Way was captivated by the beautiful young girl. "Hello I have heard so much about you; it is a pleasure to meet you at last. Please just call me Way."

After ceding to the expectations of social conduct, Louisa was anxious to learn more about Wing. She interjected, "Uncle Cheung, what can you tell me about Wing? Do you have any new information?"

Nathan appeared and greeted his guests, "Louisa will have to wait. Dinner is ready. So please join us in the dining room. I have invited some friends to join us."

As Cheung and Way entered the dining room they were introduced by Nathan to each guest. "Cheung, you know many of our guests already, or have read about the others in my correspondence, but Way knows no one. This is Mary Beckham, her son Jonathan, and her very close friend Mrs. Florence Baillie Grohman. Ming is Mary's cook. Mr. Nigel Thompson is the chief customs officer for the City of Victoria, and this is his good friend Mr. Walter Moberly, the major contractor for the Cariboo Road and a

surveyor for the Canadian Pacific Railway. Finally, this is Mr. James Fell, a local business owner. They are all privy to your recent articles posted locally in Chinatown. I translated them into English for all of our guests present here tonight."

"We are glad to see that you have returned safely," said Mary as she directed a smile at Louisa, "I am sure Louisa is very anxious to hear more about Wing. So do you have any more information?"

"Yes, Way and I searched for him in New Westminster. We offered a reward and discovered someone who witnessed how he suffered a head injury and was taken involuntarily as a replacement for an escaped railway contract labourer. His memory may have been affected by the head injury. So he is working at one of the worksites as a labourer."

"Do you know how serious his injury is, Uncle Cheung?"

"No May Yun, I do not know. He does appears to be very healthy and strong, but has lost his queue, according to one of his old friends from our village, who was working on the railway. The friend called out to him in passing, but Wing did not recognize him. He may be suffering from a memory loss. I have talked to many in the field of medicine about this type of injury. They say the time for one's memory to be restored will vary with each individual. It may occur suddenly or gradually over years. A face, a place, a name may sometimes spark instant recovery."

"Where is he? And when will you bring Wing back?" asked Louisa.

"The head office for the railway in Yale will be closed for the winter. I am expecting a friend to arrive to help with finding Wing, so I will have to wait till spring."

"Uncle Cheung he may be suffering, as you described in your posted articles."

"No, May Yun the stores in Yale will be better supplied this winter. He was not left in Yale last winter because I searched for him there. Travelling on the roads in the interior is almost impossible once snow appears. So I think looking for him now would be futile."

"Do you have any idea where he may be?" asks Louisa.

Cheung paused, looked at Nathan and decided to circumvent Louisa's concerns. "I asked the company executives when I left but they did not seem to know because there were so many sites and they do not keep track of their Chinese workers. They are all hired by labour contractors under the

control of the Six Companies in San Francisco. The head director of the Six Companies has instructed his labour agents to help me find my son. At present they do not know which site he is working at, but it should only be just a matter of time."

Nathan interrupted, "Louisa, now please eat. I am sure our guests would also like to know about Cheung and Way's recent journey to California."

"Why did you go to California?" inquired Louisa. "How could you stop looking for Wing?"

"May Yun, I had to fulfill a promise made to my father, my uncle and many others to recover their bones and send them back home to China. I am sorry that I never told you in advance about my trip, but I was concerned it would cause you too much anguish. Please forgive me but it had to be done promptly because the American government is threatening to close their borders completely to Chinese immigration very soon. May Yun, you must know how important it is for the Chinese to return the bones of relatives to the land of their ancestors?"

Louisa responded with sympathy. Her ardour subsided.

"Mr. Dai, do you really think that the Americans will exclude Chinese immigration?" asked Mary.

"Even though I hope they don't, yes, I think they will. Chinese immigrants who think that this may be their last opportunity to find jobs in America are fleeing China and flooding into San Francisco before the doors are closed completely. I think it could happen fairly soon, that is why I had to leave for California on such short notice. However, I had no idea my mission would take almost eight months to complete."

A platter of roast beef along with Yorkshire pudding, roasted potatoes, peas and carrots arrived at the table. As the guests ate, many local issues were discussed. Louisa presented her scrapbook for Cheung and Way to look at and explained how Mary and Mrs. Grohman had helped to collect articles.

Noting many empty spots in Louisa's scrapbook, Cheung remarked, " Do not worry May Yun I will bring back your missing articles. They have been safely stored in my locker in Yale. Thank you so much for all your hard work. I have a much better understanding of the problems facing the local Chinese immigrants."

During the dinner, many guests expressed concern over the mistreatment of Chinese laborers by the local community. Cheung responded. "Any mistreatment that the Chinese face here in Victoria is mild in comparison to what is happening in the United States. Chinese throughout the western states are being robbed, brutally beaten, and murdered, sometimes in mass lynchings. Their homes are being looted and burnt to the ground by anti-Chinese groups. Some towns have expelled their Chinese en masse on twenty-four-hours notice. The trend seems to be similar throughout the western states. New businesses were created and made economically feasible mainly due to the availability of cheap Chinese labour. After the railways were built, more immigrants arrived from the eastern states. They formed labour groups and demanded employers replace Chinese workers with their members. I fear the same process will occur here."

Jonathan said, "When the railway has been completed, I hope the Chinese are recognized for their contribution in keeping this country from falling into American hands. Surely this will have a profound influence on changing the attitude of all Canadians towards the Chinese."

Near the end of the meal, Mr. Moberly spoke. "Mr. Dai, I was contracted by the government as a surveyor to find a route for the railway through the Selkirk and Rockies Mountains. I resigned earlier this year when Sanford Fleming, the chief engineer of the railway, announced that the Yellowhead Pass was selected as the chosen route in opposition to my proposal of the Howse Pass. The company executives have since hired a 52 year-old American surveyor, Major Rogers, to examine the options for a more southerly route so the search continues. Apparently Rogers grew up on the plains of the American Midwest and has never seen a mountain in his life. He was once an apprentice to a ship's carpenter but later studied engineering at Brown's University. His military title was a result of his exploits as an Indian-fighter in the Sioux Uprising of 1861 and his professional reputation was gained as a surveyor for the Chicago, Milwaukee and St. Paul Railroad. He is driven by a relentless pursuit of fame. No one wants to work with him. He drives himself as a man possessed and he expects others under him to follow his example, as he torments them with profanity. He chews tobacco constantly and satisfies his meager appetite with an infrequent sea biscuit. His idea of provisions is a handkerchief of beans with a few strips of bacon. There is a strong American influence, associated

with the construction of our transcontinental railway. The newly-appointed general manager of the Canadian Pacific Railway, William Cornelius Van Horne is a 39-year-old American. Many Canadians with positions on the railway such as chief engineers, superintendents, conductors, yard masters, foremen, dispatchers, surveyors, etc. – have been replaced by Americans. Isn't it ironic that our great Canadian transcontinental railway is being constructed with American expertise so that we can avoid being assimilated by the Americans? The new contractor for the railroad company that won the 127 mile contract between Emory's Bar and Savona's Ferry is a 31-year-old American named Andrew Onderdonk. Apparently he was involved with the construction of the San Francisco seawall, the Trent Valley Canal and the first subway tunnels under New York's East River. He is always well-groomed and attired in the latest New York fashion but he remains a bit of a mystery since he confides in no one. He was selected because he is backed by a syndicate of powerful bankers who are some of the wealthiest men in America and our government chose their higher bid because they were afraid that whoever won the contract might go bankrupt. An American company, Langdon and Shepard, holds the prime contract on the prairies while a New Jersey company's bid was accepted for the mountain section north of Lake Superior. These contractors from the US proceed with reckless abandon while Canadians waste time forever squabbling and deliberating. They often succeed using brutal measures, wringing blood out of stone, so I was intrigued with your articles on how they would treat their laborers. According to my sources, your account appears to be woefully accurate. Most of the workers who served under me during the construction of the Cariboo Road were Chinese. Without their steadfast dedication this major pathway into the interior could not have been constructed within the time frame nor on the budget that was realized. During the summer when the air was thick with mosquitoes and black-flies, the natives and whites fled the campsites but the Chinese persevered without complaint. They never stole jobs from white workers, as perpetuated by the newspapers and labour groups. The great majority of the white workers I hired only supervised the Chinese who did most of the hard labour, especially the jobs that were dangerous. So I have a strong interest in how the new railway company treats their Chinese laborers."

"If you do not mind, Mr. Dai," said Mary. "I think we would all be interested in hearing about your entire account of how and when your father and uncle arrived in California and how they died and how you retrieved their bones, if it is not too painful for you to relate."

"I will be glad to share my journey with you, if you all wish to hear it?"

With unanimous consent, Cheung presented his journey, beginning with his first voyage to California. The guests were spellbound and speechless for two hours, as Cheung recounted his experiences during the California gold rush, the death of his father and uncle, his recent journey to Marysville with Way and Yuen, the recovery of bones, his visit to the Maidu village and the tong war in San Francisco.

"What a remarkable journey," said James Fell. "You inspired people with kindness and they responded by helping you fulfill a nearly impossible mission that few others would even undertake. And you made a host of friendships with extraordinary people along the way. Well done, I salute you both on a marvelous accomplishment." James raised his glass to toast Cheung and Way. The other guests did likewise.

"I agree whole-heartedly," added Nigel Thompson. "I cannot wait to relate your story to our mutual friends Captain Anderson and Dr. Mason. Mr. Dai, they told me about your assistance during your voyage on their vessel from China. They both expressed their utmost admiration for you. They have inquired about you each time they have arrived in port."

"Thank you Mr. Thompson, my feelings for them are mutual. By the way, I promised Dr. Mason that I would send him some Chinese medicine. I will have someone drop it off at your office before I leave. Would you please give it to him the next time that he arrives." Nigel agreed with a nod.

"Mr. Tan, will you also be staying in Victoria till spring?" asked Mary. "If so, I can provide accommodation for you."

"No, I plan to be leaving soon for Yale to meet up with some people from my village who have a mining operation in the interior," replied Way.

"According to our shipping schedule at the Customs office, Mr. Tan, the *Western Slope* arrives from Yale this evening and it is scheduled to return to Yale tomorrow morning at 11," said Jonathan.

"Mrs. Beckham, I know that this is your busy time of the year," said Cheung. "So I will stay at my store until I leave in the spring."

"Mr. Dai, I can always accommodate you. Please let me know, if you change your mind."

"Yes, I will let you know. Thank you for your thoughtfulness."

"Mr. Dai, I have some contacts with the railway head office," said Mr. Moberly. "If you wish I can make an inquiry about your son?"

"Thank you, Mr. Moberly, I will be grateful for any assistance in finding my son."

After the rest of the guests had departed, Cheung and Way remained behind. Nathan realized Cheung wanted to check Louisa's emotional state before leaving. Louisa sat on the sofa in front of the fireplace in the living room.

"May Yun are you alright? I hope you understand how important it was for me to go to California when I did?"

"Yes, Uncle Cheung, I understand how important it was for you to bring your father home. I am just worried what may happen to Wing before you find him in the spring. I am relieved that he is alive and well. I just hope that he will remember me."

"May Yun, how could anyone forget you? I am sure his memory will recover as soon as he sees your face. I promise you, I will find him very soon. And I always keep my promises. Every agent for the Six Companies is helping to look for Wing, it is just a matter of time. After my mission in California, this task should not pose much of a challenge."

Louisa was elated. She threw her arms around Cheung's waist. Cheung picked her up and embraced her. She kissed his cheek.

Nathan smiled. "Off to bed with you now. It's past 10 o'clock."

"Good night Uncle Cheung, good night Way, thank you for helping to find Wing. Maybe I will see you on my next visit to Chinatown. Good night father." She kissed her father in passing then ran upstairs.

Relieved Nathan sighed. "Thank you Cheung, good job."

The next morning Cheung and Way walked to the harbour. When they reached the dock, Way turned to Cheung. *Please let me know if I can help in any way. Just leave a message at the Toi San Society for me. I will wait for my friends until they arrive in Yale to replenish their supplies. You have taught me so much. My Uncle was right; you can always come up with a plan. It has been a great honour to share your journey. I am proud to bear your name.*

"In my dreams our paths will merge again. As I have told you before, Way, you have many gifts. Please don't waste them needlessly. I feel honoured also to be your friend, and I will always treasure the time that we shared together. Have a safe journey."

The men exchanged bows then shook hands. Way boarded the *Princess Louise* and waved from the promenade deck.

Two weeks later, Walter Moberly sent a message to Cheung's store to meet at Mary Beckham's boarding house. They met privately in the den. "Mr. Dai, I have some bad news. The railway company executives have been informed about your articles and have banned you from their worksites. You have thwarted their ability to recruit workers locally, and throughout the west coast. Your appearance at any of their sites may be hazardous and publishing any more articles may have dire consequences on your son. Mr. Dai, I am truly sorry to be the harbinger of this news, but I thought you should be forewarned before you approach their head office in Yale. I fear for your safety. I will continue to do whatever I can to uncover more information as to your son's whereabouts. I think that they will keep him sequestered, to muzzle your articles."

Cheung thought for a moment. "Mr. Moberly, can you please keep this private just between us? I fear this news will cause Louisa needless grief. Thank very much for the information. I am in your debt."

Moberly agreed and the men exchanged handshakes.

The next day, Cheung sent a telegram to Ti Chu describing his new predicament and requested that his articles be taken down.

Cheung met again with Moberly to inform him of his compliance and requested the information be forwarded to the railway executives. He also asked for information concerning the whereabouts of his son, but Moberly never received a response. Moberly surmised that they would be holding Wing as insurance, to prevent Cheung from creating any more problems with recruitment.

Chapter 19

Breaching Hell's Gate

THE COLONY OF VANCOUVER ISLAND WAS CREATED BY THE British in 1849 in order to maintain their sovereignty in the West. Previously known as New Caledonia, the Colony of British Columbia was formed in 1858 under a grant to the Hudson's Bay Company from the Crown. The two western colonies were amalgamated in 1866 but remained as the Colony of British Columbia. The federal Dominion of Canada was officially formed on July 1, 1867 with four provinces – Ontario, Quebec, New Brunswick and Nova Scotia. After three years of endless debate amongst local politicians and several negotiations with the federal government, British Columbia entered Confederation on July 20, 1871. The Confederation agreement between the British colony of British Columbia and Canada required the building of a transcontinental railway. An act was passed on February 15,1881 which specified exactly how the Canadian Pacific Railway was to be financed, built and operated.

It consisted of four component documents: 1. Terms of agreement of entrance of British Columbia in Union - the bargain struck between Canada and the west coast British colony. **2. An Act respecting the Canadian Pacific Railway** - the "enabling legislation" which created the Canadian Pacific Railway Company. **3. Schedule** - the contract between the

Canadian Government and the CPR Syndicate. 4. Schedule A - the agreement incorporating the CPR with regulations setting out corporate "bylaws" and procedures which could later be modified by votes of the CPR Board of Directors or CPR Shareholders.

The CPR Syndicate became the CPR Company in February 1881.

The most salient terms were:

- The Government would grant the Company a subsidy of twenty-five million dollars and twenty-five million acres of land (a land mass roughly the size of Newfoundland).

- The gifted land would be free of taxation for 20 years or until sold.

- The CPR would be given the right to issue twenty-five million dollars of land-grant bonds.

- The CPR and all stations and related grounds, workshops, buildings, yards and other property, rolling stock and appurtenances required and used for the construction and working thereof, and the capital stock of the Company, would be forever free from taxation by the Dominion, by any Province hereafter or by any Municipal Corporation.

- No duty would be placed on railway materials during construction.

- The CPR would receive all lines built with public money upon completion - a gift of approximately seven hundred miles of line: 65 mile Pembina line between Winnipeg and Minnesota; 433 mile line to be completed between Fort William and Selkirk and the 215 mile stretch to be built between Savona's Ferry and Port Moody on the Pacific coast.

- For 20 years after completion of construction of the CPR, no other railway would be constructed between the CPR and within 15 miles of the American border.

The Ottawa Free Press calculated the new Syndicate had received a cash equivalent gift of approximately 260 million dollars. The value alone of the 710 miles already laid was thought to be valued at 32 million dollars.

The first four contracts with Andrew Onderdonk were signed prior to the creation of the Canadian Pacific Railway Company. The Minister of Railways Charles Tupper had been recently embarrassed with an underfinanced contractor who had to give up on the Thunder Bay- Red River line. The government thought one firm could more adequately fulfill the terms of the four contracts as there would be less competition hiring workers. Materials could be purchased more cheaply bulk. In addition, a single firm

could make better use of the rail line already completed to cut costs and work in a more organized manner. By the time the CPR had driven its first spike in May of 1881 in the East under the new general manager William Cornelius Van Horne, Onderdonk had not laid a single mile of track. Although he had been working for over a year his first twelve months was consumed with preparing a pathway by clearing forest, blasting tunnels, draining swamps, filling gorges and building trestles and bridges. Four tunnels had to be built through mountains of solid granite, the toughest rock on earth, in the first mile and a half outside of Yale. After eighteen months only two miles of rail had been laid. In the first seventeen miles through the Fraser canyon, thirteen tunnels had to be built; between Kamloops and Port Moody twenty-seven in total. The 65 mile between Emory and Lytton was flanked by deep canyons and required 600 trestles and bridges, and one hundred bridges were needed in one 30 mile section. Excessively high freight rates of $10 per ton over short distances to construction sites along the Cariboo Road beleaguered Onderdonk who was seriously over budget. In the spring of 1882 he proposed to build a steamer to offset the cost of freight. A 250-ton craft, 127 feet long with a beam of 24 feet was to be built in Spuzzum which was 20 miles upriver from Yale. Named after a nearby creek, the *Skuzzy* was destined to operate between Boston Bar and Lytton.

Cheung and Yuen arrived in Yale at the end of March. Cheung had sent a telegram in advance to Way requesting his help and to meet with them in Yale. When the pair arrived, Way was sitting in the lobby of the tong. *"Uncle Cheung, Uncle Yuen, I am glad to see you both safe and in good health. Shall we go to the restaurant to have something to eat?"*

"Good idea," said Cheung. *"Why don't you and Yuen go to the restaurant and order while I check for messages. I am expecting one from Ti Chu. I will join you shortly."* Yuen and Way departed

Cheung showed the desk clerk Ti Chu's card. The clerk handed him an envelope. Cheung took a chair to quickly scan it.

When Cheung reached the restaurant the food was on the table. *"You didn't have to wait for me. Please eat. Here is Ti Chu's letter. I'll read it for you while you eat.*

Cheung,

I hope that you, Way and Yuen are in good health. I am sorry to hear that your articles have caused you so much hardship and stress. I have asked that

all your articles be taken down at all our affiliate offices. As for your request, I will be glad to hire Way and Yuen to act as our company representatives for the railway, so they can search for Wing. The Toi San Society in Yale has been notified, so Way and Yuen can contact them for their assignment.

The debate concerning Chinese immigration rages on in Congress. Our California senator J.F. Miller introduced a bill to bar Chinese immigration for 20 years. He wishes to preserve "American Anglo-Saxon civilization without contamination or adulteration from the gangrene of oriental civilization". This should win him a lot of votes in the next election. In opposition a senator from Massachusetts, G.F.Hoar who had opposed slavery and championed the civil rights of workers, believed that excluding people based on race made a mockery of ideals set forth in the Declaration of Independence. He blasted the hypocrisy "We boast of our democracy, our superiority, our strength. The flag bears the stars of hope to all nations. A hundred thousand Chinese land in California and everything is changed.... The self-evident truth becomes a self-evident lie." In response a Colorado lawmaker insisted the Caucasian race "has a right, considering its superiority of intellectual force and mental vigor, to look down upon every other branch of the human family." Across the West, they are burning President Arthur in effigy for vetoing a bill to exclude Chinese immigration because he praised the contributions of the Chinese in helping to build the transcontinental railway as well as developing industry and agriculture.

Personally, I think the outlook for us appears to be very grim. Anti-Chinese demonstrations grow ever larger and seem to be intensifying. If these sentiments towards us in California are perpetuated throughout the nation by the newspapers and politicians, I foresee more misery and senseless violence on the horizon. Hopefully, the situation for our people is better in Canada than here in the USA.

Good luck with your search. I hope you find your son soon. Please keep me informed and let me know if there is anything else I can do to help.

Your loyal friend,

Chung Ti Chu

"I am very thankful to have you both here to help me. I am truly in your debt."

"As friends we have to share good times and difficult times together, right?" said Yuen, "Aiya, lately it's only been difficult times. Cheung, you better come up with some good times pretty soon, or we're going to stop being friends." The three break

out in laughter. "*Way, I took your piece of jade to my friend in our village. He said that it is a lower quality of jade but it would be very worthwhile to import this jade back to China. The stones can be treated with acids and waxed to give them more value but he added where there is low quality jade there is also higher quality jade.*"

"*Thank you Uncle, that is very promising news. Did he say how much stone may be worth?*"

"*It depends on the quality of each stone but I think we can make a lot of money exporting it to China,*" said Yuen.

"*I should tell you both about my recurring dream,*" said Cheung. "*It may be helpful. I keep seeing Wing towing a heavy rope. The dream doesn't show me what is being pulled but it must be something very large because there are many other Chinese laborers behind him all helping to pull the same rope.*"

"*If we hear or see anything we will leave a message at our tong,*" said Yuen.

A couple of days later Yuen and Way were hired as labour contractors for the Six Companies under Ti Chu's head office in San Francisco. Cheung remained in Yale awaiting updates from his friends.

A continuous flow of traffic passed through Yale. Prairie schooners flowed through the main street. They entered the town empty, but as soon as they were loaded the enormous freight wagons headed north up the Cariboo Road, pulled by teams of 12 mules or 16 oxen with 6 trailing spares. Everything from cargoes of rice to heavy equipment were being transported to the construction camps. To cut costs Onderdonk built a sawmill to supply his own timber for bridges, trestles and ties as well as a dynamite factory which turned out 4000 pounds of nitro-glycerine daily.

The CPR were in desperate need of labour and accepted anyone available - bartenders, bank clerks, teachers, trappers, bakers, butchers, waiters, sailors, etc. most of whom had little to no railway experience and some had never lifted a shovel, a pick or an axe. In the spring of 1881, Onderdonk visited San Francisco where he had advertised for 3000 white workers. He also visited all of the Chinese labour agencies. As a result, 2939 Chinese laborers arrived at Yale in 1881. Six vessels from China brought 1739 laborers, 387 came from Puget Sound and 813 from San Francisco to Victoria. When 238 white workers arrived in Yale at the end of March they roared and howled through Yale, upon disembarkment. Fights broke out on Front Street, and 12 rowdies were carted off to jail. On the second night 20 more were locked up.

On the next night free liquor was terminated by the recruiting company and the town was restored to normal. The need for labour continued to persist. By mid-June 1882, 8083 more Chinese arrive from Hong Kong through the use of American labour agencies: 5297 consigned by Stahlschmidt and Ward, 929 by Tai Chong and 450 by Welch and Rithet as well as 295 from San Francisco and 280 from Puget Sound. It is estimated that at least 17,000 Chinese arrived in British Columbia between 1881 and 1884.

On May 8th Cheung received a telegram from Ti Chu:

Cheung,

As expected, on May 6, 1882, President Chester Arthur signed the Chinese Exclusion Act. No Chinese immigration (except merchants, students, teachers, & their servants) will be allowed for the next 10 years. The anti-Chinese forces are already planning a "Pia Hua" (forceful eviction) of the Chinese who still remain. All the Chinese workers who crossed the border to work on the Canadian railway will not be permitted to return to the United States.

Ti Chu

On May 4, 1882 the *Scuzzy* was launched at Spuzzum, twenty miles north of Yale. Onderdonk planned to have the vessel driven through the most treacherous section of the Fraser Canyon, Hell's Gate, a narrow passageway flowing at 10 knots with intermittent gusts up to 20 knots between twin basalt towers that stood 50 feet high and 100 feet apart. Veteran boatmen considered Hell's Gate to be impossible to navigate. Several attempts were made in vain to find an expert skipper to command the vessel during the spring flow. Onderdonk finally found one in Asbury Insley, the most experienced riverboat man on the Fraser River but he succeeded in only taking the craft two and a half miles upriver before he admitted defeat and returned back to Spuzzum. The general consensus of the experts was for Onderdonk to concede and have the *Skuzzy* scrapped, or else having her dismantled and taken overland to Boston Bar and reassembled.

A letter arrived at the Toi San tong for Cheung on June 1st from Louisa:

Dear Uncle Cheung,

I hope that you are well. I have not heard from you in awhile so I am writing to find out whether there was any news concerning Wing. Please give my warmest regards to Way and Uncle Yuen. Father and I are well. I am enjoying school and I am making many new friends. A new Chinese

theatre has opened up in Chinatown. Father and I are going to see a Chinese opera next week.

Please keep me informed about your progress.

Yours sincerely,

Louisa

(Cheung, she is doing much better. Your words of comfort have consoled her. I hope that you find Wing soon.)

Best regards,

Nathan

On September 7th five flat cars of guests passed through Yale on route to Spuzzum. Cheung stopped at On Lee's store and inquired, "*On Lee, do you know where these people are going?*"

"*Cheung, the American contractor has invited guests to witness another attempt to tame the waters of the Fraser Canyon. He has imported expert American boatmen from the upper Columbia to steer his new vessel through the rapids at Hell's Gate. The men that he hired have taken a steamer 1000 miles down the Snake River to the Blue Mountains and over the falls at Willamette, Oregon. So if they fail I doubt it can be done. Do you want to go and watch? My employees will look after the store. I can saddle a couple of my horses and we can be there in a few hours.*"

"*Why not, I have nothing else to do.*"

When the pair reached Spuzzum they followed the sound of cheering upriver. They found a good vantage point on the canyon wall from which they could see the sturdy little vessel fighting hard against the foaming turbulence. Spectators were perched on top of the high banks on both sides of the Canyon wall. Wagers of gold, timber and other merchandise were made on the outcome with odds as high as 100 to 1 against the boat completing the task but the outcome was obvious, as the vessel strained to gain only a few miles against the force of the surging rapids. On Lee and Cheung returned to Yale amused, somewhat disappointed at failing to witness a historical feat.

The crowds remained a few days as the battle continued, as the crowds slowly dwindled in size. Cheung received updates as he visited On Lee's store to check the progress. On the 9th day, On Lee informed Cheung."*Did you hear the news? The vessel has reached Hell's Gate and the American contractor is having ring-bolts driven into the canyon walls, to pull the vessel through the passageway with the help of laborers.*"

Cheung thought for a moment then remembering his dream, he gasped *"Oh, no! Can I borrow your horse tonight?"*

"Where do you want to go?"

"To Hell's Gate. I must go right away. My son may be there."

"I thought all your family was still in China."

"No, I have a son working on the railway."

"Cheung don't go in the dark, I will go with you at dawn. Now, tell me about your son."

After Cheung related the story concerning the disappearance of his son, On Lee said. *"Cheung my business has flourished thanks to you. I will do all I can to help you. Let's meet at my store early tomorrow morning."*

The company's plan to use laborers to pull the *Skuzzy* through Hell's Gate spread quickly. It was decided that four teams of workers would be chosen for the project. Due to the danger for those involved, advance information about the mission would not be disclosed to the participants and the teams would come from isolated locations sequestered from local news. The teams would be transported by flat cars with no advance warning, for the work downriver. Chinese teams were accustomed to odd job transfers on short notice. They responded faster to do urgent work since they could set up a new campsite overnight while their white counterparts would take a week.

As the site supervisor, Sam was puzzled by the company's sudden request to transport his teams downriver. Why won't they tell us where we are going or what must be done? They haven't instructed us to bring any tools so what kind of work will we have to do? The relationship between Sam and Wing had grown over the last year. They often ate their evening meals together and spent their free time hiking in the wilderness. Other workers started to join them for meals, then on outings. Sam gradually developed a closer bond with many of his laborers. As time passed, he instigated changes to improve their safety conditions.

A large crowd was assembled at the site to witness the impending disaster. Wagons and carriages were packed along the side of the Cariboo Road. The mood of the crowd was a mixture of foreboding and anticipation. Gamblers were taking bets and giving odds on blackboards. Hawkers were selling beer and sandwiches. Locals were spread out above the canyon wall in clusters at various vantage points.

When the flatcars arrived, the crowds pulled back as the teams of laborers disembarked. The new arrivals were stunned by the size of the crowd.
With the absence of advanced instructions, Sam grew more anxious wondering what the company had planned. Aware of the past failures of the
Skuzzy to ford Hell's Gate, Sam suspected the worst. He queried a young
spectator concerning the planned endeavour. "They are using the chinks to
pull the *Skuzzy* through Hell's Gate." He thought to himself, it's going to be a
disaster, but he realized protest was useless.

The *Skuzzy* was secured by ropes at the entrance to Hell's Gate from both
sides of the canyon. When Cheung and On Lee arrived at Hell's Gate they
were greeted by Yuen and Way. "*When I heard about this event from some of
the Chinese workers who secured the ring-bolts, I immediately understood the significance of your dream, so I sent a message to Uncle Yuen. Many of our workers
have taken the day off to witness this event.*"

As Cheung moved through a crowd of Chinese workers. who were
gathered at a separate location. Many of them recognized him and greeted
him with a respectful bow. The new arrivals watched from a distance, as
the company executives barked orders through a bullhorn to their subordinates. On an elevated cliff, Cheung spotted a familiar face, Samuel Harper.
He struggled through a gallery of spectators to get a closer look. The teams
were stationed at specified locations along the wall of the canyon upriver
from the narrow passageway. Stout hawsers were secured to the *Skuzzy's*
capstan and steam winch at the front of the vessel and passed through ring-
bolts then up towards the team stations. The roar of the *Skuzzy's* engine and
the thrashing of her stern wheel echoed loudly above the constant flow of
cascading rapids. The spray created by the rapids below made the footing
treacherous and the rope wet and slippery. Losing your footing could prove
fatal, especially for those at the front. Holding the wet rope steadfast on
the initial release of the moorings would be the most dangerous part of the
ordeal. The workers had no idea of how much force would be exerted by the
weight of the vessel, combined with the force of the river rapids. Would they
all be pulled over the canyon wall at the same time once the moorings were
released? Would those at the back support those at the front if the force
became too powerful? Who would release first?

Cheung struggled through the crowd, followed by his friends. On an
elevated platform, one of the executives from the Yale office recognized

him in passing and pointed him out to his superiors. They conferred for a moment, then the executive that recruited Cheung went to find Sam who was assigned a location on the eastern canyon wall. The work crews would be directed to pull in coordination with the other teams to keep the vessel in alignment. After the executive found Sam, he asked where Wing was located. Sam pointed at the end of his row. The man repositioned Wing at the front, nearest the edge of the cliff. At the other locations, workers were staggered back twenty to thirty feet from the edge of any drop-off, in case the initial force that was created when the moorings were released was too strong. Wing was placed at the edge with no margin for error. Sam balked vehemently, as the executive signaled for two others to seize Sam and keep him restrained. Cheung spotted Wing in the distance. He pushed his way frantically, through the gallery of onlookers shouting, "Wing, Wing, Dai Wing Sing."

Holding the rope, Wing instantly froze. The voice sounded familiar. He looked around scanning the crowd.

The executive quickly assigned another man to replace Sam, then signaled his cohort, who shouted into a bullhorn. "Release the moorings!" The lines tightened and suddenly surged forward ten feet. Wing was suddenly pulled off the cliff and dangled on the rope, above the river canyon. Spectators gasped in horror. The *Skuzzy* crew of fifteen worked the capstan and winch while the Chinese pulled with all of their strength. The men at the front of each team crept closer and closer to the edge of disaster. The foremen used hand signals and barked out orders for each team to "pull!" or "hold!" to keep the vessel from crashing on the walls of Hell's Gate. The ropes had been left outside overnight; they were still moist and slippery from the morning frost. Wing stared at the rapids below, as events of the past flashed through his mind. He remembered it was late at night and he was trying to escape from some men on a walkway. He remembered an upriver voyage on a steamship with a thrashing paddle-wheel. He remembered fighting rapids in a canoe. He remembered a ride on a horse-driven carriage. Where was I? Why was I there? Who are those people? His mind struggled as faces, places and events cascaded into his consciousness. It was starting to come back to him. The rope shook and vibrated in his hand, as the *Skuzzy* battled below. The vessel surged forward, then fell back, as Wing swung back and forth like a puppet on a string.

Sam struggled free from the two men holding him back while they watched Wing, wondering when he would fall. Sam moved quickly forward up the line of rope bearers and grabbed the rope at the front near the edge of the cliff. He frantically screamed, "Pull, pull, pull!" at his men. As his team responded, the vessel swerved out of alignment, but he didn't care. The other teams were ordered to pull harder to keep the *Skuzzy* from colliding with the walls of the narrow passage. When Cheung reached the landing, he positioned himself behind Sam and started to pull. Yuen, Way and On Lee rushed forward to help. Some of the Chinese workers who had come to watch, recognizing Cheung, rushed to assist. More workers started to join nearby stations, in support of their countrymen. The vessel started to move forward as Wing drew closer and closer to safety. From the look of anguish on Wing's face, Sam could see Wing's grip was starting to falter. Sensing Wing would soon fall, Sam lunged forward with his right hand and grabbed the neck of Wing's jacket, just as Wing lost his grip. Cheung quickly seized Sam's belt from behind as Sam pulled Wing back on solid ground. The disproportionate effort created by Sam's team forced the *Skuzzy* swerve out of alignment. Relieved temporarily, the team held as the other teams compensated. Once realigned, the *Skuzzy* progressed gradually through the foaming rapids. After several minutes, with the aid of the vessel's engine at full throttle, a steam winch, the support of 15 men on the capstan and a horde of Chinese workers straining to exhaustion, the *Skuzzy* finally breached the narrow passage and came to rest on calmer waters. Her hull was badly scraped and gouged almost beyond repair. The *Skuzzy* had just become the first known steamboat to pass upriver through the rapids of Hell's Gate. She would also be the last paddle-wheeler to breach Hell's Gate. The crowd rallied around the *Skuzzy* crew, congratulating them on their historical achievement. Captain S.R. Smith, his brother David Smith and engineer J.W. Burse and their 15-man crew then navigated the *Skuzzy* through to Boston Bar. The twenty-two-mile journey from Boston Bar to Lytton took over seven hours, but the return journey took only one hour and twenty-seven minutes. The exhausted Chinese remained behind the celebrants, collapsed on any patch of ground that was unoccupied.

"My son, how are you?"

"Father, it's you. Sam, this is my father." Wing embraced his father, then looked around for his friend, but Sam was gone.

"*My son, you have grown big and strong. I have been very worried about you. These are my very good friends On Lee and Tan Sun Yuen. Do you remember Way?*"

Wing smiled at his new friends and Way. "*Big brother it is very nice to see you again.*"

"*Little monkey, you have grown so much I will have to change your name.*"

Chapter 20

The Road Ahead

WHEN CHEUNG AND WING ARRIVED IN VICTORIA, NATHAN AND Louisa were waiting at the dock. As they disembarked with their luggage, Louisa ran up to Wing and gave him a hug and a kiss on the lips. Wing stood aloof and unresponsive. Wing turned to Cheung. "Father who is this girl? Do I know her?" Tears started to flow from Louisa's eyes, as Wing quickly smiled. "Okay, I was just having fun with you. How could I forget such a big trouble-maker? I hope you haven't performed too many evil deeds for me to undo? Working on the railway has been very tiring." She embraced him. For the first time, Wing allowed her to vent her emotions in public, without resistance.

"Louisa, we are in public," said Nathan. "You are not 10 anymore, please try to act your age."

Louisa brushed back her tears. "Thank you, Uncle Cheung, I knew that you would keep your promise."

Nathan smiled at Cheung, "We have arranged a dinner for tomorrow night to celebrate Wing's return. I hope that you approve."

"That will be fine Nathan. I look forward to it."

A carriage took the group to Mary Beckham's rooming house. The streets were brightly decorated with flowers and signs. They observed a forty-five

foot Chinese arch over Store Street near Johnson Street. There were smaller arches on either side, striped in green and white. Flag poles bearing the Chinese standard stood on ornamental pagoda roofs. The arch was adorned with Chinese lanterns, pictures, theatrical scenes and banners with "God Save the Queen" and "The Orient Greets the Occident." The Chinese shops on Store and Johnson Street were decorated with evergreens and Cormorant Street was lined with young fir trees.

Cheung looked at Nathan. "What is this? Is the Queen coming?"

"No, her fourth daughter, Princess Louise, and the Marquis of Lorne who is the new Governor-General of Canada are arriving soon. They are the first of the Royal Family to visit the Pacific coast. Even some Americans have come up to honour their visit. The Royals arrive September 20th and all of Victoria has gone mad with excitement. Chinatown has out-performed the rest of the city much to the chagrin of the locals."

When they arrived at the boarding house, Mary greeted them with her usual hospitality. While the adults were having tea, Louisa and Wing wandered out to Mary's backyard garden.

"Wing I really missed you. I was so scared you were dead or badly injured. I thought about you every day and night. I wanted to come to find you myself." They embraced as she kissed him on the cheek.

"I'm sorry. I'll try to warn you in advance the next time labour agents for the railway decide to kidnap me." He laughed as Louisa chased him around the yard.

She feigned anger, "I cried my eyes out almost every night and you laugh at me. I should have known better. You weren't worth it."

"I guess we can forget the last two favours that I still owe you?"

"What are you talking about? It's still five."

"Haven't you learned to count while I was gone? It was actually four when I left and then you kissed me twice when I arrived. That leaves two."

"Those don't count. Our fathers were there."

"Sorry, I'm counting them. So get yourself a lawyer. I'm not worth it anyway, remember?" She started to chase him again. After a few minutes they sat together on a bench in the garden.

"Wing, is your head okay? Can I see the wound?"

He nodded. She pulled his hair aside to study the wound. "I am glad your queue is gone. I hope you don't grow it back. It will show that you

are adapting to these new surroundings. That must have been a pretty big wound. Does it ever hurt anymore?"

"Only when I am being kissed."

Louisa playfully pouted, "You never take me seriously. One of these days you are going to regret it when I run off with someone else. There are quite a few boys at school that seem interested in me. So you better watch out."

"I doubt it, especially not after I warn them about all your evil deeds." She giggled.

"Louisa do you remember the man that threw you into the ocean?"

"Yes, how could I forget him?"

"We became very good friends when my mind wasn't right. I saved his life but he also saved mine."

"How did that happen?"

"It's a long story."

"Go ahead, I'm listening."

Wing related the story of his experiences during his work on the railway.

"You are lucky to have survived, but it must have been a very exciting adventure. All I did was go to school and cry myself to sleep every night while you scaled mountains. And you killed a wolf with a knife?"

"Yes, but the wolf never stood much of a chance."

"What do you mean?"

Wing started to laugh, "well, I had a very big knife."

Louisa burst out in laughter. "The work on the railway has made you much bigger and stronger. How about me? Have I changed much?" Louisa stood up and straightened her dress, then approached Wing with an alluring smile, expecting a compliment.

He walked around her slowly, surveying up and down. With arms crossed and a hand under his chin, he quipped. "No, not much, maybe just more evil." He chuckled, then darted off, back towards the house as she chased after him.

From an upstairs landing, Cheung watched from a window, worried about the outcome of the blossoming relationship between Wing and Louisa. He had hoped that time and distance would ease their affection for each other, but nothing had changed. After Nathan and Louisa departed, Cheung and Wing went to their room. As they unpacked, Cheung said. "My

son, you are almost a man now. There are some things that I must discuss with you concerning women."

"Yes, father I saw you at the window above, watching us in the garden earlier."

"My son, I know that you have great feelings for Louisa. However, the society that we now live in will never accept the two of you together in a lasting relationship. Any further growth in the relationship between the two of you can only end in disaster. Do you understand, my son?"

After a pause, Wing replied. "Father, I understand the danger."

"I am so glad that you have developed the wisdom to understand the danger you will face if the two of you fall in love and have a child. The child will be constantly subjected to ridicule and abuse by not only whites, but also our own people who despise the west for their treatment of our people. So you must never taste the fruits of her passion."

"Father, is there nowhere that we could live in peace?"

"My son maybe there is, but certainly not here. So please make her aware of the potential danger of a serious relationship. She is very determined and willful, so you must be very firm."

The next evening, the guests arrived. They were the same people that attended Nathan's dinner in November, with the addition of Quan Li. When all were assembled around the dinner table Nathan announced, "Wing, it is with great pleasure and relief that we have you back after such a challenging ordeal. Welcome back."

Lifting their glasses, the others repeated, "Welcome back."

"Where are Way and your friend who arrived in March?" Mary asked Cheung.

"They are mining somewhere in the interior. They have asked us to join them but Wing needs to go to school but I am not sure where he will be attending school yet," said Cheung.

"He can come to mine," said Louisa. "It is a very good school."

"Are there many Chinese children at your school, May Yun?" asked Cheung.

"No, there are none but Wing could be the first."

"May Yun, I will give the matter careful consideration."

"I think currently there is a small group of Chinese parents in Victoria who have decided to send their children to the public schools here. If they are denied entrance they are prepared to appeal in court," said James Fell.

"Wing, has your memory been fully restored?" asked Jonathan.

"Yes I think so," replied Wing in perfect English. The others were shocked by Wing's response.

"Wing, I didn't know that you could speak English. Jonathan how did you know?" asked Mary.

Jonathan winked at Wing. "It was our little secret."

"My father was afraid of that I could be kidnapped and held for ransom so he would not allow me to speak English in public before. But he is no longer concerned now that I have grown."

"Mr. Moberly," said Cheung, "I must thank you for all your help. Without your information, the consequences could have been very severe. I am truly in your debt." Cheung explained, "Mr. Moberly warned me in private that the railway executives disapproved of my articles and that attempting to return to my job was going to be very dangerous."

"Only too glad to help you, Mr. Dai. Nathan has told me that you plan to move your family to Canada. Is that right?"

"Yes, I hope so, but I am not sure. The safety and education of family members are issues that deeply concern me. Wing needs to make up time with his studies. I may have to find him a private tutor."

"Mr. Dai, I thought that you should be aware of the recent comments made by our prime minister, so I cut this article out of the newspaper for you," said Nigel Thompson. He brought out a newspaper clipping from the *Colonist* dated May 1881. He circled a portion of the article referring to the Chinese:

"Their presence, he believed, would not be a wholesome thing for the country. They were an alien race, and there could be no assimilation of the race, therefore when the temporary exigencies had been overcome, and when there was a railway stretching across the continent, and there was a means of sending in white settlers, he would be quite ready to join, to a reasonable extent, in preventing the permanent settlement in the country of Mongolians or Chinese immigrants. But at the present it was a question of Chinese labour or no railway. The government had not had its attention especially called to the matter before, but the subject would engage its attention for the future ...."

"Yes, politicians pander to fears which they have created to get elected, while the newspapers perpetuate their hate-mongering distortions and

lies," said James Fell who continued, "our new mayor of Victoria, Noah Shakespeare, is a good example. An incident occurred before he became mayor that helped to launch his political carreer. When the steamship *Quinta* arrived last July, he hounded the Chinese passengers for a $3 school tax as the ship docked, then confiscated their belongings until the tax was paid. The controversy and coverage in the newspaper elevated him as a local hero. When Mayor Turner retired, Shakespeare ran for the vacant post. His advertisement consisted of just one statement in the daily paper "Gentlemen – I am a candidate for Mayor in the ensuing municipal election" but that was all he needed. Next to the editor of our illustrious daily paper, this man is the city's greatest persecutor of the Chinese. He is a pillar of the Methodist Church, a Sunday School superintendent for 15 years, and president of the Anti-Chinese Society. In 1879, he had proudly brandished a severed Chinese queue at a meeting and announced that he would keep it as a family heirloom. The desirability of restricting Chinese immigration has been brought up in parliament consistently by our B.C. representatives, Amor De Cosmos and Arthur Bunster, but they have been ignored by the feds, who realize that Chinese labour is needed to finish the railway. De Cosmos owns the local newspaper in town, the *British Colonist*. The hypocrite also owns property in Chinatown that Chinese live in, packed like sardines, but he continues to sling mud at the Chinese at every possible opportunity to pad his political aspirations. Bunster owns the local brewery on Johnson Street. He hates and bullies everyone but mostly the Chinese, because they won't fight back."

Ming said. "According to my family in China, the situation is growing worse each day in China. Our situation here is still better than what we can hope for in China."

"Yes, we can go home and starve with our families, or stay and work to send them money to survive," added Cheung. "There may be opportunities elsewhere but the Chinese have become very distrustful. We were told that America was the land of opportunity and freedom and that all men would be treated as equals. No one specified that our skin must be the right colour, to receive these benefits. So once our countrymen find work to send money to our families, they will not risk losing their jobs. We are a very patient people. As time passes it is hope that Canadians will gain a better understanding of us and our contributions to this country. But how can we deal with the lies

and distortions perpetuated by the politicians and the newspapers ... when so few are willing to listen?"

"You are right, Mr. Dai, James gave a great speech at the Theatre Royal awhile ago, in favour of Chinese immigration. He received no support, with the exception of the few of us here tonight who attended the gathering," said Mary.

"I brought an article from the Kamloops daily that that I thought you might all enjoy. I am hopeful that others embrace the wisdom offered by the writer," said Florence Baillie-Grohman. "It is entitled the 'The Labour Question' and appeared in the Inland Sentinel on January 31, 1881. I'll read it for you : "To deny the Chinese or any other race from participating in equal advantages is to prove that the liberties we possess are for ourselves only and not for the human race in general. In fact, it is proof that our pretensions to liberty were founded on falsehood and prejudice and a terrible illusion of intolerable bigotry which liberals of every age have striven to express. If anything is reprehensible it is the conduct of writers and aspiring politicians who endeavour to make capital out of a subject they do not understand or willfully misconstrue for selfish motives."

Nathan raised his glass, "That was a great article, Florence. Here's to people with open minds." The others raised their glasses in sympathy.

"How the newspapers and politicians treat us after the completion of the Canadian Pacific Railway will give me a good indication of our future in Canada," said Cheung. "I think I shall go to observe the final ceremony when the time comes. When the Central Pacific was completed in Utah, the Chinese were excluded from the closing ceremony. They were immediately laid off afterwards and abandoned at their various worksites. Many are still there, stranded in caves, ghost-towns and empty box-cars. I will be very interested to see how Canadians respond, in comparison."

James Fell interjected, "My hope is that the Chinese receive the recognition they deserve for their service in saving confederation. Hopefully, people will change for the better. We have a colony of blacks living on Saltspring Island. We have even had a black man elected to Victoria city council a few years ago."

"The migration of negroes to British Columbia is unique," related Nigel Thompson. "The governor of Vancouver Island prior to the Fraser River gold rush was James Douglas, whose mother was a Creole woman from

Barbados. Mifflin Gibbs was an activist who toured the United States with Frederick Douglas promoting the abolition of slavery before the Civil War. After the tour, he travelled to California in 1850 and helped to establish and publish *Mirror of the Times* in San Francisco which advocated justice and equal rights for all. He later became the leader of a community of black people in California and arrived in Victoria in 1858 at the start of the gold rush. Due to the imposition of a discriminatory poll tax and being denied the right to vote in California, his community decided to emigrate. When Gibbs arrived in Victoria from California, he made a large profit selling mining equipment and goods that he brought on his voyage north. He purchased a building and established the first mercantile, outside of Fort Victoria's Hudson Bay's Company settlement. He returned to the United States in 1859 and married Mary Ann Alexander. More than 400 blacks followed him north to Vancouver Island. Gibbs helped to form an all-black volunteer militia during the threat of American aggression during a dispute over the San Juan Islands that arose in 1861. He was elected to Victoria Cily Council in 1866 and served two terms becoming the chairman of the finance committee. In 1860, he and 17 other black property owners voted en block in the election for the House of Assembly for Vancouver Island. The defeated candidate was Amor De Cosmos who launched a bitter campaign against the new immigrants in his local newspaper. Gibbs also represented Saltspring Island as their delegate at the Yale Convention which explored the prospect of joining confederation."

"This man was a very gifted and intelligent leader, experienced in dealing with adversity. His people were willing to fight for their rights. Western society admires and respects those who are willing to fight and die for their ideals, but demonizes those who cannot afford the same luxury. Black people are descendents of warriors and hunters," stated Cheung, "we are the descendants of countless generations of peasant farmers. Our country-men will not risk injury or death because they need to fulfill their labour contracts and feed their families back in China. While winning rights and equality may be essential for the future, our primary concern is the survival of our families in China now."

"Canadians are very proud of the role that they played in the Underground Railway, that helped to smuggle runaway slaves to freedom in Canada. If

our country can sympathize with one minority, it should be able to do the same for other minorities," said James Fell.

"I hope so, Mr. Fell, but the question is when," replied Cheung. "It seems ironic how the blacks run from slavery while the Chinese run towards it. Canada welcomes and honours those who have escaped slavery but they treat the Chinese worse than slaves. We cannot be sold for money, so our only value is our labour, and if we are too numerous, we become disposable."

In the days that followed, Cheung searched for a private tutor for Wing without success. Jonathan volunteered to help secure books on science, math, and English, recommended by the head nun at St. Ann's Academy. Wing spent every afternoon studying. Cheung studied the newspapers daily to glean information on the progress of the railway and updates on anti-Chinese legislation.

The Marquis and the Princess departed on December 6. James Bay in Victoria was frozen solid; while ice on the Fraser River extended down river past Port Moody. The rare frigid winter of 1883 was instrumental in shifting the terminus for the railway down the inlet, away from the proposed capital of New Westminster. With the Fraser frozen, food was in short supply upriver. Early in February, Yale's newspaper the *Sentinel* noted the deaths of many Chinese due to "a sort of scurvy or black leg". There were no facilities for treatment of the ill; Onderdonk's hospital was reserved only for the injured. In March 1883 a *Colonist* correspondent reported : "Here in Yale at the temporary hospital opened at Sam Sing's house are a number of sick, Sunday one died, Wednesday two died and others are very low. Upon enquiry we were told the dead and dying all belonged to the railway company. No medical attendance is furnished, nor apparently much interest felt for the unfortunate creatures. We understand that Mr. Onderdonk declines interfering while the Lee Chuck Company that brought many of the Chinamen from their native land refuses through his agent Lee Soon, who is running the Chinese store at Emory, to become responsible for doctor's bills or medicine. The illness is reported to be berrie-berrie or swelling of the feet, legs and eyes, getting into the body and in a few hours the victims die in great suffering."

On May 10, 1883, an altercation over wages at Camp 37 near Lytton turned violent. A gang of Chinese men attacked the foremen, timekeeper, bridge superintendent and a teamster who were forced to retreat with

minor injuries. Late that evening, a party of twenty whites crept into the Chinese camp and set fire to their log house, clubbing them as they exited. One died, and eight were badly injured. When the inquest was held, the perpetrators could not be found. Neither were there twelve men found who were willing to form the jury.

Having just won a seat in Ottawa, Noah Shakespeare proposed a motion recommending that Chinese entering the province be assessed $50 and that each ship arriving in British Columbia be restricted to one Chinese for every 100 tons. Sir John A. Macdonald insisted that they were sojourners, not settlers. They brought no wives and no children, so they would ultimately leave. It was too early, he said, to pass the motion until the railway was completed. He was paraphrased as saying "there was no fear of the degradation of the country by a mongrel race."

In Victoria's daily *British Colonist* dated June 8, 1883 , an article entitled "Chinese Immigration" claimed the following : "it was further stated that about 2000 Chinamen died last year on the railroad, but there are many others who leave helpless and sick and become a burden on the Chinese community in Victoria, which is not admired."

During 1883, Onderdonk had secured the services of 800 mechanics and 3000 white laborers from California, Nevada and Manitoba. The need for Chinese immigration had passed. Construction sites were located at various points along the planned route. As sections were completed and joined, employees were discharged. By December 1883, unemployment was widespread even though 3000 more arrived that year. Scores of Chinese were seen strung along the lower rail line penniless and starving. Hundreds were camped along the Thompson, five hundred below Savona, and over two thousand at Spence's Bridge. John Robson stated that three thousand were burrowing caves in the earth near Tilton Creek and living off the carcasses of dead spawned salmon.

Noah Shakespeare had become the great oracle who warned of the Chinese invasion. When the Legislative Assembly met in late 1883 and early 1884 more anti-Chinese legislation was proposed, but disallowed for being unconstitutional as it was so many times before. In mid-January 1884 the attorney-general A.E.B. Davie presented two bills to the provincial government. First, "The Chinese Regulation Act of 1884" with 31 clauses, which proposed that every Chinese over 14 years of age purchase a license for $100;

every employer of a Chinese worker must supply names of Chinese liable to pay the tax; Chinese exhumation must be authorized; and dwellings occupied by Chinese must contain 384 cubic feet per person with a window of at least 2 square feet. The second bill was "An Act to prevent the immigration of Chinese 1883-1884". It stated that it was unlawful for Chinese to enter the province and a fine of $50 or 6 months imprisonment would be levied on violators and any one assisting a Chinese to enter was liable to a fine of a $100. The Chinese Immigration Act and the Chinese Regulation Act were both passed unanimously by the province. On April 11, the federal government disallowed the bills.

On July 5, 1884, Joseph Chapleau, the Secretary of State, and Mr. Justice, John Hamilton Gray were appointed to head a Royal Commission on Chinese Immigration. Hearings were held in Victoria and New Westminster, with visits to Nanaimo, Yale and Portland, Oregon. Thirty-one witnesses were interviewed and thirty-nine responded to printed questionnaires.

Dr. Helmcken, aged 61 years, had spent 31 years on Vancouver Island had nothing unpleasant to say about the Chinese except "No one likes a foreigner who can speak only his mother tongue." Mr. Gray had read Arthur Bunster's evidence alleging "that white ladies are scrubbed by Chinese whilst in their bath. Is that true?" he asked Helmcken. "It is a lie" answered the doctor.

Sir Matthew Baillie Begbie, Chief Justice of the Supreme Court, stated: "Industry, economy, sobriety and law-abidingness are exactly the four prominent qualities of Chinamen as asserted by their advocates and their adversaries. Lazy, drunken, extravagant and turbulent; this is, by the voices of their friends and foes, exactly what a Chinaman is not. This, on the whole, I think, was the real cause of their unpopularity." He added that he had employed them, "for there are things that white people simply refuse to do at all, for example, wash and hew stove-wood."

Henry Pelling Perew Crease, Judge of the Supreme Court, aged 59 and a resident since 1858, stated the Chinese met "a want that had become almost intolerable." If ladies had to do their own cooking and cleaning and men had to chop their own wood, "the wail of the housewife would sweep through the land and find a very decided expression in every husband's vote at the polls."

Robert Dunsmuir, aged 60 and a resident since 1852, was the owner of the Dunsmuir coal mine and the richest man in the province. He stated that he had 700 to 800 Chinese men working in his mines and that they were as

good as whites. They were industrious, hardy, temperate, peaceable, frugal and faithful. He stated that the agitation was merely political and that no regulations were necessary.

Samuel M. Robbins was the Superintendent of the Vancouver Coal Mining and Land Company; he praised the 150 Chinese in his employ. He stated, "at the time of their coming here, my company had been suffering from a strike of white laborers, and we accepted the Chinese as a weapon with which to settle the dispute."

Andrew Onderdonk, railway contractor, responded briefly in writing, stating that the Chinese were necessary for the construction of the railway; they are harmless, faithful, law-abiding and he would need 2000 more for the spring of 1885.

The commissioners departed at the end of August in 1884. British Columbians waited to be presented with the findings of the Commission. Almost a year later the report arrived. The commissioners found that the Chinese were honest, industrious, sober peaceable, law-abiding, frugal and clean, and at the same time they pointed out that white laborers, as soon as they became contractors, were the first to employ Chinese workers. The commissioners, Chapleau and Gray, stated that there was little doubt that coal mining, fish canning and market gardening would not have progressed to their current state without Chinese labour, nor could the C.P.R. have been constructed within a reasonable length of time. The commissioners considered that anti-Chinese legislation would cause a possible loss or reduction in $1,848,587 revenue to the federal government that it received from trade with the orient. They also considered other factors: the Chinese prostitutes of which there was 70 to serve 10,500 men; the smoking of opium which was hurtful only to the user; the local manufacture of opium which cost 15 Victoria factories $500 annually for a opium license; and secret associations which exist in every society. To appease the growing public demand for anti-Chinese legislation, the commission proposed three suggestions: first, a Chinese consul be appointed to Victoria; second, a duty of perhaps $10 be charged on every Chinese man, woman or child landing in the province; and third, the sum raised be used for administration of the Chinese population such as health officers, interpreters, etc..

The Canadian Parliament passed the Chinese Immigration Act on July 20th of 1885:

"every person of Chinese origin shall pay into the Consolidated Revenue Fund of Canada, on entering Canada, at the port or other place of entry, the sum of fifty dollars, except the following persons who shall be exempt from such payment, that is to say, first: the members of the Diplomatic Corps, or other Government representatives and their suite and their servants, consuls and consular agents; and second: tourists, merchants, men of science and students..."

On September 5, 1885, 3000 workers had been released by the C.P.R.. At the end of September, a similar number of discharges was reported. The railway was nearing completion. By mid-October, the distance of separation between eastward and westward sections of the rail lines was only twenty-nine miles.

Cheung sent a telegram to Yuen and Way to arrange a meeting in Yale. Cheung and Wing arrived by train at Yale on November 1st. Yuen and Way were waiting at the train station.

"How are you my friends? You both look happy and well," said Cheung.

"Cheung we are doing very well. Let's go have something to eat. Are you hungry?"

"Yes, very hungry but we did not expect to be served in the dining car. One of the merchants in Victoria told me that he sat in the dining car on the way to Yale awhile ago and no one would serve him. So we did not bother to try our luck."

Once they arrived at the local Chinese restaurant, Cheung ordered dinner.

"There is a very important historical event that will be taking place soon. Wing and I want to be there to see whether the Chinese will receive recognition for their role in helping to build the Canadian railway. Based on what is happening around us I do not think so, but I cannot be sure. In my dreams I see great accomplishments made by our people in the future. I see Chinese lawyers, doctors, dentists, accountants, scientists, professors, members of provincial legislature, members of parliament, even a Chinese mayor of Victoria. I only hope that these dreams are not just wishful fantasies."

"Cheung your dreams have served us well in the past," said Yuen.

"Yes, they helped us find Wing," said Way, "how are you little brother?"

"I am fine but very hungry. It is nice to see you both again. How is your mining operation doing?"

"The gold is running out, so we are searching for new locations. But there is lots of jade, so we are sending shipments back to China as quietly as possible because

we don't need any rivals. Uncle Yuen has told his friend in the village to keep our operations secret. We haven't told the others because there are too many now and they objected to the inclusion of any more in our mining operation. So Uncle and I wish the two of you to join us in our new venture."

"I will think on the matter but have the two of you been keeping up with the newspapers?"

"No we have been out of touch except for your telegram that On Lee attached to our provisions."

"The Canadian government has passed a head tax of $50 on every Chinese who lands in Canada with very few exceptions."

"That is at least a whole year's savings for most laborers here," said Yuen. "Passage from Hong Kong cost me $70 and most Chinese have to save a lifetime or indenture themselves to pay that back. This new legislation will certainly slow down the flow of Chinese immigration."

"Wing and I are heading to Craigellachie to watch the Last Spike Ceremony. Would you like to join us?"

Yuen looked at Way who consented with a nod. "Yes, we will come with you. I am looking forward to riding on the new train."

The four arrived in Craigellachie on November 5th and the closing ceremony was scheduled two days later. Many dignitaries and locals from the surrounding area had gathered in anticipation. On November 7th the crowd awaited the arrival of the Hon. Donald Smith to drive in the last spike. Many Chinese workers were dressed in their best clothes and had gathered to witness and share in the monumental event. At 9:22 AM Pacific Time, Smith approached with a hammer and pounded the spike as the crowd roared loudly after each stroke. The photographer set up a group photo. All of the Chinese were forcefully ushered out of the background before the photo was taken.

**Canadian Pacific Railway Last Spike Ceremony at
Craigellachie, B.C. on November 7,1885**

Afterwards the Chinese workers gathered nearby in disgust and disappointment. Cheung approached the photographer and hired him to do another
photo. He talked to the Chinese workers and asked them if they would pose
for a photo. They happily agreed. Once the photo was taken Yuen, Way, and
Wing distributed drinks and sandwiches for the gathering.

The Forgotten Men Who Helped To Save Confederation

On the train ride back to Yale, the four men quietly sat together pondering the hopes and dreams for their families in a country that they helped to unite. *"Cheung, you knew this was going to happen, didn't you?"* asked Yuen.

"Remember Jack informed us that one of his co-workers told him later that many Chinese railway workers were proud of their contribution and wanted to be recognized at the closing ceremony of the Central Pacific in Utah. They attended the celebration with the expectation of taking part in the historical photo. Just before the photo was to be taken all the Chinese were escorted out of the procession. I had hopes that it would not happen here but I thought it might. Many of our stranded countrymen will starve. I must send Ti Chu a telegram explaining the situation at hand."

Cheung and Wing returned to Victoria. Cheung told Yuen and Way he would give serious consideration to their offer to join their new jade enterprise over the winter.

The unemployment situation in Victoria was the worst in province. In 1885, there were 3000 unemployed Chinese workers living in Victoria, 1435 were living on Cormorant Street, 556 on Fisgard Street, 373 on Government Street and 219 on Store Street. Growing desperation left only three options for most: beg, steal or starve.

James Fell was elected mayor in January 1886. The new mayor met with Chinese leaders and merchants expressing his hope that they would come to the aid of their compatriots. He gave a speech in favour of aiding the unemployed in Chinatown at a council meeting which was met with boos, hisses, groans and cries. A soup kitchen was later put in operation to feed the starving Chinese. The Six Companies of San Francisco posted a notice in Chinatown stating that they had hired four steamers which would transport those who wished to return to China at a reduced rate of $25. Those sixty years or older would be given free passage and a present of $15 and those younger if they could prove poverty could also obtain free passage and a present of $10.

Wing was studying hard as Jonathan collected several books for Wing which were recommended by St. Ann's Academy's head nun. He was gifted with an inquisitive mind and was particularly interested in learning about science and new technology. Louisa came often to visit and their relationship flourished even though Wing had related his father's warning. Louisa

said that she understood the circumstances then smiled and said "the bigger the challenge the sweeter the reward".

One evening Wing approached Cheung. *"Father, the head tax is so unfair. How can the Canadian government ever justify it to future generations? Will it ever end? If it does, will the government reimburse those who paid it?"*

"My son I have dreamt it will be increased several times before it ends. The government will make a token apology after those responsible for passing it are long gone and all those who paid it are dead. Words of apology to the dead are meaningless but can still win votes and cost nothing."

Epilogue

The poor want to be rich;
The rich want to play God.

THE LIFE OF EVERY HUMAN BEING DEPENDS ON THOSE WHO have preceded them. I am indebted to those who preceded me for the legacy of rights, freedoms and privileges with which I have been endowed. This book expresses my appreciation for those before me who suffered and persevered against an epidemic of laws and regulations imposed by various levels of government to limit their rights and economic opportunities. Token gestures of apology have been expressed concerning the mistreatment of the early Chinese immigrants to North America, but I feel that they seem so inadequate, considering what I believe is their historically unrecognized contribution to Canada and the United States. I have tried to be as historically correct as possible to present a realistic snapshot of the era in which my characters supposedly existed. I have also tried to reveal how politicians, media and governments can sway public attitudes based on personal bias. The facts and figures that I present are taken from books and internet websites, listed as follows under "References" and "Websites".

Under British rule, the colony of Australia was the first to introduce anti-Chinese legislation. The Chinese Immigration Act of 1855 levied a head tax of 10 pounds on all Chinese upon their arrival in Australia. A clause

was later added denying Chinese immigrants the right of naturalization. More anti-Chinese legislation followed in Australia such as the New South Wales Chinese Immigrants Regulation and Restriction Act of 1861, the Queensland Chinese Immigrants Regulation Act of 1877, etc. culminating in the Inter-Colonial Conference of 1888 in Sydney which recommended uniform legislation throughout Australia, prohibiting Chinese immigration.

In 1849, the state constitution of California affirmed only "white males" citizens "shall be entitled to vote at all elections". As the Chinese population increased in California, numerous anti-Chinese acts were introduced. California passed the Foreign Miner's Tax in 1852 which was implemented to discourage Chinese competition during the gold rush. By 1870, the Chinese represented approximately 9% of the population of California. As a culturally distinguishable and politically vulnerable minority, they became the sacrificial lamb of California's racialized politics. The anti-Chinese forces consisted of two main groups with different interests. Capitalists, who profited from Chinese labour, understood that disenfranchisement of the Chinese would preserve their ability to control and exploit them. The labour groups who used the anti-Chinese movement as a unifying factor, which enabled new immigrants from different ethnic backgrounds to re-invent themselves as members of the white race, de-emphasizing their ethnicity. The most significant acts of legislation were the Anti-Coolie Act of 1862, the Naturalization Act of 1870 and the Chinese Exclusion Act of 1882, which closed the door to Chinese immigration in the USA.

In Canada the Chinese Immigration Act that initiated the Head Tax was passed in 1885 to discourage Chinese immigration to Canada. The federal government was gaining a windfall profit; they would not pass their Chinese Exclusion Act until 1923. According to government figures, 81,000 Chinese immigrants paid approximately 23 million dollars between 1885 and 1923 when inflation was almost negligible. According to historical gold charts, (onlygold.com) the average price of gold in US dollars remained stagnant at $20.67 from 1878 to 1926. To understand the magnitude and significance of $23 million and the extreme hardship imposed on those who paid the tax, it should be noted that the Americans purchased Alaska in 1867 from Russia for $7.2 million. $23 million would have purchased Alaska 3 times with change leftover. The Head Tax was not terminated until 1947 after the arrival of 16,123 more Chinese immigrants. Income tax was not introduced

in Canada until 1917 during the First World War, so I assume that the revenue acquired from the Head Tax was used to fund federal projects and infrastructure, while the countless locally-imposed anti-Chinese taxes funded regional projects, lessening the burden on local residents. In addition, by working for half the normal wages the Chinese helped local businesses prosper, enabling employers to pay their non-Chinese workers higher wages, which allowed the workers and their families to maintain a higher standard of living.

During the Head Tax era, numerous schemes for assisted emigration to Canada were launched in Europe by the British and Canadian governments as well as railway and land companies, private individuals and charitable organizations. Clifford Sifton was elected as a Member of Parliament in 1896. As the new Minister of the Interior he orchestrated a vigourous campaign that encouraged immigration on a massive scale, excluding Asians, Jews and Blacks. The federal government assigned resident agents throughout the British Isles, continental Europe and the United States. The agents recruited immigrants through newspaper ads and guidebooks as well as delivering lectures on the benefits of living in Canada in the new classless society. They offered financial support, employment, free passage and land in addition to agricultural training and assistance. Between 1891 and 1914, more than three million people came to Canada. While many of the immigrants came from Britain and the United States, Canada also welcomed many dissident groups from continental Europe. After the initial land rush, many of the subsidized programs and schemes collapsed and by 1920 a massive exodus took place. From 1915 to 1925, the population of Canada decreased by 413,145 people. During this period, 829,736 Canadians emigrated to the United States. In 1936, C.W.Peterson, the territorial deputy commissioner of agriculture, stated in a paper on immigration, "When the history of the past half century comes to be written, it will reveal a colossal failure in developing our vast country, typified by an appalling lack of intelligent and continuous policy." Governments can choose what to acknowledge and what to ignore about the past. One hundred and twenty-one years after the Head Tax was first implemented, the Prime Minister of Canada, Stephen Harper, offered an apology to all Chinese Canadians and $20,000 in compensation for each victim. Only 20 Head Tax victims at that time were awarded compensation.

Children of the victims were not eligible for compensation and are still appealing for redress from the government.

An overview of anti-Chinese legislation by the BC legislative staff revealed that 89 separate bills and 49 motions were passed in the BC Legislature from 1872 to 1928. Of the 89 bills, 58 dealt with labour & employment, 12 with economic & social rights, 10 voting rights, 9 immigration issues and 1 vital statistics. The 49 motions included: 16 immigration issues, 12 labour, 8 Head Tax, 6 economics and taxes, 5 health, 2 voting rights. Outside of the discriminatory legislation against the Indigenous peoples, the Chinese were the most heavily legislated and most harshly persecuted minority in Canada. I started this book many years ago after reading Anthony Chan's "Gold Mountain: The Chinese in the New World". My primary goal was to create understanding and to expose the conspiracy of silence concerning the exploitation and abuse of a people who contributed so much to the founding of Canada and the American West. Although there have been many books written on this topic, I felt that they were never presented in a manner to maintain the interest of mass readership, so I endeavoured to create a storyline with characters that would appeal to readers who shared some commonality with my personal background. To create greater empathy, my main characters are highly westernized and devoid of stereotypical traits. My intent was to give the reader a history lesson and explain how the philosophical differences between the East and West evolved. Human beings must adapt to their environment to survive. Over centuries, hostility and peace will produce contrasting societies with different philosophies, different values, different strengths and different weaknesses. I believe that the major factors influencing the historical development of humanity are necessity and greed. That which has served us in the past may be a detriment in the future. The cold war mentality spawns paranoia and weapons of mass destruction are non-partisan.

The main characters in my story are fictitious creations. Many like Chun Ti Chu, William Ellis, Jack Ellis, James Fell, Mrs. Baillie Grohman and Walter Moberly did exist and I wanted to commemorate their "humanality" and their contribution in supporting and helping the Chinese in the face of overwhelming ignorance. I struggled for months to find an appropriate photo of a Chinese gathering of CPR workers without finding one. Although I wanted to be as historically correct as possible the final photo of

the supposed CPR workers is actually a photo of the Chinese workers for the Great Northern Railway circa 1909. I also had a white worker deleted on the top row. The political characters in my story who thrived and exploited the Chinese for personal gain also existed. The owner of the *British Colonist* and Member of Parliament, Amor De Cosmos (Lover of the World) who demonized the Chinese, was one of the most vehement advocates of anti-Chinese legislation.

This 1879 cartoon depicts Amor de Cosmos telling a Chinese immigrant to leave B.C. because he refuses to assimilate. "You won't drink whiskey, and talk politics and vote like us," he says.

Most books about the construction of Canadian Pacific Railway glorify Andrew Onderdonk. None of my research revealed that he showed any compassion or concern for the needs or safety of his Chinese workers. According to James Morton's "In the Sea of Sterile Mountain" and the *British Colonist*

(November 14, 1885) approximately 1500 Chinese died during the construction of the CPR. This was probably a conservative estimate. In *The CPR West*, Patricia E. Roy states the Chinese merchants in Victoria estimated 2200 Chinese railway workers died in 1882. This may have been based on data from the bone storage facility in Victoria. In "Canadian Pacific Railway – Heritage Series" Christine Welldon states "about 4000 died during railway construction because of unsafe and unhealthy working and living conditions". No formal records have ever been documented. During the ten days prior to the final breach of Hell's Gate in 1882, the Skuzzy made several attempts to pass through. I could find no record of these attempts. The best description that I found in my research of the Skuzzy episode at Hell's Gate was a 1952 poem by EJ Pratt entitled "Toward The Last Spike" :

"......Two engines at the stern, a forrard winch,

Steam-powered, failed to stem the cataract.

The last resource was shoulders, arms and hands.

Fifteen men at the capstan, creaking hawsers,

Two hundred Chinese tugging at shore ropes

To keep her bow-on from the broadside drift,

The Skuzzy under muscle and steam took

The shoals and rapids, and warped through the Gate,

Until she reached the navigable waters - -

The adventure was not sailing: it was climbing."

My hypothesis about totem poles was inspired by University of Victoria's Dr. David Chuenyan Lai's "The Forbidden City" which displays the pailau and huabiao. I did not intend to give the Chinese credit for native artwork; I only propose that shipwrecked and abandoned Chinese sailors may have helped to inspire it. The story about "Chop Suey" was inspired by an Asian

Studies professor Rene Goldberg whose class I attended at the University of British Columbia in 1975.

In times of crisis, human beings regress to survive. The sense of right and wrong is clouded by fear. Governments designate scapegoats to blame for their own ineptitude. When a single minority is blamed for the misfortunes and failures of government, please remember the exploitation, misdeeds and injustice that I have described which were perpetrated in the past. Hopefully I have inspired readers to re-evaluate the past. Did the Chinese contribute in helping to build North America? If the doors of immigration had been open to Chinese immigration would North America have been better or worst than today? If the Chinese had not been marginalized how would they have influenced the prevailing attitudes? By exposing historical inequities, I am hopeful that my children and others will be spared the racial biases of the past during the turbulent times ahead. When rivals of the West are demonized by the media, please remember how governments and the media can evade accountability by creating scapegoats for their own misdeeds. It is my personal opinion that the sectarian barriers that seek to divide us – religion, nationalism, politics, racism, greed – must be relinquished for the betterment of humanity.

In an age dominated by national self-interest and corporate greed, conflicts never end. Individuals who value peace and freedom must look beyond their own self-interest, beyond their borders and beyond their God. The goal of peaceful co-existence cannot be achieved without truth, goodwill and understanding. We cannot change the past, only the present, to enhance the future for the benefit of all.

The title of my book , Yut Di - One Earth, reflects the common need for goodwill, peace and harmony for all who share the earth.

Thank you for your kind indulgence,

Ed Ho

Food for Thought

"Human progress cannot advance without change; and without dissent change is suppressed."

TWO OF THE MAJOR OBSTACLES BLOCKING THE PATH TO PEACE-ful co-existence are religion and nationalism. Historically, governments and politicians have used these devices to pacify and exploit the public, to serve their own self-interest. Unifying others through lies, fear and greed can only lead to eventual conflict.

Historical lies, distortions and omissions allow governments to instill a false sense of national pride. Nationalism and religion have been used throughout history, to recruit the young to fight wars, in order to enslave others, steal their land and plunder their resources. Today, multi-national corporations supported by their governments exploit less developed nations without public awareness of truthful motives.

Religion substitutes futility and guilt with a promise of paradise. It allows those in power to manage and manipulate the masses to protect their mandate and fulfill their vision for the future. Under freedom of religion, people can believe whatever they want to believe, but blind faith in government and the media empowers others to exploit us. My fear is that anyone who will sacrifice his son based on hearing a voice will also press a button

on command, regardless of consequences. Books purported to be the word of God have been written, translated, and amended by countless scholars throughout history. Believe whatever you want, just try not to be misled or influenced by those who will profit or be empowered by your beliefs. Personally, I believe in re-incarnation and that there is a realm beyond physical existence and that life is a form of energy, which continues after death but needs to be revitalized through life in the physical world. It is my personal belief that the spiritual and physical realms co-exist, without one the other cannot exist because common sense dictates that nothing lasts forever. I also believe in the law of karma and that we are all eventually accountable for the choices that we have made.

The major theme of my book has been the conflict of greed and self-interest versus truth and understanding. Historically the strong have always ruled the weak until the weak become strengthened by adversity. Throughout history, many forms of government have maintained their mandates for long durations but they eventually all fall victim to arrogance and overconfidence. Any system of government is only as good as the leaders that run it. The form of government that any nation chooses to adopt should be based on economic circumstance, free of all foreign influence. The rivalry between communism and capitalism created during the Cold War was a battle for control of world influence through ideology. The horrendous cost in resources related to this rivalry could have resolved many of the inequities facing humanity today such as world hunger, clean water, free education. If some of these Cold War expenditures had been directed elsewhere, would peace be less distant than it is today? Instead of creating peace, altruistic world organizations became pawns, mired in the struggle for global control. Proxy wars, instigated by major powers, were justified under a banner of democracy and freedom, as trillions of dollars were spent over a misunderstood battle of greed. During the Cuban Missile Crisis, two nations brought the world to the brink of annihilation for the sake of national pride. What kind of insanity grants two individuals the right to decide the fate of humanity? Wars do not determine righteousness, only strength.

The popular trend of today flows towards democratic forms of government. A history professor at the University of Edinburgh named Alexander Tyler stated in 1887, "A democracy is always temporary in nature; it simply

cannot exist as a permanent form of government. A democracy will continue to exist up until the time that voters discover that they can vote themselves generous gifts from the public treasury. From that moment on, the voters always vote for the candidates who promise the most benefits from the public treasury, with the result that every democracy will finally collapse over loose fiscal policy, which is always followed by a dictatorship." It is doubtful that this inherent weakness can be remedied until voters understand the danger of this fundamental flaw. Another concern is the trend of having military personnel serve as government leaders, since they are more prone to use force rather than diplomacy to resolve disputes. Those, trained in the art of warfare, may foster a more aggressive geopolitical point of view. The evolution of the world's precarious state of affairs may be a reflection of this trend. What kind of leadership is best suited for human survival in the nuclear age, the leadership of hawks or the leadership of doves?

As long as the poor and the underprivileged represent the majority, history will continue to repeat itself. The rivalry between capitalism and socialism is nothing more than a struggle between the rich and the poor. Although greed undoubtedly inspires the advancement of technology, how these advances are used to benefit the future of humanity is questionable. With the emergence and proliferation of weapons of mass destruction the future of our planet is threatened as never before. Regardless of the benefits of new technology, collateral side-effects are not always foreseeable. Sometimes they emerge much later with catastrophic effects. In the past, the rich have always exploited the poor, to fight their wars. With modern technology and nuclear weapons, the enemy can be eliminated by pressing a button. As the gap between the rich and the poor widens the possibility of nuclear warfare draws ever closer to reality. Nuclear weapons were first used in 1945. Throughout history, once new weaponry has proven to be effective, other nations race to exploit the new technology. Leadership provided by the biggest bully is only temporary. Great leadership is founded on wisdom, not power. To lead a nation one must abandon personal interests; to lead the world one must abandon national interests.

Some governments use military force, some use technology, some use religion, some use nationalism, some use alliances and some use propaganda to prolong their mandate. Today most use all these devices to control and indoctrinate the masses. Indoctrination is the process of planting ideas

and attitudes in the mind of others through education and the media. It is used to train individuals in "what to think and not how to think", as I have tried to demonstrate in my book. With the use of indoctrination, any individual can be trained to hate and kill without remorse, to serve the will of others. Monopolized ownership of media can subvert freedom of the press, the watchdog of democracy. Biased reporting can be tailored to justify any event or government decision. Children can be trained to be acquiescent at an early age. Education and indoctrination are strangers, the former seeks to enlighten while the latter seeks to control. When the public is taught to accept lies without question & allow governments to operate in secrecy, the rights and freedom of every individual are jeopardized. Democracy is a sham, when voters cannot distinguish between lies and the truth.

Until lies and secrecy cease, governments and those who control them can fulfill clandestine agendas with impunity as radicals who attempt to expose government fraud are ostracized, ridiculed and labeled "conspiracy theorists". Without radical thought, America would still be a British colony. The internet is the last bastion of radicalism. Governments may tamper and apply more restrictions on the use of the internet, to track and silence dissenters. Freedom of speech and critical thinking may be subverted, under the guise of national security. When governments infringe on the right to privacy, they will be empowered to identify and eliminate radicalism. America's greatest conspiracy theorist once stated:

> **"For we are opposed around the world by a monolithic and ruthless conspiracy that relies primarily on covert means for expanding its sphere of influence – on infiltration instead of invasion, on subversion instead of elections, on intimidation instead of free choice, on guerrillas by night instead of armies by day. It is a system which has conscripted vast human and material resources into the building of a tightly knit, highly efficient machine that combines military, diplomatic, intelligence, economic, scientific and political operations.**
>
> **Its preparations are concealed, not published. Its mistakes are buried, not headlined. Its dissenters are silenced, not praised. No expenditure is questioned,**

no rumor is printed, no secret is revealed. It conducts the Cold War, in short, with a war-time discipline no democracy would ever hope or wish to match."

– John F. Kennedy

I think that JFK was determined to do something about it, unfortunately, he died under a cloud of controversy. Governments can no longer be trusted when they operate in secrecy, regardless of their justification for their actions and decisions. Technology can be hidden for ulterior motives, or used to enable those in power and their allies. Events can be staged to create mass fear and hatred, to support hidden motives. The general public can be led to believe whatever their governments do is justified and morally righteous. Today, lies, misdirection and propaganda cloud common sense and critical thought. The pursuit of truth requires careful research and analysis. Lies become reality if they persist long enough without opposition, but the seeds of peaceful co-existence can only flourish in a field of truth.

 "When I despair, I remember that all through history the way of truth and love have always won. There have been tyrants and murderers, and for a time, they can seem invincible, but in the end, they always fall. Think of it-always."
 -Mahatma Gandhi

 Good always triumphs over evil because fear can only create temporary alliances so evil must eventually stand alone. "Freedom, Justice & Equality for all" were the moral principles that helped to liberate the New World from the chains of tyranny. For every step forward, we take two steps back. Will history repeat itself? Writers can only light the fire, attempting to inspire others. Hopefully, I have encouraged you to re-evaluate the past and reflect on how it impacts the future.

 May truth & wisdom guide you.
 Yutdi.com

References

Barde, Robert Eric. **Immigration at the Golden Gate: passenger ships, exclusion, and Angel Island**, 2008 published by Praeger Publishers, Westport, Connecticut

Berton, Pierre. **The Last Spike**, 1971 published by McClelland and Stewart Limited, Toronto, Ontario

Chan, Anthony. **Gold Mountain : The Chinese in the New World**, 1983 published by New Star Books Vancouver, B.C.

Chang, Iris. **The Chinese in America: A Narrative History**, 2003 published by Viking 2004 published by Penguin Books, New York, N.Y.

Chen, Jack. **Chinese of America**, 1980 published by Harper& Row, Publishers San Francisco, California

Choy, Philip P. **San Francisco Chinatown**, 2012 published by City Light Books, San Francisco, California

Choy, Philip, Lorraine Dong, and Marlon K. Hom. **Coming man : 19th century American perceptions of the Chinese**, 1995 published by University of Washington Press, Seattle Washington

Dempsey, Hugh A. (Editor). **The CPR West : The Iron Road and The Making of a Nation**, 1984 published by Douglas & McIntire Ltd., Vancouver, B.C.

Johnson, Paul C. **Pictorial History of California**, 1970 published by Random House Value Publishing USA

Kung, Shien-Woo. **Chinese in American life : some aspects of their history, status, problems, and contributions**, 1962 University of Washington Press

Lai, David Chuenyan **Chinatowns : Towns Within Cities in Canada**, 1988 The University of British Columbia Press, Vancouver, B.C.

Lai, David Chuengyan. **The Forbidden City**, 1991 Orca Book Publishers, Victoria B.C.

Lee, Rose Hum Lee. **Chinese in the United States of America**, 1960 published by The Hong Kong University Press, Hong Kong China

McCunn, Ruthanne **Illustrated history of the Chinese in America**, 1979 published by Design Enterprises of San Francisco, San Francisco, California

McLeod, Alexander. **Pigtails and Gold Dust**, 1948 published by The Caxton Printers Ltd. Caldwell, Idaho

Mau Dicker, Laverne ; with a pref. by Thomas W. Chinn. **Chinese in San Francisco : A Pictorial History**, 1979 published by Dover Publications, Inc., New York, N.Y.

Morton, James. **In the Sea of Sterile Mountains :The Chinese in British Columbia**, 1974 published by J. J. Douglas Ltd. Vancouver, B.C.

Pfaelzer, Jean. **Driven out : the forgotten war against Chinese Americans**, 2007 published by University of California Press, Oakland, California

Roy, Patricia E. Roy. **A White Man's Province: British Columbia Politicians & Chinese & Japanese Immigrants**, 1858-1914, 1989 published by University of British Columbia Press, Vancouver, B.C.

Segger, Martin & Douglas Franklin **Victoria : A Primer for Regional History in Architecture**, 1979 published by Milestone Publications, Victoria, B.C.

Steiner, Stan. **Fusang : The Chinese Who Built America** , 1979 published by Harper and Row Publishers, New York, N.Y.

Ward, W. Peter. **White Canada Forever**, 1978 published by McGill - Queen's University Press, Montreal, Quebec

Wickberg, Edgar editor - Harry Con, Ronald J. Con, Graham Johnson, Edgar Wickberg, William E. Willmott. **From China to Canada**, 1982 published by McClelland & Stewart Ltd. in association with the Canadian government Publishing Centre, Toronto , Ontario

Yee, Paul - Diary of Lee Heen-gwong 1882 **Blood and Iron: Building of the Railway**, 2010 published by Scholastics Canada Ltd., Toronto, Ontario

Websites

**Victoria's Chinatown – A Gateway to the
Past & Present of Chinese Canadians :**

http://chinatown.library.uvic.ca/chronology

The Chinese Canadian Historical Society of BC :

https://www.facebook.com/cchsbc

The Ties That Bind :

http://mhso.ca/tiesthatbind/

University of Victoria Library's Chinese Canadian Collection website :

http://www.uvic.ca/library/featured/collections/asian/Chinese-Canadian.
php

Dr. Henry Yu Website:

http://www.history.ubc.ca/people/henry-yu

A Journey Into Time Immemorial:

http://www.sfu.museum/time/en/panoramas/beach/spiritual-beliefs/

Royal BC Museum :

http://royalbcmuseum.bc.ca/bcarchives/

BC History Portal :

http://bchistoryportal.tc.ca/SPT--AdvancedSearch.
php?Q=Y&F3=Chinese&RP=5&SR=0

British Columbia Historical Federation :

http://bchistory.library.ubc.ca/?db=bchf

An Act Respecting the Canadian Pacific Railway :
http://members.kos.net/sdgagnon/cpa.html

The Bristish Colonist :
http://www.britishcolonist.ca/

The Chinese in California, 1850-1925 :
http://memory.loc.gov/ammem/award99/cubhtml/chron.html

The History of Yuba County :
http://www.yubaroots.com/history/hycch-iii.htm

Chinese American Museum of Northern California
http://www.chineseamericanmuseum.com/

Chinese Canadian Stories – Chinese Head Tax Searchable Database
http://ccs.library.ubc.ca/en/headtax/beginnings.html.